Algorithmic Regulation

Algorithmic Regulation

EDITED BY

KAREN YEUNG
MARTIN LODGE

OXFORD
UNIVERSITY PRESS

OXFORD

UNIVERSITY PRESS

Great Clarendon Street, Oxford, OX2 6DP,
United Kingdom

Oxford University Press is a department of the University of Oxford.
It furthers the University's objective of excellence in research, scholarship,
and education by publishing worldwide. Oxford is a registered trade mark of
Oxford University Press in the UK and in certain other countries

Published in the United States of America by Oxford University Press
198 Madison Avenue, New York, NY 10016, United States of America

British Library Cataloguing in Publication Data
Data available

Library of Congress Control Number: 2019938554

ISBN 978–0–19–883849–4

Printed and bound by
CPI Group (UK) Ltd, Croydon, CR0 4YY

To Erica and Fei

To Fabian

Summary Contents

Detailed Contents

Table of Cases

INTERNATIONAL

European Court of Justice

NATIONAL COURTS

United Kingdom

United States of America

Table of Legislation

List of Contributors

Leighton Andrews is Professor of Practice in Public Service Leadership and Innovation at Cardiff Business School.

Irina Brass is Lecturer in Regulation, Innovation and Public Policy at the Department of Science, Technology, Engineering and Public Policy (STEaPP) at University College London.

Lee A Bygrave is Professor of Law and Director of the Norwegian Research Center for Computers and Law (NRCCL) in the Department of Private Law at the University of Oslo..

Andrew Charlesworth is Professor of Law, Innovation and Society, School of Law at the University of Bristol.

Natalia Criado is Lecturer in Computer Science in the Department of Informatics and Co-Director of the UKRI Centre for Doctoral Training in Safe and Trusted Artificial Intelligence at King's College London.

Nello Cristianini is Professor of Artificial Intelligence in the Faculty of Engineering at the University of Bristol.

John Danaher is Senior Lecturer in the School of Law at NUI Galway.

Alex Griffiths is Chief Technical Officer (CTO) at Statica Research and Visiting Fellow, Centre for Analysis of Risk and Regulation (**carr**), London School of Economics and Political Science.

Martin Lodge is Professor of Political Science and Public Policy and Director of the Centre for Analysis of Risk and Regulation (carr) at the London School of Economics and Political Science.

Jason D Lohr is a Partner at the global law firm Hogan Lovells, specializing in intellectual property and technological innovation.

Winston J Maxwell is Director, Law & Digital Technology Studies, Telecom Paris, Institut polytechnique de Paris.

Andrea Mennicken is Associate Professor of Accounting in the Department of Accounting and Deputy Director of the Centre for Analysis of Risk and Regulation (carr) at the London School of Economics and Political Science.

Teresa Scantamburlo is a post-doctoral researcher at the Department of Computer Science at the University of Bristol.

Jose Such is Reader in Security and Privacy in the Department of Informatics and Director of the Cybersecurity Centre at King's College London.

Michael Veale is Digital Charter Fellow, The Alan Turing Institute, London, UK; Honorary Research Fellow, Birmingham Law School, University of Birmingham, Birmingham, UK; Doctoral Researcher, Department of Science, Technology, Engineering and Public Policy (STEaPP), University College London, London, UK.

Peter Watts is a Partner at the global law firm Hogan Lovells, specializing in technology and media.

Karen Yeung is Interdisciplinary Professorial Fellow in Law, Ethics and Informatics at Birmingham Law School and School of Computer Science, University of Birmingham. She is also Distinguished Visiting Fellow at Melbourne Law School.

1

Algorithmic Regulation

An Introduction

Karen Yeung and Martin Lodge

1. Introduction

Imagine the following scene during a recent political science conference. Among all the conference activities, which include panels concerning the future of democracy, the decline of social democracy, and geo-political tensions in South East Asia, one panel is dedicated to the implications of digitalization on public administration. Paper after paper draws attention to the relationship between technology and its social context, with many highlighting how technology shapes, and is shaped by social processes, and the tendency of technological systems to reinforce and accentuate existing power relations and disparities in its distribution. During the questions and answers session, the discussion turns to 'algorithms'. Across all panelists, there is shared consensus: algorithms are already beginning to, and will inevitably continue to, drive radical changes to the way in which societies, including public administration, will be organized, often in unexpected and hitherto unimaginable ways.

At a nearby conference of legal scholars, another panel is also grappling with understanding the implications of digitization of society for law and legal institutions. One tranche of these papers focuses on the ambiguities and challenges associated with reform of contemporary data protection legislation, in which the enactment of the EU's General Data Protection Regulation (GDPR) often takes centre-stage, alongside concerns about the implications for privacy more generally. The discussion invariably turns to the slippery and problematic legal characterization of digital data, with participants routinely acknowledging that data has become the 'new oil', with frequent analogies drawn between the mining giants of a pre-digital age and the emergence of a handful of 'Digital Titans' whose power is now global in scale and reach. Yet the size, scale, profitability, market capitalization, and revenue generation streams produced by the platforms controlled by the Digital Titans are of a magnitude that the oil magnates of an earlier industrial age could scarcely have contemplated.

Another tranche of papers also makes frequent mention of algorithms, appearing in the ruminations of labour and employment lawyers in seeking to grapple with the implications and challenges associated with the rise of the 'sharing economy' particularly given the precariousness of the conditions under which individuals who contribute their services now typically work, or debate amongst competition law scholars in seeking to reckon with the realities of 'platform power' and the 'data monopolies' which they enable, seeking to evaluate the capacity of contemporary competition law to respond to the practices of data extraction and the complex data ecosystem upon which it relies. Yet in the adjacent conference room focused on exploring contemporary challenges in public law, the word algorithm is rarely mentioned. In those discussions, there is little by way of recognition (at least in the Anglo-Commonwealth community of public law scholars) that a revolution in the process of governing might be afoot, perhaps because it has been private sector entrepreneurship that has been most visible in shaping the digital transformations that are currently unfolding (cf Mazzucato 2018).

Like their political science counterparts, an increasing number of legal scholars are now turning their attention to algorithms, questioning their implications for existing legal frameworks in ways that might threaten some of law's most foundational concepts, including the rule of law and fundamental rights. Yet for lawyers concerned with the digitization of society, the public sector has not hitherto occupied centre-stage, given that modern data protection law applies to all those engaged in the task of data processing, irrespective of the characterization of the processor as governmental or otherwise, and that the rise of the digital platform has been overwhelmingly dominated by commercial rather than governmental players.

But attempts at wrestling with the social implications of algorithms are not solely the province of academics. Policy-makers in Europe and elsewhere are also turning their attention to the challenges associated with the widespread and increasingly pervasive use of algorithms across an almost limitless range of social domains. But even leaving aside difficulties in fully comprehending how algorithmic systems operate, given the technical sophistication and mathematical logic upon which they rest, policy-makers of democratic market economies often find themselves caught between a rock and a hard place. In an age pervaded by economic austerity, a declining tax base, poor GDP growth, and an increasing recognition of the seriousness and magnitude of the adverse implications of climate change and other 'global societal challenges' on human societies, technological solutions offer the promise of economic growth through renewed investment and entrepreneurship, but also a fervent (and undoubtedly naïve) hope that technological solutions will deliver us from our contemporary social ills. At the same time, however, the techno-utopian vision that accompanied the enthusiastic claims peddled by the High Priests of Silicon Valley portraying their entrepreneurial activities as primarily concerned with serving the interests of humanity, thereby 'making the world a better place', no longer holds sway (Taplin 2017). In the last two years, this techno-utopian vision has given way to growing (at times, dystopian) recognition that although the digital services wrought by the age of the algorithm may bring myriad conveniences and efficiencies to the daily lives of the inhabitants of industrialized economies which many find it increasingly impossible to live without, these technologies have a dark side (Bridle 2018). Growing public anxiety associated with the 'rise of the machines' and what they may portend has therefore led to increasing calls for regulation. Yet the merest whiff or hint of regulation by policymakers typically provokes a chorus of opposition from commercial interests, particularly the tech industry (and their army of well-paid lobbyists), loudly chanting the familiar refrain that 'regulation stifles innovation', tapping into a deeply held contemporary fixation in which innovation is unthinkingly regarded as a synonym for social good (Ford 2017).

These various snapshots reveal that algorithms are now widely seen as a 'gamechanger' (Council of Europe 2019), even for those who are typically rather sceptical about the transformative impact of technologies for societies. Although algorithms simply refer to a set of steps or instructions for carrying out a specific task, in contemporary parlance, algorithms are typically associated with computational algorithms. Many of the current discussions often focus on the use and implications of machine learning algorithms, which, when powered by massive data sets supported by powerful computational processing capacities, are capable of generating new and often unexpected insight which might then be harnessed in productive (and often highly lucrative) ways (Zuboff 2019).

This book provides for a set of interdisciplinary perspectives on algorithms in contemporary debates, which we have gathered together under the broad notion of 'algorithmic regulation'. Initial discussions by scholars from a wide range of disciplines including law, politics, applied philosophy, computer science, organizational sociology, and public administration suggested that algorithmic regulation provoked a range of challenging and important questions ripe for searching and sustained interrogation.[1] In an age of near-daily headlines about the power of continuous and highly granular surveillance by both state and non-state entities alike, and the promises and pitfalls of algorithmic systems, this volume seeks to provide a stepping stone towards a richer, more structured cross-disciplinary and integrated conversation. Our workshop discussions revealed the high level of interest in algorithmic regulation across different scholarly disciplines, yet which had not, however, crossed departmental and disciplinary silos in a significant way. Instead, academic interest in algorithmic regulation has been largely carried forward by different disciplinary outlooks, ranging from those in the fields of programming and engineering to those from legal and political science viewpoints. Largely

---

[1] These discussions originated in a joint workshop we convened under the auspices of the Centre for Technology, Ethics, Law and Society ('TELOS'), King's College London and the Centre for the Analysis of Risk and Regulation (**carr**) at the London School of Economics in the summer of 2017. **carr** gratefully acknowledges financial support by the ESRC under its seminar series competition scheme ('Regulation in crisis?').

absent from these discussions has been a systematic move towards fostering genuinely interdisciplinary conversations between these different perspectives so as to avoid inevitable conceptual confusion, cross-disciplinary 'ignorance' of different research dynamics as well as the creation of potential research 'underlap' where certain critical questions fall between the cracks of different disciplinary concerns.

This introductory chapter develops its argument in a number of steps. First, we explore what we mean by 'algorithmic regulation'. Second, we reflect on how debates regarding algorithmic regulation relate to wider debates about the interaction between technology and regulation. Third, we consider algorithmic systems as potentially novel types of *large technical* systems (Hughes 1983). In doing so, we highlight the growing consensus regarding critical challenges for the regulation and governance of algorithmic systems, but also note the lack of agreement regarding potential solutions. Finally, we introduce the contributions to this volume.

2. What is Algorithmic Regulation?

We use the term 'algorithmic regulation' to refer to the underlying phenomenon of interest which conceptually unites the diverse concerns and perspectives represented in this collection. Although the term 'algorithmic regulation' was popularized by Silicon Valley entrepreneur Tim O'Reilly in 2013 (O'Reilly 2013), the idea that computational algorithms might be understood as a form of social ordering was proposed some time earlier by sociologist A. Aneesh in 2009 in the context of an ethnographic analysis seeking to understand how Indian workers providing IT services to a North American firm were coordinated (Aneesh 2009). Aneesh argued that the underlying logic of the software programming schedules through which globally dispersed labour was maintained was *mathematical,* and hence distinct from bureaucratic forms of organization, which he dubbed 'algocracy'. It is the computerization of society that is crucial to the increasing digitization and 'datafication' of social and economic life, and which has in turn, generated the burgeoning contemporary interest in algorithms. While the resulting computational turn is vividly reflected in the widespread take-up of 'smart' devices by individuals and the 'internet of everything' that is sweeping through advanced industrialized economies, these connected devices rely on an underlying and universal data infrastructure that emerged from the development and implementation of the internet which allows for the collection, processing, and remote storage of digital data both in real time, and at a planetary scale. As Gillespie observes, when describing something as 'algorithmic' our concern is with the insertion of procedure that is produced by, or related to, a socio-technical information system that is intended by its designers to be functionally and ideologically committed to the *computational generation of knowledge* (Gillespie 2014).

For the purposes of this collection, however, our interest is narrower and more specific than a diffuse and general interest in connected computational devices and systems. As one of us has argued elsewhere, algorithmic regulation points to regulatory governance systems that utilize *algorithmic decision-making* (Yeung 2018), in which 'algorithmic decision-making' refers to the use of algorithmically generated knowledge systems to execute or inform decisions. Although the scope and meaning of the terms 'regulation' and 'regulatory governance' are contested (Baldwin et al 2010; Koop & Lodge 2017), we adopt a broad understanding of regulation (or regulatory governance) as intentional attempts to manage risk or alter behaviour in order to achieve some pre-specified goal. Accordingly, because regulation is also pursued by both state and non-state actors and entities (Black 2008), so too is algorithmic regulation. For example, Facebook regulates the posting and viewing behaviour of users through the use of algorithmic decision-making systems to optimize returns to the company, in the same way that a public transport authority may regulate vehicle movement to optimize traffic flow. At the same time, the size of the regulated 'population' may refer to the intentional actions of one person who adopts some system or strategy to regulate some aspect of her own behaviour (such as an individual who uses a fitness tracking device to help her ensure that she attains a minimum level of daily physical activity), through to regulatory systems that seek to direct and influence the behaviour of a large number of people or entities, (such as algorithmic systems employed by digital car-sharing platform, Uber, to enable drivers to offer motor vehicle transport services to individuals at a pre-specified fee without having had any previous relationship). Critical to all these systems is the need for some kind of system 'director' (or 'regulator') to determine the overarching goal of the regulatory system, given that regulation is above all an *intentional* activity directed at achieving a pre-specified goal, often by seeking to effect the modification of behaviour (of other people, phenomena, or things). Thus, this volume adopts Yeung's definition of algorithmic regulation, referring to decision-making systems that regulate a domain of activity in order to manage risk or alter behaviour through continual computational generation of knowledge from data emitted and directly collected (in real time on a continuous basis) from numerous dynamic components pertaining to the regulated environment in order to identify and, if necessary, automatically refine (or prompt refinement of) the system's operations to attain a pre-specified goal (Yeung 2018).

Although various scholars have critically reflected upon and developed this notion of idea of algorithmic regulation which goes beyond the ambitions of this introductory chapter (eg Zweig et al 2018; Carsten Stahl & Wright 2018; Hildebrandt 2018; Ulbricht 2018), four features are worth highlighting. Firstly, algorithmic regulation draws upon a modality of control that regulatory governance scholars sometimes refer to as 'architectural' or 'design-based' techniques of control (Yeung 2008, 2015). On this view, algorithmic regulation is simply an application of the use of design for regulatory purposes, building on the logic of the water-lock, devised by the Ancient Egyptians over 3,000 years ago to prevent unauthorized entry to a protected space without the need for human intervention (Beniger 1986). Secondly, as we have already noted, attempts to coordinate the activity of multiple individuals or other non-human agents through the use of algorithmic systems might be understood as a distinctive form of social ordering. Seen in this light, algorithmic regulation might be associated with a distinct set of political, normative, or ideological commitments, as has been the case with other forms of social ordering, such as markets and bureaucratic hierarchy (Yeung 2018).

Thirdly, there is no doubt that, at least in the Western industrialized world, the Digital Titans that have established the global digital platforms are at the forefront of cutting-edge applications of algorithmic regulatory systems, despite the frequency of the claimed benefits that can be expected to accrue in the governmental domain through the use of data-driven insight. Indeed, as Griffith's contribution to this volume highlights, applying the logic of algorithmic regulation to public sector decision-making is far more challenging than the policy rhetoric would have us believe. Fourthly, it is worth recognizing that emerging critiques of algorithmic systems generally, and algorithmic regulation in particular, has hitherto been largely dominated by perspectives drawn from a political perspective focused on their application to highly industrialized, democratic societies. Although there is a distinct and growing interest in 'data for development' or data for 'social good', the widespread implementation of algorithmic regulation as a feature of daily life remains largely the province of wealthy industrialized states. As the contributions to this volume demonstrate, the emergence of algorithmic regulation is something of a double-edged sword, rich with the potential to deliver great benefits, yet equally rich with potential threats and hazards. At the same time, the promises, benefits, and dangers which the computational turn has hitherto generated are unequally distributed, highlighting the need to acquire a richer and more sophisticated understanding of the rise of algorithmic power and its implications.

3. Anything New under the Sun?

Algorithmic regulation may appear to be something inherently novel, and can therefore be expected to generate novel issues and challenges for both individuals and society more generally. For some, it offers for the first time, the capacity to generate accurate behavioural predictions, providing an evidence-based foundation for anticipatory intervention. For public administrators, this opens up the possibility that, armed with large data sets germane to their domain of oversight, public actors will be able to steer their attention to those hotspot issues and areas which warrant particular attention. Private actors, too, can rely on data-driven profiling techniques to pinpoint the preferences, interests, and concerns of consumers and at a highly granular level, enabling them to offer bespoke services to users on a personalized basis, and in real time. For others, however, it offers the bleak prospect of a fully automated, totalizing surveillance society that drastically curtails scope for human freedom and autonomy (Zuboff 2019).

A related debate concerns the relationship between regulation and technology. Technology is frequently regarded as emerging and existing outside regulatory systems. Consequently, technology is often seen as driving social change, with regulatory approaches seeking to play a game of inevitable and potentially doomed 'catch up' (Bennett Moses 2007). Based on this premise of technological determinism, a number of arguments emerge. One is to criticize all forms of regulation as 'stifling' technological development, placing barriers for innovation on entrepreneurs and citizens alike (cf Ford 2017). Those with a less entrepreneurial orientation might nevertheless suggest that given the inevitable 'laggard' nature of regulation in relation to technological change, producers of new technology are in an inevitably powerful position, seeking out grey zones and blind spots in existing regulatory frameworks to their (commercial) advantage (Taplin 2017). Such conditions often result in patchwork responses with regulators responding to 'today's crisis' before being distracted by the next. Furthermore, given the inherent informational advantages of the producers of new technologies, they are well placed to capture regulators. According to this view, regulation is, at best, seen as being subject to the whims of powerful corporate interests that are likely to shape social relations according to their preferences. A more differentiated form of this argument highlights how sophisticated corporate actors seek to innovate *around* regulation that is intended to constrain their behaviour, opportunistically harnessing regulatory rules in ways that circumvent their protective intentions and thereby substantially undermining the achievement of regulatory goals (Ford 2017).

A contrasting perspective highlights the inherently social nature of technological developments. Technologies do not just emerge out of nowhere, they are a result of, if not response to, existing regulatory frameworks and social norms. Accordingly, technologies evolve and respond to dominant social structures and existing regulatory approaches. An example of the former is the development of the contraceptive pill as a result of male-dominated scientific laboratories and other institutions of knowledge and power. An example of the latter is the regulatory standards for the emerging railway technology in the early nineteenth century that drew on waterways- and turnpike-related regulatory approaches. According to this perspective, technologies and their regulation often emerge and develop by applying frameworks developed for technologies deemed sufficiently analogous to enable 'cross-reading'. These initial categorization efforts represent 'critical junctures' in the evolution of technologies, helping to explain why certain paths of technological evolution and application are taken and others are not.

Discussions about algorithmic regulation are characterized by elements from both these perspectives. Some of the most penetrating and nuanced perspectives examine the ways in which technology and their social contexts (which includes the humans who interact with those technologies) are 'co-produced', with one influencing the other in a dynamic interaction, recognizing the non-linear and often unexpected trajectory through which they emerge and develop over time. In the case of algorithmic regulation, one can easily identify aspects that are shaped by social structures and norms, whether, for example, it is by the shared characteristics of those programmers creating algorithms (white, male) or the 'freemium' business models that have emerged as the predominant approach adopted by commercial providers enthusiastically seeking to deploy algorithmic regulation. There are, however, also certain technological properties that shape algorithmic regulation, namely their reliance on the vast computational processing power that enables the utilization of data sets in ways that were hitherto infeasible. In other words, algorithmic regulation is about technology and social phenomena at one and the same time, hence the increasing reference to complex 'socio-technical' systems and phenomena, in which technology and society are understood as deeply intertwined rather than separate and distinct. In light of this, insights from Science and Technology Studies ('STS'), a well-established strand of inquiry within the sociology of science, may have much to offer those concerned with critically investigating algorithmic regulation, particularly their exploration of complex socio-technical systems. The following discussion draws on seminal work by Thomas Hughes in his analysis of large technical systems as a springboard for reflecting upon their continuities and discontinuities with forms of algorithmic regulation that have emerged in recent years.

4. Understanding Algorithmic Regulation as a Complex Socio-Technical System

According to Thomas Hughes, large technical systems are defined by a number of characteristics: they are at the centre of a wider, integrated social and technical system, they perform standardized operations that rely on integration with other social processes, and their operation is legitimized by their supposedly impersonal and objective rationality (Hughes 1983; Joerges 1988). These systems also have considerable (redistributive) social impact, interdependencies, and reinforcing social dynamics, some of which are beneficial and welcome, whilst others are detrimental and unwelcome. These impacts and are both direct, indirect and often unanticipated by their designers. Large technical systems of this kind are usually associated with nineteenth-century technologies, be it railways, electricity networks, or sewerage systems. The pipes and wires that constitute their core networked infrastructure seem somewhat distant from the world of algorithmic regulation which is typically less visible, with its reliance upon computing power (often located in remote destinations), multiple large data sets, often gathered from diverse sources, and the internet's global networked data infrastructure. Despite their somewhat different appearances, however, several features of algorithmic regulation relate directly to the concept of large technical systems, particularly given their shared network characteristics. Algorithmic regulation provides a powerful mechanism for coordinating activity across networks, in which its power and reach increases the greater the number of connected network nodes, a feature which it shares with other communication networks. Just as large technical systems shape attention, structure decision-making, and generate effects across multiple settings and across time, so too does algorithmic regulation, albeit at lightning speed and in a much more fine-grained and targeted manner. At the same time, both algorithmic regulation and large technical systems of this kind usually work in the background (even if their user interfaces are highly visible) typically in a taken-for-granted (or 'seamless', in contemporary parlance) way. And, like large technical systems, algorithmic regulation shapes, facilitates, and constrains the interactions and relationships between individuals and their social and economic lives.

Similarly, debates about algorithmic regulation resonate with earlier debates about large technical systems in terms of their social implications, and the dispute over the nature of the technology's operations as 'objective' in character. Likewise, concerns about the magnitude of corporate and state-based power that is associated with the owners of large technical systems, and the resulting opportunities for exploitation, abuse, and their impact on distributive justice also feature in debates about algorithmic regulation that emerge throughout the contributions to this volume. For example, there are considerable privacy and competition-related concerns regarding the power and practices of the Digital Titans to exploit their privileged access to the massive data sets they accrue from tracking the digital traces of individual activity online. More specific concerns about the ways in which the forms of algorithmic regulation operated by the Digital Titans rest on a 'freemium' or 'free services' model in which the individual receives ostensibly 'free' digital services in return for offering both their personal data to the service provider and their 'eyeballs' to advertisers. For commercially driven algorithmic regulatory systems, configured in accordance with the uncompromising logic of capitalism, the result has been a concern by owners of these systems to maximizing user time on site (thereby maximizing opportunities for advertising revenue generation). While the drive for revenue maximization is hardly surprising, this has resulted in unintended but potentially profound consequences at both the individual and collective level, ranging from alarm about individual addiction (and associated mental health concerns) to fears about the expansion and rapid spread of sensationalist content and misinformation online, and the use of political micro-targeting at an unprecedented scale in ways that not only diminish the quality of public debate and deliberation, but may threaten the very fabric and integrity of democracy itself. Concerns of this kind are a manifestation of a wide variety of fears about the impact of algorithmic regulation, provoking increasing calls for mechanisms and institutions that can secure 'algorithmic accountability', including concerns about the lack of accountability surrounding the collection, processing, and transfer of personal data, or algorithmic decision-making systems which are used to make decisions about individuals which can be highly consequential, yet often reached without the provision of adequate explanation or recourse to those affected (O'Neil 2016). These debates can be understood, in essence, as ultimately concerned with the legitimacy and legitimization of algorithmic regulation, particularly given the apparent objectivity that accompanies it, concealing the grittier, and often grimier, political realities that lie beneath the technology's shiny veneer.

At the same time, algorithmic regulation displays some genuinely novel features, many of which are examined in the chapters of this volume. One is machine learning via high speed and distributed information processing, allowing for systems of classification and recommendation, and commonly used to profile individuals in order to computationally identify and evaluate their personality traits, interests, preferences, and spending priorities based on data patterns rather than any underlying causal reasoning. While sorting, classification, and scoring processes are not new, the scale (both in terms of speed and potential distance between sorter and sortee) and the level of granularity and dynamism at which these processes can now be undertaken, represent a qualitative and quantitative change (see Bachmann & Bowker 2019). In addition, these algorithmic techniques, applied to large unstructured data sets, are capable of identifying hidden patterns and correlations in the data which would be beyond the capacity of human cognition, or even ordinary computing techniques. The application of algorithmic techniques generates the capacity to make calculated *predictions* about future behaviours and states of the world. It is the combination of these features that arguably underpins algorithmic regulation's novelty and power, enabling them to re-organize social life in accordance with the values and preferences of those who control the systems' parameters while creating, organizing, and pre-emptively acting upon the new knowledge thereby generated. This paves the way for highly targeted, dynamic interventions in markets and other social relations yet at a global scale and in real time (Yeung 2017). At the same time, machine learning systems are also novel in that their outputs are not deterministic (unlike the rule-bound computational systems that preceded them), due to the continual 'updating' of the algorithm in response to feedback from their environment, and which are not directly controlled by those who devise and configure them, raising challenging questions about initial standard-setting and subsequent account-holding for the results of their algorithmic calculations and their consequences (Council of Europe 2018).

But the novelty of the issues and challenges raised by algorithmic regulation are potentially even more far-reaching that the preceding paragraphs suggest. Although we have emphasized the similarities between algorithmic regulation and the large technical systems originating in the nineteenth century which Hughes focused upon, particularly their networked nature, there are two highly significant differences. The first lies in the character of the 'raw material' flowing through and across these networks, the second is their capacity to undertake and automate the functions previously performed by humans. While digital data is now commonly described as the 'new oil', the properties of data are quite different from the essential inputs that flow through our networked utilities infrastructures, such as gas, electricity, or water. These materials are all perishable and excludable: one unit consumed by me is one less unit available for others to consume. In contrast, the digital data that someone shares with you, whether it is a chocolate cake recipe, an unflattering image of a mutual acquaintance captured on one's smartphone, or the results of an individual's recent medical examination, can be shared billions of times over, without any loss in the quality or utility of the original data. At the same time, data sets can be reused and repurposed to produce new insight in ways that neither the data subject, nor those who originally collected the data, could have anticipated or imagined. When the data pertains to specific, identifiable individuals (ie it constitutes personal data), this data can be subject to algorithmic analysis when merged with other data sets in ways that enable highly intimate information about individuals to be inferred with remarkably high degrees of accuracy (Kosinski et al 2013). It is therefore hardly surprising that contemporary data protection law has acquired considerable importance as a vehicle through which concerns about risks and threats associated with the rise of algorithmic regulation might be tamed. Yet it is fair to say that despite the recent reform of EU data protection law in the form of the GDPR, debates about data governance are far from settled. As one leading behavioural economist and privacy scholar put it when the power of big data analytics started to emerge in public consciousness, 'one of the defining fights of our times will be the fight for the control over personal information, the fight over whether big data will become a force for freedom, rather than a force which will hiddenly manipulate us' (Acquisti 2013).

The second highly significant difference lies in the automated processing capabilities and their real-world applications which machine learning systems now make possible. The functions performed by nineteenth-century network utilities infrastructure were, viewed through a twenty-first century lens, fairly basic and rudimentary, even though they revolutionized social, economic, and political life. They were, in essence, carriers of the raw material that flowed across the network, transporting it from its original source (after being appropriately filtered and refined) to the point at which it could be consumed, in which the function of terminal interfaces was simply to switch the flow on or off, as desired. This lies in sharp contrast to the highly complex ways in which digital data is algorithmically processed by machine learning systems: for algorithmic regulation is not merely about the flow of data, for it also subjects this data to algorithmic analysis in order to inform and automate *decision-making*, and to do so at scale. These highly sophisticated decision-making systems can now perform an enormous range of functions that were previously undertaken by human operators, resulting in growing public awareness and anxiety about the so-called 'rise of the machines'. While contemporary fears of the inevitable redundancy of human workers reflects previous periods of social anxiety associated with earlier waves of automation of manual tasks throughout history, what is distinctive about contemporary debates is the almost limitless domains in which algorithmic systems may be shown to 'outperform' humans on a very wide range of tasks across multiple social domains that have previously been understood as requiring human judgement and intelligence. Because the power and sophistication of these machines has no historical antecedents, the need to understand their implications for both individuals and society more generally has become a matter of pressing importance, given that these machines are now routinely used to make highly consequential decisions in ways that ordinary users may be unaware, let alone fully comprehend.

The nature and critical importance of this challenge has been put most starkly by Shoshana Zuboff, who mounts a powerful and rather chilling argument, claiming that the logic of global capitalism driving the design, configuration, and evolution of complex algorithmic systems that have become ubiquitous in the daily lives of those living in highly industrialized contemporary societies has generated new forms and structures of power that are completely unprecedented, such that they cannot be adequately grasped via our existing concepts (Zuboff 2019). For Zuboff, the logic of capitalism that drives algorithmic regulatory systems has given rise to a distinctive form of capitalism which she dubs 'surveillance capitalism', in which the overarching goal of surveillance capitalists is not only to *know* our behaviour, but to *shape* our behaviour at scale. From the perspective of those seeking to regulate the behaviour of others, algorithmic regulatory systems offer possibilities that have hitherto emerged only in the fantasies of science fiction writers, giving birth to what Zuboff regards as a new species of power that she calls *instrumentarianism*—a power which 'knows and shapes human behavior towards others' ends' (Zuboff 2019: 8). According to Zuboff, for surveillance capitalists 'it is no longer enough to automate information flows *about us*; the goal is now to *automate us*' (Zuboff 2019: 8).

In sum, therefore, a volume on algorithmic regulation can be situated in established literatures, revealing how contemporary concerns about 'big data' and machine learning have direct resonance with earlier discussions surrounding the emergence of 'disruptive technologies' of an earlier age. In other words, a 'nothing new under the sun' perspective may serve as a warning against heightened excitement about the latest technological fad. Yet, at least for one of us, Zuboff's call to arms, based on clear-eyed acknowledgement that the algorithmic age we now inhabit is unprecedented and for which a new conceptual apparatus is required if we are to undertake penetrating critical evaluation, is far more compelling. This volume can therefore be understood as a response to her call for critical, interdisciplinary reflection in order to understand and reckon with the distinct properties of algorithmic regulation, especially in view of both its predictive capacities, and the scale and speed at which it may operate, across a growing number and variety of social domains. The global scale of the technologies upon which algorithmic regulation rests is worth emphasizing. In particular, it has become commonplace in policy circles to portray the US and China as locked in a global arms race in the field of artificial intelligence in the quest for technological superiority in which European players have struggled to establish themselves as serious competitors. When these techniques and technologies are employed for the purposes of algorithmic regulation, they invariably generate concerns about the use of data for predictive purposes, particularly when employed to shape and constrain the behaviour and opportunities of individuals. This, in turn, has given rise to ethical concerns about the ways in which corporate and state power may intervene with constitutional rights in ways that potentially threaten the very socio-technical foundations upon which individual freedom and human rights are anchored (Council of Europe 2018). Yet there remains an acute and as yet unresolved tension: between the clamour for more and better data upon which to train machine learning algorithms in the race for technological advantage on the one hand, and a need for meaningful and enforceable safeguards around the collection and exploitation of data and the threat of pervasive and ubiquitous surveillance for constitutional democracies committed to respect for human dignity and individual freedom.

Within both the burgeoning policy literature and expanding scholarship associated with 'critical algorithm studies' (or 'critical data studies') there is increasing recognition and consensus about many of the problems and concerns associated with the rise of algorithmic systems. These challenges might be understood as 're-verse salients' which, according to Hughes (1983), refer to features of a system that hold back the overall technology's development. In this particular case, the reverse salients might appear to rest on the social implications of particular applications, rather than inherent to the technology itself. Having said that, one critical property of these technological applications is their capacity to scale, and to do so at an unprecedented speed. Yet although there is a growing consensus about the kinds of problems and concerns that algorithmic systems generate, the same cannot be said of discussions about how we ought collectively to respond to these concerns, including questions about whether, and in what way, algorithmic regulation should itself be regulated. This is perhaps hardly surprising, given the speed and scale at which these complex socio-technical systems have emerged. Algorithmic regulation is already seriously challenging the capacity of our existing institutions of governance to exert meaningful oversight, raising questions about the adequacy of existing national and transnational regulatory systems to address particular issues and concerns, and how regulatory intervention might be legitimated. In many ways, then, we are 'flying blind', highlighting both the urgency and importance of the need for serious and critical interdisciplinary engagement, to which we hope this volume will contribute.

5. The Organization and Content of this Volume

This volume is grouped in three broad sections, beginning with contributions concerned with seeking to understand why algorithmic decision-making might be a serious source of concern and which might warrant some kind of regulatory or other public policy response. Yeung's opening contribution poses a deceptively simple question: what, precisely, are we concerned with when we worry about decision-making by machine? Focusing her attention on fully automated decision-making systems, she suggests that there are three broad sources of ethical anxiety arising from the use of algorithmic decision-making systems: (a) concerns associated with the decision *process*, (b) concerns about the *outputs* thereby generated, and (c) concerns associated with the use of such systems to *predict and personalize services* offered to individuals. Each of these concerns is critically examined, drawing on analytical concepts that are familiar in legal and constitutional scholarship, often used to identify various legal and other regulatory governance mechanisms through which the adverse effects associated with particular actions or activities might be addressed. The chapter by Scantamburlo and her colleagues enriches Yeung's analysis in several dimensions, offering a highly accessible explanation of how machine learning works and, as a result, how decisions are made by modern intelligent algorithms or 'classifiers'. They then critically evaluate a real world 'classifier', the Harm Assessment Risk Tool (HART)—an algorithmic decision-making tool employed by the Durham police force to inform custody decisions concerning individuals who have been arrested for suspected criminal offences. They identify various technical features of the tool: the classification method, the training data and the test data, the features and the labels, validation and performance measures, and they evaluate the tool by reference to four normative benchmarks (a) prediction accuracy, (b) fairness and equality before the law, (c) transparency and accountability, and (d) informational privacy and freedom of expression. Their examination clearly demonstrate how the technical features of the tool have important normative dimensions that bear directly on the extent to which the system can be regarded as a viable and legitimate support for, or even alternative to, existing human decision-makers. Such and Criado's contribution focuses on one particular normative concern associated with machine decision-making that has attracted considerable attention in policy debate—the problem of bias in algorithmic systems, which, in turn, gives rise to various forms of 'digital discrimination'. They highlight various forms and sources of digital discrimination, pointing to a rich and growing body of technical research seeking to develop technical responses that are aimed at correcting for, or otherwise removing, these sources of bias.

While the problem of bias may arise in any form of algorithmic system, Danaher's contribution focuses on one specific application of algorithmic regulation: the use of artificial intelligence (AI)-based personal digital assistants. Rather than being employed as a tool for shaping the behaviour of others, these algorithmic tools are employed by individuals to assist them in their own self-regarding decision-making and goal achievement. While individuals have long used a great variety of tools to enrich their own decision-making and task performance, from familiar 'to do' lists hastily scribbled on a notepad by pen and ink through to the use of electronic spreadsheets to assist in managing our household budgets and expenditure, the capacity of AI-driven personal digital assistants can be understood as genuinely novel, owing to differences in scope, scale, speed, the centralization and monopolization of power in Big Tech, and the algorithmic processing of behavioural data about an individual across a population to predict and pre-empt and personalize the user's decision-making and behaviour. Accordingly, he concludes that these algorithmic tools provoke genuine concerns about user manipulation in ways that may undermine personal freedom and autonomy. Nevertheless, he also emphasizes that because individuals are not compelled to use these AI-driven personal digital assistants, the threat to autonomy which they ultimately may pose is relatively weak.

The contributions in the second part of the volume focus on the use of algorithmic regulation in the public sector. The chapter by Veale and Brass highlights the range of ways in which algorithmic regulation has been harnessed in the public sector, highlighting myriad ways in which the turn to automation (to *streamline* public service delivery) and machine learning systems (to *augment* or improve public service delivery) can be seen as both continuous with, and antagonistic towards, long-standing concerns in public sector administration (particularly with NPM logics) yet raises genuinely novel challenges. Griffith's chapter focuses on one particularly salient application of algorithmic regulation in the public sector—for the purposes of risk assessment to inform decisions about the allocation of enforcement resources, focusing on their accuracy and effectiveness in risk prediction. Drawing on two UK case studies in health care and higher education, he highlights the limited effectiveness of algorithmic regulation in these contexts, drawing attention to the prerequisites for algorithmic regulation to fully play to its predictive strengths. In so doing, Griffiths warns against any premature application of algorithmic regulation to ever-more regulatory domains, serving as a sober reminder that delivering on the claimed promises of algorithmic regulation is anything but simple, straightforward or 'seamless'. The final contribution to Part II by Lodge and Mennicken returns to questions of regulation, in particular the use of machine learning algorithms in the regulation of public services. They highlight the ways in which algorithms provide for an extension of regulatory systems, yet are associated with properties that are qualitatively different and distinct from existing regulatory instruments and approaches.

The third and final part of the volume considers potential responses to many of the concerns raised in the earlier chapters, beginning with Andrews' discussion of the UK's state of 'governance readiness', asking whether existing administrative capacity is sufficient to respond to the various threats and harms raised by the rise of algorithmic regulation, including biases caused by a lack of information on part of the 'user' while drawing attention to limitations of current systems in standing up to dominant providers of information services. In contrast, Lohr, Maxwell, and Watts focus on the extent to which 'private' solutions in the form of contractual risk management techniques can be invoked by commercial and other organizational actors involved in the development, deployment, and use of algorithmic systems, identifying a range of novel legal challenges that arise from algorithmic regulation. They note that while private law solutions have considerable scope to respond to these risks, there are a number of areas where state-based (public) regulatory interventions may be needed. It is the latter issue which Bygrave takes up in his contribution, by offering a critical assessment of the ability of critical provisions of the EU's GDPR to regulate algorithm-driven decisional processes involving profiling to ensure the protection of human rights and freedoms from threats of automated systems. He argues that many of the rules that are intended to provide safeguards against various practices and outcomes that might threaten human rights suffer from significant flaws, which are a function both of internal factors as well as external impediments to effectiveness, such as the increasing complexity and opacity of algorithm-driven 'black box' decision-making, the fickleness of consumer concerns for privacy, and the basic logic of the 'internet economy'.

The ambition of this volume is not to develop a unified position on the study of algorithmic regulation, a phenomenon that has already attracted considerable attention from both policy-makers and scholars alike. This volume (and indeed this introductory chapter) illustrates differences in perspective between those emphasizing the genuine novelty of algorithmic regulation and related unprecedented challenges and those searching for similarities and differences with earlier transformative technologies. Such differences do not prevent a common interest and conversation in the kind of tensions and conflicts that the emergence of a novel technology encourages. As we have already observed, interest in algorithmic regulation has occurred largely (although not exclusively) in isolated silos reflecting the disciplinary backgrounds and interests of different authors. This volume aspires to bring together different disciplinary perspectives so as to prepare the ground for a more sustained and integrated conversation across disciplines. Of course, this volume cannot aspire to provide a fully comprehensive perspective, and we must acknowledge distinct biases given that authors to this volume are drawn from Western hemisphere backgrounds living in highly industrialized economies. However, the much-needed trans-disciplinary conversation needs to start somewhere, and we hope that the contributions to this volume, individually and collectively, offer the basis for continued and enhanced interdisciplinary efforts in the study of algorithmic regulation.

Bibliography

Acquisti A, 'What Would a World without Secrets Look Like?' TEDGlobal 2013 <https://www.ted.com/talks/alessandro_acquisti_why_privacy_matters?language=en> accessed 22 February 2019.

Aneesh A, 'Global Labor: Algocratic Modes of Organization' (2009) 27 Sociological Theory 347.

Bachmann A and Bowker GC, 'Unsupervised by any Other Name: Hidden Layers of Knowledge Production In Artificial Intelligence on Social Media' (2019) 6(1) Big Data & Society 1 <https://doi.org/10.1177/2053951718819569> accessed 30 July 2019.

Baldwin R, Cave M, and Lodge M (eds), *Oxford Handbook of Regulation* (Oxford University Press 2010).

Beniger J, *The Control Revolution: Technological and Economic Origins of the Information Society* (Harvard University Press 1986).

Black J, 'Constructing and Contesting Legitimacy and Accountability in Polycentric Regulatory Regimes' (2008) 2 Regulation & Governance 137.

Bridle J, *New Dark Age: Technology and the End of the Future* (Verso Books 2018).

Carsten Stahl B and Wright D, 'Ethics and Privacy in AI and Big Data: Implementing Responsible Research and Innovation' (2018) 16(3) IEEE Security & Privacy 26 doi: 10.1109/MSP.2018.2701164.

Council of Europe, 'A Study of the Implications of Advanced Digital Technologies (including AI systems) for the Concept of Responsibility within a Human Rights Framework' MSI-AUT (2018) 05 rev.

Council of Europe, 'Governing the Game Changer—Impacts of Artificial Intelligence Development on Human Rights, Democracy and the Rule of Law' High Level Conference, co-organized by the Finnish Presidency of the Council of Europe Committee of Ministers and the Council of Europe (26–27 February 2019)<https://rm.coe.int/draft-programme-governing-the-game-changer-impacts-of-artificial-intel/168091fff8> accessed 20 February 2019.

Ford C, *Innovation and the State* (Cambridge University Press 2017).

Gillespie T, 'The Relevance of Algorithms' in T Gillespie, PJ Boczkowski, and KA Foot (eds), *Media Technologies: Essays on Communication, Materiality and Society* (MIT Press 2014).

Hildebrandt M, 'Algorithmic Regulation and the Rule of Law' (2018) 376(2128) Philosophical Transactions of the Royal Society A: Mathematical, Physical and Engineering Sciences 20170355 doi: 10.1098/rsta.2017.0355.

Hughes T, *Networks of Power; Electrification in Western Society, 1880–1930* (Johns Hopkins University Press 1983).

Joerges B, 'Large Technical Systems: Concepts and Issues' in R Mayntz and T Hughes (eds), *The Development of Large Technical Systems* (Campus 1988).

Koop C and Lodge M, 'What is Regulation?' (2017) 11(1) Regulation & Governance 95.

Kosinski M, Stillwell D, and Graepel T, 'Private Traits and Attributes are Predictable from Digital Records of Human Behaviours' (2013) 110 Proceedings of the National Academy of Science 5802.

Mazzucato M, *The Value of Everything: Making and Taking in the Global Economy* (Allen Lane 2018).

Moses LB, 'Why Have a Theory of Law and Technological Change' (2007) 8 Minnesota Journal of Law Science & Technology 589.

O'Neil C, *Weapons of Math Destruction* (Crown Publishing 2016).

O'Reilly T, 'Open Data and Algorithmic Regulation' in B Goldstein and L Dyson (eds), *Beyond Transparency: Open Data and the Future of Civic Innovation* (Code for America Press 2013).

Taplin J, *Move Fast and Break Things* (Little, Brown and Company 2017).

Ulbricht L, 'When Big Data Meet Securitization. Algorithmic Regulation with Passenger Name Records' (2018) 3(2) European Journal for Security Research 139 doi: 10.1007/s41125-018-0030-3.

Yeung K 'Towards an Understanding of Regulation by Design' in R Brownsword and K Yeung (eds), *Regulating Technologies: Legal Futures, Regulatory Frames and Technological Fixes* (Hart Publishing 2008).

Yeung K, 'Design for Regulation' in J van den Hoven, PE Vermaas, and I van de Poel (eds), *Handbook of Ethics, Values and Technological Design* (Springer 2015).

Yeung K, 'Hypernudge: Big Data as a Mode of Regulation by Design' (2017) 20 Information, Communication & Society 118.

Yeung K, 'Algorithmic Regulation: A Critical Interrogation' (2018) 12(4) Regulation & Governance 505.

Zuboff S, *The Age of Surveillance Capitalism* (Profile Books 2019).

Zweig KA, Wenzelburger G, and Krafft TD, 'On Chances and Risks of Security Related Algorithmic Decision Making Systems' (2018) 3(2) European Journal for Security Research 181 doi: 10.1007/s41125-018-0031-2.

PART I
NORMATIVE CONCERNS

2

Why Worry about Decision-Making by Machine?

*Karen Yeung**

1. Introduction

The capacity to collect, store, and process digital data in real time on cloud servers, and to utilize vast data sets to train and feed machine learning algorithms that rely upon feedback loops to improve their own performance, have enabled the development of machines that are capable of making decisions across an almost limitless array of potential application domains. These range from systems that offer guidance on which consumer products to purchase; identifying whether human tissue is cancerous; deciding whether to grant (or refuse) an individual's application for a loan, job, or university place; through to those designed to direct the speed, direction, and movement of autonomous vehicles. Given the power and scale of these technologies, it is hardly surprising that ethical anxiety has continued to foment in the public mind about the so-called 'rise of the machines' and what they may portend.

But what, precisely, are we concerned with when we worry about decision-making by machine? Aside from widespread concerns about the potential loss of jobs from increasing reliance on automated systems, academic and public policy literature have hitherto discussed these concerns primarily under the broad rubric of 'data ethics' or, more recently, 'AI ethics'.[1] Within legal scholarship, the debate has focused primarily on whether contemporary data protection law (particularly the EU's new General Data Protection Regulation (GDPR)) will adequately address some of these anxieties.[2] Although significant progress has been made in

* An earlier version of this chapter was presented at The Royal Society and Israel Academy of Sciences and Humanities, Ralph Kohn Memorial Seminar Series on Science, Technology and Ethics, 25–26 October 2017, Jerusalem, Israel and at the Melbourne Law School staff seminar, Melbourne, 13 April 2018. I am indebted to participants at both seminars, and particularly to Mark Taylor and Andrew Kenyon, and also to Andrew Howes for comments on earlier drafts.

[1] See eg Mittelstadt et al (2016). This strand of literature can be situated within a broader interdisciplinary literature that is sometimes referred to as 'critical data studies' or 'critical algorithm studies', including the literature referred to in Social Media Collective (2018).

[2] The General Data Protection Regulation EU 2016/679 L 119/1 applies to the collection and processing of 'personal data' (see n 4 below). Arts 15 and 21–22 include explicit provisions concerning fully automated decision-making systems, although there remains considerable uncertainty about how these provisions will be interpreted and applied by courts.

identifying and articulating ethical concerns about decision-making by machine, these discussions have hitherto tended to focus on specific issues or issue sets. For example, considerable attention has been given to concerns about algorithmic transparency (including whether a 'right to an explanation' for particular decisions exists[3]), bias and discrimination, or the evaluation of particular socio-technical applications of algorithmic systems (such as data-driven media content engines), while other concerns have not attracted sustained academic attention (such as concerns about the 'dehumanization' of decision-making processes). Accordingly, the purpose of this chapter is both to draw together existing critiques and to supplement and clarify the nature, magnitude, and source of concerns about machine decision-making by reference to analytical constructs that are well established within legal and socio-legal scholarship. Simply put, this chapter asks: what, precisely, do we worry about, when we worry about decision-making by machine? It offers a conceptual framework that identifies three broad sources of normative anxiety arising from the use of algorithmic decision-making systems: (a) concerns associated with the decision *process*, (b) concerns about the *outputs* thereby generated, and (c) concerns associated with the use of such systems to *predict and personalize services* offered to individuals. This chapter proceeds by examining each class of concern, before subjecting those concerns to critical legal and constitutional scrutiny. The final section concludes.

This chapter focuses primarily on automated algorithmic decision-making systems rather than on recommender systems in which a human operator retains formal discretion to decide whether to accept those recommendations. Its scope includes both simple automated systems which display 'automaticity' (or 'functional autonomy'), referring to the capacity of a machine to activate and achieve its purposes without further human intervention (eg a landmine), and more sophisticated systems which rely upon machine learning algorithms and thus display 'decisional autonomy' insofar as they are designed to adapt dynamically to their environment, hence the processing of inputs and the determination of outputs partly independent of their human designers, with the resulting system displaying 'emergent' behaviour (Liu 2015: 325–44). Accordingly, the outputs of these systems are indeterminate at the outset and hence not fully predictably, creating difficulties in anticipating how an input will be handled, or in seeking to explain how a particular decision was made (Millar & Kerr 2016; Burrell 2016: 1–12). My examination extends to both algorithmic decision-making systems that rely upon the processing of personal data,[4] that is data pertaining to a specific, identifiable individual, as well

---

[3] See eg Goodman & Flaxman (2016), Wachter et al (2017), Selbst & Powles (2017), Mendoza & Bygrave (2017), and Edwards & Veale (2017).

[4] Art 4(1) GDPR defines 'personal data' as 'any information relating to an identified or identifiable natural person ("data subject")'; an identifiable natural person is one who can be identified, directly or indirectly, in particular by reference to an identifier such as a name, an identification number, location data, an online identifier or to one or more factors specific to the physical, physiological, genetic, mental, economic, cultural, or social identity of that natural person.

as those which do not. As we shall see, some concerns are rooted in the reliance on machines to make decisions, others are rooted primarily in the personal nature of the data upon which many of these systems rely upon, and many arise from the combination of both these elements and their capacity to antagonize fundamental rights.

Many of the concerns discussed below apply to both fully automated decision-making systems and algorithmic recommender systems. However, recommender systems generate additional normative concerns associated with the role of the 'human in the loop', but these are excluded from this examination simply for reasons of scope and length. Nor does the focus on machine decision-making imply that human decision-making systems are necessarily superior from an ethical or legal standpoint. On the contrary, it is widely accepted that human decision-making processes and outcomes are far from perfect and often deeply flawed. But contemporary legal systems have a wealth of experience in confronting flaws in human decision-making, at least in the context of decisions by governmental authorities, and it is the task of identifying, responding to, and remedying these flaws that has become the staple diet of modern administrative law (Oswald 2018). Much of this extensive body of jurisprudence is directed towards identifying when decisions of public authorities can be challenged by judicial review, enabling a court to invalidate the decision for failing to comply with the requirements of lawful administrative decision-making. Contemporary equality legislation has also wrestled with and responded to allegations about the discriminatory nature of decisions more generally, in response to claims that a decision has been made on the basis of so-called legally 'protected' grounds, or, because the indirect effect of the decision is to discriminate against legally protected groups. Although we have a reasonably well developed understanding of the flawed nature of human decision-making in these contexts, and a set of legal and institutional mechanisms intended to provide safeguards against the worst of their excesses, imperfect though they may be, we lack an equivalent comprehensive and systematic account and experience of the potential flaws and drawbacks associated with machine decision-making, and systematic and effective institutional mechanisms to guard against them. By developing an analytical framework to understand why automated decision-making raises ethical concerns, drawing selectively on legal literature concerned with impropriety or other unfairness in human decision-making, this chapter seeks to contribute towards filling this important and increasingly urgent gap.

2. Worries about Automated Decision-Making Systems

The section identifies and critically examines various ethical concerns about machine decision-making: some have attracted considerable attention while others have not. For this purpose, the use of these systems for intentionally malign or hostile purposes is excluded from the analysis (Brundage et al 2018) Rather, this analysis assumes that algorithmic decision-making systems are employed for legitimate social purposes, typically with the aim of improving the quality, accuracy, efficiency, effectiveness, and timeliness of decision-making. For this purpose, I construct an analytic framework that distinguishes between three broad kinds of concern associated with algorithmic decision-making systems, those associated with:

(a) the decision-making *process*;
(b) the *outcome or outputs* of that process; and
(c) the *predictive personalization* of services.

2.1 Process-Based Concerns

The following concerns are 'procedural', arising primarily in connection with the decision process rather than the substantive content or outcome of the decision.

2.1.1 No Human Actor Capable of Taking Responsibility for Decision

Many concerns about automated decision-making systems rest on a perceived ethically significant difference between automated and human decision-making processes. In particular, there are worries that mistakes may arise in the decision-making process, including circumstances involving the correct application of decision-criteria in the strict sense but which, in the particular circumstances of the case, may be inappropriate.[5] These concerns are partly rooted in the legitimate interests of individuals in being able to identify a competent human person to whom they can appeal in contesting the decision, and who can investigate, and if necessary override, automated decisions. The nature of this concern, and the extent to which it might be satisfactorily overcome, may depend upon whether it relates to:

- the *analytical or reasoning process* that is intended to inform the decision-making process by providing insight based on data through the application of computational algorithms; and/or
- the *task* of decision-making.

If the underlying reasoning process rests on simple rule-based algorithms (rather than utilizing machine learning algorithms) and the task of decision-making is automated, then putting a human in the loop may help to address these concerns. For example, automated ticket gates now being rolled out at the entrance and

---

[5] See discussion of erroneous and inaccurate decisions at section 3.1 below.

exit barriers to train platforms throughout the UK railway network are typically overseen by a human atttendant to supervise their operation, who can assist those with mobility difficulties and help to identify whether the automated reasoning has malfunctioned and if so, can override the machine's refusal of access (ie false negatives), although the human attendant is not well placed to identify erroneously granted access (ie false positives).

By contrast, if the logic underpinning a machine-generated decision is based on dynamic learning processes employed by various forms of machine learning algorithms, then meaningful human oversight and intervention may be impossible because the machine has major informational advantages over a human operator due to its capacity to process thousands of operational variables ('features') at very high speed, so that it is beyond the capacity of a human meaningfully to monitor the accuracy and quality of the system's outputs in real time. Accordingly, at the point at which these decisions are implemented, there may be no practical way to demonstrate trustworthiness of outputs (Matthias 2004).[6] Human oversight might nevertheless be worthwhile, at least to the extent that a natural person is entrusted with, and can be seen to be taking responsibility for, the final decision and to whom the affected individual can appeal.[7] Whether or not such oversight is meaningful must be assessed in a context-specific manner, particularly in light of the well-documented problem of automation bias (Skitka et al 2000: 701–17) In other words, human oversight at the point of decision is at best a partial and incomplete mechanism for addressing these concerns, suggesting that *ex post* mechanisms for ensuring decision-making accountability are likely to be particularly important in these contexts.

2.1.2 Lack of Participation, Due Process, or Opportunities for Contestation

Directly related to concerns about the inability of machines to 'take responsibility' for their outputs are concerns that automated decision-making systems deny those affected by them the opportunity to contest, challenge, or otherwise participate in the decision (Veale & Edwards 2018).[8] This worry is exacerbated where those decisions are based on analysis performed by machine learning algorithms that cannot be explained in terms that are comprehensible and intelligible to the affected individual, making the resulting decision very difficult for the individual to challenge

---

[6] Although the establishment and maintenance of systematic regulatory scrutiny to provide appropriate assurances concerning the integrity and accuracy of the algorithms might be introduced as a governance mechanism in order to provide an evidential basis for at least partial faith in the operation of machine learning algorithms, rather than 'blind' faith.

[7] There may, however, be considerable value in providing *ex post* explanations that can be revised after the fact. See discussion of due process at section 2.1.4 below.

[8] If decisions which produce legal or other 'significant affects' are made about an individual based 'solely on automated processing, including profiling', Art 22(3) GDPR provides that 'the data controller shall implement suitable measures to safeguard the data subject's rights and freedoms and legitimate interests, at least the right to obtain human intervention on the part of the controller, to express his or her point of view and to contest the decision'.

(Hildebrandt 2017). By denying the affected individual a 'right to be heard' and to contest the decision, the foundational interests underlying an individual's basic right to be recognized and treated as a moral agent (ie a person with views of her own and capable of acting on the basis of reasons) and thus entitled to dignity and respect is undermined (Gardner 2006: 220–42). At the same time, denying the affected individual an opportunity to be heard may preclude the decision-maker from acquiring relevant information that may be germane to the decision at hand and thus risks undermining the accuracy and quality of the resulting decision (Galligan 1997).

The so-called 'right to be heard' forms one of the two core principles underlying the English administrative law doctrine of 'natural justice', which provides that individuals whose rights and interests are adversely affected by a proposed decision should be entitled both to (1) a fair hearing, including the right to participate in the making of that decision, which includes a right to be informed of the case against her, and (2) the decision-maker should be impartial and unbiased (Endicott 2015). Both these principles are implicated in algorithmic decision-making systems, and have emerged as a focus of concern in academic critiques. While the fair hearing requirement is most acute in relation to decisions which interfere with an individual's fundamental rights (such as a person accused of a serious criminal charge who would if, convicted, be deprived of his or her liberty), it applies whenever those whose rights, interests, or legitimate expectations may be adversely affected by a public authority's decision. So, for example, EU law institutionalizes enforceable 'rights' to participate in the governance of new technologies although some criticize these rights as unduly narrow in their scope and content (Lee 2017). In particular, legal and Science and Technology Studies scholar Sheila Jasanoff has repeatedly highlighted how our technological environment and the technological systems that we employ distribute power and have differential affects on groups and individuals, yet for which responsible governance is vital but sorely and strikingly absent from the processes through which technological innovations are developed and applied in society (Jasanoff 2016). Hence she advocates an urgent need for participation mechanisms for engaging publics to play more active roles in the design and management of their technological futures, a theme that I briefly return to in the concluding section.

2.1.3 Unlawful or Unfairly Discriminatory Input Variables and/or Algorithms

The second limb of the right to due process, requiring unbiased decision-making, has also been raised in academic and policy debates, framed primarily in terms of the potential of algorithmic processes to entail unfair or unlawful discrimination. Discrimination is inevitable when making selection decisions about individuals, so that those who are not selected for a job, for example, suffer a setback to their interests. Discrimination is not, however, morally or legally problematic unless it is *unfair or otherwise unlawful* and this depends largely upon whether the criteria upon which the evaluation was made are 'relevant' to the matter being decided. Lord Justice Warrington in *Short v Poole Corporation* [1926] Ch 66, 90–91 offered a celebrated example of a red-haired teacher being dismissed because she had red hair as a decision so absurd that no reasonable person could dream that it lay within the powers of the decision-making authority, and thus would be invalidated by a court on an application for judicial review. Such a decision is unfair because we typically regard hair colour as morally and causally irrelevant to a person's professional competence as a teacher. A teacher dismissed solely on account of her hair colour suffers not only the direct harm associated with losing her job, but also moral harm because her dismissal was *arbitrary* and therefore unfair (Endicott 2005: 27–48).

Under English law, only public authorities are required by administrative law to consider relevant considerations, and to avoid taking irrelevant considerations into account, in the exercise of their decision-making power (Endicott 2005: 27–48). In contrast, private persons and institutions typically enjoy considerable decision-making freedom provided that they comply with general laws, such as legal obligations arising under equality legislation. The use of predictive analytics is particularly problematic because variables that would ordinarily be regarded as morally and/or causally irrelevant may have a very high degree of predictive value (ie statistical relevance). Is it ethically acceptable to base a decision on an underlying logic that is concerned with identifying reliable predictors of job performance, irrespective of whether those predictors have any causal relevance to the job itself? On the one hand, the affected individual has a legitimate interest in not being evaluated and assessed on the basis of considerations that are not causally relevant to the decision. On the other hand, a prospective employer has a legitimate interest in adopting the most reliable methods for evaluating the 'fit' and likely success of the candidate for the purposes of their enterprise.[9]

Resolving this conflict depends firstly on whether the affected individual has a fundamental and legal right not to be discriminated against on the basis of the variable in question. In this case, because there is no right to be free from discrimination on the basis of one's hair colour, it may be *legally* acceptable to take hair colour into account although it may nevertheless be *ethically* spurious—and it also raises questions about the *explainability* of the decision and the decision-maker's concomitant duty to give reasons.[10] But that is not the end of the matter, because hair colour (a legally permissible basis for discrimination) may be directly correlated to race (black people rarely have blonde hair, while those with dark hair are

---

[9] As Oswald observes, relevance is not an easy concept to define—it means different things to different people—and there seems to be much work to do in achieving understanding between the various disciplines involved in the creation, deployment, and regulation of algorithms, and in particular to determine the desirability of practices which are key to predictive accuracy: Oswald (2018: 12).

[10] See section 2.1.4.

more likely to be black). If so, then it may be legally and ethically necessary to employ techniques for discrimination-free data mining in order to avoid violating the right of individuals not to be subject to unlawful discrimination and the consequential harm associated with such treatment (Kamiran & Zliobaite 2012).

2.1.4 Transparency, Explainability, and Reason-Giving

Algorithmic systems have attracted persistent concerns about their opacity, reflected in depictions of algorithms as 'black boxes' (Pasquale 2015). Transparency concerns are especially acute when the resulting decisions are made on the basis of algorithmic analysis of personal data in order to determine, or to make recommendations concerning, an individual's access to benefits or other opportunities, but they also arise in relation to these systems more generally (Yeung 2018a). Not only are the algorithms employed in decision-making processes typically concealed from public view, often legally protected as trade secrets (Pasquale 2015), but even if the algorithms were disclosed, they would be meaningless to all but those with the specialist technical expertise needed to decipher them, particularly for data mining algorithms that are configured to identify unexpected ('hidden') patterns and correlations in massive (and often multiple) data sets. Organizations using these systems may be reluctant to disclose these predictive variables both to reduce the prospect of gaming by individuals, and because the absence of any necessary causal relationship between the those variables and the phenomenon of interest may provoke distrust and concern amongst affected individuals for whom the reasoning may seem highly spurious (illustrated by the example referred to above in which hair colour might be identified as a reliable predictor of teaching competence).

Although there are legitimate concerns about 'gaming' in certain circumstances (Weller 2017: 530), the lack of any causal or 'common sense' relationship between the variable and the outcome it is claimed to predict may not justify withholding an explanation of the basis for the decision: the teacher dismissed on account of her hair colour should nevertheless be informed of the reasons for her dismissal. Yet difficulties associated with explaining the basis of a decision (and, in the case of some forms of machine learning algorithms, particularly those which rely on neutral networks and back propagation, cannot readily be explained, even by the algorithm's developers) may result in a failure to take adequate account of the legitimate interests of those adversely affected by algorithmic decisions to know and understand the reasons for the adverse decision in terms that are intelligible and comprehensible to them.[11] In contrast, within conventional human decision-making processes, humans can (at least in principle) articulate the reasons for their

---

[11] There is growing recognition of the importance of developing 'explainable AI' (XAI), and this has opened up a significant field of computational research: see eg Samek et al (2017) and Wierzynski (2018).

decision when queried, although there is no guarantee that reasons thereby offered will be a true and faithful representation of the 'real' basis upon which the decision was made (Weller 2017).

2.1.5 Dehumanized Decision-Making

Fully automated decision-making systems may also preclude important moral ('soft') values from being incorporated into the decision-making process (Roth 2016). Although the removal of human discretion from decision-making processes can reduce the possibility of arbitrariness and both conscious and sub-conscious bias and prejudice that may infect human decision-making, it also eliminates the *virtues* of human discretion, judgement, and agency, which have long been recognized in socio-legal scholarship as vital in overcoming the inevitable imperfection associated with legal rules (Black 1997). This objection can be considered from at least three perspectives, from the perspective of (a) the decision-maker, (b) the individual about whom the decision is made, and (c) the relational dimensions of human decision-making.

(a) The Decision-Maker

From the decision-maker's perspective, discretion in decision-making allows scope for the harshness of rules to be tempered by considerations of compassion, sympathy, morality, and mercy in particular cases. In contrast, decisions made by machine are based on a cold, calculating logic applied with relentless consistency. While consistency is a morally desirable property of decision-making systems, and one of the virtues associated with rule-based decision-making, there may nevertheless be occasions when it may be legitimate to depart from the strict application of a rule. For example, Roth observes that in certain American school districts, automated attendance systems are used to refer students to truancy court automatically when the student has accrued a certain number of absences, a system which has been criticized by one disability rights group on the basis that it 'leaves no room for correction if an absence should be excused because it is related to a student's disability' (Roth 2016). Although data scientists might respond that we could identify those factors and then add them to the model to improve its performance, it is questionable whether such messy 'real life' factors can be readily and faithfully translated into machine readable data and programmes (Oswald 2018: 14–15).

In a different, but related, vein is growing anxiety that automating important decisions (particularly when they are life critical, such as making the 'kill' decision to trigger lethal weapons) may eliminate the decision-maker's capacity to rely upon her own moral sense of right and wrong to inform her decision-making. For a decision that may have very significant adverse effects on a particular individual, then the latter might regard the decision-maker's personal morality and desire to do what is right as an important safeguard that may help assure affected individuals and others that such decisions are ethical and appropriate. Hence in deciding whether, for example, to target a lethal weapon towards another, the human solider can be expected to recognize the target as a human being with whom he shares the common bond of humanity and must forever bear the physical, moral, and emotional consequences of his decision. This a fully automated lethal weapon cannot and will not do.[12]

(b) The Affected Individual

While concerns about algorithmic decision-making systems' capacity to discriminate against groups that have historically been disadvantaged are prominent in contemporary debates, often overlooked is their capacity to discriminate against an individual *qua* individual. Because the models underlying these techniques are based on the assumption that past behaviours are the most reliable predictors of future behaviours, they fail to take account of the nature of individuals as moral agents, as persons with wills of their own and the capacity to break free of past habits, behaviours, and preferences. Although we, as humans, may be predictable (and predictably irrational—Ariely 2009) and our behaviours deeply patterned— nonetheless we remain self-reflective moral agents, capable of making active choices and exercising self-control so as to resist temptation and forge a new path through which we can seek to alter ourselves and our anticipated future provided we have sufficient courage and determination to do so (Hildebrandt 2017).[13] If critical decisions about us are left wholly to algorithmic evaluation, then we risk become trapped in algorithmic prisons that are, in one sense, of our own making (Davidow 2014: 4). We have no hope of redemption or reinvention via the exercise of our own moral determination and courage to break out of our past habits and attitudes. In short, algorithmic decision-making systems that employ behavioural profiling may undermine our right to be treated with dignity and respect, and risk eroding our capacity for autonomy and self-determination.[14]

(c) The Relational Dimension of Human Decision-Making

Related but distinct from both these perspectives are concerns that reliance on algorithmic decision-making systems may eliminate the relational, communicative character of human decision-making processes which plays a vital role in our collective life. Consider, for example the value of the so-called 'right to be heard', which is recognized as an essential element of the right to due process and fair procedure. Although its primary value lies in giving the affected individual an opportunity to offer her own views on the matter, which may provide the decision-maker with information that is relevant to the decision at hand, value also lies in giving

---

[12] See eg Anderson & Waxman (2017) and the literature cited therein.
[13] Hildebrandt refers to this quality as the 'inherent indeterminacy' of the human which, she suggests, constitutes the essence of our humanity.
[14] See discussion at section 3.1 below.

the affected individual the subjective experience of *being listened to* by a fellow human being. Human decision-making processes provide the decision-maker with an opportunity to acknowledge—and to empathize with—the subjective reality of that individual's experience. In arriving at decisions that are associated with grief, anguish, and distress, including the kind of decisions that often arise for determination in family courts, for example, but perhaps most vividly revealed in the ongoing public inquiry into London's Grenfell tower blaze in June 2017 in which seventy-one people lost their lives, it may be especially important that those directly affected by a decision feel that they have been *listened* to by the relevant decision-makers, in which their subjective experience has been properly acknowledged: this requires recognition of the emotional cost and *meaning* of the events in question for which empathy and compassion is the morally appropriate response (Jack 2018), irrespective of the outcome of the decision-making process (Parens 2010: 99–107). While AI systems are increasingly capable of simulating human emotions and responses,[15] they are artificial and inferior substitutes for authentic empathy, compassion, and concern of those with whom we share the common bonds of human experience.

2.2 Outcome-Based Concerns

In addition to these procedural concerns are concerns about the substantive content or outcome generated by algorithmic decision-making systems, to which I now turn.

2.2.1 Erroneous and Inaccurate Decisions

Understandable concerns arise concerning the possibility that decisions generated by algorithmic decision-making systems may be erroneous or inaccurate. These errors may have serious adverse consequences, depending upon the application in which those systems are embedded: so, for example, if they are embedded in safety critical systems, such as those which inform the operation of autonomous vehicles, those errors can have fatal consequences. Other kinds of errors may appear relatively trivial, for example, algorithmic decision-making recommender systems for consumer products. Yet even then, as the Cambridge Analytica scandal illustrates, algorithmic systems that deliver media content recommendations might, in the aggregate, have highly consequential results, with the potential to skew the results of democratic elections. For individuals, errors arising from the use of data-driven personal profiling may be highly consequential, particularly when employed to inform judgements about people on the basis of group characteristics which may

---

[15] See eg <https://www.soulmachines.com/> accessed 6 July 2018.

not accurately reflect the individual's particular characteristics or circumstances, and hence lead to erroneous decisions about that individual. In such cases, the immediate harm to the individual lies in the inaccurate or erroneous decision. The relative severity and seriousness of the harm will depend upon the (tangible and intangible) consequences of the error: while the deprivation of the individual's fundamental rights and freedoms lies at the most serious end of the scale, decisions which result in the deprivation of legal rights, or reduction or denial of the life chances, opportunities, and benefits and other forms of adverse treatment associated with erroneous classification (stigma, stereotyping) can also have substantial adverse consequences for those directly affected (Davidow 2014).

2.2.2 Biased/Discriminatory Outputs Generating Injustice/Unfairness

Unlawful discrimination (discussed above) is one of several bias problems that can affect algorithmic decision-making. Biased decisions can also arise if the data mining techniques used to inform decision-making encode biases, due to hidden bias in the design of the algorithms (Roth 2016); if the training data is biased; or if the data fed into the system is biased, resulting in biased outcomes. Where those outcomes have a direct impact on individuals, this can cause harm and injustice, depending upon the consequence of the biased decision for the affected individual.

Related but distinct risks can arise where the underlying data is biased, or the way in which the algorithm itself operates in a biased manner, resulting in biased and inaccurate outcomes. These problems are general in nature, and may arise whether or not the data is personal data. For example, an image classification algorithm may be biased in favour of emphasizing particular features of a landscape (eg tends to over-identify man-made objects whilst underemphasizing features of the natural landscape)—so that its outputs are skewed in favour of man-made objects. This may not give rise to any harm or other adverse consequences in and of itself, but might do so if that output is used in ways that directly and differentially affect individuals and/or communities. For algorithmic systems that process personal data to inform and automate decisions that directly affect individuals, then such discrimination is a significant concern due to the biased and inaccurate outcomes that they generate and can cause substantial injustice (O'Neil 2016).[16]

A different but related problem arises if particular groups (eg based on race, religion, ethnicity etc) have historically suffered disadvantage. In these circumstances, even when the algorithms and underlying data are accurate and the algorithm is

---

[16] The making of an erroneous decision about an individual may itself be regarded as a moral harm, depending upon the decision in question. For example, as Galligan (1997) observes, there is a particular moral harm involved in an erroneous decision to convict an innocent person, which is not present in an erroneous decision to allow a guilty offender to go free.

itself untainted by bias, profiling techniques can inadvertently create an evidence base that leads to discrimination, perpetuating and deepening past patterns of discrimination against these groups and generating related harms. For example, experiments using an algorithmic decision-making model based on Google's Adfisher system resulted in male users being shown high-paying job ads six times more often than they were displayed to female users (Datta 2015: 92–112). This problem is not attributable to the algorithm per se, but with the way in which it replicates and reinforces historic discrimination and disadvantage, thereby perpetuating injustice against disadvantaged groups and associated stereotypes and stigmatization.

2.2.3 Imitating Human Traits and Affective Responses

The discriminatory effects of algorithmic decision-making systems are often unintended. Rather different concerns arise when systems are intentionally designed to imitate the affective responses of others in ways that might be deceptive or might exploit user vulnerability (Boden et al 2011). Concerns of this kind have been expressed primarily in relation to robots, particularly when designed to provide care or companionship to vulnerable individuals. Fears have been expressed that if a robot's appearance and behaviour is designed to simulate that of a living creature (such as a human or animal), in order to increase user take-up and attachment, this might be considered deceptive and therefore ethically dubious (Boden et al 2011).[17] While these concerns may appear, at first blush, unlikely to attach to algorithmic decision-making systems per se, more recent work recognizes how these systems can be utilized to simulate the voice of a particular individual. These systems could then be used to deceive individuals, who are led to believe that they are speaking directly with the individual whose voice is being simulated, typically a person known to them, such as a particular friend or family member (Brundage et al 2018). Even leaving aside concerns about the potential for these applications to be harnessed by malign actors, there are worries that even well-intentioned use of these systems to imitate the behaviour of humans or animals might induce false beliefs in the mind of users, constituting a form of deception and thus ethically problematic (Boden et al 2011).[18]

---

[17] Of the list of principles advocated by Boden et al (2011), Principle 5 noted that although it might be permissible and even sometimes desirable for a robot to sometimes give the impression of real intelligence, anyone who owns or interacts with a robot should be able to find out what it really is and perhaps what it was really manufactured to do. Robot intelligence is artificial, and the authors suggested that the best way to protect consumers was to remind them of that by guaranteeing a way for them to 'lift the curtain' (to use the metaphor from The Wizard of Oz).

[18] See eg principle 5 of the proposed 'principles of robotics' proposed by this interdisciplinary group of academics, which calls for transparency in robot design and prohibits deception of the vulnerable. In essence, they argue that users should always be able explicitly to identify that they are dealing with a machine rather than a human being.

3. Data-Driven Prediction and Personalized Information Services

3.1 Predictive Personalization and Data-Driven 'Hypernudging'

Additional ethical anxiety arises from the growing use of algorithmic decision-making systems which rely on the real-time collection and mining of personal data gathered from the digital traces of everyday behaviours from individuals across a population in order to provide 'personalized' services to individual users, typically on a predictive basis. Well-known examples include algorithmic consumer product recommendation engines such as those provided by Amazon, the 'News Feed' system used by social media giant Facebook to push media content to users, and the 'Up Next' system employed by YouTube automatically to identify and play video content algorithmically identified as relevant to the user. These are but a few examples of machine learning systems now employed within a very wide and diverse range of commercial applications, ostensibly on a 'free services' basis, that is, without requiring the payment of a monetary fee, but instead offering to provide the service in exchange for the right to access, process, and re-use the user's personal data (Acquisti et al 2015: 509–14). These systems rely on advanced data mining techniques to create profiles of individuals (based on group traits or characteristics) identified through the algorithmic mining of data left by the digital traces acquired from continuous, real-time tracking of a very large number of individuals (Hildebrandt & Gutwirth 2010). They can be configured to offer services that are 'personalized' to fit the inferred interests and habits of users, offering efficiency and convenience in seamlessly navigating through the vast volume of digital information that is now currently available and which would be effectively unmanageable without the kind of powerful algorithmic tools now available.

Although portrayed by providers as offering users a more 'meaningful' experience, algorithmic personalization differs from traditional, handcrafted personalization in that algorithmic personalization is typically based on the preferences and interests which the service provider has *inferred* about the individual, with services offered *pre-emptively* without any express request for service by the individual. Because the individual has not explicitly stated her preferences and interests about the service (indeed, she may not want the service at all), the ethical concerns associated with predictive personalization become apparent once we attend to the underlying aim of these systems. What is it, precisely, that these systems seek to optimize, and who has the power to specify that overarching goal? These systems are intended to channel the user's behaviour and decisions in the *system owner's* preferred direction, and thus commercial systems are intentionally configured to optimize whatever variables will generate maximum commercial returns to its owner. Because these systems are aimed primarily to optimize the long-term interests of the system owner, there is no guarantee that they align with the longer-term interests and welfare of users whose decisions and behaviours these systems are aimed at influencing (Yeung 2012: 122–48; 2017).

Although individuals formally retain the freedom to decide whether to consume these services, it is important to recognize the powerful, subtle, and typically subliminal way in which these systems operate via reliance on 'nudging' techniques (Thaler & Sunstein 2008) which seek to exploit the systematic tendency of individuals to rely on cognitive heuristics or mental short cuts in making decisions, rather than arriving at them through conscious, reflective deliberation. Not only are many nudging techniques ethically problematic because they can be understood as manipulative and lacking in transparency (Yeung 2017), but owing to their capacity continually to reconfigure networked services in light of real-time feedback from individuals who are concurrently tracked on a population-wide basis, this qualitatively enhances their manipulative power, which I have referred to elsewhere as 'hypernudging' (Yeung 2017: 118–36). Owing to the overwhelming dominance of the 'free services' business model for the provision of online services in which providers earn revenue from advertising and by exploiting the value of their customer data, these algorithmic systems are typically configured to maximize users' 'time on site' in order to maximize returns, for the longer users linger, the greater the opportunity the user has to view (and click on) ads and the more extensive the opportunities for the service-provider to collect and analyse more data from continuously tracking user behaviour. Many commentators have therefore highlighted how these systems foster addictive behaviours, designed to optimize user engagement in ways that are not typically in the longer-term interests of users themselves, offering endless engaging distractions, diverting their attention from their own personal goals and projects (Williams 2018). Taken together, there is a substantial concern that our increasingly smart environments, rooted in reliance on *pre-emptive, predictive* orientation of machine profiling techniques that are configured to personalize our surroundings and the opportunities and obstacles that emerge from our digital encounters, might both fail to respect, and serve to erode, our individual freedom and autonomy (Yeung 2017: 118–36; Zuboff 2019).

3.2 Population-Wide Dataveillance and Algorithmic Regulation

Not only does the continuous, systematic nature and highly invasive digital surveillance ('dataveillance') upon which behavioural profiling relies and that these processes typically entail raise ethical concerns, but they also invite consideration of a further series of questions, including: who has the capacity to engage in algorithmic decision-making? How is that power exercised, in relation to whom, and for what purposes? While conventional objections to population-wide surveillance, whatever its technological forms, are typically expressed in terms of its impact on the right to privacy[19] it is doubtful that privacy concerns can be satisfactorily overcome on the basis that individuals consent to digital tracking in order to avail themselves of 'free' digital services that granting access to their personal data makes possible. Not only are the intractable challenges associated with obtaining meaningful consent to data sharing well known (and the associated 'transparency paradox'—Nissenbaum 2011: 32–48; Cranor et al 2013–14: 781–812), but given that the power to develop and implement these systems rests almost exclusively in the hands of large, wealthy, and powerful organizations, this generates chronic asymmetries in the encounters arising between the large institutions (both commercial and governmental) that employ these technologies to guide, inform, and execute decisions and the individuals whose lives they affect and about whom decisions are made.

Because even the most innocuous data about our daily activities, when aggregated and algorithmically mined by reference to similar highly granular behavioural data gathered across populations, may reveal (with high degrees of accuracy) very intimate information about us, including our gender, sexual orientation, religious and political beliefs, ethnicity, and so forth, to which only large powerful institutions have access, this generates acute risks that this information might be used against us in ways that may be difficult (if not impossible) to detect and of which we are completely unaware (Kosinski et al 2013: 5802–05). This capacity to make probabilistic yet reasonably reliable inferences about intimate aspects of ourselves not only constitutes a straightforward violation of individual privacy, but once we become aware of the power of behavioural profiling to influence the decisions that are made about us across a wide range of domains, this is likely to alter our sense of our practical freedom, to play around with who we are, and to develop our sense of ourselves. In other words, the pervasive surveillance upon which behavioural profiling relies may have a corrosive chilling effect on our capacity to exercise our human rights and fundamental freedoms, particularly our capacity to engage in activities through which we can develop our sense of ourselves through the creative forms of action, expression, and experimentation within an environment in which we have confidence that will not be observed by others in ways that might increase our exposure to the potential adverse effects of algorithmic decision-making. (Richards 2013: 1934).

Not only does pervasive tracking and pre-emptive prediction threaten our agency and autonomy (Hildebrandt 2015), but when personalized pre-emption is scaled up and applied on a population-wide basis, it might be understood as

---

[19] See eg Joined Cases C-293/12 and 594/12 *Digital Rights Ireland and Seitlinger and Others* (the 'Digital Rights Ireland' case) in which the European Court of Justice held that the EU Data Retention Directive violated the EU Charter on Fundamental Rights and Freedoms, notably Art 7 (the right to private life) and Art 8 (the right to data protection).

antithetical to the principle of universal and equal treatment that we have come to associate with the contemporary rule of law ideal, in which the same general legal standards are applied to all legally competent adults as the basis for evaluating past behaviour, regardless of status, wealth, or other idiosyncratic beliefs or inclinations. For me, the use of automated personalization techniques raises thorny questions concerning whether, in what ways, and under what circumstances, personalization may be regarded as compatible with, or antagonistic to, the basic right of all human beings to be treated with equal concern and respect (Yeung 2012: 122–48; 2018b). I suspect that these questions can only be answered in the specific social and political contexts in which machine-driven personalization techniques are employed. To this end, Helen Nissenbaum's concept of 'contextual integrity' may have a valuable role to play in identifying the limits of acceptable personalization by helping to illuminate the underlying normative assumptions operative in any given domain. (Nissenbaum 2011). Accordingly, the adverse effects associated with predictive personalization of individuals' informational environment recently highlighted by the use of 'fake news' and other misinformation circulating on social media in the run up to both the UK referendum concerning Brexit, and the 2016 US presidential election (Wardle & Derakhshan 2017) are likely to be quite different from those associated with the use of predictive policing by law enforcement authorities (Ferguson 2017), personalized pricing employed by online retailers (Townley et al 2017: 683–748) or the provision of automated legal advice on a personalized basis (Casey & Niblett 2016: 429–42). My worry is that, as fears about algorithmic 'filter bubbles' and 'echo chambers' portend, when employed systematically on a population-wide basis, data driven personalization has the potential to corrode the social foundations of individual autonomy, social solidarity, and democratic community (Yeung 2018b).

4. How Should We Respond to these Concerns: Towards a Vocabulary of Justice, Rights, Wrongs, Harms?

The preceding section has highlighted a wide range of ethical concerns associated with the use of algorithmic decision-making. In order to respond effectively to these concerns, I suggest that both scholars and policy-makers urgently need to move beyond the language of 'data ethics' or 'AI ethics'. Although these terms are useful in highlighting how computational systems may have potentially negative implications for normative values, we cannot identify meaningful, effective, and legitimate governance institutions and mechanisms to address and mitigate them unless and until we clarify the nature, magnitude, and source of those concerns (Floridi & Taddeo 2016; Anderson & Anderson 2011). To this end, significant progress might be made by drawing upon analytical constructs that are well established within legal and constitutional scholarship (including contemporary

data protection legislation and the emerging jurisprudence concerning its interpretation) and which is starting to emerge in discussions about the 'human rights'
dimensions of algorithmic systems.[20] In this final section, I offer some brief reflections concerning how the ethical concerns raised in the preceding section might be
framed and conceptualized in terms familiar to lawyers, including 'justice', 'rights',
'wrongs', and 'harms'.

4.1 Justice, Democracy and Freedom in a Data-Driven Machine Age

Many of the concerns discussed in section 3 are amplified in their seriousness
and severity by the chronic asymmetry of power between those who design,
own, and implement these algorithmic decision-making systems and have
access to the voluminous and valuable data upon which they rely, and the individuals whose lives they affect. This asymmetry fuels acute disparity in the
distribution of the potential burdens and benefits associated with algorithmic
decision-making systems. Although users derive significant benefits from these
systems, largely in the form of the efficiency, speed, and convenience they provide, given that it is now effectively impossible to navigate the world of digital
information super-abundance that we now inhabit, their potential adverse effects are unevenly distributed. Not only do these systems have the capacity to
directly and adversely affect individuals when used to inform and automate the
tasks of selection, and to condition and distribute access to opportunities, resources, benefits, and burdens, but these adverse effects may also directly affect
groups and society more generally.

The way in which benefits and burdens are distributed across society, including those associated with the rise of algorithmic decision-making systems, raises fundamental questions of justice: and these are ethical concerns
of the highest order. At the same time, it should be evident from the preceding
analysis that there are a number of subtle yet powerful and potentially systematic ways in which algorithmic decision-making systems have the potential to diminish the practical capacity for individuals and groups to exercise
their freedom and autonomy, as active participants and authors of their own
lives and which, over time and as these systems penetrate every aspect of our
everyday lives, could seriously threaten our democratic and political foundations (Yeung 2011: 1–29).

---

[20] See eg Nemitz (2018), Hildebrandt (2015), Australian Law Reform Commission (2018), and Raso et al (2018).

4.2 From 'Data Ethics' to Institutional Safeguards: Rights, Risks, Harms, and Wrongs

One important institutional mechanism for safeguarding against some of these risks lies in the protection offered by contemporary data protection law. Yet, some of the terms and phrases employed in the EU's new GDPR are a potential source of confusion. Although the approach to data protection adopted by the GDPR remains anchored in the so-called Fair Information Principles,[21] it also introduces a new emphasis on 'risk' and on risk management techniques as part of the introduction of so-called 'accountability' obligations on data controllers to demonstrate compliance.[22] This includes placing a legal duty on data controllers to undertake a 'data protection risk assessment' in certain circumstances[23] and to implement, review, and update appropriate technical and organizational measures to ensure and be able to demonstrate that data processing is performed in accordance with the GDPR.[24] Although risk-based approaches to data protection are far from new within informational privacy discourse, there is a striking lack of consensus or coherence concerning what the concept of 'risk' refers to in this context and a surprising lack of attention devoted to identifying in more precise and concrete terms

---

[21] Art 5 of the GDPR provides that 'personal data shall be (a) processed lawfully, fairly and in a transparent manner in relation to individuals; (b) collected for specified, explicit and legitimate purposes and not further processed in a manner that is incompatible with those purposes; further processing for archiving purposes in the public interest, scientific or historical research purposes or statistical purposes shall not be considered to be incompatible with the initial purposes; (c) adequate, relevant and limited to what is necessary in relation to the purposes for which they are processed; (d) accurate and, where necessary, kept up to date; every reasonable step must be taken to ensure that personal data that are inaccurate, having regard to the purposes for which they are processed, are erased or rectified without delay; (e) kept in a form which permits identification of data subjects for no longer than is necessary for the purposes for which the personal data are processed; personal data may be stored for longer periods insofar as the personal data will be processed solely for archiving purposes in the public interest, scientific or historical research purposes or statistical purposes subject to implementation of the appropriate technical and organisational measures required by the GDPR in order to safeguard the rights and freedoms of individuals; and (f) processed in a manner that ensures appropriate security of the personal data, including protection against unauthorised or unlawful processing and against accidental loss, destruction or damage, using appropriate technical or organisational measures'.

[22] Art 5(2) GDPR provides that 'The controller shall be responsible for, and be able to demonstrate compliance with, paragraph 1 ("accountability")'. See also GDPR Arts 24–25.

[23] Art 35(1) GDPR provides that 'Where a type of processing in particular using new technologies, and taking into account the nature, scope, context and purposes of the processing, is likely to result in a high risk to the rights and freedoms of natural persons, the controller shall, prior to the processing, carry out an assessment of the impact of the envisaged processing operations on the protection of personal data. A single assessment may address a set of similar processing operations that present similar high risks.'

[24] Art 25(1) GDPR provides that 'Taking into account the state of the art, the cost of implementation and the nature, scope, context and purposes of processing as well as the risks of varying likelihood and severity for rights and freedoms of natural persons posed by the processing, the controller shall, both at the time of the determination of the means for processing and at the time of the processing itself, implement appropriate technical and organisational measures, such as pseudonymisation, which are designed to implement data-protection principles, such as data minimisation, in an effective manner and to integrate the necessary safeguards into the processing in order to meet the requirements of this Regulation and protect the rights of data subjects.'

the potential harms associated with the algorithmic processing of personal data (Kuner et al 2015: 95–98).[25] Within conventional risk assessment methodologies (which draw heavily on a family of methods for the calculation of risk based in the statistical sciences), before any risk calculation can be made, it is first necessary to identify the relevant unwanted event (Power 2007; Allhoff 2009). This entails identifying the relevant *harm*. Yet the GDPR does not define the concept of 'risk', but merely offers interpretative guidance in Recital 75 which opens with the claim that,

> (t)he risk to the rights and freedoms of natural persons, of varying likelihood and severity, may result from personal data processing which could lead to physical, material or non-material damage. (Art 29 Data Protection Working Party 2017)[26]

But what exactly are we concerned with when we speak about 'risk' in the context of the algorithmic processing of personal data? To what extent are these risks concerned with decision-making by machine per se, rather than with decision-making systems that rely upon the processing of personal data? Is our concern with risks understood as potential *harm or damage* (which is the standard focus of attention in conventional risk analysis—Allhoff 2009), or is our concern with potential *wrongs*, understood in terms of violations of legal and fundamental rights, or might our concern be with both *wrongs and harms*? As philosophers of crime have emphasized, harms and wrongs are distinct concepts (Duff 2001–02: 14–45). A's actions might cause harm to B without engaging in any wrongdoing (eg if A is stung by a wasp and involuntarily jerks her arm away in pain, striking B in the face), while X might wrong Y by violating Y's rights without Y suffering any concrete harm (eg if X trespasses on Y's property but causes no damage to the land or obstructs no activity that Y carries out on that land). In short, wrongs might not be harmful (because they may not give rise to tangible harm in the form of damage to life, limb, or property), whilst actions sounding in harm or damage might not be wrongful (because an action might cause harm yet not entail any violation of an underlying right). Accordingly, identifying whether 'risks' in the context of personal data protection refers to potential harms, or potential wrongs (ie rights violation), is of considerable importance.

Rather than describing ethical concerns and their potential implications in terms of 'risks' above, in relation to individuals and groups, I suggest that these may

---

[25] As Kuner and his colleagues have observed, there has been a failure to articulate a comprehensive framework of harms or other impacts of personal data processing, and that although harms from security breaches are generally well understood, much work remains to be done to identify the relevant impacts that should be considered in risk management: Kuner et al (2015).

[26] Although the EU's Art 29 Data Protection Working Party has recently issued guidelines concerning data protection risk assessment required by the GDPR, these consist of identifying and elaborating a series of 'risk factors' associated with personal data processing, rather than clarifying the nature of the underlying 'risk'.

be better described and understood in terms of the concepts and language of *rights, harms*, and *wrongs*. In so doing, this would help draw attention to the *distribution* of burdens across and between individuals, groups and society generally.

(a) **Individuals:** may be adversely affected by algorithmic decision-making systems that unfairly deny them access to critical opportunities (eg access to jobs, educational opportunities, housing, loan finance, and insurance). These adverse effects might be better described and understood as 'wrongs', for the underlying ethical concern lies in their potential to violate an individual's fundamental moral right to be treated with equal concern and respect (Dworkin 1985). This right is ultimately rooted in the basic principle of respect for persons, and can plausibly be interpreted to include recognition of an individual's prima facie right to be provided with reasons for actions which directly and adversely affect her, her entitlement to contest such decisions, and who, as a moral agent, has the capacity to be treated as capable of making active decisions and to exercise control over her own behaviour in significant, unpredictable, and sometimes transformative ways.

(b) **Groups:** may be adversely affected by bias in the design and operation of algorithms themselves, or in the underlying data on which they operate or have been trained. Groups that have historically been marginalized and disadvantaged may be particularly prone to the adverse effects arising from such biases, resulting in discriminatory decisions that may replicate and reinforce patterns of historic disadvantage and discrimination. Similarly, algorithmic decision-making systems may fail to exclude legally protected characteristics from the decision-making process, even though their exclusion might reduce the accuracy of the resulting predictions (Schauer 2007). Group-based discrimination may also generate intangible but nonetheless real and significant adverse effects which, again, might be better described as potentially wrongful rather than 'risky', by virtue of its communicative dimension, expressing demeaning and derogatory views, reinforcing negative stereotypes, and stigmatizing individual members of the group by virtue of their group identity and upon which a legitimate claim of right by the group may be grounded.

(c) **Society:** Taken together, the cumulative effect from widespread and systematic reliance on algorithmic decision-making could erode and destabilize the core constitutional, moral, political, and social fabric upon which liberal democratic societies rest and upon which our shared values are rooted (Yeung 2018b). While it might be possible to speak in terms of 'intergenerational rights', a term intended to refer to the duties owed by the present generation of rights-holders to future generations, the concept and language of rights fits uncomfortably in this context because these future rights-holders have not yet come into being. (Weiss 1990: 198–207). Because the collective moral, political, and constitutional values that constitute the social foundations of modern liberal democratic societies are potentially destabilized and eroded by the cumulative, aggregate effect of the increasing turn to machine decision-making in a data-driven age, these concerns might be usefully characterized as 'risks' of a 'systemic' nature. Thus, in the same way that systemic risks to financial markets are considered to be of paramount concern due to the potential for catastrophic system-wide failure should those risks materialize in ways that threaten to bring down the entire financial system, we might also regard these risks associated with algorithmic decision-making systems as systemic in character and which, if we fail to ensure that adequate safeguards are put in place, may erode our moral, cultural, and political foundations (the 'commons') which could fatally undermine our democratic political system and with it our individual freedom, autonomy, and capacity for self-determination which our socio-cultural infrastructure ultimately seeks to nurture and protect (Yeung 2012:122–48; 2018b). Failing systematically to allow scope for 'soft' but nonetheless important moral values such as compassion, mercy, and forgiveness to infuse the decision-making process may erode the fabric of our shared moral life that is rooted in the bonds of our common humanity and character as a moral community of responsible agents and which can be understood as a 'systematic risk' to our democratic system which is essential for flourishing communities in which both solidarity and individual freedom and self-development are cherished and nurtured.

These observations suggest ways in which both the language and concepts of 'rights' and 'risks' might be utilized more thoughtfully and carefully to give more concrete content and precision to the ethical concerns associated with machine decision-making, particularly in characterizing their nature, scope, and severity. We should then be better placed to identify, construct, and assess the range of institutional governance mechanisms by and through which these ethical concerns might be prevented, addressed, and/or mitigated. So, for example, whether or not the turn towards risk-based approaches to data protection, including data protection risk assessments, which the GDPR now requires in certain circumstances, will in practice play a significant role in safeguarding the rights and interests of individuals and society and thereby help secure algorithmic accountability depends critically on how the concept of data protection 'risks' is understood and operationalized, both by those engaged in data handling, and those empowered to enforce compliance with data protection law. Although risk-based approaches to data protection are far from new, there has been a striking (and perhaps puzzling) lack of attention to what the concept of 'risk' refers to, nor attempts to identify in more concrete terms the potential harms associated with the algorithmic processing of data generally, or personal data in particular. It is impossible to imagine how risk-based approaches to data protection can succeed unless and until we can understand and identify in more concrete terms the potential harms and wrongs associated with machine decision-making.

5. Conclusion

In this chapter, I have outlined a tripartite analytical framework for understanding the ethical concerns associated with the use of machine decision-making, encompassing:

(a) **process-based concerns**, which may interfere with the fundamental right of individuals to be treated with dignity and respect, without necessarily generating material harm or damage. Accordingly, they may be understood as *risks to rights*, reflecting the language of GDPR Recital 71 (including moral and legal rights to due process and participation, to be provided with an explanation of the reasons for adverse decisions, and to respect for one's dignity and responsibility as a moral agent with capacity for self-reflection and self-control). Yet the intangible nature of these adverse effects, associated with being treated as a 'thing', an object to be controlled, nudged, and manipulated, rather than, as Isaiah Berlin put it, a 'thinking, willing, active being bearing responsibility for my choices and able to explain them by reference to my own ideas and purposes'(Berlin 1998: 191), is no less real or serious simply because it is intangible. For this reason, the language of potential 'wrongs' may be a better descriptor, highlighting the potential interference with an underlying right rather than that of 'risks' to rights.

(b) **Outcome-based concerns** in the form of erroneous or otherwise inaccurate outcomes (including discriminatory outcomes) and the adverse consequences that arise from mistaken decision-making (whether in the form of denial of job or educational opportunities, access to insurance, loan finance, or other benefits and facilities) and which could reinforce and perpetuate past patterns of injustice against groups that have historically been marginalized and disadvantaged. In addition, ethical concerns about the use of machine decision-making systems to imitate the speech and behaviours of living creatures generally, and identifiable individuals known to the user, may also be regarded as outcome-based insofar as these outputs might be considered deceptive and potentially exploitative of human vulnerability. These more tangible harms may be difficult to quantify in monetary terms and might also be understood as *wrongful*, in that they may also interfere with the fundamental moral right of all individuals to be treated with dignity and with equal respect and concern, even though they might not entail any violation of strict legally enforceable or constitutional rights.

(c) Ethical concerns associated with **pre-emptive, prediction-oriented per-sonalization** of our informational environments and the opportunities and obstacles that configure our digital encounters, which, when employed systematically on a population-wide basis, might best be understood as systematic 'risks' that have the potential to corrode the social foundations of individual autonomy, social solidarity, and democratic community and upon which our collective freedom and the social bonds of our common humanity are ultimately rooted (Yeung 2018b).

Taken together, these ethical concerns risks may directly effect the well-being, autonomy, and flourishing of individuals, groups and of society more generally, yet they are unevenly and unequally distributed. Identifying how the benefits and burdens associated with machine decision-making are distributed, particularly the severity and probability of the burdens which they may generate for particular individuals, groups, and society, is only possible by attending to the particular context and consequences of a given decision-making system. The way in which I have conceptualized these concerns draws attention to their potential tangible and intangible adverse effects, highlighting how any of these concerns can be understood as undermining fundamental rights and which might therefore more appropriately be described as potential *wrongs* rather than *risks to rights*. Having said that, one advantage of adopting rights-based language and framing may lie in highlighting the *systemic risks* associated with algorithmic processing, understood in terms of their potential to undermine the moral, cultural, and democratic fabric ('the moral and democratic commons') which makes both individual freedom and democratic society possible. At the same time, it is important to recognize that human-decision making suffers from many weaknesses, and these are ultimately attributable to problems associated with the exercise of discretionary human judgement.

I have not, however, made any attempt to assess the benefits associated with algorithmic decision-making systems, let alone attempt to posit what a meaningful algorithmic risk assessment might consist of. There is no doubt that algorithmic decision-making systems offer considerable benefits in terms of their capacity to enhance the efficiency and accuracy of decisions, including their capacity to personalize and accurately anticipate our preferences, behaviours, and habits in ways that we might, at least theoretically, harness to foster our individual self-development and democratic participation. Nevertheless, Jasanoff's call to action is worth reflecting and recalling in concluding:

It would be foolish at best and dangerously innocent at worst to deny the advantages of the human-made instruments and infrastructures that make up the environments of modernity. Yet, whether we treat technology as a passive backdrop for a society that evolves according to unconstrained human choice or attribute to technology superhuman power to shape our destinies, we risk making conceptual errors that threaten our well-being. Centuries of invention have not only made human lives more pampered, independent and productive; they have also perpetuated forms of oppression and domination for which classical political and social theory barely has names, let alone principles of good government. Unless we understand better how technologies affect basic forms of social interaction, including structures of hierarchy and inequality, words like 'democracy' and 'citizenship' lose their meaning as compass points for a free society. (Jasanoff 2016)

Bibliography

Article 29 Data Protection Working Party, Guidelines on Data Protection Impact Assessment (DPIA) and determining whether processing is "likely to result in a high risk' for the purposes of Regulation 2016/679. Working Paper 248, 4 April 2017.

Acquisti A, Brandimarte L, and Lowenstein G, 'Privacy and Human Behavior in the Age of Information' (2015) 347(6221) Science 509.

Allhoff F, 'Risk, Precaution, and Emerging Technologies' (2009) 3(2) Studies in Ethics, Law and Technology 1.

Anderson M and Anderson S (eds), *Machine Ethics* (Cambridge University Press 2011).

Anderson K and Waxman MC, 'Debating Autonomous Weapons Systems, Their Ethics and Their Regulation Under International Law' in R Brownsword, E Scotford, and K Yeung (eds), *The Oxford Handbook of Law, Regulation and Technology* (Oxford University Press 2017).

Ariely D, *Predictably Irrational: The Hidden Forces that Shape Our Decisions* (Harper Collins 2009).

Australian Law Reform Commission, 'Human Rights and Technology—Issues Paper' (July 2018).

Berlin I, 'Two Concepts of Liberty' in H Hardy and R Hausheer (eds), *The Proper Study of Mankind* (Pimlico 1998).

Black JM, *Rules and Regulators* (Oxford University Press 1997).

Boden M, Bryson J, Caldwell D, et al, 'Principles of Robotics' Engineering and Physical Sciences Research Council (2011) <www.epsrc.ac.uk/research/ourportfolio/themes/engineering/activities/principlesofrobotics/> accessed 16 August 2016.

Brownsword R, Scotford E, and Yeung K (eds), *The Oxford Handbook of Law, Regulation and Technology* (Oxford University Press 2017).

Brundage M, Avin S, Clark J, et al, 'The Malicious Use of AI: Forecasting, Prevention and Mitigation' (2018) <https://maliciousaireport.com/> accessed 6 July 2018.

Burrell J, 'How the Machine "Thinks": Understanding Opacity in Machine Learning Algorithms' (2016) 3 Big Data & Society 1.

Casey AJ and Niblett A, 'Self-Driving Laws' (2016) 66 University of Toronto Law Journal 429.

Cranor L, Frischmann BM, Harkins R, et al, 'Panel I: Disclosure and Notice Practices in Private Data Collection' (2013–14) 32 Cardozo Arts & Entertainment Law Journal 781.

Datta A, Tschantz MC, Datta A, 'Automated Experiments on Ad Privacy Settings' (2015) 1 Proceedings on Privacy Enhancing Technologies 92.

Davidow B, 'Welcome to Algorithmic Prison—The Use of Big Data to Profile Citizens is Subtly, Silently Constraining Freedom' (2014) The Atlantic <https://www.theatlantic.com/technology/archive/2014/02/welcome-to-algorithmic-prison/283985> accessed 30 July 2019.

Duff RA, 'Harms and Wrongs' (2001–02) 5 Buffalo Criminal Law Review 14.

Dworkin R, *A Matter of Principle* (Harvard University Press 1985).

Edwards L and Veale M, 'Slave to the Algorithm? Why a "Right to an Explanation" is Probably Not the Remedy You Are Looking For' (2017) 16(1) Duke Law and Technology Review 1.

Endicott T, 'The Value of Vagueness' in V Bhatia, J Engberg, M Gotti, and D Heller (eds), *Vagueness in Normative Texts* (Peter Lang 2005).

Endicott T, *Administrative Law* (3rd edn, Oxford University Press 2015) Chs 4–5.

Ferguson AG, 'Policing Predictive Policing' (2017) 94 Washington University Law Review 1115.

Floridi L and Taddeo M, 'What is Data Ethics?' (2016) Philosophical Transactions of the Royal Society A. 371: 20160360.

Galligan D, *Due Process and Fair Procedures* (Oxford University Press 1997).

Galligan DJ, *Discretionary Powers in the Legal Order* (Oxford University Press 1986).

Gardner J, 'The Mark of Responsibility (With a Postscript on Accountability)' in MW Dowdle (ed), *Public Accountability* (Cambridge University Press 2006).

Goodman B and Flaxman S, 'European Union Regulations on Algorithmic Decision-Making and a "Right to Explanation"' ICML Workshop on Human Interpretability in Machine Learning (2016) arXiv:1606.08813 (v3).

Hildebrandt M, *Smart Technologies and the End(s) of Law* (Edward Elgar 2015).

Hildebrandt M, 'Privacy as Protection of the Incomputable Self: From Agnostic to Agonistic Machine Learning' Paper presented at The Problem of Theorizing Privacy (8–9 January 2017) The Buchmann Faculty of Law, Tel Aviv University, available via SSRN network accessed 24 October 2018.

Hildebrandt M and Gutwirth S (eds), *Profiling the European Citizen* (Springer 2010).

Jack I, 'I Feared the Grenfell Tributes Would Be Mawkish. I Was Wrong' *The Guardian* (26 May 2018) <https://www.theguardian.com/commentisfree/2018/may/26/grenfell-tower-tributes-titanic-victims> accessed 6 July 2018.

Jasanoff S, *The Ethics of Invention* (WW Norton & Co 2016).

Kamiran F and Zliobaite I, 'Explainable and Non-explainable Discrimination in Classification' in B Custers, T Calders, B Schermer, and T Zarsky (eds), *Discrimination and Privacy in the Information Society* (Springer 2012).

Kosinski M, Stillwell D, and Graepel T, Private Traits and Attributes Are Predictable from Digital Records of Human Behaviours' (2013) 110 Proceedings National Academy of Science 5802.

Kuner C, Cate FH, Millard C, et al, 'Risk Management in Data Protection' (2015) 5(2) International Data Privacy Law 95.

Lee M, 'The Legal Institutionalization of Public Participation in the EU Governance of Technology' in R Brownsword, E Scotford, and K Yeung (eds), *The Oxford Handbook of Law, Regulation and Technology* (Oxford University Press 2017)

Liu H-Y, 'Refining Responsibility: Differentiating Two Types of Responsibility Issues Raised by Autonomous Weapons Systems' in N Bhuta, S Beck, R Geiss, H-Y Liu, and C Kress (eds), *Autonomous Weapons Systems: Law, Ethics, Policy* (Cambridge University Press 2015).

Matthias A, 'The Responsibility Gap: Ascribing Responsibility for the Actions of Learning Automata' (2004) 6 Ethics and Information Technology 175.

Mendoza I and Bygrave LA, 'The Right Not to Be Subject to Automated Decisions Based on Profiling' in T Synodinou et al (eds), *EU Internet Law: Regulation and Enforcement* (Springer 2017).

Millar J and Kerr I, 'Delegation, Relinquishment and Responsibility: The Prospect of Expert Robots' in R Calo, M Froomkin, and I Kerr (eds), *Robot Law* (Edward Elgar Northampton 2016).

Mittelstadt BD, Allo P, Taddeo M, et al, 'The Ethics of Algorithms: Mapping the Debate' (2016) 3(2) Big Data & Society 205395171667967s.

Nemitz P, 'Constitutional Democracy and Technology in the Age of Artificial Intelligence' (2018) Philosophical Transactions of the Royal Society A 376.

Nissenbaum H, 'A Contextual Approach to Privacy Online' (2011) 140(4) Daedalus 32.

O'Neil C, *Weapons of Math Destruction: How Big Data Increases Inequality and Threatens Democracy* (Allen Lane 2016).

Oswald M, 'Algorithm-Assisted Decision-Making in the Public Sector: Framing the Issues Using Administrative Law Rules Governing Discretionary Power' (2018) Philosophical Transactions of the Royal Society A doi: 10.1098.

Parens E, 'The Ethics of Memory Blunting and the Narcissism of Small Differences' (2010) 3(2) Neuroethics 99.

Pasquale F, *The Black Box Society* (Harvard University Press 2015).

Power M, *Organised Uncertainty* (Oxford University Press 2007).

Raso F, Hilligoss H, Krishnamurthy V, et al, *Artificial Intelligence and Human Rights: Opportunities and Risks* (Berkman Klein Center for Internet & Society 25 September 2018).

Richards NM, 'The Dangers of Surveillance' (2013) 126 Harvard Law Review 1934.

Roth A, 'Trial by Machine' (2016) 104 Georgetown Law Journal 1245.

Samek W, Wiegand T, and Müller K-R, 'Explainable Artificial Intelligence: Understanding, Visualizing and Interpreting Deep Learning Models' (2017) Special Issue No 1 ITU Journal: ICT Discoveries 1.

Schauer F and Zeckhauser R, 'Regulation by Generalization' (2007) 1 Regulation & Governance 68.

Selbst AD and Powles J, 'Meaningful Information and the Right to Explanation' (2017) 7(4) International Data Privacy Law 233.

Skitka LJ, Mosier K, and Burdick MD, 'Accountability and Automation Bias' (2000) 52 International Journal of Human-Computer Studies 701.

Social Media Collective, *Critical Algorithm Studies: A Reading List* <https://socialmediacollective.org/reading-lists/critical-algorithm-studies/> accessed 6 July 2018.

Thaler R and Sunstein C, *Nudge* (Penguin Books 2008).

Townley C, Morrison E, and Yeung K, 'Big Data and Personalized Price Discrimination in EU Competition Law' (2017) 36(1) Yearbook of European Law 683.

Veale M and Edwards L. 'Clarity, Surprises, and Further Questions in the Article 29 Working Party Draft Guidance on automated Decision-Making and Profiling' (2018) 34 Computer Law & Security Review 398.

Wachter S, Mittelstadt B, and Floridi L, 'Why a Right to Explanation of Automated Decision-Making Does Not Exist in the General Data Protection Regulation' (2017) 7(2) International Data Privacy Law 76.

Wardle C and Derakhshan H, 'Information Disorder: Towards an Interdisciplinary Framework for Research and Policy Making' Report DGI (2017) 09, Council of Europe, Strasbourg.

Weiss EB. 'Our Rights and Obligations to Future Generations for the Environment' (1990) 84 American Journal of International Law 198.

Weller A, 'Challenges for Transparency' Paper presented at 2017 ICML Workshop on Human Interpretability in Machine Learning (WHI 2017) Sydney, NSW, Australia, <arxiv.org/pdf/1708.01870.pdf> accessed 30 July 2019.

Wierzynski C, 'The Challenges and Opportunities of Explainable AI' (12 January 2018) <https://ai.intel.com/the-challenges-and-opportunities-of-explainable-ai/> accessed 27 March 2018.

Williams J, 'Technology is Driving Us to Distraction' *The Observer* (27 May 2018) <https://www.theguardian.com/commentisfree/2018/may/27/world-distraction-demands-new-focus> accessed 6 July 2018.

Yeung K, 'Can We Employ Design-Based Regulation While Avoiding Brave New World?' (2011) 3(1) Law, Innovation and Technology 1.

Yeung K, 'Nudge as Fudge' (2012) 75(1) Modern Law Review 122.

Yeung K, '"Hypernudge": Big Data as a Mode of Regulation by Design' (2017) 20(1) Information, Communication & Society 118.

Yeung K, 'Algorithmic Regulation: A Critical Interrogation' (2018a) 4 Regulation & Governance 505.

Yeung K, 'Five Fears about Mass Predictive Personalization in an Age of Surveillance Capitalism' (2018b) 8(3) International Data Privacy Law 258–69.

Zuboff S, *The Age of Surveillance Capitalism* (Profile Books 2019).

3

Machine Decisions and
Human Consequences

Teresa Scantamburlo, Andrew Charlesworth, and Nello Cristianini*

1. Introduction

The recent 'machine learning' data revolution has not just resulted in game-playing programs like AlphaGo, or personal assistants like Siri, but in a multitude of applications aimed at improving efficiency in different organizations by automating decision-making processes. These applications (either proposed or deployed) may result in decisions being taken by algorithms about individuals which directly affect access to key societal opportunities, such as education, jobs, insurance, and credit. For, example, job applications are often screened by intelligent software[1] for shortlisting, before being seen by human recruiters;[2] college admissions are increasingly informed by predictive analytics,[3] as are mortgage applications,[4] and insurance claims.[5] In those circumstances, individuals are usually voluntarily

* Teresa Scantamburlo and Nello Cristianini were funded by the ERC Advanced Grant ThinkBIG.

[1] A note on terminology: throughout the chapter we will use the expressions 'intelligent software' and 'intelligent algorithms' to refer to the products of AI methods and specifically of machine learning. While we will use the terms 'machine decision' and 'machine decision-making' to indicate the application of machine learning techniques to decision-making processes.

[2] The human resource software market includes applicant tracking systems, resume screening tools, talent matching, and candidate relationship systems. Many companies use proprietary software eg *JobVite* (<https://www.jobvite.com/>) or free applications eg *MightyRecruiter* (<https://www.mightyrecruiter.com/>), which, collect and manage applicants' data, but can also provide functions for parsing and classifying applicants' resumes. Other software such as *Belong* (<https://belong.co/>) can perform more personalized search by analysing candidates' behaviour on social media platforms like Facebook or Twitter.

[3] eg consulting firm EAB (<https://www.eab.com>) provides technological solutions to enable colleges and universities to achieve the desired target of applicants, track students' activities, and offer personalized advises. Institutions using these, or similar tools, include Georgia State University, (<https://www.eab.com/technology/student-success-collaborative/ssc-wsj-oct-13>), and Saint Louis University, which has developed its own data-driven approach for finding successful students in existing and new geographic markets (Selingo 2017).

[4] eg *Experian* (<http://www.experian.com>), one of the largest UK Credit Reference Agencies, is using machine learning to approve or deny mortgage applications reducing processing time (see eg <http://www.experian.com/blogs/news/2017/05/25/information-data/>). Other lending platforms, like *Upstart* (https://www.upstart.com/) and *SoFi* (<https://www.sofi.com>) make their assessment also based on an applicant's career and education. For a list of companies using machine learning and AI in lending see (Payne 2017).

[5] eg SAS (<https://www.sas.com/>) provides Detection and Investigation for Insurance which uses automated business rules, embedded AI and machine learning methods, text mining, anomaly

engaging with the organization utilizing the software, although they may not be aware of its use (Eubanks 2018). However, predicative analytics are increasingly in use in circumstances where the individual's engagement with the organization is largely or wholly involuntary, for example in areas of state intervention such as child safeguarding and access to welfare benefits.[6]

A controversial area of application is that of criminal justice, where use of intelligent software may not directly impact the wider population, but the outcome of the decisions made are of critical importance to both the rights of those subject to the criminal justice system, and to the public's perception of the impartiality and fairness of the process.[7] Software tools are already used in US and UK courts and correctional agencies[8] to support decision-making about releasing an offender before trial (eg custody and bail decisions), and to determine the nature and length of the punishment meted out to a defendant (eg sentencing and parole). Such software, usually referred to as 'risk assessment tools', have become the focus of public attention and discussion because of claims about their associated risks (Angwin et al 2016; Wexler 2017) and benefits.[9]

In a democratic society, when a human decision-maker, such as a judge, custody officer, or social worker evaluates an individual for the purposes of making a decision about their entitlement to some tangible benefit or burden with real consequences for the relevant individual, it is understood that they should do so in accordance with a commonly understood set of normative principles, for example:

- justice (eg equality before the law, due process, impartiality, fairness);
- lawfulness (eg compliance with legal rules);
- protection of rights (eg freedom of expression, the right to privacy).

It is expected that not only will a decision-maker normally act in conformity with those principles, but also that the exercise of their decision-making powers can, when challenged, be exposed and subjected to meaningful oversight. This requires that the system within which they operate is subject to certain normative

---

detection, and network link analysis to automatically score claims records <https://www.sas.com/en_us/software/detection-investigation-for-insurance.html>.

[6] eg in the United States, Allegheny County was the first jurisdiction to use a predictive-analytics algorithm to identify families most in need of intervention (Hurley 2018). See the Allegheny Family Screening Tool <http://www.alleghenycounty.us/Human-Services/News-Events/Accomplishments/Allegheny-Family- Screening-Tool.aspx>. In the UK '… at least five local authorities have developed or implemented a predictive analytics system for child safeguarding. At least 377,000 people's data has been incorporated into the different predictive systems'. (McIntyre & Pegg 2018).

[7] eg the case of Eric Loomis in Wisconsin, USA (Liptak 2017).

[8] For a survey of the tools used in US see Electronic Privacy Information Centre <https://epic.org/algorithmic- transparency/crim-justice/>. In the United Kingdom, eg, see the Harm Risk Assessment Tool examined below. Similar tools, such as actuarial methods, have been used in England and Wales since the 1990s and are reviewed in a Ministry of Justice (UK) report (Moore 2015).

[9] For a brief examination of the benefits and risks in criminal justice, see the White House Report on Algorithmic Systems, Opportunity, and Civil Rights (2016: 19).

obligations, for example, that it is transparent and accountable, and as such facilitates public participation and engagement.

Many decisions will not be subject to specific review or scrutiny processes as a matter of course. Thus, the legitimacy of the system within which they are made rests both upon the reliance we are willing to place on the decision-makers internalizing and applying the normative principles—that is our having a rational basis on which to develop trust; and the system's effective observance of the normative obligations which provide the capacity and capability to criticize and question— that is our having a meaningful ability to exercise distrust. Decision-making systems in which the ability of the public to effectively develop trust or exercise distrust is significantly attenuated are likely to be perceived as illegitimate, and probably dysfunctional.

Ensuring that machine decision-making operates in accordance with normative principles, and takes place within a system that incorporates normative obligations, will be an important challenge, particularly as the precise nature and degree of observance of those principles and obligations may vary according to cultural and disciplinary expectations.[10] The current generation of intelligent algorithms make decisions based on rules learnt from examples, rather than explicit programming, and often these rules are not readily interpretable by humans. There is thus no guarantee that intelligent algorithms will necessarily internalize accurately, or apply effectively, the relevant normative principles, nor that the system within which they are embedded will have the means to facilitate the meaningful exercise of particular normative obligations.

This chapter focuses on the example of criminal justice, because it highlights many of the concerns shared by other applications of machine learning to human decision-making: how are these decisions made? How will this impact our ability to develop trust or exercise distrust effectively? What do we know about the accuracy, fairness, and transparency of such decisions? Can biases affect intelligent algorithms, due to their training examples or the conditions in which they are used? What kind of analogies might we use to think about these situations? What technical or legal solutions should be developed?

The principle underlying the use of machine decisions, that a score can be used as an indicator of the risk that a given person will behave in a certain way over a period of time (eg she will commit a crime, graduate successfully, or fulfil assigned tasks) remains the same for a broad range of uses, even if the consequences of a decision vary significantly in context. Depending on the score produced, the algorithm triggers a determinate response action such as 'detaining an offender'

---

[10] eg obligations such as transparency and accountability may be more highly valued in some countries, or in decision-making systems, than in others; and understanding of the meaning and/or application of terms such as 'privacy' or 'equality' can differ between lawyers, computer scientists, and laypersons.

or 'rejecting a loan application'. But a lack of general understanding of how these algorithms work and the impact they may have on people's lives, combined with limited access to information about software and outcomes, renders such decision-making processes opaque, even as an increasing reliance upon algorithms suggests a need for in-depth examination.

There is a need for discussion of the individual and social consequences of increased reliance on machine decision-making, and whether systems predicated upon such consequential decisions can support the necessary elements for the development of trust, or exercise of distrust, that are fundamental to the legitimacy of the criminal justice process, or to the legitimacy of administrative decision-making, when humans play a decreasing (or no) role in the process. The requirements for developing trust and exercising distrust in such systems will extend beyond simple guarantees of accuracy, to encompass guarantees that they operate according to key normative principles, such as justice, lawfulness, and protection of specific rights. Such limits might include not making use of information that is normatively excluded when reaching a given decision (eg the use of 'gender' or 'sexual orientation' in recruitment decisions), respecting some predetermined notion of fairness, and providing evidence both about how a decision was reached, and that the system was operated within the range of conditions for which it was designed and authorized.

Four benchmarks derived from the normative principles/objectives, which we consider both common to consequential decision-making relating to individuals, and critical to development of appropriate trust relations between stakeholders, are used here to exemplify the claim that a knowledgeable critical assessment of the interplay of key technical and normative concepts is required for the effective and legitimate application of machine decision-making. These benchmarks are accuracy, transparency/accountability, fairness/equal treatment, and rights to privacy/free expression. It is not suggested that these are the only possible or necessary benchmarks, but they are arguably the most representative elements of the public concerns about the encroachment of technology into social structures that permeate the zeitgeist of the 'big data' era. The main objectives here are to demystify the technology behind machine decisions, making it comprehensible and accessible to a non-technical audience, and to suggest how complementary technical and normative perspectives can help us to articulate and interlink specific requirements and remedies.

The following sections describe how a class of algorithms called 'classifiers' work (section 2), examine how they operate in practice in the Harm Assessment Risk Tool (HART), a real-life implementation in the criminal justice sector (section 3) and hypothesize how the four benchmarks might be used to effect and evaluate meaningful trust relations between stakeholders in the context of available legal and technical remedies (section 4).

2. Machine Decisions: The Technology

2.1 Machine Learning

Artificial intelligence (AI) is concerned with the study and design of systems that can perform complex actions, such as translating a text, driving a car, blocking unwanted emails, or recommending a book. An important type of action routinely performed by intelligent software is that of classification: assigning an item to one of many possible categories. This includes, as a special case, the task of making discrete decisions:[11] for example, about blocking or recommending a web page, or diagnosing a patient. While decisions can be made based on various mechanisms, modern AI methods are often created by exposing a learning algorithm to large numbers of training examples, a procedure known as 'machine learning'.

In the language of AI, the properties used to describe the item to be classified are often called 'features' and the classes that are assigned to each item are called 'labels'. So, we could describe an email by the words it contains, a patient by the outcome of a set of clinical measurements, a client by a set of parameters describing their track record of payments. The labels applied to an email can be, for example, 'spam' or 'ham', those applied to a patient could be 'diabetic' or 'healthy', those for the loan-client could be 'safe' or 'risky'. The goal of a learning algorithm is to build a function (a 'classifier') that assigns a class label (eg 'spam' or 'ham') to any object (eg emails) that has not yet been labelled.

2.2 Performance of Classifiers

The performance of any given classifier is defined in terms of the mistakes it makes on new and unseen data (called a 'test set'), and it can be estimated on a data set of known cases (called 'training set'). For example, given a set of emails already labelled as 'spam' or 'ham', how many errors does the classifier make, of each type, when it is run on a set of unlabelled emails? In this two-class example, mistakes can be either false positives (eg 'ham' emails mistakenly classified as 'spam') or false negatives (eg 'spam' emails incorrectly labelled as 'ham') and can have different costs (deleting a valid email might be more costly than keeping an unwanted one). The confusion matrix (see Table 3.1) is a data structure that keeps track of the four possible outcomes:

---

[11] The output of a classification algorithm might be considered a decision since it results from choosing among a set of categories or a score that puts an item within a certain category. This should be distinguished from the consequential decision that usually humans make after consulting algorithmic output (eg doctor's decision of requiring further screening to a patient based on the algorithmic output classifying that patient into a 'malignant tumour' category.

Table 3.1 2×2 confusion matrix

	True Spam	True Ham
Predicted spam	True Positive (TP)	False Positive (FP)
Predicted ham	False Negative (FN)	True Negative (TN)

Future performance is what matters when deploying such a system, and this is where significant work has been done in the theory of machine learning: what can past performance tell us about future performance? This is typically quantified in terms of probability: the probability of a given type of mistake being made, under certain (controllable) conditions.

In home pregnancy tests the labels are 'pregnant' and 'non-pregnant' and only one feature is used: the concentration of certain hormones in urine. The test can lead to false positives and false negatives, each with a different cost. (Is it better to miss a pregnancy or to raise a false alarm? This depends of course on the usage situation.) Past performance of this test on a sample of patients can give us information about its future performance, but only under the strong assumption that the subjects were selected in the same way. For example, if we test it on teenagers and then we use it on middle-age subjects, it might not have similar levels of performance.

To quantify the probability that a certain type of mistake is made in the future, we need to make some assumptions about the source presenting the future items to the classifier, as mistakes can occur with different probability. A typical statement that can be made in statistical learning is: if the future data are sampled according to a distribution of probability which is the same as that used in the test phase, then with high probability the error rates will be close to those observed in the test phase.

A technical detail that will be relevant later in this chapter is that many (but not all) binary classifiers work in two steps: first a real valued score is computed for the item to be classified, then that score is compared with a threshold, or cut-off point, and the item is assigned to one class or the other, based on where it falls. That real valued score could informally be thought of as a probability, though it is not necessarily formally a probability. For this specific case, there is an extra consideration: by moving the threshold we have a trade-off between false positives and false negatives. In the clinical example of pregnancy testing this could be captured by the notions of sensitivity or recall (ie the true positive rate: $TP/(TP + FN)$) and specificity (ie the true negative rate: $TN/(TN + FP)$).

Other common performance measures are: overall accuracy ($(TP + TN)/(TP + FP + TN + FN)$), which tell us how often the algorithm classifies items correctly, and precision (ie the positive predicted value: $TP/(TP + FP)$), which estimates the fraction of relevant positive instances returned by the algorithm. For our case study other relevant metrics are the probability of mistakes: the false discovery rate (ie the expected proportion of discoveries which are false, FP/(TP + FP)) and the false omission rate (ie the expected proportion of discoveries which are omitted: FN/(FN + TN)).

While this threshold must be set before the system is deployed, when engineers compare the merits of different scoring methods they often compare all possible error rates for all possible thresholds: in other words, by moving the threshold from the minimum to the maximum level, they generate pairs of true positives rate (sensitivity)—false positive rate (the probability of false alarm) that are plotted on a diagram called a receiver operating characteristic (ROC) curve, whose mathematical properties are well known.

ROC analysis can add further insights into model performance enabling the algorithm designer to visualize different trade-offs between the benefits (the true positive rate) and the costs (the false positive rate) of a classifier. Often ROC performance is reduced to a scalar value, the so-called area under the curve (AUC), which can range between 0 and 1, where 1 indicates a perfect classification and 0.5 a random guess.

2.3 Learning to Classify

In most practical cases, the designers of an AI system decide the features that are used to describe an item, and the classes that are available, but they do not design the actual decision function. This is automatically generated by a learning algorithm which has access to many training examples: large sets of labelled data which can guide the learning algorithm towards the best configuration of parameters, to maximize some measure of performance. This is why the design of automated classifiers is really a branch of machine learning,[12] and also why training data is such a valuable commodity.

It is important to notice that the system designer makes another important choice: the class of possible decision functions that can be output by the system. This may be a very large space, which the learning algorithm will have to explore, guided by the training data, but will necessarily be a subset of all possible decision functions.

As the decision function has been selected by an algorithm based on training data, the assessment of its performance on new unseen data is particularly

---

[12] This is the automation of statistical work previously done by actuarial scientists, statisticians, etc. There is a lot of overlap—but with machine learning this happens on a very large scale and in a largely autonomous manner, and the effects of the scale, automation, and future development of the field is the concern of this chapter.

important. Statistical Learning Theory[13] provides guidance for this step: if a classifier is tested on data that was never seen during its training phase and is of sufficient size, and it is found to perform well, then we can expect it to perform well on future data that was obtained in the same way as the test set.

The crucial points above are: (a) the test set needs to be of sufficient size; (b) it should not have been used for training; and (c) the future data must be obtained in the same way as the test set. Violating those requests means that we do not have a reliable assessment of the future performance of the classifier.

For the spam filter, a certain combination of words might appear to be associated with spam emails, but on a small test sample this might also be a coincidence. This kind of coincidence becomes more probable if the test data was already seen in the training phase (a problem known as 'overfitting'[14]), or—equally—if changes are made to the classifier in response to the test data. Finally, even if the classifier performs well on a large number of new and unseen test emails, its performance cannot be guaranteed if it is applied to a different source of data. For example, if something is found to be effective in detecting spam in emails from 1995, it might still fail on emails from 2017.

It is worth noting that there are many types of functions that can be used to map features to classes. The most common ones are based on linear functions (class is predicted based on a score that is a linear combination of features), neural networks (the class-score is a non-linear function of features), decision trees, and various types of combinations and committees of those. Interpreting how the classification function combines the various input features to compute a decision is not an easy task, in general, and goes beyond the boundaries of Statistical Learning Theory.

2.4   Correlation vs Causation

These important effects (like overfitting) are all related to the key fact that, at present, classifiers make predictions based on statistical correlations discovered between the features and the labels associated with the training items, not on any causal relations. So, it is possible that a statistical relation may disappear if the sampling distribution is changed, or that a spurious relation may appear as the result of what statisticians call 'multiple testing'—that is when testing multiple hypotheses simultaneously which are actually non-significant but can produce a significant result just by chance. The scoring function will not capture the essence of what makes

---

[13] Statistical Learning Theory is a mathematical framework for the field of machine learning which became popular with the development of the so-called Support Vector Machines (Vapnik 1995).

[14] Overfitting is the result of a statistical model which performs well over the training sample but generalizes poorly to new data. Underfitting occurs when the model does not capture the underlying structure of data (eg when a linear model is applied to non-linearly separable data).

a spam email but will be able to predict—and bet—based on indirect clues that associate with the labels.

To summarize, overfitting and out-of-domain application are both the result of the system relying on associations that appeared to be informative in the training or evaluation stage but are no longer informative during the deployment of the system.[15]

However, this is also part of the success of machine learning: predictions can be made based on combinations of features that somehow end up correlating with the target signal. This is the way in which purchase behaviour might be informative about voting intentions,[16] and therefore valuable.

When the machine cannot explain the reasons behind a guess, we cannot interpret its motivations, we can only assess its input-output, we talk about a 'black box'—the email might have been removed, but we will not know why. In other words, machine learning predictions or classifications are educated guesses or bets, based on large amounts of data, and can be expected to work subject to certain assumptions.

Often the specific blend of features that happens to correlate with the target signal has no real meaning to us. For example, a home pregnancy test is not based directly on the cause of pregnancy, but on correlating hormonal factors. However, what if we had a pregnancy test based on email content? The frequency of certain expressions might suggest an increased probability of pregnancy (eg morning sickness) in the general population, but this would not be causal, and the application of this general rule to a specific population—say medical students' inboxes—might fail entirely.[17]

2.5 On Bias

The fact that we trust certain correlations, or a class of possible decision functions, largely depends on a series of assumptions and inductive bias (Mitchell 1997). The term 'bias' is used with different meaning in different contexts. Informally, 'bias' is used to indicate any deviation from neutrality (or uniformity), any preference (or preconception), but its technical use in probability, statistics, machine learning,

---

[15] Overfitting was one of the reasons that led Google Flu trends to predict 'more than double the proportion of doctor visits for influenza like-illness (ILI) than the Centers for Disease Control and Prevention (CDC)' (Lazer et al 2014: 1203).

[16] eg according to Kantar UK Insights: <https://uk.kantar.com/ge2017/2017/what-your-shopping-basket-says-about-how-you-vote/>: 'Conservatives buy more products from the alcohol and fresh fish categories' whereas 'Labour supporters put more toiletries into their trolley'.

[17] However, consider the notorious case where Target, the US discount store, was able to predict a teenage girl was pregnant, before her own family knew, based on the analysis of historical purchase data for women who had signed up for Target baby registries in the past (Duhigg 2012). Purchase data were correlated to pregnancy and so they were able to predict it but, of course, the data played no causal role.

and social sciences can be very specific. 'Bias' is not used in a pejorative way in the STEM literature.

For example, in the theory of probability the term 'bias' is often used to indicate the probability associated with a binary event such as a coin toss. The bias of a coin is its probability of landing on head, and a coin is called 'unbiased' or 'fair' when that probability is 1/2.

In statistics, where we usually estimate a property of a distribution, the notion of bias refers to an estimator.[18] If the expected value of that estimator is the same as the true value of the quantity being estimated, the estimator is said to be unbiased. Sometimes biased estimators are preferred to unbiased ones. This occurs when biased estimators, for increasing sample size, converge to the true value faster than unbiased ones.

In machine learning a related concept is used: learning a concept from a finite sample requires making some assumptions about the unknown concept, so as to reduce the search space, and reduce the risk of overfitting the training set. This is done by knowingly introducing a bias in the system, that is a preference for a certain type of outcome.[19] For example, we can force a spam filter to only use linear combinations of word frequencies, or to prefer simple decision rules, thus reducing the options of the learning algorithm. Occam's razor, the principle that the simplest hypothesis is to be preferred, all else being equal, is a classic example of bias in machine learning.

3. Machine Decisions in Criminal Justice

3.1 Risk Assessment Tools

The development of risk assessment tools has an established tradition in criminal justice and, since the early 1980s, actuarial methods have been used to inform decision-making in correctional institutions (Feeley & Simon 1994). In the justice system, risk assessment tools are used to measure the future behavioural risk posed by a defendant and to inform a variety of decisions at different steps of the criminal justice process and in several types of crime. For example, risk assessment tools have been deployed in pretrial release,[20] in parole and probation[21] (ie to identify

---

[18] eg if we are estimating the expectation of a random variable based on a finite sample, the estimator might be the average of that sample.

[19] It is known in machine learning that without such a learning bias the general problem of learning from finite data is ill-posed. See the so-called 'inductive learning hypothesis' (Mitchell 1997).

[20] The Public Safety Assessment tool, developed by Laura and John Arnold Foundation (<http://www.arnoldfoundation.org/>) is used by twenty-one jurisdictions including three entire states, ie Arizona, Kentucky, and New Jersey (Christin et al 2015).

[21] The Correctional Offender Management Profiling for Alternative Sanctions (COMPAS) which has been developed by a for-profit company, Northpointe (now Equivant), is one of the most popular risk assessment tools in the United States (<http://www.equivant.com/solutions/inmate-classification>).

the most appropriate supervision), and criminal sentencing.[22] There are also tools developed for specific types of crimes, such sex offences,[23] youth delinquency,[24] or domestic violence.[25]

In this section we will review the Harm Assessment Risk Tool (HART) (Urwin 2016; Barnes 2016) as a recent example drawn from a huge literature[26] and, most importantly, as a concrete application of machine decision-making. In the light of the technical descriptions outlined in the previous section, we will try to point out the main components of the tool, ie the classification method, the features used, the training and the test sets, the implied assumptions and the performance measures.

3.2 The Harm Assessment Risk Tool (HART)

Launched in May 2017 to extensive media coverage (eg Baraniuk 2017; Sulleyman 2017), HART is an application developed by Durham Constabulary and Cambridge University to support police officers with custody decisions.[27] The model predicts the likelihood that an arrestee will commit a serious offence (high risk), non-serious offence (moderate risk), or no offence (low risk), over a two-year period after the current arrest.

3.3 The Classification Method

HART is built using random forests, a machine learning method that results from the combination of hundreds of decision trees (Oswald et al 2018; Urwin 2016). A decision tree is a popular algorithm where classification can be thought of as a series of if-then rules (Mitchell 1997: 52). Each node of the tree tests some attribute

---

[22] Pennsylvania is in the process of extending the use of risk assessment tools for sentencing decisions (Barry-Jester et al 2015) and, interestingly, also the state of Wisconsin is using COMPAS for sentencing (Tashea 2017).

[23] Static-99/R is the most widely used sex offender risk assessment instrument in the world and is used extensively in the United States, Canada, the United Kingdom, Australia, and many European nations. For more details see the website: <www.static99.org>.

[24] Many risk assessment tools offer versions for young offenders, such as COMPAS (<http://www.equivant.com/solutions/case-management-for-supervision>) and the Violence Risk Scale (<http://www.psynergy.ca/VRS_VRS-SO.html>).

[25] The Ontario Domestic Assault Risk Assessment (ODARA) predicts the risk of future domestic violence <http://odara.waypointcentre.ca/> and is available for police, victim support, and health services. It was developed by the Ontario Provincial Police and the Research Department at Waypoint. Other similar tools are the Violence Risk Appraisal Guide Revised (see the official website <http://www.vrag-r.org/>) and the Domestic Screening Violence Inventory (see Williams & Grant 2006).

[26] See examples in footnotes 2–6 and 20–25.

[27] HART was introduced as part of the Checkpoint programme, an initiative within Durham Constabulary which aims to reduce reoffending by offering moderate risk offenders an alternative to prosecution. See (Oswald et al 2018) and Durham Constabulary website: <https://www.durham.police.uk/Information-and- advice/Pages/Checkpoint.aspx>.

of the item to be classified (eg, age, gender, years in jail, etc) and each descending branch represents a possible value for the considered attribute/node (eg for gender there might be two values: 'female' or 'male', for age there might be some predefined intervals such as '0–18', '19–30', '31–50', and so on). Starting from the root, each instance is sorted at each node based on the value taken by the specified attribute moving down until a leaf, that is the terminal node containing a class label, is reached. Usually, we refer to classification trees when the labels take discrete values ('Yes'/'No' answers or integers) while we talk about regression trees when the labels take continuous values (usually real numbers).

Random forests construct a multitude of decision trees trained on random subsamples of the training set and using a random subset of features. Predictions of each individual tree can be averaged (with regression trees) or aggregated by taking the majority vote (in the case of classification trees). HART consists of 509 decision trees, each one producing a separate forecast that counts as one vote out of 509 total votes and outputs the forecast that receives the most votes (Oswald et al 2018; Urwin 2016).

A key feature of random forests is the out-of-bag error, which provides an estimate of the generalization error during the training phase. When a random sample is drawn to grow a decision tree a small subset of data is held out (usually one third of the sample) and used as a test set of that tree. This process, commonly known as 'Out of Bag (OOB) sampling', is used internally, during the run of the model, to estimate an approximation of model accuracy.

Another property is the ability to balance different types of errors, so that mistakes with highest costs occur less frequently than those less costly. For example, classifying a future serious offender into a lower risk category (false negative, ie someone classified as low risk who commits a crime in the follow-up period) is considered costlier than misclassifying a non-serious offender into a high-risk category (false positive, ie someone flagged as high risk who does not commit any crime in the follow-up period).[28] In HART these two errors are termed 'dangerous error' and 'cautious error' respectively (Oswald et al 2018: 227; Urwin 2016: 43) and their costs vary accordingly.

As Oswald et al (2018) pointed out, the set-up of cost ratios is a policy choice that was taken prior to the model's construction with the involvement of senior members of the constabulary. In these respects, HART intentionally prefers (ie applies a lower cost ratio to) false positives (the so-called cautious error) over false negatives (the so-called dangerous errors). In this way, 'the model produces roughly two cautious errors for each dangerous error' (Oswald et al 2018: 227).

---

[28] From a technical point of view a way to build the costs of classification errors is to alter the prior distribution of the outcomes so as to reflect the desired policy. For example, suppose that 30 per cent of the offenders in the training set 'fail' and 70 per cent do not. By this procedure the prior proportions can be changed so that failures are made relatively more numerous (Berk 2012).

3.4 The Training and the Test Sets

The training data set is composed of 104,000 custody events from a period be-tween January 2008 and December 2012. A custody event is defined as 'the dis-posal decision taken by the custody officer following arrest at the end of the first custody period' (Urwin 2016: 37). The output of a custody decision could be: 'to bail (conditional or unconditional), remand in custody, taken no further action, administer an out of court disposal/diversion scheme or prosecute the suspect with a decision to bail (conditional or unconditional)' (Urwin 2016: 37).[29]

The model was validated in two steps. A preliminary validation has been made with the aforementioned 'Out of Bag sampling' procedure, thus with random samples of the construction (training) data set. A more recent validation (Urwin 2016) has been conducted by using a separate test set composed of 14,882 custody events occurred in 2013. All data sets were drawn from Durham Constabulary management IT system.

3.5 The Features and the Labels

The training set includes thirty-four features regarding offenders' demographics and criminal history (see Table 3.2). Note that the feature set also includes two types of residential postcodes. The former ('CustodyPostcodeOutwardTop24') contains the first four characters of the offender's postcode, while the latter ('CustodyMosaicCodeTop28') can take a value from twenty-eight available codes providing information about most common socio-geo demographic characteristics for County Durham.[30]

While acknowledging the ethical implications of including offender's postcode among predictors—this could give rise to a feedback loop that may reinforce pos-sible existing biases, so that people living within areas targeted as 'high risks' would undergo closer scrutiny than those living in other areas (more will be said on the dimension of fairness in the following section)—Oswald et al (2018) argue that the nature of random forests would prevent a single feature, like postcode, from

---

[29] Note that the custody events of the training and the test sets are supposed to regard decisions with an observable outcome (eg 'released on bail')—indeed for those suspects who remain in jail we have no observation.

[30] According to Big Brother Watch (2018) the second postcode feature refers to Experian's Mosaic data. Mosaic UK is Experian's tool providing a classification of UK households relating socio-demographic characteristics to postcodes (<http://www.experian.co.uk/marketing-services/products/mosaic-uk.html>). The Mosaic system generates information about typical individuals and families in postcode areas (common social types are: 'World-Class Wealth', 'Disconnected Youth', 'Low Income Workers', etc). Widely used for marketing purposes, it can also be used for credit scoring and crime mapping.

determining the entire forecasted outcome.[31] Yet, Oswald et al (2018) reported that one of the two postcodes could be removed in a later iteration.

The model uses three labels reflecting the classification of offenders: (1) high risk = a new serious offence within the next two years; (2) moderate risk = a non-serious offence within the next two years; (3) low risk = no offence within the next two years.

3.6 Validation and Performance Measure

In Urwin's validation study (2016), HART's performance has been assessed with respect to both the Out of Bag samples (OOB construction data) and the separate test set (2013 validation data). For each dataset a 3 x 3 confusion matrix (see Tables 3.3 and 3.4) keeps track of the standard error measures expressed in per cent values and conditional to the three possible labels (high risk/moderate risk/ low risk).[32]

Among cautious and dangerous errors two notions are distinguished (Urwin 2016: 54–55):

- 'very dangerous error' = a suspect being labelled as 'low risk' commits a serious offence in the next two years (see cells marked with '+' in Tables 3.3 and 3.4)
- 'very cautious error' = a suspect being labelled as 'high risk' does not commit any crime in the next two years (see cells marked with '*' in Tables 3.3 and 3.4)

In the table below, we report some performance measures of HART (see Table 3.5 which was created by combining tables 6 and 9 in Urwin 2016: 52, 56)—note that they can be easily computed by using the terminology introduced in the previous section of this chapter.

To the best of our knowledge, ROC analysis and the AUC value are not provided in the validation study (Urwin 2016).

---

[31] Indeed, 'algorithms such as random forests are based upon millions of nested and conditionally-dependent decisions points, spread across many hundreds of unique trees ... It is therefore the combination of variables, and not the variable in isolation, that produced the outputted risk level' (Oswald et al 2018: 228).

[32] Note that the validation study also assessed to what extent the custody officers' decisions agree with HART predictions. Using a separate data set consisting of 888 custody events for the period: 20 Sept 2016–9 Nov 2016), the study suggested that the highest level of agreement is in the moderate category, at 39.86 per cent, while clear disagreement emerges in the high-risk category—the police and the model agree only at 1.58 per cent (Urwin 2016: 71–72).

Table 3.2 List of features used to train HART (Urwin 2016)

FEATURE	DESCRIPTION
1. Custody Age	Age at presenting custody event
2. Gender	Male or female
3. Instant Any Offence Count	Count of any offences at presenting custody event
4. Instant Violence Offence Binary	A yes/no binary value is used to define the present offence in terms of violence
5. Instant Property Offence Binary	A yes/no binary value is used to define the present offence in terms of property offence.
6. Custody Postcode Outward Top 24	The 25 most common 'outward' (first 3–4 characters) postcodes in County Durham. If the offender's postcode is outside of County
7. Custody Mosaic Code Top 28	The 28 most common socio-geo demographic characteristics for County Durham
8. First Any Offence Age	The suspect's age at first offender regardless of juvenile or adult
9. First Violence Offence Age	The suspect's age at first violent offence regardless of juvenile or adult
10. First Sexual Offence Age	The suspect's age at first sexual offence regardless of juvenile or adult
11. First Weapon Offence Age	The suspect's age at first weapon offence regardless of juvenile or adult
12. First Drug Offence Age	The suspect's age at first drug offence regardless of juvenile or adult
13. First Property Offence Age	The suspect's age at first property offence regardless of juvenile or adult
14. Prior Any Offence Count	The number of offences prior to the presenting offence for the suspect
15. Prior Any Offence Latest Years	The number of years since any offence—if there is no offence history, Null value is returned
16. Prior Murder Offence Count	The number of murder offences prior to the presenting offence for the suspect
17. Prior Serious Offence Count	The number of serious offences prior to the presenting offence for the suspect
18. Prior Serious Offence Latest Years	The number of years since the most recent custody instance in which a serious offence was committed— if there is no serious offence history then a code of 100 years is used.
19. Prior Violence Offence Count	The number of violence offences prior to the presenting offence for the suspect
20. Prior Violence Offence Latest Years	The number of years since the most recent custody instance in which a violence offence was committed—if there is no violence offence history then a code of 100 years is used.

Continued

Table 3.2 *Continued*

FEATURE	DESCRIPTION
21. Prior Sexual Offence Count	The number of sexual offences prior to the presenting offence for the suspect
22. Prior Sexual Offence latest Years	The number of years since the most recent custody instance in which a sexual offence was committed—if there is no sexual offence history then a code of 100 years is used.
23. Prior Sex Reg Offence Count	The number of sex offender register offences prior to the presenting offence for the suspect
24. Prior Weapon Offence Count	The number of weapon offences prior to the presenting offence for the suspect
25. Prior Weapon Offence Latest Years	The number of years since the most recent custody instance in which a weapon offence was committed—if there is no weapon offence history then a code of 100 years is used
26. Prior Firearm Offence Count	The number of firearms offences prior to the presenting offence for the suspect
27. Prior Drug Offence Count	The number of drug offences prior to the presenting offence for the offender
28. Prior Drug Offence Latest Years	The number of years since the most recent custody instance in which a drugs offence was committed—if there is no drugs offence history then a code of 100 years is used
29. Prior Drug Dist Offence Count	The number of drug distribution offences prior to the presenting offence for the offender
30. Prior Property Offence Count	The number of property offences prior to the presenting offence for the offender
31. Prior Property Offence Latest Years	The number of years since the most recent custody instance in which a property offence was committed—if there is no property offence history then a code of 100 years is used.
32. Prior Custody Count	The number of custody events prior to the presenting offence for the offender
33. Prior Custody Latest Years	The number of years since the most recent custody instance—if there is no custody event history then a code of 100 years is used
34. Prior Intel Count	The number of intelligence submissions at nominal level. The offender at nominal level will have a unique identifier, the submissions are counted within the forecasting model

Table 3.3 Confusion matrix for the training set (see table 7 in Urwin 2016: 54)

OOB Construction Data	Actual High	Actual Moderate	Actual Low	Total
Forecast High	8.12%	6.80%	1.80%*	16.72%
Forecast Moderate	2.25%	34.09%	12.19%	48.53%
Forecast Low	0.82%+	7.65%	26.28%	34.75%
Total	11.18%	48.54%	40.27%	100% = 104,000 custody events

* percentage of very cautious error
+ percentage of very dangerous error

Table 3.4 Confusion matrix for the test set (see table 8 in Urwin 2016: 54)

2013 Validation	Actual High	Actual Moderate	Actual Low	Total
Forecast High	6.26%	10.01%	2.23%*	18.49%
Forecast Moderate	4.88%	32.53%	13.55%	50.95%
Forecast Low	0.73%+	5.81%	24.02%	30.55%
Total	11.86%	48.35%	39.79%	100% = 14,882 custody events

* percentage of very cautious error
+ percentage of very dangerous error

Table 3.5 Some performance measures of HART extracted from tables 6 and 9 in Urwin (2016: 52, 56)

	OOB construction data	2013 validation data	
Overall accuracy: what is the estimated probability of a correct classification?	68.50%	62.80%	
Sensitivity/recall: what is the true positive rate for each class label?	72.60%	52.75%	HIGH
	70.20%	67.28%	MODERATE
	65.30%	60.35%	LOW
Precision: what is the rate of relevant instance for each class label?	48.50%	33.83%	HIGH
	70.20%	63.84%	MODERATE
	75.60%	78.60%	LOW
Very dangerous errors: of those predicted low risk, the percent that was actually high risk (subset of the false omission rate)	2.40%	2.38%	
Very cautious errors: of those predicted high risk, the percent that was actually low risk (subset of the false discovery rate)	10.80%	12.06%	

3.7 Operationalizing Trust: Four Normative Benchmarks for Machine Decision-Making

As noted above, HART is a case study drawn from a wider reality and, in addition to criminal justice, many other domains are reframing routine decisions in machine learning terms (education, recruitment, health care, government, etc). This reframing is premised on the fact that machine learning captures the general mechanism underlying common 'diagnostic questions' (Swets et al 2000): Will this person commit violence? Will this student succeed? Will this candidate meet current and future company's needs? Which customers will best match your business? Which persons will be more likely to develop depression? Which citizens should be prioritized in tax exemption? Usually all these questions call for a positive or negative decision about the occurrence of future event (student's success, employee's achievements, the rise of depression …) or the presence of specific conditions (eg for accessing a tax reduction programme or other public services).

Many argue that a thoughtful application of machine learning to (diagnostic) decisions might improve public policy (Kleinberg et al 2016). But, while the study of the effective advantages of machine decisions need further investigation,[33] the overall assessment of these technologies should extend beyond accuracy guarantees. When machine learning software evaluates an individual for the purposes of making a decision about their entitlement to some tangible benefit or burden, the operating procedures and consequences of their use should be evaluated according to the principles and values of democratic society.

In the following sections we will examine four benchmarks derived from the normative principles/objectives discussed above that may help stakeholders, including practitioners and citizens, answer the following question: How does one create an effective trust framework (eg one that permits rational development of trust and efficient exercise of distrust) that will legitimize the augmentation, or replacement, of human decision-making by machine decision-making? These benchmarks are derived from established normative principles and reflect the primary factors in the contemporary debate surrounding the quality of machine

---

[33] eg on one hand, Kleinberg et al (2017a) showed that machine learning could provide important economic and welfare gains in bail decisions, on the other, Dressel & Farid (2018) revealed that machine learning algorithms (eg COMPAS), when applied to pretrial decision-making, are no more accurate and fair than untrained (Mechanical Turk) workers. Urwin (2016) also addressed the problem of human vs machine predictions, but the results of such analysis are not yet available as the forecasts were made in 2016 and the follow-up period has not yet passed (see the written evidence submitted by Sheena Urwin, Head of Criminal Justice at Durham Constabulary, in relation to the enquiry into Algorithms in Decision-Making of the Science and Technology Committee, House of Commons, UK: <http://data.parliament.uk/writtenevidence/committeeevidence.svc/evidencedocument/science-and- technology-committee/algorithms-in-decisionmaking/written/78290.pdf>).

decisions. We believe these could form the basis of minimum requirements for legitimating the use of machine decision-making and, hence, set a standard for current and future applications. The benchmarks are explored here in the light of the HART case study, but their use as an analytical tool to inform regulatory theorizing is extensible beyond the criminal justice sector, and has potential for cross-domain application.

3.8 Prediction Accuracy

As discussed above, there are many ways to quantify the performance of a classifier and various aspects to consider when model accuracy is reported. Two important pieces of information are: which performance measure is used (eg overall accuracy? 'area under the curve' (AUC)?); and how was this measured (how large was the test or validation set; how was it formed?). Let us consider these questions in the light of our running example.

HART was validated by using two datasets: the construction sample (used also for training) and the validation sample (not used for training). The validation study provided several measures such as overall accuracy, sensitivity, precision and the expected probability of two specific mistakes, ie 'very dangerous' and 'very cautious errors'.[34]

When comparing model performances with the two datasets (ie training and test sets) the classification accuracy declines (see Urwin 2016: 50–52). This holds for both overall accuracy which falls from 68.50 per cent (in the OOB construction data) to 62.80 per cent (in the 2013 validation data), and sensitivity (the true positive rate) which gets worst with the high-risk category (it passes from 72.60 per cent to 52.75 per cent). So, one might ask whether using HART provides real advantages (greater accuracy) with respect to a more trivial decision mechanism (the so-called 'baseline'): Would it perform better than a random guesser? Computing the prediction of a random baseline we observe that HART sensitivity would be definitely more accurate. If the percentage of actual outcomes is known the accuracy of a random baseline can be calculated by using the rules of probability.

We denote Y as the actual outcome and $\hat{Y}$ as the prediction of a random guesser which is picked from the population of the 2013 validation dataset (comprising 11.86 per cent of high risk, 48.35 per cent of moderate risk and 39.79 per cent low risk offenders). Then the accuracy of the random guesser is:

---

[34] For an extensive account of the metrics computed, see Urwin (2016).

$$[P(Y = \text{"high"}) * P(\hat{Y} = \text{"high"})] + [P(Y = \text{"moderate"}) * P(\hat{Y} = \text{"moderate"})]$$
$$+ [P(Y = \text{"low"}) * P(\hat{Y} = \text{"low"})] = [0.1186 * 0.1186]$$
$$+ [0.4835 * 0.4835] + [0.3979 * 0.3979] = 0.406 = 41\%$$

The decline of accuracy might relate to the differing of offender samples (ie OOB construction sample vs 2013 validation sample)—indeed the frequency of serious crimes increased between 2013 and 2015.[35] Thus, it might be the case that HART captured statistical relations that were more effective in classifying offenders in the training set, but that were less significant in the test set.

As we have seen before, the statistical associations found in the training phase might also become less informative because of an out-of-domain application, that is when sampling conditions vary. In the case of criminal justice, we might ask: Are judges' decisions made in the same way? Did they predict the same outcome? Have the regulatory bodies' practices changed (rules, police routines, etc)? For instance, a risk assessment tool trained on a population of parolees might not be appropriate to inform bail decisions (the two populations have different characteristics: usually parolees have already spent time in jail) and thus provide poor or wrong predictions (Berk 2012). Note that in the case of HART these problems might be kept under control if, as Oswald et al (2018) reported, the data are drawn only from the Durham Constabulary system and not from other sources, such as local agencies in Durham or national IT systems.

The characterization of a model's performance, as we have noted above, depends also on the fact that not all mistakes are equal: for binary classifiers, one would need to separate the effect of false positives and false negatives; for multi-class classifiers, there would be many combinations and types of error, potentially each with different cost. For example, HART's developers have deliberately weighted more false negatives than false positives. This, as Oswald et al (2018) stressed, is a policy choice rather than a design strategy reflecting specific social needs and preferences (eg that of safeguarding citizens from potential harms). This choice is reflected in HART's performance: The percentage of very dangerous errors is lower than that of very cautious errors and the former remains the same in both data sets (very cautious errors slightly increase).[36]

---

[35] See the percentages of recorded crimes in Urwin (2016: 47).

[36] Specifically, 'the model was able to ensure the likelihood of very dangerous errors occurring was just 2%. Therefore, the organisation can be 98% sure that a very dangerous error will not occur.' (Urwin 2016: 85). Technically speaking, this result says that 98 per cent of the time that the model predicts somebody as low risk, they will not commit a serious crime (see the Cambridge Centre for Evidence-Based Policing video: <https://www.youtube.com/watch?v=zc8x5P7suuo&featur e=youtu.be>) Hence, she/he will be a moderate or low-risk offender. This is not the same as the media claim that 'forecasts that a suspect was low risk turned out to be accurate 98% of the time' (Baraniuk 2017).

3.9 Fairness and Equality

The findings of *ProPublica*'s analysis (Larson et al 2016) suggested that the use of risk assessment tools might bring about social discrimination.[37] Social disparities are not new in online advertising (Sweeney 2013; Datta et al 2015) and computer systems (Friedman & Nissenbaum 1996).

All these findings naturally raise questions for machine decision-making: can AI systems discriminate? How do they do it? Which technical, legal, and social remedies exist to avoid algorithmic discrimination? Which criteria can help us to inform such remedies?

A basic intuition underlying the notion of fairness is that all human beings must be treated equally before the law. This idea is deeply rooted in human rights documents which acknowledge that 'all are entitled to equal protection against any discrimination' (UN Universal Declaration of Human Rights, Article 7). Generally, we consider fairness as a comparative notion:[38] what counts for a person is to be treated equally with respect to other people who are subject to the same procedure. Thus, when a person or a group is unjustifiably differentiated and, because of this, put in unfavourable conditions, they are discriminated against.

What discrimination is and how it occurs is a controversial issue. Often the law, rather than providing a definition, prefers to indicate a non-exhaustive list of prohibited attributes that cannot be used to ground decisions in various settings (such as housing, education, employment, insurance, credit, etc). Typically, the list includes: race, colour, sex, religion, language, political or other opinion, national or social origin, property, birth or other status.[39] These attributes are then used to characterize groups of people which are recognized as important to the structure of a society and, hence, worthy of a special protection ('protected groups').

Algorithmic discrimination[40] can arise at different stages of the design process (Barocas & Selbst 2016). For instance, when forms of social bias are incorporated in the training data, the classifier is likely to reproduce the same bias (see, eg, Caliskan et al 2017 for the case of language).[41] Other pitfalls might be found during

---

[37] In short, the analysis found that COMPAS made more mistakes with black defendants as compared to their white counterparts, ie the false positive rate was higher with black defendants and the false negative rate was higher with white defendants.

[38] For an alternative view, see also Hellman (2016).

[39] These characteristics are referred to, in the context of non-discrimination, in international human rights documents such as the International Covenant on Civil and Political Rights (Art 26), and European Convention on Human Rights (Art 14). Most are also to be found in international data protection agreements, eg The Council of Europe's Convention for the Protection of Individuals with regard to Automatic Processing of Personal Data (Art 6), and the EU General Data Protection Regulation (Art 9), as personal data to which special safeguards should be applied.

[40] For a survey on this topic, see also Romei & Ruggeri (2013) and Zliobate (2015).

[41] Caliskan et al (2017) have documented how standard natural language processing tools, which are trained on large corpora derived from the Web, reflect the same implicit bias found in language by the Implicit Association Test. For instance, European American names are more likely than African American names to be associated with pleasant terms—eg health, peace, honest, etc—than unpleasant terms—eg abuse, murder, accident, etc.

the feature selection process—when sensitive attributes in the feature set correlate to a classification outcome (eg when gender attribute is systematically associated to lower paid jobs)[42]—and sampling—when certain protected groups are underrepresented as compared to others.[43]

Building fair (or non-discriminating) algorithms supposes the implementation of an equality principle which can be intended in various ways. From a purely formal point of view, equality is achieved when alike cases are treated as alike.[44] From a social perspective, equality is concerned with the distribution of goods and services. Its meaning has been specified in two competing conceptions:

- *Equality of outcomes*: everyone should receive the same levels of good or services. A straightforward example is the ideal that all receive the same income.
- *Equality of opportunities*: everyone should have the same chances of success irrespective of sensitive attributes or those that are irrelevant for the task at hand.

These principles inspire different fair practices. For example, a system of quotas (eg jobs for specific groups) would enforce equality of outcomes; a system that screens CVs only based on relevant attributes would enforce equality of opportunities. The same holds true also for the development of non-discriminating algorithms where different fairness criteria relate to different notions of equality.

A technical measure that relates to equality of outcomes is *statistical or demographic parity*. The latter requires that the portion of individuals classified as positive (eg 'hired' or 'high risk offenders') is the same across the groups (eg 'male' and 'female'). However, statistical parity is subject to several objections since ensuring the same portion of positive outcomes among groups does not guarantee the same level of accuracy, ie when there is an imbalance in the training set, the algorithm will learn and perform better with member of the overrepresented group (Dwork et al 2012; Hardt et al 2016). Moreover, a system of quotas might not be desirable in certain contexts such as that of criminal justice (Chouldechova 2017).

On the other hand, the implementation of equality of opportunity requires an in-depth consideration of how the classifier behaves across the groups (eg is the

---

[42] Note that a sensitive attribute can be redundantly encoded in other features. Thus, the algorithm may discover these encodings even if the sensitive attribute has been removed, eg, even though the gender attribute is dropped from the feature set, other attributes encoding gender (eg 'cooking', 'shopping', 'family', 'children') may correlate to jobs with lower salaries.

[43] If we have sample size disparities (ie a social group is overrepresented), the algorithm will learn statistical correlations that will badly transfer to the minority group (Hardt 2014). For example, if a credit score algorithm is trained on a data set which disproportionally represents a segment of the population (eg 'Caucasian individual with long credit history'), it could be error-prone on underrepresented groups (eg 'Hispanic individuals with short credit history'). Similar effects were found in computer vision algorithms (see Dwoskin 2015 for a review).

[44] This principle has been formulated by Aristotle in the Nicomachean Ethics. For an extensive account of the notion of equality, see Gosepath (2011).

error rate the same across the groups? Is precision or sensitivity the same?). For example, popular metrics are:[45]

- *Calibration* which requires that the fraction of relevant instances among positive predicted outcomes (eg the fraction of predicted 'high-risk' offenders which are indeed 'high-risk') is the same across the groups. In other terms this notion requires equal precision across the groups.
- *Equalized odds* (Hardt et al 2016) which, roughly speaking, enforces that the true positive rate is equally high in all groups. This corresponds to require equal levels of sensitivity and specificity in all groups.[46]
- *Error rate balance* (Chouldechova 2017) which requires that the classifier produces equal false positive and false negative rates across the groups. This is comparable to requiring equal misclassification rates (see the notion of disparate mistreatment in Zafar et al (2017) and balance for positive and negative class (Kleinberg et al 2017b). Note that controlling the error rate balance is complementary to the notion of equalized odds.

Note that all these notions, being comparative, require information about the size of the protected groups within the dataset (eg how many 'women' and 'men'). In the case of HART this information was not provided, and so no conclusion can be drawn.

Overall, the literature discussing these notions pointed out that it is impossible to satisfy multiple criteria at the same time. For example, Kleinberg et al (2016) showed that there is no method to satisfy simultaneously calibration and the balance for positive class and the balance for the negative class. Similar conclusions were achieved by Chouldechova (2017), which considered the specific case of risk assessment tools, and Berk et al (2017).

3.10 Transparency and Accountability

Transparency is a desirable property of legal and administrative systems. It can be understood as the right of citizens to access information about the procedures and data which lead to certain decisions affecting them. It is beneficial for several reasons: on the one hand, it can help organizations to account for the performed tasks, that is keeping track of the entire process that has led to a specific output (accountability), and, on the other, it can support citizens in understanding and questioning processes and outcomes (participation).

---

[45] For an extensive account of available metrics based on accuracy measures, see Berk et al (2017).
[46] In a binary classifier when the aim is to identify a 'favourable' outcome (eg 'admission' or 'release', etc) this notion is called 'equal opportunity'.

While a right to transparency may not be explicitly expressed in human rights documents such as the UN Declaration of Human Rights and European Convention on Human Rights, it is arguable that without transparency as a penumbral, or background right, it would be difficult for an individual to ensure that those rights that are explicitly protected have been respected. Modern data protection legislation is explicit about the need to observe a principle of transparency in personal data processing (eg EU GDPR Recital 58 and Article 12; Council of Europe Draft Protocol amending the Convention for the Protection of Individuals with regard to Automatic Processing of Personal Data, Article 7).

The idea of transparency often implies an oversight body (eg audit commission or regulatory office) that can shed light on potential abuses or discriminations and, if necessary, motivate corresponding sanctions. For example, under the EU GDPR, ensuring compliance with transparency obligations will be part of the responsibility of an organization's data protection officer, and will be subject to scrutiny by national supervisory authorities.

Usually transparency supports the design of accountable systems which allow one to detect responsibilities when some failures occur (eg when some records are lost or when they contain errors). Although transparency and accountability refer to distinct problems (what is called 'inscrutable evidence' and 'traceability' respectively in Mittelstadt et al (2016)) they are both directed at the diagnosis of potential or actual harms caused by a decision system. Indeed, when information is accessible and open to scrutiny it should be easier to understand where and why harms arise (ie doing system debugging) and, most importantly, who should be held responsible for them (Mittelstadt et al 2016)

In the context of machine decisions, disclosing information may introduce new problems (Kroll et al 2017). For example, if key factors, such as features and labels, are revealed, it may become possible to 'game the system' by seeking to alter variables that might influence the final output (see, eg search engine optimization). Other obvious concerns arise from the publication of the data set where sensitive information is used as input. However, the disclosure of the system's source code, while it may impact legitimate commercial interests (ie protecting a competitive advantage), does not necessarily imply transparency in the sense of intelligibility of the process or outcomes. Source code is usually incomprehensible to non-experts and even experts may not be able to predict algorithm behaviour just by examining the code (Kroll et al 2017).

In addition, when approaching the transparency of machine decisions, we face another challenge that does not simply relate to the ability of reading a piece of code, but it refers instead to the mismatch between data-driven machine learning methods and the demands of human interpretation (Burrell 2016). Since machine learning methods are designed to discover subtle correlations, and not to understand the causes behind any phenomenon being studied, the resulting classifiers often take the form of complicated formulae that are not explainable to the general user. While it is true that these formulae can be proven to be predictive and, under certain assumptions, even optimal, it is not possible for an individual decision to be explained. A random forest, a boosted combination of trees, or even a linear combination, cannot provide a unvarnished explanation for a citizen whose liberty has been denied by the algorithm.

Returning to the HART case study, it would be unfeasible for a human being to look for an explanation in nearly 4.5 million nested and conditionally dependent decision points spread across many hundreds of unique trees (Oswald et al 2018). Paraphrasing Burrell (2016), we might say that when HART learns and builds its own representation of a classification decision, it does so without regard for human comprehension. So, even if a learnt representation was available it would be extremely difficult, even for an expert, to fully understand and interpret the decision process (eg to understand the impact of a specific feature).

In recent years the research community has developed several ways to characterize and improve the transparency of machine decisions (Lipton 2018). Some of these amount to post-hoc interpretations, ie separate models which furnish verbal justifications or more simple representation of algorithmic output (eg visualization of active nodes in a neural network). Other approaches try to justify a decision by reporting analogous cases (ie a model generating examples that are similar). An alternative strategy is to build systems that ensure *procedural regularity,* by verifying that an automated decision meets specific policy goals through software verification and cryptographic techniques (Kroll et al 2017).

As well as technical remedies, transparency might be supported by sectoral laws, such as the US Fair Credit Reporting Act 1970 (through the creation and maintenance of a consumer report), or by laws of general application such as the EU GDPR, which acknowledges the right of the data subject to access personal data which have been collected concerning them (Article 15), and requires data controllers to implement appropriate measures to safeguard the data subject's rights and freedoms and legitimate interests, including the right to obtain human intervention on the part of the controller (Article 22 and Recital 71).

3.11 Informational Privacy and Freedom of Expression

The type of input data in risk assessment tools like HART largely reflect information that police officers collect about inmates at specific steps of the justice process (eg at intake), such as a suspect's demographics and criminal history.[47] This data collection is mandated and/or supported by legislative provisions, but the ability to

---

[47] The business of risk assessment tools is associated with the development of information management systems (sometimes the former is considered an extension of the latter, see eg CourtView Justice Solutions: <http://www.courtview.com/court>).

integrate heterogeneous sources of information and other social factors (eg greater levels of perceived vulnerability among citizens) might suggest further directions. For example, in New Orleans a software program (owed by Palantir) is in use by the police department to identify connections between individuals and gang members by analysing both criminal histories and social media activity (Winston 2018). This has implications for both privacy and freedom of expression—if individuals are aware of the fact that their behaviour or interactions with others may be used to make predictions about them and that consequential decisions may be made about them as a result of those predictions, they may be caused to consciously or subconsciously alter those behaviours and interactions. In the case of the New Orleans example, this might involve possible targets not using social media, or changing the style or content of their communication with the consequence of 'silencing' them or restricting their ability to communicate effectively.

The use of personal data in machine decision-making raises serious privacy concerns: what data are admissible? In which contexts? Should public expressions of a citizen be permitted to be used as part of computing his risk or credit score? More generally, can personal private online activities be used as an element in assessing the score of individuals? Might this directly or indirectly undermine their right to expression?

The right to (informational) privacy is commonly reframed as the 'right to control over personal information'[48] which refers to each piece of data that can be linked to a person ('data subject') such as date of birth, social security number, fingerprint, etc.[49] Note that when personal data refers to intimate aspects of life or valuable information such as ethnicity, political opinions, religious or philosophical beliefs, biometric data, sexual orientation, etc is also called 'sensitive data'.

From a technical standpoint, the field of computer science has been developing privacy enhancing technologies for many years, for instance, introducing privacy concerns in data release and processing (eg k-anonymity and differential privacy) or addressing the problem of data disclosure in social networking platforms. All these efforts have produced an exceptional stock of tools for those who would be willing to take up privacy by design[50] and, considering the growing concerns about information privacy and security, we would expect further progress on this camp.

The simplest method to tackle privacy is to de-identify data, ie to remove, generalize or replace with made-up alternatives explicit identifiers such as name, social security number, address, phone number, etc (Sweeney 1997). Unfortunately,

---

[48] For a different account of privacy, see Nissenbaum (2010).

[49] In the EU legal terms personal data indicates 'any information relating to an identified or identifiable natural person ("data subject")' where 'an identifiable natural person is one who can be identified, directly or indirectly, in particular by reference to an identifier such as a name, an identification number, location data, an online identifier or to one or more factors specific to the physical, physiological, genetic, mental, economic, cultural or social identity of that natural person' (GDPR).

[50] Privacy by design is a methodological approach that supports the inclusion of privacy into the whole lifecycle of IT systems (Cavoukian 2009).

de-identification is often a limited solution since the combination of de-identified databases with other publicly available data ('auxiliary information') can reveal subjects' identity or reduce uncertainty on a subset of subjects in the data set.[51]

Another technical approach is provided by the model of k-anonymity (Sweeney 2002), a property that characterizes the degree of privacy protection in the release of a database. Roughly speaking, k-anonymity requires that every combination of the values reported in the data released can be indistinctly matched to at least k individuals in the database. However, k-anonymity also presents some weaknesses as it assumes restrictions on auxiliary information (ie an attacker's knowledge may be greater than what is supposed to be) and does not perform well in high-dimensional data sets (Narayanan & Shmatikov 2008).

Contrary to traditional models, the framework of differential privacy (Dwork 2006) shifts the focus from database to computation by drawing on randomized response in the structured interview (a technique that allows study participants to answer embarrassing questions while maintaining confidentiality). Differential privacy aims at the same time to maximize the accuracy of data analysis and minimize the risk of re-identification. Given a database and a series of queries, differential privacy ensures that 'that any sequence of outputs (responses to queries) is "essentially" equally likely to occur, independent of the presence or absence of any individual' in the database (Dwork & Roth 2014). Note that while the theoretical research has rapidly grown, the concrete application of differential privacy started more recently.[52]

4. Concluding Remarks

Machine decision-making is set to become an increasing factor in our lives. The calculation whether to adopt such technology may be driven by considerations of promised accuracy and efficiency gains, or simply by the attraction of downsizing and cost savings. Yet the social impacts of removing or reducing human interventions in decision-making that will impact individual rights and personal opportunities, as well as the collective good, will be wide-ranging. To date, the speed of adoption of such technologies in sensitive administrative and criminal decision-making processes has clearly outpaced evaluation of, and reaction to, those impacts. Contemporary research raises issues as diverse as the deskilling and devaluation of certain types of employment, eg social workers become call centre workers (Eubanks 2018); loss of social connection, critical judgement, and empathy as decisions become divorced from personal interactions (Turkle 2015); and

---

[51] The release of AOL web search data (Hansell 2006) and the Netflix competition (Narayanan & Shmatikov 2008) are two popular examples of failed anonymization.

[52] See, eg Apple's announcement (Greenberg 2016).

social exclusion of the poorly educated or those in poverty who lack the resources to identify, understand, and challenge system errors and failings (Eubanks 2018).

This chapter addresses one of these impacts: where algorithms make decisions that seek to evaluate individual persons for the purposes of making a decision about their entitlement to some tangible benefit or burden, it is essential that those decisions and the system within which they are made remain capable of incorporating and acting upon appropriate normative principles and obligations. While machine decisions are often judged based solely on their accuracy, in such circumstances there are wider normative considerations. Thus, the use of machine learning-based decision-making in criminal justice decisions about bringing criminal charges, length of prison sentence, eligibility for parole, or state administrative decisions about child safeguarding and eligibility for welfare benefits differs fundamentally from its use in other spheres, even those that may also have a positive or negative impact on individuals, such as medical diagnosis decisions.[53]

This chapter reviewed some technical aspects of machine decisions and suggests that when seeking to develop or maintain a trust framework that supports the social legitimacy of criminal justice or state administrative decision-making systems using machine decision-making, it is helpful to do so by reference to key representative benchmarks. Such benchmarks are common to consequential decision-making relating to individuals, and critical to development of appropriate trust relations between stakeholders, and include accuracy, transparency/accountability, fairness/equal treatment, and rights to privacy/free expression. They reflect the main tracks around which research communities have articulated the main social and ethical implications of learning algorithms in the big data context (eg Fairness, Accountability, and Transparency in Machine Learning (FAT/ML) scholarship). In a similar vein, Mittelstadt et al (2016) have framed the discourse with a distinctive vocabulary highlighting both epistemic and normative concerns.

Each of these benchmarks may incorporate a multitude of interrelated aspects: legal concepts, metrics, (technical and legal) procedures, values, rights, existing laws, pragmatic concerns, etc. In this chapter we have tried to demonstrate some of the connections between these aspects to shed light on the variety of (human) choices involved in the design, assessment, and deployment of such systems (eg dealing with fairness requires consideration for different notions of equality and, in some contexts, existing laws, understanding of distinct technical criteria and techniques, etc). Choosing which set of notions or procedures to follow calls for in-depth analysis, assessment of commitments, and delicate balance. Of course, the benchmarks identified here do not exist independently of one another. Rather they are in constant interaction and many problems arise out of their fuzzy

---

[53] As opposed to medical treatment decisions—whether a person has a particular form of cancer is a different question to whether the person should receive treatment for the cancer, and if so, what that treatment should be.

boundaries, consider the use of sensitive data in decision-making and the risk of discrimination. This also has consequences for the search for, and the implementation of, remedies for particular problems, eg an intervention on data protection/privacy may impact negatively on concerns regarding fairness.

It is recognized that while 'trust' is frequently referenced when members of a society are affected by the deployment of novel infrastructures, such as sociotechnical systems, the precise meaning and nature of trust has been debated and contested at length in the social sciences literature. We appreciate that the brief discussion here of the relationship of trust/distrust to the legitimacy of criminal justice or state administrative decision-making systems, and to the utility of the suggested benchmarks, cannot begin to do justice to that literature. Nevertheless, we would argue that the inclusion of the normative principles and obligations reflected in the benchmarks is critical to the social acceptance of those systems. The principles and obligations provide rational grounds to engage with such decision-making systems and to accept their decisions: providing a reason to trust. They also facilitate meaningful criticism and oversight of decision-making processes within those systems: permitting the ability to distrust.

Most of the social and ethical issues raised by these benchmarks have also been tackled by Oswald et al (2018), who developed a framework (ALGO-CARE) drawing on the experience of Durham Constabulary. The framework translates key ethical and legal principles in considerations and questions for supporting the assessment of predictive tools like HART. We hope that this chapter can contribute to the discussion and the development of guidelines like ALGO-CARE with a synthesis of relevant technical and legal notions. A purely algorithmic solution to these problems is not likely to be sufficient, as many of these problems require the development of legal and cultural tools and available metrics cannot capture the entire spectrum of human values and principles. Our ambition was to disclose important parts of the process implied in assessing our trust in machine decision-making, and to make accessible some conceptual tools that are necessary to approach the issues raised by machine learning algorithms.

Bibliography

Angwin J, Larson J, Mattu S, et al, 'Machine Bias' *ProPublica* (23 May 2016) <https://www.propublica.org/article/machine-bias-risk-assessments-in-criminal-sentencing> accessed 30 May 2017.

Baraniuk C, 'Durham Police AI to Help with Custody Decisions' *BBC Online* (10 May 2017) <https://www.bbc.com/news/technology-39857645> accessed 1 June 2017.

Barnes G, 'Focusing Police Resources: Algorithmic Forecasting in Durham' 9th International Conference on Evidence-Based Policing, Cambridge, United Kingdom (16 July 2016).

Barocas S and Selbst A, 'Big Data's Disparate Impact' (2016) 104(3) California Law Review 671.

Barry-Jester AM, Casselman B, and Goldstein D, 'The New Science of Sentencing. Should Prison Sentences Be Based on Crimes That Haven't Been Committed Yet?' *The Marshall Project* (4 August 2015) <https://www.themarshallproject.org/2015/08/04/the-new-science-of-sentencing> accessed 24 September 2017.

Berk R, *Criminal Justice Forecasts of Risk. A Machine Learning Approach* (Springer 2012).

Berk R, Heidari H, Jabbari S, Kearns M, and Roth A, 'Fairness in Criminal Justice Risk Assessments: The State of the Art' Sociological Methods & Research [online] (2 July 2018).

Big Brother Watch, 'Police use Experian Marketing Data for AI Custody Decisions' (6 April 2018) <https://bigbrotherwatch.org.uk/all-media/police-use-experian-marketing-data-for-ai-custody-decisions/> accessed 10 April 2018.

Burrell J, 'How the Machine "Thinks": Understanding Opacity in Machine Learning Algorithms' (2016) 3 Big Data & Society 1.

Caliskan A, Bryson JJ, and Narayanan A, 'Semantics Derived Automatically from Language Corpora Contain Human-Like Biases' (2017) 356(6334) Science 183.

Cavoukian A, 'Privacy by Design. The 7 Foundational Principles' (2009) <https://www.ipc.on.ca/wp-content/uploads/resources/7foundationalprinciples.pdf> accessed 14 October 2017.

Chouldechova A, 'Fair Prediction with Disparate Impact: A Study of Bias in Recidivism Prediction Instruments' (2017) <https://arxiv.org/abs/1610.07524> accessed 30 July 2019.

Christin A, Rosenblat A, and boyd d 'Courts and Predictive Algorithms, Data & Civil Right: A New Era of Policing and Justice' (2015) <http://www.datacivilrights.org/pubs/2015-1027/Courts_and_Predictive_Algorithms.pdf> accessed 10 September 2017.

Datta A, Tschantz MC, and Datta A, 'Automated Experiments on Ad Privacy Settings' (2015) 2015(1) Proceedings on Privacy Enhancing Technologies 92.

Dressel J and Farid H, 'The Accuracy, Fairness, and Limits of Predicting Recidivism' (2018) 4(1) Science Advances <https://www.ncbi.nlm.nih.gov/pmc/articles/PMC5777393/> accessed 13 March 2018.

Duhigg C, 'How Companies Learn your Secret' *New York Times* (16 February 2012) <https://www.nytimes.com/2012/02/19/magazine/shopping-habits.html> accessed 15 June 2017.

Dwork C, 'Differential Privacy' in M Bugliesi, B Preneel, V Sassone, and I Wegener (eds), Automata, Languages and Programming ICALP 2006, *Lecture Notes in Computer Science*, vol 4052 (Springer 2006).

Dwork C and Roth A, *The Algorithmic Foundation of Differential Privacy* (NOW Publishers 2014).

Dwork C, Hardt M, Pitassi T, et al, 'Fairness through Awareness' Proceedings of the ACM (ITCS 2012) 214 (2012).

Dwoskin E, 'How Social Bias Creeps into Web Technology. Software Can Lead to Unintended Errors, Potentially Unfair Outcomes' *The Wall Street Journal* (21 August 2015) <https://www.wsj.com/articles/computers-are-showing-their-biases-and-tech-firms-are-concerned-1440102894> accessed 29 August 2017.

Eubanks V, *Automating Inequality: How High-Tech Tools Profile, Police, and Punish the Poor* (St Martin's Press 2018).

Executive Office of the President, *Big Data: A Report on Algorithmic Systems, Opportunity and Civil Rights* (The White House Washington May 2016) <https://obamawhitehouse.archives.gov/sites/default/files/microsites/ostp/2016_0504_data_discriminati on.pdf> accessed 21 May 2017.

Feeley M and Simon J, 'Actuarial Justice: The Emerging New Criminal Law' in D Nelken (ed), *The Futures of Criminology* (Sage 1994).

Friedman B and Nissenbaum H, 'Bias in Computer Systems' (1996) 14(3) ACM Transactions on Information Systems 330.

Gosepath S, 'Equality' in EN Zalta (ed), *The Stanford Encyclopedia of Philosophy* (Spring 2011 edn) <https://plato.stanford.edu/archives/spr2011/entries/equality/> accessed 7 October 2017.

Greenberg A, 'Apple's Differential Privacy is About Collecting Your Data—But not Your Data' *Wired* (13 June 2016) <https://www.wired.com/2016/06/apples-differential-privacy-collecting-data/> accessed 10 February 2018.

Hansell S, 'AOL Removes Search Data on Vast Group of Web Users' *New York Times* (8 August 2006) <https://www.nytimes.com/2006/08/08/business/media/08aol.html> accessed 18 September 2017.

Hardt M, 'How Big Data Is Unfair. Understanding Unintended Sources of Unfairness in Data Driven Decision Making' *Medium* (26 September 2014). <https://medium.com/@mrtz/how-big-data-is-unfair-9aa544d739de> accessed 9 June 2017.

Hardt M, Price E, and Nathan S, 'Equality of Opportunity in Supervised Learning' in DD Lee, M Sugiyama, UV Luxburg, I Guyon, and R Garnett (eds), Advances in Neural Information Processing Systems 29 (2016) arXiv:1610.02413 <http://papers.nips.cc/paper/6374-equality-of-opportunity-in-supervised-learning> accessed 3 November 2017.

Hellman D, 'Two Concepts of Discrimination' (2016) 102(4) Virginia Law Review 895.

Hurley D, 'Can an Algorithm Tell When Kids Are in Danger?' *New York Times Magazine* (2 January 2018) <https://www.nytimes.com/2018/01/02/magazine/can-an-algorithm-tell-when-kids-are-in-danger.html> accessed 21 January 2018.

Kleinberg J, Ludwing J, and Mullainathan S, 'A Guide to Solving Social Problems with Machine Learning' *Harvard Business Review* (8 December 2016) <https://hbr.org/2016/12/a-guide-to-solving-social-problems-with-machine-learning> accessed 20 September 2017.

Kleinberg J, Lakkaraju H, Leskovec J, et al, 'Human Decisions and Machine Predictions' (2017a) 133(1) The Quarterly Journal of Economics 237.

Kleinberg J, Mullainathan S, and Raghavan M, 'Inherent Trade-Offs in the Fair Determination of Risk Scores' in CH Papadimitriou (ed), 8th Innovations in Theoretical Computer Science Conference (ITCS 2017b) Article No. 43 arXiv:1609.05807 <http://drops.dagstuhl.de/opus/volltexte/2017/8156/pdf/LIPIcs-ITCS-2017-43.pdf> accessed 22 October 2017.

Kroll JA, Huey J, Barocas S, et al, 'Accountable Algorithms' (2017) 165(3) University of Pennsylvania Law Review 633.

Larson J, Mattu S, Kirchner L, et al, 'How We Analysed the COMPAS Recidivism Algorithm' *ProPublica* (23 May 2016) <https://www.propublica.org/article/how-we-analyzed-the-compas-recidivism-algorithm/> accessed 2 June 2017.

Lazer D, Kennedy R, King G, et al, 'The Parable of Google Flu: Traps in Big Data Analysis' (2014) 343(6176) Science 1203.

Liptak A, 'Sent to Prison by a Software Program's Secret Algorithm' *New York Times* (1 May 2017) <https://www.nytimes.com/2017/05/01/us/politics/sent-to-prison-by-a-software-programs-secret-algorithms.html> accessed 22 June 2017.

Lipton Z, 'The Mythos of Model Interpretability' (2018) 16(3) ACM Queue arXiv:1606.03490 <https://queue.acm.org/detail.cfm?id=3241340> accessed 19 July 2018.

McIntyre N and Pegg D, 'Councils Use 377,000 People's Data in Efforts to Predict Child Abuse' *The Guardian* (16 September 2018) <https://www.theguardian.com/society/2018/sep/16/councils-use-377000-peoples-data-in-efforts-to-predict-child-abuse> accessed 17 September 2018.

Mitchell T, *Machine Learning* (McGraw-Hill 1997).

Mittelstadt B, Allo P, Taddeo M, et al, 'The Ethics of Algorithms: Mapping the Debate' (2016) 3(2) Big Data & Society 1.

Moore R (ed), *A Compendium of Research and Analysis on the Offender Assessment System 2009–2013* Ministry of Justice (NOMS July 2015) <https://www.gov.uk/government/publications/research-and-analysis-on-the-offender-assessment-system> accessed 1 December 2017.

Narayanan A and Shmatikov V, 'Robust De-anonymization of Large Sparse Datasets' Proceedings of the 2008 IEEE Symposium on Security and Privacy 111 (2008) arXiv: cs/0610105.

Nissenbaum H, *Privacy in Context: Technology, Policy and the Integrity of Social Life* (Stanford University Press 2010).

Oswald M, Grace J, Urwin S, et al, 'Algorithmic Risk Assessment Policing Models: Lessons from the Durham HART Model and 'Experimental' Proportionality' (2018) 27(2) Information & Communications Technology Law 223.

Paine J, '10 Companies Using Technology to Disrupt the Lending Industry' *Inc.com* (25 August 2017) <https://www.inc.com/james-paine/10-companies-using-technology-to-disrupt-the-lendi.html> accessed 7 November 2017.

Romei A and Ruggieri S, 'A Multidisciplinary Survey on Discrimination Analysis' (2013) 29(5) The Knowledge Engineering Review 582.

Selingo J, 'How Colleges Use Big Data to Target the Students They Want' *The Atlantic* (11 April 2017) <https://www.theatlantic.com/education/archive/2017/04/how-colleges-find-their-students/522516/> accessed 3 October 2017.

Sulleyman A, Durham Police to Use AI to Predict Future Crimes of Suspects, Despite Racial Bias Concerns' *The Independent* (12 May 2017) <https://www.independent.co.uk/life-style/gadgets-and-tech/news/durham-police-ai-predict-crimes-artificial-intelligence-future-suspects-racial-bias-minority-report-a7732641.html> accessed 19 June 2017.

Sweeney L, 'Weaving Technology and Policy Together to Maintain Confidentiality' (1997) 25(2&3) Journal of Law, Medicine & Ethics 98.

Sweeney L, 'K-Anonymity: A Model for Protecting Privacy' (2002) 10(5) International Journal on Uncertainty, Fuzziness and Knowledge-Based Systems 557.

Sweeney L, 'Discrimination in Online Ad Delivery' (2013) 56(5) Communication of the ACM 44 arXiv:1301.6822.

Swets JA, Dawes RM, and Monahan J, 'Psychological Science Can Improve Diagnostic Decisions' (2000) 1(1) Psychological Science in the Public Interest 1.

Tashea J, 'Courts Are Using AI to Sentence Criminals. That Must Stop Now' *Wired* (17 April 2017) <https://www.wired.com/2017/04/courts-using-ai-sentence-criminals-must-stop-now/> accessed 9 June 2017.

Turkle S, *Reclaiming Conversation: The Power of Talk in a Digital Age* (Penguin Press 2015).

Urwin S, 'Algorithmic Forecasting of Offender Dangerousness for Police Custody Officers: An Assessment of Accuracy for the Durham Constabulary' (Master's Thesis, Cambridge University, UK 2016) <http://www.crim.cam.ac.uk/alumni/theses/Sheena%20Urwin%20Thesis%2012-12-2016.pdf> accessed 16 June 2017.

Vapnik V, *The Nature of Statistical Learning Theory* (Springer Verlag 1995).

Wexler R, 'Code of Silence' *Washington Monthly* (August 2017) <https://washingtonmonthly.com/magazine/junejulyaugust-2017/code-of-silence/> accessed 13 September 2017.

Williams KR and Grant SR, 'Empirically Examining the Risk of Intimate Partner Violence: The Revised Domestic Violence Screening Instrument (DVSI-R)' (2006) 121(4) Public Health Reports 400.

Winston A, 'Palantir Has Secretly Been Using New Orleans to Test its Predictive Policing Technology' *The Verge* (27 February 2018) <https://www.theverge.com/2018/2/27/17054740/palantir-predictive-policing-tool-new-orleans-nopd> accessed 7 March 2018.

Zafar MB, Valera I, Rodriguez MG, et al, 'Fairness beyond Disparate Treatment & Disparate Impact: Learning Classification without Disparate Mistreatment' Proceedings of the 26th International Conference on World Wide Web 1171 (2017) arXiv:1610.08452.

Zliobate I, 'A Survey on Measuring Indirect Discrimination in Machine Learning' (2015) arXiv:1511.00148.

4

Digital Discrimination

Natalia Criado and Jose M Such*

1. Introduction

Digital discrimination is a form of discrimination in which automated decisions taken by algorithms, increasingly based on artificial intelligence techniques like machine learning, treat users unfairly, unethically, or just differently based on their personal data (Such 2017) such as income, education, gender, age, ethnicity, religion. Digital discrimination is becoming a serious problem (O'Neil 2016), as more and more tasks are delegated to computers, mobile devices, and autonomous systems, for example some UK firms base their hiring decisions on automated algorithms (BBC 2016).

In this chapter, we briefly introduce the notion of unlawful discrimination based on current legislation in selected jurisdictions, and consider how that notion is currently extended to the digital world in the form of digital discrimination. Then we show some of the most relevant digital discrimination examples studied in the literature. We also review advances in research in seeking to address digital discrimination, and outline a research roadmap to tackle the challenges to detect and address digital discrimination.

1.1 Discrimination

Many nations and international organizations have enacted legislation prohibiting discrimination; for example the International Covenant on Civil and Political Rights, the US Civil Rights Act, the European Convention for the Protection of Human Rights, the UK Equality Act 2010, and so on and so forth. However, there is not a universally accepted definition of discrimination, what it is, and when it happens. Indeed, it is a concept very much shaped by culture, social and ethical perceptions, and historical and temporal considerations. Most anti-discrimination legislation simply consists of a non-exhaustive list of criteria or protected attributes (eg race, gender, sexual orientation) on the basis of which discrimination

* We would like to thank the EPSRC for supporting this research under grant EP/R033188/1 'DADD: Discovering and Attesting Digital Discrimination'.

is forbidden. Thus, discrimination refers to actions, procedures, etc., that disadvantage citizens based on their membership of particular social groups defined by those attributes.

Legal systems traditionally distinguish between two main types of discrimination (Altman 2016):

(a) **Direct discrimination** (also known as disparate treatment) considers the situations in which an individual is treated differently because of their membership of a particular social group. This ultimately means that different social groups are being treated differently, with some of them effectively being disadvantaged by these differences in treatment. A clear example of direct discrimination would be a company having the policy of not hiring women with young children. Note, however, that direct discrimination does not necessarily involve intentionality or that the discrimination process is explicit. In particular, direct discrimination is a more complex phenomenon that can take many shapes regardless of discrimination being explicit or intentional. There are therefore two dimensions of discrimination outlined below.

   (i) **Explicit/implicit.** Direct discrimination can be explicit, exemplified in the previous case of a member of a particular social group (women with young children) explicitly disadvantaged by a decision process (hiring policy). More subtle cases of direct discrimination can also occur in which the disadvantaged group is not explicitly mentioned. For example, the same company may replace the explicit hiring policy with a policy of not hiring candidates who have had a career break in recent years. The new policy does not explicitly refer to the relevant social group. Instead, it employs some facially neutral criteria that accomplish the same discrimination aim. This is an example of implicit direct discrimination as the alternative policy was created with the aim of discriminating against women with young children (who are statistically more likely to have had a recent career break).

   (ii) **Intentional/unintentional.** Direct discrimination is not just intentional discrimination, for example a teacher who encourages male students to support and help the only female student in the class may be unintentionally discriminating by adopting a patronizing attitude towards that female student. In this situation, the offending agent may not be aware of the discriminatory motive behind their act, for example they may not be aware of the fact that they prejudice women as being weaker and in need of support as the reason for their act.

(b) **Indirect discrimination** (also known as disparate impact) considers the situations in which an apparently neutral act has a disproportionately negative effect on the members of a particular social group. This is considered discrimination even if there is no intention to discriminate against that particular group or even in the absence of any unconscious prejudice motivating the discriminatory act. For example, a company policy to consider only customer satisfaction scores when awarding promotions may disproportionately impact women, as there is empirical evidence suggesting that women are under evaluated when compared to their male counterparts with a similar objective performance.[1] In this case, the company may not have an intention to discriminate against female employees, but the promotion criteria may effectively disadvantage women disproportionately.

1.2 Digital Discrimination

The term digital discrimination (Wihbey 2015) refers to those direct or indirect discriminatory acts that are based on the automatic decisions made by algorithms.[2]

Increasingly, decisions (even very important ones) are delegated to algorithms, such as those that use artificial intelligence techniques such as machine learning. From the jobs we apply for, to the products we buy, to the news we read and to the persons we date, many sensitive decisions are increasingly delegated to or, at least, influenced by those systems. Machine learning is a subfield of artificial intelligence that focuses on the study of computer algorithms that improve automatically through experience. Machine learning algorithms are classified into unsupervised algorithms (eg those used in data mining) that find patterns in a given data set; and supervised algorithms that are presented with example inputs and their desired outputs to learn a general rule that maps inputs to outputs. What is predicted by the supervised algorithm is known as the target variable. This target variable can be nominal, that is its value is known as the class category and the machine learning task is known as classification; or numeric, that is the machine learning task is known as regression. For example, an algorithm trying to predict political affiliation from social network data has a nominal target variable where the possible values are the different political parties, whereas an algorithm trying to predict income from purchase data has a numeric target variable.

The automated decisions made by algorithms, including those based on machine learning, are sometimes perceived as faultless, not having most of the shortcomings that we humans have (eg tiredness or personal prejudices); and their decisions may be less scrutinized, that is decisions made by algorithms may be less closely examined than the decisions made by humans (Angwin et al 2016). However, automated decision-making, and in particular machine learning algorithms, are likely

---

[1] <http://www.wordstream.com/blog/ws/2014/05/13/gender-bias> retrieved 30 May 2019.
[2] Note the term digital discrimination has also been used to define traditional discrimination practices facilitated by online information (Edelman & Luca 2014) or a discriminatory access to digital technologies or information (Weidmann et al 2008), which we are not using here.

to inherit the prejudices of programmers, previous decisions, users and/or the society. This leads to discriminatory outcomes (Pasquale 2015; O'Neil 2016). Indeed, machine learning algorithms have the potential to discriminate more consistently and systematically and at a larger scale than traditional non-digital discriminatory practices.

The literature in the area of digital discrimination very often refers to the related concept of algorithmic bias (Danks & London 2017). Despite playing an important role in digital discrimination, algorithm bias does not necessarily lead to digital discrimination per se, and this distinction between bias and actual discrimination is crucial:

1. In algorithmic terms, a bias means a deviation from the standard, but it does not necessarily entail a disadvantageous treatment to particular social groups. For example, an autonomous car that is biased towards safe driving decisions may deviate from the standard driving norms, but it is not discriminating against users.

2. Algorithms need some degree of bias. If the decision that an algorithm models is always aligned with the standard and/or it is random to some extent, then it makes little sense to use an algorithm to make that decision. Indeed, machine learning algorithms rely on the existence of some statistical patterns in the data used to train them, so that an algorithm can learn to predict or make the most suitable decision.

Therefore, while bias is a very useful concept and it is indeed related to digital discrimination, we focus in this chapter on the problematic instances of bias, and on the extent to which bias may lead to digital discrimination. There are different causes for digital discrimination which can be categorized into:

- **Modelling**: machine learning algorithms are usually used to make predictions or recommendations based on some data. Note for some problems there may be an objective and unambiguous definition of the target variable and its values; for example an algorithm trying to predict age from images, since there is a measurable and clear definition of age. For other problems the target variable and its categories are artefacts defined by the designer of the algorithm, for example the classification of potential employees into good/bad candidates is a socially constructed feature for which there is no clear and unambiguous specification. The creation of these artificial variables and categories may lead to discrimination. For example, the definition of what makes a particular candidate suitable to be hired, and hence, the definition of that category in machine learning terms, is based on subjective assessments of current and previous successful candidates. These subjective assessments are very likely to include prejudices. Even more, if by any chance the definition of what makes a particular candidate suitable to be hired relates to some sort of personal or sensitive information (such as ethnicity) or proxies to this sensitive information (eg the postcode and income can be a good predictor of race), this can also lead to digital discrimination.

- **Training**: In addition to, or in spite of, how the modelling has been done, machine learning algorithms learn to make decisions or predictions based on a data set that contains past decisions. This data set may be provided to the machine learning algorithm offline or online:

  - In offline training, the machine learning algorithm undergoes a learning phase where a prediction model is built based on the information in the training data set. Obviously, the system will likely learn to make discriminatory decisions if that data set reflects existing prejudices of decision-makers (eg only candidates from a particular group are identified as appointable candidates), underrepresents a particular social group (eg a data set that does not contain information about a particular social group is likely to lead to inaccurate decisions for that social group), over-represents a particular social group (eg, usually people who do not adhere to stereotypes for a particular profession are disproportionately supervised and their mistakes and faults will be detected at higher rates), or reflects social biases (eg particular social groups will have fewer opportunities to obtain certain qualifications).

  - In online training, the machine learning algorithms learn as they are used. For example, reinforcement learning algorithms (Kaelbling et al 1996) are rewarded for good decisions and punished for bad ones. These types of systems are not free from discrimination. In some cases, the data collected online may be unrepresentative (eg some disadvantaged social groups may be excluded from interacting with the data collection system), in other cases the data is representative but discriminatory (eg women, who are more likely to be specialized in low paid sectors, may click more frequently on adverts for low-paid jobs, which may reinforce the algorithmic rule to suggest these types of job offers to women).[3] Similarly, machine learning algorithms have been demonstrated to inherit prejudices when being trained with online text (Caliskan et al 2017) or by interacting with users.[4]

---

[3] <https://www.technologyreview.com/s/539021/probing-the-dark-side-of-googles-ad-targeting-system/> retrieved 30 May 2019.

[4] A prominent example that was featured extensively in the media was the case of the Microsoft Tay Chatbot (<http://www.bbc.co.uk/news/technology-35890188> retrieved 30 May 2019). Tay was a machine learning chatbot that was designed to interact and engage with users on Twitter to 'entertain and connect with others online through casual and playful conversation'. It turned out that through interactions with other users, it learned from them in a bad way, and it went rogue and started swearing and making racist remarks and inflammatory political statements. Microsoft finally took Tay down and cancelled the project.

- **Usage:** A non-discriminatory machine learning algorithm can also lead to discrimination when it is used in a situation for which it was not intended. For example, an algorithm utilized to predict a particular outcome in a given population can lead to inaccurate results when applied to a different population, which may also disadvantage this population over others and cause discrimination. For example, a natural language processing tool that is trained on the data shared online by a given social group may not be able to process the online communications produced by another social group, even if both groups share the same language; for example research (Eisenstein et al 2014) suggests that different groups use different dialects and word-choices in social media.

2. Examples of Digital Discrimination

Digital discrimination has been mostly studied and demonstrated in the context of gender, race, income, location, and lifestyle. In the following, we briefly describe some of the most relevant discrimination examples studied in the literature.

Gender. Digital discrimination based on gender has been widely documented in research (Datta et al 2015; Kay et al 2015; Wagner et al 2015). All of these studies show that machine learning algorithms have the potential to exacerbate and perpetuate gender stereotypes and increase gender segregation. In particular, Datta et al (2015) demonstrated that Google showed males adverts encouraging the use of coaching services for high-paying jobs more frequently than females, which may lead to discrimination against women and increase the gender pay gap. Due to the opacity of the advertisement recommendation system, the authors could not determine the causes of this effect; it may be that the policy of the advertiser algorithm is to tailor the adverts shown based on gender, which is not illegal or discriminatory per se; or that differences on the online behaviour shown by males and females has driven the algorithm to show these coaching services to men as they are more likely to click on them.

Kay et al (2015) studied gender representation in image search results for different professions. Their study showed a slight underrepresentation of women (when compared to actual gender distributions of the different professions considered in the study) and that the female gender for a given profession was usually depicted less professionally. Wagner et al (2015) studied the representation of women and men in Wikipedia. Their findings suggest that women are well covered by Wikipedia; however, there are significant differences in the way in which they are portrayed. Women's pages contain more information about their personal lives and their pages are less central in the network of pages when compared to male pages. This example may not be considered as digital discrimination as the information on Wikipedia has been produced by human users, not an algorithm and in that sense it does not differ from traditional discrimination. However, when existing algorithms (eg search engines) use that information to compute their results they could discriminate against women who can be underrepresented (eg search algorithms use network centrality measures to rank the results of a given query).

Race. Other well-known examples of digital discrimination are related to race discrimination (Sweeney 2013; Angwin et al 2016). Sweeney (2013) demonstrated that advertisements suggestive of arrest records appear more often with searches of black-sounding names than white-sounding names, regardless of the existence of arrest records for those names. The causes of this discrimination are not clear: (i) it may be the case that advertisers have defined particular search terms as the target of their adverts (note that targeting is critical to advertising and is not illegal); or (ii) it may be the case that user behaviour (eg clicks received by each advertisement) has driven the machine learning algorithms to make these suggestions with particular names. Angwin et al (2016) demonstrated that one of the crime prediction algorithms most widely used in the US criminal justice system is not only inaccurate, but discriminatory. For example, evidence shows that black subjects are more likely to be wrongly assessed with a high risk of reoffending, whereas white subjects are more likely to be wrongly assessed with a low risk of reoffending. Although race is not itself a feature used to generate this risk score, some of the features used (eg information about job status, family conviction antecedents) may be highly correlated with race, which may explain the accuracy difference across different races.

Income, Location, and Lifestyle. Aspects related to income, location, or lifestyle may also lead to digital discrimination. A very clear example of intentional direct discrimination is the current practice of targeting the low-income population with high-interest loans.[5] Discrimination based on location, which may not be perceived as illegal or unfair, may also lead to discrimination based on income. For example, Valentino-Devries et al (2012) demonstrated that an online pricing algorithm considering the proximity of users to competitors' stores discriminated against low-income users who are more likely to live far from these competitors' stores. More subtle cases of digital discrimination are related to the underrepresentation of some groups of people in data sets due to their income, location, and/ or lifestyle. For example, Lerman (2013) has reflected on the dangers of exclusion from data collection processes. As more and more decisions both in the private and public spheres are informed by data collected from citizens, there is an increasing risk of not considering particular disadvantaged groups who may not be able to participate in data collection processes; for example they may not have access to the technology that is used to collect the data. This has the potential to not only ignore the needs and views of these marginalized groups in critical policy-making

---

[5] Retrieved 30 May 2019, from <https://www.nytimes.com/2015/07/10/upshot/when-algorithms-discriminate.html>.

and industry-related decisions about housing, health care, education, and so on, but also to perpetuate existing disadvantages.

3. Research on Addressing Digital Discrimination

Previous machine learning research has focused on two main streams: detecting discrimination and avoiding discrimination. In the following we review the main works in these two areas.

3.1 Detecting Discrimination

The first line of defence against discrimination is the development of metrics and processes to detect discrimination. Discrimination detection metrics can also be used in developing and implementing techniques aimed at avoiding discrimination in selecting an optimization criteria when preprocessing data sets or training algorithms.

Within this line of research, Zliobaite (2015) surveys different metrics that have been proposed to measure indirect discrimination in data and the decisions made by algorithms. The study also discusses other traditional statistical measures that could be applied to measure discrimination. In particular, discrimination measures are classified by the authors into: statistical tests, which indicate the presence of discrimination at data set level; absolute measures, which measure the magnitude of the discrimination present in a data set; conditional measures, which capture the extent to which the differences between groups are due to protected attributes or other characteristics of individuals; and structural measures, which identify for each individual in the data set if they are discriminated. Similarly, Tramer et al (2017) proposed FairTest, a methodology and toolkit combining different metrics to detect what they call *unwarranted association*, a strong association between the outputs of a machine learning algorithm and features defining a protected group. In Datta et al (2016) the authors proposed quantitative metrics to determine the degree of influence of inputs on outputs of decision-making systems. Their paper is not primarily intended to detect discrimination, but the measures they propose have the potential to increase transparency of decisions made by opaque machine learning algorithms, which in turn may provide useful information for the detection of discrimination.

All of these measures assume that the protected ground (ie the protected characteristics such as race or sex in which decisions cannot be based on; or the protected groups which cannot receive a disparate impact and what counts as disparate impact) are externally proscribed, for example, by a law. However, as noted in section 1.1 discrimination laws are not exhaustive in terms of all potential instances of discrimination or the grounds that may lead to discrimination. Thus, the applicability of these detection measures is limited by the lack of a clear definition of a protected ground for a given problem.

3.2 Avoiding Discrimination

Work on avoiding discrimination can be further classified according to the way in which discrimination is prevented: modifying the problem model, preprocessing the data to be used to train the algorithm, and modifying the algorithm to include non-discrimination as a criterion to maximize together with prediction accuracy.

3.2.1 Problem Model

One of the first attempts to avoid discrimination in algorithms consisted in modifying how the problem at hand is modelled, so that the protected information is not available. For example, research has been conducted on the use of machine learning itself, but with the aim to learn new representations of a problem that minimize the inclusion of sensitive characteristics, while still allowing for good performance in the original prediction task (Edwards & Storkey 2015; Zemel et al 2013; Louizos et al 2015). Although these approaches achieve a relatively good trade-off between prediction accuracy and non-discrimination, it has been shown that the representations learned are not completely free from sensitive information. Another problem with these approaches is that they cannot address classification tasks that are highly dependent on the sensitive characteristics. In such tasks there is a need for a better understanding of what counts as discrimination.

3.2.2 Data Preprocessing

These techniques are somewhat independent of the algorithm used to make predictions about the data, as they focus on modifying the data set that is used for training algorithms—see section 1.2 for an explanation of the different types of uses of data sets for training machine learning algorithms. This has the advantage that once the data set has been modified to avoid discrimination, it can be reused to train other algorithms, even regardless of the type of algorithm.

Discriminatory data sets normally have biases, so that when they are used for training machine learning algorithms, this leads to disfavouring particular users or groups of users. One example is that of unbalanced data sets, which contain more instances for particular types of users than others. The problem of unbalanced data sets (ie data sets that do not contain a realistic distribution of the data) is not exclusive to digital discrimination. Within the more traditional machine learning and data mining areas, different techniques have been proposed to deal with unbalanced data sets such as: oversampling (which replicates data elements that are underrepresented), undersampling (which eliminates data elements in the over-represented class), and resampling (which consists in exchanging labels on data elements).

Within the digital discrimination domain, the methods proposed consist of relabelling the data elements to ensure fairness (Zhang et al 2006), which has similarities to the resampling methods aforementioned. Other proposals have particularly focused on removing disparate impact (or indirect discrimination) from data sets (Feldman et al 2015). In particular, the authors propose a test to detect disparate impact based on the '80% rule' advocated by the US Equal Opportunity Employment Opportunity Commission.[6]

Detecting the extent of biases that may lead to discrimination in other types of data such as unstructured data, hyperlinks, text, etc is ever more complicated. For example, textual data may also encode existing biases in a more subtle way (eg with text that may reinforce gender stereotypes) and algorithms trained to make decisions based on this data will inherit such biases. One of the most common ways to process textual data such that it can be used by an machine learning algorithm are word embeddings (Goldberg & Levy 2014), a framework to represent text as vectors. In Bolukbasi et al (2016) the authors proposed a methodology to modify embeddings to remove discriminative associations between words that encode gender stereotypes. This allows the modification of the vectors (ie the data set) used to feed the machine learning algorithms.

3.2.3 Algorithm Modification

This area of research, also known as fair algorithms or fair machine learning, has significantly expanded over the last years, giving rise to modifications and extensions of existing machine learning and data mining algorithms, which specifically aim to prevent discriminative outcomes.

One of the first works on the definition of fair algorithms was made in Dwork et al (2012). In this work, the authors propose a classification technique ensuring that similar individuals are treated similarly (regardless of their belonging to protected groups). This work assumes the existence of a task-specific metric determining the similarity between individuals. Note the creation of this metric is problematic, since there may be no unambiguous definition of what constitutes similarity (eg how similarities between job applicants can be defined), the definition of such metric can incorporate existing decision-making prejudices about similarity (eg not all candidates willing to work longer hours may achieve the same productivity) or even worse, it can entail a disparate impact (or indirect discrimination) to particular groups (eg considering a qualification as a criterion may have a

---

[6] The 80 per cent rule states that the selection rate of a protected group should be at least 80 per cent of the selection rate of the non-protected group. Note there is significant controversy about this rule: a recent memorandum from the US Equal Employment Opportunities Commission suggests that a more defensible standard would be based on comparing a company's hiring rate of a particular group with the rate that would occur if the company simply selected people at random.

significant negative impact on a particular group of the population less able to obtain it, regardless of their capability to perform well in the job). On the other hand, the elicitation of a similarity metric, if feasible, can help detect and reveal existing prejudices and discrimination in decision-making practices.

In Calders et al (2013) the authors proposed a method to control the effect of different attributes in linear regression models. A linear regression model tries to predict a numeric outcome based on a set of attributes. In this work, the authors proposed methods to ensure that the differences among the mean prediction in different groups, which are defined in terms of attribute values, are explained in terms of non-protected attributes and to ensure that the prediction errors for the different groups are also explained by non-protected attributes. In both cases, there is a need for a definition of protected and non-protected attributes. Note also that non-protected attributes may be highly correlated with protected ones and, therefore, become a proxy for discrimination.

Raff et al (2017) proposed a method to minimize discrimination by tree-based algorithms, which are machine learning algorithms that provide a degree of interpretability, which also has a positive impact in decision transparency. In particular, their method allows for the protection of both nominal and numeric protected attributes, whereas most of the existing literature only focuses on nominal protected attributes.

4. Unresolved Issues Surrounding Digital Discrimination

Despite the existing research on digital discrimination, some of which we summarized in the previous section, there are still several unresolved issues. One particular area of interest for us, and a very important step towards understanding and avoiding digital discrimination, is how to attest digital discrimination, that is testing whether existing or new algorithms and/or data sets contain biases to the extent that make them discriminate against users. While previous research on detecting digital discrimination can indeed measure and/or limit the extent of bias of an algorithm/data set, the lingering questions needing urgent attention are: how much bias counts as digital discrimination? That is, how much bias is too much? There are different measures proposed to quantify bias and unwanted associations between user attributes/variables—as detailed in section 3.1, but they are not sufficient to fully understand whether digital discrimination is present or not from a legal, ethical, and/or socially acceptable point of view. Therefore, what constitutes digital discrimination and how to translate that into automated methods that attest to digital discrimination in data sets and algorithms is a very important and difficult challenge. This requires cross-disciplinary collaboration enabling a synergistic and transformative social, legal, ethical, and technical approach, which will ultimately allow the design of ground-breaking methods to certify whether or not data sets and algorithms discriminate by automatically verifying computational non-discrimination norms. In particular, we discuss below four cross-disciplinary challenges towards this endeavour.

4.1 Socio-Economic and Cultural Dimensions of Digital Discrimination

There is recent research concerned with understanding users' perceptions of digital discrimination, particularly with regards to concrete domains like online targeted advertising (Plane et al 2017) and criminal risk prediction (Grgi´c-Hla˘ca et al 2018). For instance, the second case focuses on why people perceive certain features as fair or unfair to be used in algorithms. While this is indeed going in the right direction and it represents a very good start, more research is needed to produce a strong empirical base to understand the socio-economic and cultural dimensions of digital discrimination. This should entail not only survey-based studies, but also the definition of spaces for both co-creation, bringing together researchers and technical and non-technical users; and cross-disciplinarity, drawing on expertise from a diverse research team including experts in machine learning, human-computer interaction, law, ethics, philosophy, social sciences, and so on. These spaces should bring the social, economic, and cultural dimensions of digital discrimination by examining datasets, algorithms, and processes. Techno-cultural approaches such as Coté and Pybus (2016) seem particularly suitable for this purpose.

4.2 Legal-Ethical Digital Discrimination Frameworks

As mentioned earlier in section 1.1, there is legislation around the globe that already targets discrimination, though in some instances it is not completely specified when it comes to identifying the legally protected ground. In addition, there is no universally accepted definition of discrimination, in relation to both identifying what it is and when it occurs. Indeed, it is a concept very much shaped by culture, social and ethical perceptions, and time. Most anti-discrimination legislation simply consists of a non-exhaustive list of criteria or protected attributes (eg race, gender, sexual orientation) on the basis of which discrimination is forbidden. Therefore, there is a need for a legal and ethical framework that articulates, defines, and describes digital discrimination. This entails the development of a new way of understanding discrimination from the perspective of decision-making algorithms. Based on a review of discrimination law and the socio-economic and cultural empirical base mentioned above, critical reflection about the concept of discrimination and anti-discrimination within a digital context is needed. The reflection should address issues such as: discrimination vs freedom of choice, positive discrimination, and intersectionality and seek to formulate an initial set of ethical norms covering legislative gaps and clarifying misconceptions. Argumentation processes, through cases and counter-examples must be used to enable these ethical norms to be interrogated and critically evaluated in a systematic manner. Finally, this challenge also entails the interrogation of the assumptions under which non-discrimination norms are computable; that is under which circumstances an effective algorithm can determine whether or to what extent a decision-making algorithm or data set abides by a non-discrimination norm.

4.3 Formal Non-Discrimination Computational Norms

Following the legal-ethical framework discussed above, a formal definition of norms that capture the requirements for non-discrimination should be defined. In particular, this challenge may consider research in the area of normative multi-agent systems (Criado et al 2011), which combines normative systems with intelligent systems, by considering norms that are inherently subjective and ambiguous. Norms and normative systems have been extensively studied in recent years, particularly as a way of limiting the autonomy of autonomous systems to adhere to acceptable behaviours. Norms are usually defined formally using deontic logic to state obligations, prohibitions, and permissions, but other modalities such as commitments and other formalizations such as soft constraints have also been considered. Norms could be used to define non-discriminatory behaviours, for example norms could define acceptable treatment of users, so that other non-acceptable behaviours would be prohibited. Norms have the added benefit that they can be used to govern and promote appropriate behaviours considering the whole socio-technical spectrum, from non-autonomous to autonomous algorithms and systems to human users (Singh 2013), and they could be very useful as a common language for humans and machines, which could foster transparency and accountability in turn. The formal representation of non-discrimination norms will also pave the way for the development of novel verification methods to determine whether instances of discrimination occur in algorithms and data sets.

4.4 Automated Certification of Non-Discrimination Norms

Following from the previous challenge, once it is necessary to formalize non-discrimination norms based on socio-economic, cultural, legal, and ethical dimensions, the next step would be to design automated methods to verify and certify that data sets and algorithms satisfy the non-discrimination computational norms, identifying the causes of discrimination otherwise. This will support an integrated and multi-level view of discrimination, that is from the formal norm being violated, down to the instantiation of the norm, and to the specific rules, variables, and/or associations causing discrimination. This challenge would entail both white-box and black-box scenarios.

For white-box scenarios —that is algorithms the code of which can be inspected and comprehended (eg they can be expressed as decision trees) or data sets that are used to train algorithms are available—it is possible to take a model checking approach (non-discrimination norms are operationalized as formal properties) and/or mathematical approach (non-discrimination norms are operationalized as mathematical formulas defined over data sets). Note that the tools developed for white-box scenarios would be particularly useful to algorithm developers and data curators in businesses or the public sector to make sure algorithms/datasets will not discriminate before releasing them.

For black-box scenarios—that is the cases in which the algorithm or the data set used to feed or train the algorithm is not available for inspection (eg in auditing scenarios, because of IP reasons), two different cases must be considered: (i) that the algorithm can be isolated and put into a testing environment (eg by an independent auditing party); and (ii) that there are only limited opportunities to interact with an algorithm, with limited or non-direct observability of input-output sequences and limited control of inputs provided. The tools that would be developed for black-box scenarios would be particularly useful to regulatory, auditing, and certification bodies, law enforcement, and non-governmental organizations to certify the presence (or the absence) of digital discrimination.

5. Conclusion

In this chapter, we introduced the problem of digital discrimination. Firstly, we briefly revisited how the term discrimination is used in the law, and how that might extend to the digital world. In particular, we reviewed some prominent examples of digital discrimination. After this, we reviewed the main research streams in digital discrimination, and outlined a roadmap to one such research streams which is how to assess whether a particular algorithm or data set discriminates against users. Because of the very nature of digital discrimination, which encompasses social, cultural, legal, ethical, and technical aspects, we very much encourage cross-disciplinary research to address the challenges to detect and address digital discrimination, which would ultimately create the new transdisciplinary field of attesting digital discrimination.

Bibliography

Altman A, 'Discrimination' in EN Zalta (ed), *The Stanford Encyclopedia of Philosophy* (Winter 2016 edn, Metaphysics Research Lab, Stanford University) <https://plato.stanford.edu/archives/win2016/entries/discrimination/> accessed 30 May 2019.

Angwin J, Larson J, Mattu S, et al, 'Machine Bias: There's Software Used across the Country to Predict Future Criminals. And Its Biased against Blacks' *ProPublica* (23 May 2016) <https://www.propublica.org/article/machine-bias-risk-assessments-in-criminal-sentencing> accessed 30 July 2019.

Blansett J, 'Digital Discrimination' (2008) 133(13) Library Journal 26.

Bolukbasi T, Chang K-W, Zou JY, et al, 'Man Is to Computer Programmer as Woman Is to Homemaker? Debiasing Word Embeddings' Proceedings of the 30th Conference on Neural Information Processing Systems, Barcelona (2016).

Calders T, Karim A, Kamiran F, et al, 'Controlling Attribute Effect in Linear Regression' Proceedings of the IEEE 13th International Conference on Data Mining (2013).

Caliskan A, Bryson JJ, and Narayanan A, 'Semantics Derived Automatically from Language Corpora Contain Human-Like Biases' (2017) 356 (6334) Science 183.

Coté M and Pybus J, 'Simondon on Datafication. A Techno-Cultural Method' (2016) 2(2) Digital Culture & Society 75.

Criado N, Argente E, and Botti V, 'Open Issues for Normative Multi-Agent Systems' (2011) 24(3) AI Communications 233.

Danks D and London AJ, 'Algorithmic Bias in Autonomous Systems'. Proceedings of the 26th International Joint Conference on Artificial Intelligence 469 (2017).

Datta A, Tschantz MC, and Datta A, 'Automated Experiments on Ad Privacy Settings' (2015) 1 Proceedings on Privacy Enhancing Technologies 92.

Datta, A, Sen S, and Zick Y, 'Algorithmic Transparency via Quantitative Input Influence: Theory and Experiments with Learning Systems' Proceedings of the IEEE Symposium on Security and Privacy (2016).

Day P, Can a Computer Really Recruit the Best Staff?' *BBC* <http://www.bbc.co.uk/news/business-36129046> accessed 30 May 2019.

Dwork C, Hardt M, Pitassi T, et al, 'Fairness through Awareness' Proceedings of the 3rd Innovations in Theoretical Computer Science Conference (2012).

Edelman BG and Luca M, 'Digital Discrimination: The Case of airbnb.com' Harvard Business School NOM Unit Working Paper (2014).

Edwards H and Storkey A, 'Censoring Representations with an Adversary' (2015) arXiv preprint arXiv: 1511.05897.

Eisenstein J, O'Connor B, Smith NA, et al, 'Diffusion of Lexical Change in Social Media' (2014) 9(11) PloS one e113114.

Feldman M, Friedler SA, Moeller J, et al, 'Certifying and Removing Disparate Impact' Proceedings of the 21th ACM SIGKDD International Conference on Knowledge Discovery and Data Mining (2015).

Goldberg Y and Levy O, 'word2vec Explained: Deriving Mikolov et al.'s Negative-Sampling Word-Embedding Method' (2014) arXiv preprint arXiv: 1402.3722.

Grgi´c-Hla˘ca N, Redmiles EM, Gummadi KP, et al 'Human Perceptions of Fairness in Algorithmic Decision Making: A Case Study of Criminal Risk Prediction' (2018) arXiv: 1802.09548.

Kaelbling LP, Littman ML, and Moore AW, 'Reinforcement Learning: A Survey' (1996) 4 Journal of Artificial Intelligence Research 237.

Kay M, Matuszek C, and Munson SA, 'Unequal Representation and Gender Stereotypes in Image Search Results for Occupations' Proceedings of the 33rd Annual ACM Conference on Human Factors in Computing Systems (2015).

Lerman J, 'Big Data and its Exclusions' (2013) 66 Stanford Law Review 55.

Louizos C, Swersky K, Li Y, et al, 'The Variational Fair Autoencoder' (2015) <https://arxiv.org/abs/1511.00830> accessed 30 July 2019.

O'Neil C, *Weapons of Math Destruction: How Big Data Increases Inequality and Threatens Democracy* (Broadway Books 2016).

Pasquale F, *The Black Box Society: The Secret Algorithms that Control Money and Information* (Harvard University Press 2015).

Plane AC, Redmiles EM, Mazurek ML, et al, 'Exploring User Perceptions of Discrimination in Online Targeted Advertising' (2017) Proceedings of the 26th USENIX Security Symposium (2017) <https://www.usenix.org/conference/usenixsecurity17/technical-sessions/presentation/plane> accessed 30 July 2019.

Raff E, Sylvester J, and Mills S, 'Fair Forests: Regularized Tree Induction to Minimize Model Bias' (2017) arXiv preprint arXiv: 1712.08197.

Singh MP, 'Norms as a Basis for Governing Sociotechnical Systems' (2013) 5(1) ACM TIST 21.

Such JM, 'Privacy and Autonomous Systems' Proceedings of the 26th International Joint Conference on Artificial Intelligence (2017).

Sweeney L, 'Discrimination in Online Ad Delivery' (2013) 11(3) Queue 10.

Tramer F, Atlidakis V, Geambasu R, et al, 'Fairtest: Discovering Unwarranted Associations in Data-Driven Applications' Proceedings of the IEEE European Symposium on Security and Privacy (2017).

Valentino-Devries J, Singer-Vine J, and Soltani A, 'Websites Vary Prices, Deals Based on Users Information' (2012) 10 Wall Street Journal 60.

Wagner C, Garcia D, Jadidi M, et al, 'It's a Man's Wikipedia? Assessing Gender Inequality in an Online Encyclopedia' ICWSM (2015).

Weidmann NB, Benitez-Baleato S, Hunziker P, et al, 'Digital Discrimination: Political Bias in Internet Service Provision across Ethnic Groups' (2016) 353(6304) Science 1151.

Wihbey J, 'The Possibilities of Digital Discrimination: Research on E-commerce, Algorithms and Big Data' (2015) Journalists Resource <https://journalistsresource.org/studies/society/internet/possibilities-online-racial-discrimination-research-airbnb/> accessed 30 July 2019.

Zemel R, Wu Y, Swersky K, et al, 'Learning Fair Representations' International Conference on Machine Learning (2013).

Zhang H, Berg AC, Maire M, et al, 'SVM-KNN: Discriminative Nearest Neighbor Classification for Visual Category Recognition' Proceedings of the IEEE Conference on Pattern Recognition Vol 2 (2006).

Zliobaite I, 'A Survey on Measuring Indirect Discrimination in Machine Learning' (2015) arXiv preprint arXiv: 1511.00148.

5

The Ethics of Algorithmic Outsourcing in Everyday Life

John Danaher*

1. Introduction: Algorithmic Tools and Everyday Life

Today, I went for a run. As per usual, I brought my smartphone with me, plugging in my earphones as I went out the door. The rain was pouring down and the wind was swirling in my face, but I was determined to beat my personal best. A little voice in my ear told me I could do it. It told me how far I had run, what my average speed per kilometre was, whether I was beating my previous split times. With these constant, encouraging reminders I knew not to get disheartened by the conditions. I persevered. In the end I did indeed beat my personal best. The app from which the encouraging voice emanated pinged me with a gold merit badge as a reward. It also immediately informed all my followers on social media of my success. A congratulatory cycle soon followed.

My experience is one of millions of similar experiences that take place everyday. We live in a world in which a vast ecosystem of algorithmic tools are used to incentivise, control, nudge, and manipulate our behaviour (Pasquale 2015; Wu 2017; Alter 2017; Crawford 2015). Whether it is planning a journey using Google Maps, recording workouts and sleep data with a FitBit, or browsing through film and book choices on Amazon or Netflix, it is hard to avoid the influence of these algorithmic tools. Indeed, so pervasive are they that I even use an algorithmic tool to block access to all the other algorithmic tools that might distract me from my daily tasks. I am using it right now, in a desperate attempt to finish writing this book chapter.

The pervasiveness of these algorithmic tools raises several important social, legal, and regulatory questions, many of which are addressed in this book. People worry about the impact they have on our privacy and data protection (Polonetsky & Tene 2013; Hartzog 2018), on biased and unequal access to social services and goods (Noble 2018; Eubanks 2018; O'Neil 2016), and on the transparency and

* I would like to thank Karen Yeung for her helpful comments on a previous draft of this chapter. I would also like to thank the attendees at a Whitaker Institute seminar at NUI Galway for their criticisms and questions about the main arguments given above.

legitimacy of public and political decision-making (Danaher 2016; Danaher et al 2017; Burrell 2016; Pasquale 2015). In this chapter, I want to focus on the impact of these algorithmic tools at a different scale: in the day-to-day activities of our personal lives. What happens when we outsource or share many of our daily tasks and objectives to digital assistants and other algorithmic tools? In particular, what happens to our autonomy and freedom of choice? Algorithmic tools affect our choice environments: they pre-filter and highlight options; they 'ping' us with reminders or incentives; and they sometimes even make choices on our behalf, giving us (if we are lucky) the power to veto those choices.

Does this mean that individual autonomy is under a significant new, technological threat? How should we as individuals and societies respond? Do we need reformed legal and regulatory systems to address this threat? This chapter defends three claims by way of response. First, it argues that autonomy is indeed under threat in some new and interesting ways. To be precise, it identifies two interesting mechanisms through which algorithmic tools can manipulate and undermine our autonomy. Second, it evaluates the claim that we shouldn't overestimate these new threats because the technology is just an old wolf in a new sheep's clothing. In other words, that it is no different from historical threats to autonomy. It challenges this by arguing that there are some distinctive qualities to the threats posed by algorithmic outsourcing tools, even though it is also important to bear in mind the various ways in which algorithmic tools can promote individual autonomy. Third, and finally, it looks at responses to these threats at both the individual and societal level. It argues that we shouldn't encourage an attitude of 'helplessness' among the users of algorithmic tools—there are ways in which they can personally adapt their behaviour to address the new threats—but there may also be an important role for legal and regulatory responses to these threats, ones that go beyond what are currently on offer.

The chapter is divided into four parts. First, I provide a framework for thinking about algorithmic tools and the various ways in which they can affect individual autonomy. This will give us a sense of the diverse strategies employed by the makers of algorithmic devices to control our choice environments and so help us to appreciate some of the complexities in how users relate to algorithmic tools. Second, I introduce the argument for thinking that these algorithmic tools pose a significant threat to autonomy, focusing on two particular mechanisms for this. Third, I look at the sceptical response to that argument—the one that claims we have seen it all before. And fourth, I consider the possible individual and social responses.

2. Understanding Algorithmic Tools

We need to start by clarifying the phenomenon of interest. This chapter is concerned with the threat that algorithmic tools pose to our autonomy. The use of the word 'tools' to describe the phenomenon is somewhat controversial in this context. A tool is typically understood as something that an agent controls; not something that controls and manipulates an agent. Take a simple example. A hammer is a tool used for driving nails into hard surfaces. It enhances the autonomy of the user, enabling them to do things that were previously impossible. It does not 'shout' at the user, demanding that they hammer more nails, or 'scold' them if they miss a certain target number of hammered nails for the day. There is, consequently, no sense in which it could be thought to undermine an individual's autonomy.

But think about it again. The mere presence of the hammer in your workshop might make the option of driving nails into surfaces more attractive (if only because it becomes less difficult). In other words, the presence of the tool could change the cost/benefit ratio associated with certain options and, consequently, 'nudge' you to make choices that you otherwise would not have made (Morrow 2014). So although talk of algorithmic tools might seem misleading at first glance—since tools are autonomy-enhancing not autonomy-threatening—there is in fact a dual character to even the simplest of tools: they enable, incentivize, and therefore influence, our choices. Furthermore, algorithmic tools are clearly a bit different from traditional tools like hammers. Digital assistants such as Alexa or Siri, or ranking algorithms such as those used by Google and Facebook, are 'tool-like' in the sense that we can use them to accomplish goals, for example finding useful information, connecting with our friends, scheduling calls and meetings. But they go beyond this. They don't just enhance our agency; they also do things on our behalf. They constrain the range of options with which we are confronted, make some information more manageable and more salient, and ease some of our cognitive burden (Brundage & Danaher 2017). Sometimes they go even further. Fitness and productivity apps often come equipped with behaviour-change algorithms that try to explicitly prompt and encourage us to do certain things. If instead of the traditional, inert hammer, we had a modern 'smart' hammer in our workshops, coded with some behaviour-change algorithm, then we might very well expect it to start shouting at us and demanding that we hit a certain target for the day. It would still be a tool, but it would also be much more than that: it would be a device for regulating and governing our behaviour. It would also not just be a self-imposed tool for regulating and governing our behaviour. It would be one whose software and programming is controlled by third parties. It would not be entirely *ours*; it would be *theirs* as well.

So why stick with the term 'algorithmic tool'? I do so because using the term highlights the fact that algorithms still function as tools—as things that enable us to accomplish our goals—and it is important that we don't lose sight of that fact. Indeed, it is a fact to which I will return below. Nevertheless, the term must be used with some caution, and with the proviso that it is understood that algorithmic tools often have a regulatory or governance dimension. Furthermore, I want to be clear that I am not interested in all possible algorithmic tools. The term 'algorithm' is vague and could be used to describe any set of rules that transforms a defined set of inputs into a set of outputs. A recipe in a cookbook could, consequently, count as an algorithmic tool. I am not concerned with such cases in this chapter. I am concerned with algorithmic tools that are incorporated into information technology devices (personal computers, smartphones, smartwatches, and so on). The algorithmic tools embedded in such devices typically rely on data capture and data mining and are often networked and cloud-based. To avoid doubt or confusion I will provide a precise definition of the concept of an algorithmic tool that will be used for the remainder of this chapter:

Algorithmic tool: Any computer-coded algorithm embedded in an information technology device that is used to generate and act upon knowledge that can be used to aid decision-making and goal achievement, and that functions in part by regulating and governing behaviour.

This definition blends together a distinction that Yeung (2017b: 3) makes between *algorithmic decision-making* (decision-making that is aided by algorithmically generated knowledge) and *algorithmic regulation* (regulatory systems that utilise algorithmic decision-making). This blending together is deliberate. It is the very fact that these systems combine tool-likeness and with regulation and governance that makes their impact on the day-to-day activities of our lives, and on individual autonomy so difficult to determine. I discuss this in more detail below.

Now that we have a clearer sense of what an algorithmic tool is (in the abstract) we can introduce some additional distinctions. For not all algorithmic tools are created equal. They often function in different ways and these differences can be relevant to any discussion of their autonomy-promoting and autonomy-undermining effect. There has been some interesting recent work on this very issue. Gal (2017) argues that there are at least four different kinds of algorithmic tool, each of which has a distinctive effect on individual choice. The four kinds are: (i) 'stated preference' algorithmic tools, for which the individual specifies exactly what they want the algorithm to do and the algorithm assists in achieving this outcome; (ii) 'menu of preferences' algorithmic tools, for which the individual doesn't specify their preferred outcome but chooses from a menu of options provided to them by the algorithm; (iii) 'predicted preference' algorithmic tools, for which the algorithm, based on data-mining (often from other individuals), tries to predict what the user will want and target options at them accordingly; and (iv) 'self-restraint preference' algorithmic tools, for which the algorithm functions as a pre-commitment device, favouring the user's long-term interests (perhaps stated; perhaps predicted) over their immediate interests. As you might imagine, these different kinds of algorithmic tool have different consequences for individual autonomy. A stated preference algorithm, for example, would seem to be obviously autonomy-enhancing; a predicted preference algorithm much less so.

In a similar, but more complex, vein, Yeung (2017b) describes a 'logical space' of possible algorithmic tools, focusing specifically on their use in regulatory systems that try to enforce certain behavioural standards. This logical space has three dimensions to it, each of which has two 'settings', making for eight possible forms of 'regulation by algorithmic tool'. The first dimension concerns the nature of the algorithmic tool itself. Is it fixed or adaptive? The second dimension concerns the way in which the algorithmic system monitors individual behaviour. Does it 'react' to the user's violation of its behavioural standards or does it try to predict and pre-empt the user? The third dimension concerns the role that human regulators play in the system. Does the system automatically enforce its standards (perhaps giving humans a veto power) or does it simply recommend (perhaps strongly) enforcement options to them? Again, the different settings on each of these dimensions would appear to be relevant when it comes to assessing the impact of these systems on individual choice and autonomy, even in cases where we impose regulatory tools on ourselves. Intuitively, it seems like a system that anticipates and pre-empts violations of prescribed standards, and that automatically enforces sanctions on those violations, poses more of a threat to autonomy than a system that simply reacts and recommends. Yeung's discussion seems to suppose that these tools are imposed on us by outside regulators, but it seems obvious that we can self-impose them too by 'voluntarily' adopting more tools into our lives.

The taxonomies proposed by Gal and Yeung are useful because they encourage nuance and complexity in how we consider the impact of algorithmic tools on our behaviour. They inspire and guide the analysis that follows.

3. Do Algorithmic Tools Undermine Autonomy?

So what about the impact of algorithmic tools on our day-to-day behaviour? If we make excessive use of them, will they significantly undermine autonomy or could they actually enhance it? To answer that question we need to bear in mind both the complex nature of algorithmic tools—as suggested by both Gal and Yeung—and, perhaps more importantly, the complex nature of autonomy itself as a value.

There is no shortage of material written about the nature of autonomy. Everyone agrees on the basic idea—to be autonomous means that you are, in some sense, the 'author' of your own life—but there are differences when it comes to the critical sub-conditions of autonomy. This is where the complexity comes in. Many sub-conditions have been identified over the years, leading some people to propose quite complicated theories of autonomy as a result (eg Killmister (2017) proposes a four-dimensional theory of autonomy). Acknowledging this complexity, in this chapter I will adopt and adapt a theory of autonomy that was first proposed by Joseph Raz back in the 1980s. This theory focuses on three conditions that need to be satisfied if a particular choice/life is to count as autonomous. The following quote from Raz sets them out:

If a person is to be maker or author of his own life then he must have the mental abilities to form intentions of a sufficiently complex kind, and plan their execution. These include minimum rationality, the ability to comprehend the means required to realize his goals, the mental faculties necessary to plan actions, etc. For a person to enjoy an autonomous life he must actually use these faculties to choose what life to have. There must in other words be adequate options available for him to choose from. Finally, his choice must be free from coercion and manipulation by others, he must be independent. (Raz 1986: 373)

The three conditions of autonomy embedded in this quoted passage are: (a) the autonomous person must have the minimum rationality to plan actions that will allow them to achieve their goals; (b) they must have an adequate range of options available to choose from; and (c) they must be independent, which Raz takes to mean free from *coercion* and *manipulation* when making and implementing their choices, but which we can take to mean freedom from interference or domination in a broader sense (Pettit 2014).

What I like about Raz's theory is that it captures both the essence of autonomy, while at the same time allowing for considerable differences in how the conditions are interpreted or understood. For example, you could understand them as minimal or threshold conditions. In other words, you could say that once a minimal degree of rationality is achieved, once there is an adequate range of options available, and once there is independence from others (in some appropriately defined sense) then a particular choice (or set of choices) is, indeed, autonomous. That's all there is to it. But it is also possible, I believe, to understand these three conditions as defining a dimensional space of possible degrees of autonomy. In other words, to hold that the higher the degree of rationality and independence, and the more options available to you, the more autonomous you become.

That said, if one embraces this dimensional view of autonomy, one must be sensitive to the possibility that once you go beyond a certain level of independence, rationality, and optionality, you may start to experience *diminishing marginal returns*. Indeed, at extreme levels it is possible that there is an inverse relationship between an increase along those dimensions and autonomy. An example of this inverse relationship might be the so-called 'paradox of choice' (Schwartz 2004). This is an effect that has been discussed by psychologists which suggests that if you have too much choice (too wide a range of adequate options) you become unable to make a decision. Inability to decide is clearly not compatible with autonomy. I return to this point below.

Relatedly, it could be that some infringement of one of the conditions is necessary if we are to achieve the right overall balance of autonomy. We can see this most clearly with the independence condition. This states that in order to live an autonomous life you must be free from interference and domination by others. While this certainly seems like a plausible requirement, it should be noted that some degree of external interference may be necessary in order to achieve one's goals. This is, in fact, a central paradox underlying liberal modes of government. Many prominent liberal authors argue that some coercion by the state is necessary if you are to be free from coercion and manipulation by your fellow citizens. This is, for example, the classic Hobbesian argument justifying the need for a coercive state. There is undoubtedly something faintly paradoxical about this but its truth seems to be borne out by our collective history: a lingering threat of coercive interference by the state (or other institutional actor) seems to be integral to maintaining peace and stability. Furthermore, not all autonomy-undermining interferences and dominations are going to come from other people. Sometimes we are our own worst enemies. We have cognitive and motivational biases that draw us away from doing what we most want to do. Weakness of the will and procrastination are obvious examples of this. It's possible that by consenting to some degree of external constraint we may be able to overcome these internal interferences and allow ourselves to do what we most want to do. My use of an algorithm to block access to other algorithmic tools is an example of this. I know that my distractibility and lack of focus are my own worst enemies and so I deliberately restrict myself in order to accomplish my goal of finishing this chapter. It is a classic pre-commitment device that promotes rather than undermines autonomy.

We can reinterpret the Razian account to incorporate these considerations and use it to formulate a test for autonomy:

Autonomy: If you have (a) the rationality to select the appropriate means to your desired ends; (b) an adequate range of options; and (c) are free from most external and internal sources of interference with, and coercion and manipulation of, your will, then you are autonomous. Indeed, the more you have of each, the more autonomous you are (up to some point of diminishing returns).

We can then use this test to assess the threat posed by algorithmic tools to our autonomy. Whenever we are confronted by a particular tool we can ask ourselves the three questions prompted by the Razian definition: does the tool undermine minimum rationality? Does it undermine optionality? And does it undermine independence? If the answer is yes to all three, then the tool clearly undermines autonomy. If it is yes to some but no to others, then we have some tricky and nuanced judgments to make. How significantly does the tool affect the relevant conditions? How important are those conditions, overall, to our understanding of autonomy? The answers will determine our assessment of the impact of the tool on autonomy.

Given the way in which I am talking about it, it's pretty obvious that I don't think a global assessment of the threat that algorithmic tools pose to autonomy is possible. Each tool has to be considered on its own merits. They could pose a threat, sometimes, depending on the context in which they are used and the way in which they function. It all depends. Nevertheless, it is possible to get a sense of the possibilities and trends by comparing the impact of algorithmic tools on each of the three conditions identified above. In doing so, I think it is possible to identify some of the particular, and distinctive mechanisms through which these tools might pose a threat to our autonomy.

First, let's consider the impact that they might have on the rationality condition. This consideration can be brief: I am generally inclined to discount any claimed impact that algorithmic tools might have on this condition. Why so? Well, because it seems unlikely to me that algorithmic tools of the sort under consideration could completely undermine our capacity to plan and execute complex intentions. Personal digital assistants, and the like, are all premised on the fact that we have complex intentions/goals that we need machine assistance to realize. They work with a presumption of minimal rationality, not against. They provide us with both the information and the means we need to make use of that rationality. That said, if we follow the arguments of Nicholas Carr (2014)—who claims that the persistent use of tools might degenerate our cognitive faculties—or the arguments of Frischmann and Selinger (2018)—who claim that such tools may actually programme us to act as simple stimulus-response machines—there may well be some negative impact on our capacity for rationality. Nevertheless, I think it is much more plausible to suppose that automating technologies will impact on the optionality and independence conditions, either by limiting and constraining our options or interfering (directly or indirectly) with our exercising of those options. It's there that the real effects on autonomy are likely to be felt.

Let's consider the limitation of options. David Krakauer has expressed some fears about this, specifically in relation to the widespread deployment of artificial intelligence (AI) decision-support tools. He uses the Homeric story of the Lotos Eaters to make his point:

> In Homer's The Odyssey, Odysseus's ship finds shelter from a storm on the land of the lotus eaters. Some crew members go ashore and eat the honey-sweet lotus, 'which was so delicious that those [who ate it] left off caring about home, and did not even want to go back and say what happened to them.' Although the crewmen wept bitterly, Odysseus reports, 'I forced them back to the ships … Then I told the rest to go on board at once, lest any of them should taste of the lotus and leave off wanting to get home.' In our own times, it is the seductive taste of the algorithmic recommender system that saps our ability to explore options and exercise judgment. If we don't exercise the wise counsel of Odysseus, our future won't be the dystopia of Terminator but the pathetic death of the Lotus Eaters. (Krakauer 2016)

As evidenced in this quote, Krakauer is particularly concerned about AI 'recommender' systems that block us from exploring an adequate range of options. He thinks we are fed recommendations by such systems on a daily basis and that this 'saps us' of our will. This certainly chimes with my everyday experience. When I go shopping on Amazon, I am immediately presented with a list of 'recommended' products, allegedly based on my past purchases (and the purchases of other, like-minded, people); when I go to watch a movie on Netflix, I am fed different menus of options with titles like: 'currently trending', 'because you watched Fargo ...', 'films with a strong female lead', and so on; and when I am trying to find my way around a strange city, Google Maps tells me which route to take, and which routes have a similar ETA. This is just a small sample of recommender systems. Similar systems are also widely deployed in business and government. Each of these systems could have a negative impact on the optionality condition. They all work by designing the 'choice architecture' in which we select our preferred options (Thaler & Sunstein 2009). The major problem is that the range of options made available to us through such recommender systems might be quite limited, not 'adequate' to our preferred self-conception. It might be more reflective of the needs and interests of the corporations who control the recommender systems than ourselves. In extreme cases, the choice architecture might be so limited as to give us only one 'live' option to choose from, thereby effectively 'forcing' a single choice out of us. Google Maps sometimes has this effect due to the way in which it highlights a preferred route. In even more extreme cases, the system might block us completely from making a choice among available options and simply make the choice for us. This can happen if the default setting of the algorithmic tool is to *act* rather than to *omit*.

It is important, however, not to overstate the impact of algorithmic tools on the optionality condition. As hinted at above, there are ways in which AI recommender systems could help to promote autonomy by filtering and pre-selecting options. It's long been noted that having a range of valuable options is no good by itself: you have to be able to search through those options and exercise judgment in selecting the ones you prefer. Too many options could actually hinder us from doing this. I could be presented with ten million randomly arranged movies on Netflix and quickly get overwhelmed. I might get 'stuck' in the choice architecture, hovering between all the possibilities, like a modern-day version of Buridan's Ass. The psychologist Barry Schwartz calls this the 'paradox of choice' and he and others have documented it in a series of experimental studies (Schwartz 2004; Scheibehenne et al 2010). Some of these studies suggest that it has a significant impact on our capacity to choose; others suggest it has a more modest effect (Scheibehenne et al 2010). Either way, AI recommender systems could help to overcome the paradox of choice by limiting our options and making it easier for us to navigate through the choice architecture. They could also help us to sustain and develop our capacity for choosing among valuable options by reducing our cognitive burden in certain tasks (Brundage & Danaher 2017).

That leaves us with the independence condition. At first glance it might seem like the personal use of algorithmic tools is entirely consistent with our independence—after all, most of the time *we* voluntarily choose to use them to accomplish *our* goals. But things are not so straightforward. As noted in the previous section, the tools are not just ours; they are *theirs* too. We don't retain full ownership and control once we start using them. The companies and programmers who designed them continue to monitor and update their functionality, and they often transfer (with our explicit consent or otherwise) the data they collect to other interested parties. As we get comfortable with outsourcing some of the cognitive burden of choice to the AI assistant, we become more trustworthy. This trust can be abused. This can lead to some important negative effects on autonomy.

Some of these are pretty obvious. Some algorithmic tools can be designed to coerce you into acting in a certain way, that is threaten you with some adverse outcome if you fail to act in a prescribed way. This is already beginning to happen to some extent. Health and car insurance companies already 'offer' better deals to people if they agree to use algorithmic monitoring tools that track their driving and health-related behaviours. We might initially view these 'offers' as autonomy-enhancing (and hence not a form of coercion) but given the way in which insurance markets function (ie given the widespread adverse selection and information problems), a failure to consent to algorithmic monitoring could very quickly take on significance in the calculation of premiums. This could turn what seemed like an offer into a coercive threat. There is also even the possibility of turning this from purely financial coercion into actual physical coercion, if the algorithmic tool is joined up with some robotic technology that can physically interfere with the human user. This is not completely far-fetched. The Pavlok behaviour change bracelet, for example, shocks its user if they don't follow through on certain commitments. For the time being, this system is something that an individual chooses to impose on themselves; not something that is imposed on them by some outside force. Consequently it may not undermine freedom. Nevertheless, it is not that hard to imagine an insurance company (or a more nefarious third party) coopting such a system to physically coerce its users in an autonomy-undermining way.

More important than explicit coercion, however, are the subtle forms of manipulation and decisional interference that are made possible through the use of algorithmic tools. Yeung (2017a) argues that modern algorithmic tools enable 'hypernudging', which is a kind of behaviour-change technique that operates beneath the radar of conscious awareness and happens in a dynamic and highly personalised fashion. Nudging is a concept that was made popular by Cass Sunstein and Richard Thaler (2009). It involves using insights from behavioural science to construct choice architectures that 'nudge' people towards actions that are welfare-maximising or that serve the common good. For example, setting the default on retirement savings to 'opt-out' rather than 'opt-in', or placing healthy foods at eye level and unhealthy ones below or above, makes it more likely that people will choose options that are in their long-term interests. Nudges usually operate on subconscious biases in human reasoning. Sunstein and Thaler maintain that nudging is not freedom-undermining because it is still possible for people to identify and reject the 'nudges'. Others are more doubtful and argue that nudges are highly manipulative (Sunstein 2016). Whatever the merits of nudging, Yeung's point is that algorithmic outsourcing technologies bring nudging to an extreme level of precision. Instead of creating a one-size-fits-all choice architecture that is updated slowly, if ever, you can create a highly personalised choice architecture that learns and adapts to an individual user. Hypernudging consequently looks like a distinctively algorithmic mechanism for undermining autonomy. It is definitely not something that is possible with older forms of technology.

Algorithmic tools can also enable distinctive forms of domination. Domination is a kind of power. It arises from asymmetrical relationships between two or more individuals or groups of individuals. The classic example of such an asymmetrical relationship is that between a slave and his/her master, but there are many others. If you live your life constantly in the shadow of such a master, then you cannot be free, even if the master never explicitly interferes with or manipulates your choices. This is the central insight of modern neo-republican political theory, which argues that 'non-domination' is an essential condition for individual autonomy (Pettit 2001, 2011, 2014). Recently, some scholars have argued that in making use of algorithmic tools we may be letting algorithmic masters into our lives. Hoye and Monaghan (2015) and Gräf (2017), for instance, both argue that the systems of mass surveillance and big data analytics that undergird modern AI tools are domination-facilitating. The idea they share is that by welcoming such tools into our lives we facilitate the construction of a digital panopticon around our activities. We are all watched over by algorithmic tools of loving grace, each of which is standing in wait to nudge us back on track if we ever try to escape. Evgeny Morozov (2013) has captured this problem in an evocative metaphor, suggesting that the Big Data systems that surveil and govern our lives, function like 'invisible barbed wire'. They enclose and constrain our space of autonomy, without us even realising what they are doing.

I believe it is important that we understand the precise mechanisms of this algorithmic domination. It is not a crude and explicit form of domination—like that of the master over the slave. It is more subtle than that. It is what I would call a form of 'algorithmic micro-domination'. 'Micro-domination' is a concept that I take from the work of Tom O'Shea (2018), who uses it to understand the forms of domination experienced by people with disabilities. He argues that people with disabilities often suffer from many small-scale instances of domination. If they live in an institutional setting, or are heavily reliant on care and assistance from others, then large swathes of their daily lives may be dependent on the goodwill of others. They may need these others to help them when they wake up, when they go to the bathroom, when they eat, when they go outside, and so on. Taken individually, these cases may not seem all that serious, but aggregated together they take on a different guise:

> The result is often a phenomenon I shall call 'micro-domination': the capacity for decisions to be arbitrarily imposed on someone, which, individually, are too

minor to be contested in a court or a tribunal, but which cumulatively have a major impact on their life. (O' Shea 2018: 136)

The pervasive use of algorithmic tools across all domains of our personal lives can, I believe, give rise to a similar phenomenon. Many small-scale, arguably trivial, choices in our everyday lives might be executed with the help of an algorithmic tool: what route to drive, what news stories to read, who to talk to on social media, what film to watch next, and so on. The resulting network of algorithmic tools would monitor and track our behaviour and send us prompts and reminders. This means that we would then be the 'subjects' of many algorithmic masters. They would surveil our lives and create a space of permissible/acceptable behaviour. Everything is fine if we stay within this space. We can live happy and productive lives (perhaps happier and more productive than our predecessors), and to all intents and purposes, these lives may appear to be autonomous. But if we step out of line we may be quick to realise the presence of the algorithmic masters. There are already some cautionary tales to this effect. Consider, Janet Vertesi's experiences in trying to 'hide' her pregnancy from the algorithmic tools that enable online shopping and that undergird social media (Vertesi 2014). Vertesi, an expert in Big Data, knew that online marketers and advertisers like to know if women are pregnant. She decided to conduct an experiment in which she would hide her own pregnancy from them. This turned out to be exceptionally difficult. She had to avoid all credit card transactions for pregnancy-related shopping and all social media mentions of her pregnancy. In the end, her attempt to avoid algorithmic domination led to her behaviour being flagged as potentially criminal. Suddenly, the domination was made visible.

Taken together this assessment of the impact of algorithmic tools on autonomy seems to be negative. Although there is hope when it comes to the rationality and optionality conditions, there is a reasonable case to be made for thinking that algorithmic tools can negatively impact on the independence condition for autonomy. Furthermore, there might some distinctive and novel mechanisms—hypernudging and algorithmic micro-domination—through which this negative impact is realised. That makes it sound like we should avoid algorithmic tools if we care about our autonomy.

4. But is it any Different this Time Round?

There is, however, a sceptical view that is worth considering. This sceptical view maintains that the analysis given above is overhyped and overstated. Algorithmic tools are just an old wolf in new clothing. As Ord and Bostrom have argued (2006), it is essential in any debate about a new technology (or indeed any new policy), to avoid unwarranted status quo bias. This arises whenever you fixate on identifying the risks and benefits of the new technology but ignore the risks and benefits of the status quo (and the best available alternative). The status quo is never value neutral—this is one of the central insights of Thaler and Sunstein (2009) in their defence of 'nudging'. It could be that the status quo is much worse than the new reality that is being offered to us, even if that new reality has its flaws.

Applying this insight to the argument about autonomy, we have to accept that the world we currently inhabit is filled with threats to autonomy. Our decisions are constantly coerced, manipulated, and dominated by others. We are being bought and sold competing ideologies all the time. We are pushed into alliances and factions that are not of our own choosing at our births. We persuade and overwhelm one another's intellectual resistance. We have been at this for centuries. Nothing about the new technology changes that. Algorithmic tools are just that: tools that humans use to do what they have always done. If we fixate on the 'threats' posed by these tools—or, indeed, the fancy new mechanisms through which they act—we will lose sight of this larger reality and dangerously overstate and overhype the risk to autonomy. This could be made even worse if we fixate on the threats while ignoring the opportunities for enhanced rationality and/or optionality made possible by these tools, coupled with the fact that they might eliminate forms of manipulation or decisional interference that were once in the ascendancy. This is not purely hypothetical. The information made accessible through algorithmic behaviour-change tools, for example, can wean us off of old, irrational habits, or cause us to question routines and beliefs that have been handed down to us by others. In other words, algorithmic tools, even if they do somehow negatively affect autonomy, might be simply replacing or offsetting other autonomy-undermining practices. This doesn't mean that we should welcome them with open arms, of course, but it does suggest that we should be wary of overstating the problem.

In response to this sceptical view, we need to consider whether there is something genuinely different about the ways in which algorithmic tools undermine autonomy. These 'genuine differences' must be differences in effect, not just differences in form. You can use two different tools to achieve the same result; it's only if the results differ that we should really be concerned. Are there any such 'genuine differences'? There are three that might be worth considering:

Differences of scope, scale, or speed: algorithmic tools undermine autonomy at a scale, scope, and/or speed that is truly unprecedented. The tools are everywhere; they are used across many domains of activity; and they operate (and update) at a speed that is completely incomprehensible to human beings.

Differences having to do with the centralisation/monopolisation of power: algorithmic tools are controlled by relatively few actors (ie large tech enterprises like Amazon, Google, and Facebook) and so when they undermine autonomy they do so by enabling and growing the power of these few institutional actors.

Differences having to do with the distinction between personalisation and manipulation: algorithmic tools tend towards personalisation (ie they try to adapt to and predict our preferences) rather than outright manipulation (ie the imposition of external preferences over our own).

Each of these has a whiff of plausibility so it's worth considering them in some more detail.

With regards to differences of scope, scape, and speed, there is definitely something distinctive here. This is, essentially, what Yeung (2017a) is getting at in her description of hypernudging. We are used to dealing with interferences in our decision-making that emanate from other human beings or institutions, not from a superfast technological infrastructure. We are also used to interferences that manifest and act at human speeds. When this happens we are able to spot the interferences, and potentially respond to them before it is too late (or before the interference shifts and takes on a new form). With algorithmic interference, this is no longer the case. Our brains just can't compete and we can't easily escape the oversight of the algorithmic masters. Our natural, evolved forms of resistance are overwhelmed. This means the net effect of algorithmic interference might be far more pernicious than the traditional and more familiar kinds.

With regards to the centralisation of power, there is also definitely something to this. Companies like Google, Facebook, and Amazon (and other tech giants) really do control large swathes of our digital lives. They are empowered and enriched when we make use of their algorithmic tools. Our individual lives can seem very small by comparison. You could argue that when human beings are manipulating and interfering with one another there is at least greater competition for and fragmentation of power. And so there are differences in effect with important moral consequences. The differences here are not so much to do with how the algorithmic tools affect us on an individual scale, but how the empowerment of the tool-makers could have other spillover effects, particularly relating to the inequality of wealth and political power. That said, I tend to think the concern about the centralisation of power is not that compelling. There have been some very centralized, and very powerful underminers of autonomy in human history. Churches and states have, historically, wielded outsized influence over human actors. Sometimes that influence has been extremely pervasive and invasive. At one point in time, the Catholic Church played a significant role in constructing the choice architectures of many Europeans. It did this from dawn to dusk and birth to death. The same was true for other religious organisations and doctrines elsewhere on the globe. Although it is right to be concerned about the outsized influence of tech giants, it's not clear that they threaten something genuinely new and different. On the contrary it seems like the choice architectures of the typical, modern European (to stick with that example), even if they are the result of algorithmic tools, are much more diverse than used to be the case, and that the power landscape is much more fragmented than it once was.

Finally, with regards to the personalisation of algorithmic tools, it is hard to know whether that is a net positive or net negative difference. On the one hand, you could argue that the personalisation that is made possible by algorithmic tools is exactly what we would want if these tools are to respect and promote individual autonomy. Being authentic to oneself and acting in ways that are consistent with one's higher order preferences is generally thought to be conducive to autonomy (Frankfurt 1971) (and, probably, well-being if we go with the general presumption that we are the best judges of what is in our interest). If algorithmic tools are just enabling this, then what's the problem? On other hand, you could argue that algorithmic tools typically don't work by enabling us to act in a manner that is consistent with our higher order preferences. On the contrary, they are customised to our lower order instincts and practices. They perpetuate us at our worst, not at our best. In addition to this, through personalisation, these apps undermine solidarity and the sense of collective identity (Harari 2018: 67). Instead of being the common victims of shared masters we each become the unique victims of a personalised algorithmic master. This can be disempowering and thus disabling of another natural form of resistance to the corrosion of autonomy. (It is also, however, worth noting that the actual degree of personalisation made possible by algorithmic tools can be overstated since most of these tools are trained by making statistical generalisations from patterns spotted in very large, aggregated, and de-personalised data sets; this can actually lead to systematic oppression (Noble 2018).)

In summary, despite the sceptical view, it may genuinely be different this time. The actual effects of algorithmic tools (and not just their mechanisms of action) may be different. Still, even if we take this insight onboard, it is difficult to make a global assessment about the impact of these tools on our autonomy since the net effects could be both positive and negative.

5. How Should We Respond?

How should we respond to this? If the widespread use of algorithmic tools poses new and distinctive threats to autonomy (at the same time as it introduces some opportunities for autonomy enhancement) what should we do to make the best of it? It's worth considering the potential responses at a both a personal and social level.

Let's start at the personal level. It's important not to overlook this. There is a tendency in discussions of algorithmic governance and algorithmic regulation to presume that we are helpless victims of technological overlords.[1] This may be true

---

[1] Some of my previous work has tended toward this view. See Danaher (2016) for more.

in some contexts, but when it comes to the algorithmic tools under discussion in this chapter—the digital assistants, and productivity, health and fitness apps that we use to accomplish our daily goals—this is not true. We still exercise considerable discretion when it comes to the acceptance of these tools into our lives. Some of this discretionary power is boosted by existing legal regimes, such as the revised General Data Protection Regulation (GDPR), but even when those regimes are in place it is important that we don't forget that it is we as individuals that have the ultimate power to accept or reject the influence of these algorithmic tools. To presume otherwise is to foster an attitude of helplessness, which will never be conducive to autonomy. So we need to empower individuals to make autonomy-enhancing decisions about when to accept algorithmic tools into their everyday lives. To do this, we need to encourage them to think about the overall importance of the goals they want to achieve with the help of the tools (of course) and whether the tools do this in an autonomy-undermining or promoting way. Sensitivity to the different dimensions and conditions of responsibility will be critical in this regard. If an individual has a goal of significant importance to them, and if to achieve that goal they must navigate a complex choice architecture with many thousands of options, some algorithmic assistance could be quite beneficial. It might make them less confused and more rational. This may come at the expense of some independence, but this could be worth it when we think about the other conditions of autonomy. On the other hand, if the individual uses an algorithmic tool to accomplish a goal of little overall importance, and that wouldn't be that difficult to achieve in the absence of the tool, they may be sacrificing their independence for minimal gain. They should think twice about running the risk. In between these two extreme cases, there will be plenty of room for individual judgment to be exercised.

None of this is to deny that individuals may need help. If, as was argued above, algorithmic tools act at a speed, scope, and scale that is truly unprecedented, and thus wears down our natural forms of resistance, some external assistance may be required to promote individual autonomy. This assistance could take a number of different forms. It could come direct from the marketplace for algorithmic tools. In other words, if there are fears about the erosion of autonomy, and these are taken seriously, we might expect the marketplace to self-correct (to some extent) and for companies that offer tools that are autonomy-preserving to gain a competitive advantage. This has already happened with respect to privacy. Apple, for example, now markets itself as a privacy-protecting company, relative to its peers in Google, Facebook, and Amazon, which rely more heavily in data mining and surveillance to make their money. Could we see something similar happening with respect to autonomy? Perhaps, though I wouldn't be too confident of this. Many of the tech giants work off advertising and marketing-based business models. These business models have always depended on the capacity to manipulate and persuade potential consumers. Consequently these companies are deeply committed to practices that are, shall we say, not always respectful of autonomy: they want to capture our attention and influence our behaviour (Wu 2017; Bartholomew 2017; Alter 2017; Crawford 2015). If they don't do this, they won't make money. Unless the successfulness of this business model is completely undermined, we can't expect the market to easily correct itself.

This means we may have to look to other legal and regulatory responses. Recent changes to data protection law in Europe are certainly helpful in this regard insofar as data is the fuel that feeds the fire of algorithmic manipulation, but other legal responses may need to be contemplated. Changes to laws on monopoly power and anti-competitiveness might be needed to break up the powerful tech giants and address concerns about the centralization of power. More precise regulations on the speed, scope, and scale of algorithmic interference might also be required. Perhaps algorithmic tools that update and adapt at speeds that erode natural forms of resistance will need to be banned (in much the same way as subliminal advertising was banned in the past)?[2] Perhaps stated preference algorithms (which we might expect to map onto our higher order preferences) should be encouraged and promoted, while predictive preference algorithms (which we might expect to map onto our lower order preferences) should be discouraged? This is to say nothing of bans or limitations on the more extreme and coercive forms of algorithmic interference, for example those made available through insurance markets.

Perhaps we should also consider recognizing new fundamental rights? Frischmann and Selinger (2018) have argued as much, suggesting that we need to recognise the 'right to be off' if we are to retain our sense of agency and autonomy in the twenty-first century. The right to be off is, as the name suggests, a right to live a life without any algorithmic tools being foisted upon you. In a similar vein, I have argued that we may need to recognise a right to attentional protection to address the impact of algorithmic tools on autonomy.[3] The idea behind this is that attention is the thing that tech companies try to capture and control through their algorithmic tools (Wu 2017; Bartholomew 2017; Alter 2017; Crawford 2015). Without capturing our attention, and slowly eroding our capacity to ignore digital distractions, these companies would be much less successful and much less able to interfere with our autonomy. By targeting our legal interventions at the capacity to pay attention, we can address one of the root causes of the potential problem. This is not a completely unprecedented idea. As Tran (2016) notes, there are many legal doctrines that already target attention. For example, informed consent laws are, at least in part, about requiring us to pay attention to certain things, and giving us the right to ignore others. By creating a new right to attentional protection you can unify and bring order to these disparate areas of law, and address the threats to autonomy posed by algorithmic tools.

We may also need to consider more radical social responses. Throughout this chapter I've been assuming that individual autonomy is something that we want

---

[2] See Bartholomew (2017: 11, 112–17) on this point.
[3] Danaher (2017), working off of Tran (2016). My argument is partly influenced by the right to data protection which has only been identified and recognized in the recent past.

to protect and preserve, but maybe that is not the case. Maybe autonomy competes with other important values (eg individual well-being and flourishing) or maybe it is only valuable to the extent that it helps bring about other values. Some prominent legal philosophers have argued as much, holding that freedom is only instrumentally valuable to the extent that it improves well-being (Leiter 2016). If that's the case, maybe the algorithmic threat is exactly the excuse we need to push us towards a post-autonomy society (Harari 2016, 2018), just as digital convenience and mass surveillance have encouraged some people to argue for a shift to a post-privacy society (eg Brin 1998).

6. Conclusion

It is time to draw together the strands of argument from the preceding discussion. In brief, I have argued that algorithmic tools play an increasingly important role in how we live our daily lives. I have suggested that they are tools—insofar as they enable us to fulfil our goals—but that they also have a regulatory and governance dimension—insofar as they can be used by ourselves and third parties to manipulate, nudge, incentivize, and control our behaviour. Consequently, I believe they can have an impact on our autonomy. I have tried to clarify the nature of that impact, without overstating it. I have used Joseph Raz's three conditions of autonomy (rationality, optionality, and independence) to assess the likely impact of algorithmic tools on autonomy. In doing so, I identified two novel mechanisms through which algorithmic tools can undermine our independence—Yeung's 'hypernudging' and O'Shea's 'micro-domination'—whilst also emphasising the positive impact these tools could have on our optionality and rationality. I have also considered the extent to which algorithmic tools threaten something genuinely new and concluded that they may do so due to their speed, scope, and scale and the way in which this overwhelms our natural forms of resistance to outside interference. Finally, I have argued that we need to consider responses to these threats at both an individual and societal level. Individuals should be empowered to make informed choices about when using an algorithmic tool might undermine their autonomy. And societies should consider new regulatory responses and fundamental rights (such as the right 'to be off' or the right to 'attentional protection'), as well as the possible need for a radical shift in values to a post-autonomy society.

Bibliography

Alter A, *Irresistible* (The Bodley Head 2017).
Bartholomew M, *Adcreep: The Case Against Modern Marketing* (Stanford University Press 2017).

Brin D, *The Transparent Society* (Basic Books 1998).

Brundage M and Danaher J, 'Cognitive Scarcity and Artificial Intelligence: How Assistive AI Could Alleviate Inequality' (*Philosophical Disquisitions*, 15 May 2017) <http://philosophicaldisquisitions.blogspot.com/2017/05/cognitive-scarcity-and-artificial.html> accessed 10 June 2019.

Burrell J, How the Machine Thinks: Understanding Opacity in Machine Learning Systems' (2016) Big Data and Society doi: 10.1177/ 2053951715622512.

Carr N, *The Glass Cage: Where Automation is Taking Us* (The Bodley Head 2014).

Crawford M, *The World Beyond Your Head* (Farrar, Strauss and Giroux 2015).

Danaher J, 'The Threat of Algocracy: Reality, Resistance and Accommodation' (2016) 29(3) Philosophy and Technology 245.

Danaher J, 'The Right to Attention in an Age of Distraction' (*Philosophical Disquisitions*, 19 May 2017) <http://philosophicaldisquisitions.blogspot.com/2017/05/the-right-to-attention-in-age-of.html> accessed 31 July 2019.

Danaher J, Hogan M, Noone C, et al, Algorithmic Governance: Developing a Research Agenda through the Power of Collective Intelligence' (2017) 4(3) Big Data and Society doi: 10.1177/2053951717726554.

Eubanks V, *Automating Inequality: How High-Tech Tools Profile, Police and Punish the Poor* (St. Martin's Press 2018).

Frischmann B and Selinger E, *Re-Engineering Humanity* (Cambridge University Press 2018).

Gal M, 'Algorithmic Challenges to Autonomous Choice' (2017) Michigan Journal of Law and Technology https://papers.ssrn.com/sol3/papers.cfm?abstract_id=2971456##, accessed 10 June 2019.

Gräf E, 'When Automated Profiling Threatens Freedom: A Neo-Republican Account' (2017) 4 European Data Protection Law Journal 1.

Harari YN, *Homo Deus* (Harvill Secker 2016).

Harari YN, *21 Lessons for the 21st Century* (Jonathan Cape 2018).

Hartzog W, *Privacy's Blueprint* (Harvard University Press 2018).

Hoye JM and Monaghan J, 'Surveillance, Freedom and the Republic' (2015) European Journal of Political Theory doi: 10.1177%2F1474885115608783.

Killmister J, *Taking the Measure of Autonomy: A Four-Dimensional Theory of Self-Governance* (Routledge 2017).

Kitchin R, 'Thinking Critically about and Researching Algorithms' (2017) 20(1) Information, Communication and Society 14.

Krakauer D, 'Will AI Harm Us? Better to Ask How We'll Reckon with Our Hybrid Nature' *Nautilus* (6 September 2016) <http://nautil.us/blog/will-ai-harm-us-better-to-ask-how-well-reckon-with-our-hybrid-nature> accessed 10 June 2019.

Leiter B, 'The Case Against Free Speech' (2016) 38 Sydney Law Review 407.

Morrow DR, 'When Technologies Makes Good People Do Bad Things: Another Argument against the Value-Neutrality of Technologies' (2014) 20(2) Science and Engineering Ethics 329.

Morozov E, 'The Real Privacy Problem' (2013) MIT Technology Review <http://www.technologyreview.com/featuredstory/520426/the-real-privacy-problem/> accessed 10 June 2019.

Noble S, *Algorithms of Oppression* (NYU Press 2018).

O'Neil C, *Weapons of Math Destruction* (Penguin 2016).

Ord T and Bostrom N, 'The Reversal Test: Eliminating Status Quo Bias in Applied Ethics' (2006) 116 Ethics 656.

O'Shea T, 'Disability and Domination' (2018) 35(1) Journal of Applied Philosophy 133.

Pasquale F, *The Black Box Society* (Harvard University Press 2015).

Pettit P, *Republicanism: A Theory of Freedom and Government* (Oxford University Press 2001).

Pettit P, 'The Instability of Freedom as Non-Interference: The Case of Isaiah Berlin' (2011) 121(4) Ethics 693.

Pettit P, *Just Freedom: A Moral Compass for a Complex World* (WW Norton and Co 2014).

Polonetsky J and Tene O, 'Privacy and Big Data: Making Ends Meet' (2013) 66 Stanford Law Review 25.

Raz J, *The Morality of Freedom* (Oxford University Press 1986).

Rouvroy A, 'Algorithmic Governmentality and the End (s) of Critique' (2013) 2 Society of the Query 163.

Rouvroy A, 'Algorithmic Governmentality: A Passion for the Real and the Exhaustion of the Virtual' All Watched over by Algorithms, Berlin (29 January 2015) <https://www.academia.edu/10481275/Algorithmic_governmentality_a_passion_for_the_real_and_the_exhaustion_of_the_virtual> accessed 31 July 2019.

Scheibehenne B, Greifeneder R, and Todd PM, 'Can There Ever Be Too Many Options? A Meta-Analytic Review of Choice Overload' (2010) 37 Journal of Consumer Research 409.

Schwartz B, *The Paradox of Choice: Why Less Is More* (Harper Collins 2004).

Sunstein C, *The Ethics of Influence* (Cambridge University Press 2016).

Thaler R and Sunstein C, *Nudge: Improving Decisions about Health, Wealth and Happiness* (Penguin 2009).

Tran J, 'The Right to Attention' (2016) 91(3) Indiana Law Journal 1023.

Vertesi J, 'My Experiment Opting Out Made Me Look Like a Criminal' *Time* (1 May 2014) <https://time.com/83200/privacy-internet-big-data-opt-out/> accessed 31 July 2019.

Wu T, *The Attention Merchants* (Atlantic Books 2017).

Yeung K, 'Hypernudge': Big Data as a Mode of Regulation by Design' (2017a) 20(1) Information, Communication and Society 118.

Yeung K, 'Algorithmic Regulation: A Critical Interrogation' (2017b) Regulation and Governance doi: 10.1111/rego.12158.

Zarsky T, 'Automated Predictions: Perception, Law and Policy' (2012) 15(9) Communications of the ACM 33.

Zarsky T, 'Transparent Prediction' (2013) 4 University of Illinois Law Review 1504.

PART II
PUBLIC SECTOR APPLICATIONS

6

Administration by Algorithm?

Public Management Meets Public Sector Machine Learning

Michael Veale and Irina Brass*

1. Introduction

Public bodies and agencies increasingly seek to use new forms of data analysis in order to provide 'better public services'. These reforms have consisted of digital service transformations such as 'e-government 2.0' and the creation of 'integrated data infrastructures' (Statistics New Zealand 2016), generally aimed at 'improving the experience of the citizen', 'making government more efficient' and 'boosting business and the wider economy' (Manzoni 2017).

It is not a new observation that administrative data—data collected by or for public bodies for registration, transaction, and record keeping—might be mined for better understanding of societal patterns, trends, and policy impacts, or sanitized and released to fuel innovative products and services. A plethora of government reviews and initiatives have, especially over the last decade, led to the establishment of centres, networks, and infrastructures to better understand societal phenomena using these data (Woollard 2014). Yet more recently, there has been a push to use administrative data to build models with the purpose of helping make day-to-day operational decisions in the management and delivery of public services, rather than providing general evidence to improve strategy or government-citizen interaction.

These new operational models are designed to serve as decision support or even to trigger automatic action. These are systems built primarily using *machine learning* techniques: algorithms which seek to identify patterns in data sets and render them into a usable form. In this chapter, we focus on this trend, and attempt to answer elements of several important questions for the scholarship and practice of public administration:

* Both authors are supported by the Engineering and Physical Sciences Research Council (EPSRC): [MV] under grants EP/M507970/1 and by the Alan Turing Institute under the grant EP/N510129/1, and [IB] under EP/N02334X/1.

A. What are the drivers and logics behind the use of machine learning in the public sector, and how should we understand it in the contexts of administrations and their tasks?
B. Is the use of machine learning in the public sector a smooth continuation of 'e-Government', or does it pose fundamentally different challenges to the practice of public administration?
C. How are public management decisions and practices at different levels enacted when machine learning solutions are implemented in the public sector?

We first explain the types of machine learning systems used in the public sector, detailing the processes and tasks that they aim to support. We then look at three levels of government—the macro, meso, and the street-level—to map out, analyse, and evaluate how machine learning in the public sector more broadly is framed and standardized across government considering unintended consequences (macro level), how it is designed and monitored in relation to proposed policy initiatives and existing public performance measurements, management and risk assessment mechanisms (meso level), and how it is implemented in the daily practices of frontline public service providers (micro level). We conclude that, while the use of machine learning in the public sector is mostly discussed with regard to its 'transformative effect' versus 'the dynamic conservatism' characteristic of public bureaucracies that embrace new technological developments (Hood 2008), it also raises several concerns about the skills, capacities, processes, and practices that governments currently employ, the forms of which can have value-laden, political consequences.

Information technology is supposed to be a 'central force' to transformations in public management (Hood 2000: 17), although despite decades of promise of transformation, these tools usually fused onto existing practices rather than altering them at a deeper level (Margetts 1999). Scholars have argued that in recent years technologies have taken centre stage and repositioned some of the trajectories of New Public Management into 'digital era governance'. They point to trends such as the digital re-integration of siloed services, data sharing practices aimed at creating a 'one-stop-shop' and 'end-to-end' service delivery with minimal repeated information gathering, and briefly discuss the rise of interest in 'zero touch technologies' (today often referred to as automated decision-making, following the EU Data Protection Directive 1995 and the later General Data Protection Regulation (GDPR)). This integration of digital technological developments in the public sector have led some to claim that 'technological change influences administrative capacity in public organisations', as the routines and capabilities of public organizations 'co-evolve with technology while being influenced by the wider institutional context (ie innovation systems)' (Lember et al 2017). However, this raises the question whether information technologies and digital processes augment administrative capacity, leading to better management and delivery of public services?

Recently, machine learning powered, algorithmic tools[1] have garnered a great deal of attention due to public and private entities' drive to obtain value from large and increasingly well-structured data sets they hold, combined with a range of narrow discoveries in the machine learning field, primarily indicating that tasks we thought were computationally very difficult, such as certain types of image recognition or strategic board-game play, might be less so. In order to understand how governments increasingly administer by algorithm, we now distinguish between two main types of systems using machine learning for operational purposes: *automation systems* and *augmentation systems*.

2. Automation Systems

Automation systems attempt to increase the quantity or efficiency of routine public sector operations through computation. Here, machine learning is used to enable the automation of tasks which have complicated elements but a straightforward and relatively objective outcome—such as triaging phone-calls or correspondence to the right points of contact. The incremental automation of rule-based processes is far from new, with public institutions such as tax agencies seeing it as an organizational ambition over many decades, with varying success (Margetts 1999). For processes that can be translated to rule-based systems with completeness and fidelity, progress continues at a slow-burn pace. Many barriers to rote automation surround classic challenges of legacy systems, as well as the slow and surprising creep of information technology in government over time, which has seen a greater fusion of data systems onto locked-in or slow-moving existing practices, rather than the transformative effect that had long been anticipated (cf Downs 1967; Dunleavy et al 2006). New technologies such as robotic process automation have already further aided integration by using computational techniques to automatically connect systems that do not naturally work together (Willcocks & Lacity 2016). Similarly, machine learning technologies provide improved tools, such as translation, image, or handwriting recognition, which can be 'plugged in' to chains of automation for straightforward tasks. This follows the 'transformative vision' of information and communication technologies in the public sector, whereby technological innovations can lead to new 'government instrumentalities and operations', creating

[1] In this work, 'algorithm' and its derivative terms are used as a shorthand for machine learning technologies and models, computational methods that, in practice, allow fine-grained patterns to be discerned in data sets and acted upon. This differs from a historical computer science definition of algorithms, which refers to repeatable computational processes, and which are not unfamiliar to government, business, or practice.

more effective ways of managing public portfolios, and more efficient and personalized public service delivery (Hood 2008).

Yet many administrative tasks are not straightforward and easily reduced or defined. Issues concerning operational decision-makers that might seem rote and 'objective' may be less so on closer inspection, and instead contain highly subjective and political aspects. Some researchers have historically pointed to a subset of tasks that therefore resist automation. An early empirical study of information systems in US cities concluded that the political nature of some tasks, such as measuring internal departmental goals or deciding on external decisions (eg planning), may never allow them to be dramatically affected by computerization—and that '[p]lanners and policy makers are especially cognizant of this reality' (Northrop et al 1990: 512). 'Such models', they argued, 'would require criteria for defining problems and evaluating solutions, analysis of data in several files, and information that cannot be automated, such as interest group feelings about problems or support for various solutions'. Given the trend they saw to 'devalue community statistics and, instead, to emphasize the opinions of the affected citizens', they claimed 'it is likely that computerized information will have little impact on city planning decisions in the near future' (Northrop et al 1990: 510). This sentiment has a longer history in public administration. Michael Lipsky, for example, claimed that 'the nature of service provision calls for human judgment that *cannot be programmed and for which machines cannot substitute*' (Lipsky 2010: 161) [emphasis added].

The implication is that equitable and effective public services require judgement that cannot be quantified, reduced, or encoded in fully automated systems. These are issues familiar from the study of artificial intelligence and the law in the early 1990s, when it became clear that the application of these systems led to grey zones of knowledge in problem-solving, and that, formally, codification was only effective in 'some highly specific, syntactically complex but semantically untroubling domains' (Edwards & Veale 2017: 24). This in turn is connected to the indeterminacy of law: particularly the prevalence of terms with an 'open textured' nature, where the term's use or extension cannot be determined in advance of its application (Bench-Capon & Sergot 1988); where the connections between terms are vague in nature (Prakken 1997; Zeleznikow 2004); or where a series of factors are expected to be weighted and have relative importance assigned in a manner difficult to prescribe or render replicable (Christie 1986). At a larger, more strategic scale, the literature on the governance of socio-technical problems has similarly emphasized the intractability of 'unstructured' or 'semi-structured' problems where there is a lack of consensus around appropriate means and/or ends, and how participatory processes that open up rather than close down are required to socially reach more navigable issues (Hoppe 2010).

Automation systems always bring politicized elements in the public sector, from encouraging the shifting and avoidance of blame, the increased rigidity of rules, and the types of 'edge cases' on which the systems will fail (Smith et al 2010).

They also serve to prioritize some public values, such as consistency and efficiency, above others (Hood 1991). However, where approaches with significant grey zones are automated, the value-laden nature of automation is accentuated, as the systems have to determine on which basis to make decisions within the grey zones of decision-making. This makes it necessary to ensure that automation systems, particularly ambitious ones, are well encompassed by frameworks for suitable accountability.

Others have taken a different stance in relation to grey areas (Martinho-Truswell 2018), arguing that tasks that previously appeared to require human judgement, can now be *better* decided upon with the help of statistical models such as machine learning systems. This leads to the second category: *augmentation systems*.

3. Augmentation Systems

This second category of technological solutions, which we term *augmentation systems*, stems from a belief that machine learning does not just help cheapen or hasten decision-making, but can *improve it*.

What would it be to improve a decision? It is useful to point to a definition of machine learning from Mitchell (1997):[2] we say that a machine learns when its *performance* at a certain *task* improves with *experience*. Here, performance, task, and experience are captured through data, which are determined by designers. Improvement, or learning, can only be discussed once these three areas *at the very least* are accurately implemented. At a minimum, this requires that the aims of policy are quantifiable and quantified: a highly value-laden task in and of itself.

Traditionally, ensuring that policy is implemented with fidelity and legitimacy, and that public service delivery decisions are made in an equitable, effective, and efficient manner, has fallen within the remit of 'bureaucratic professionalism', which itself carries tensions between responsiveness, as a means of enacting professional judgement, and standardized performance, as a means of ensuring best practice (Kearney & Sinha 1988; Stivers 1994). 'Bureaucratic professionalism' has itself changed from the Weberian model of administrative integrity and impartiality in the public interest, to (new) public management (Dahlström et al 2011) and there has been growing recognition of its limitations (Bevan & Hood 2006; Dunleavy & Hood 1994; Hood & Peters 2004; Lapsley 2009). This shift has not only led to increased questioning of the effectiveness of measuring, standardizing, and auditing public sector performance for the public interest, but also brought about new conceptions of the role of the bureaucrat as negotiator and co-creator of public values with the citizens (JV Denhardt & Denhardt 2007; RB Denhardt & Denhardt 2000).

---

[2] This definition of machine learning has been popularized in the social, legal, and philosophical studies of the technology by Mireille Hildebrandt, eg in Hildebrandt (2015).

In this respect, one could argue that this shift to new public service (NPS) is supporting the public servant's professional responsibility for more responsiveness in the management and delivery of public services, which augmentation systems could support.

Interestingly, in studies of digitization of government (eg Dunleavy et al 2006), there seems an almost complete omission of anticipation of the augmentative and predictive logics we have seen draw attention today. Programmes such as the *Integrated Data Infrastructure* in New Zealand (2016) have been designed not (just) for the purpose of creating 'one-stop shops' for accessing and delivering public services via interoperable, cross-departmental solutions (ie e-government 1.0 and 2.0), but for the purpose of 'informing decision-makers to help solve complex issues that affect us all, such as crime and vulnerable children'. Such programmes are thus established in order to augment the analytic and anticipatory capacity of contemporary governments 'to systematically use knowledge to inform a more forward-looking and society-changing style of policy-making' (Lodge & Wegrich 2014). These augmentations are hoped to help governments navigate coupled and complex problems that have ramifications outside the siloed organizational and decisional structures in which government departments still operate (ie wicked problems) (Andrews 2018).

The nature of the analytic capacity that algorithmic augmentation systems are supposed to improve, particularly in the context of linked administrative data combined with additional data sources, is that it is possible to 'mine' data for insights public professionals alone would miss. In areas such as tax fraud detection, ambitions do not stay at replicating existing levels of success with reduced staff cost, but to do 'better than humans' (Milner & Berg 2017: 15). In highly value-charged areas where accuracy costs live, such as child welfare and abuse, it is common to hear calls after a scandal that a tragedy 'could have been prevented', or that the 'information needed to stop this was there'.[3] Increased accuracy and the avoidance of human bias, rather than just the scalability and cost-efficiency of automation, is cited as a major driver for the development of machine learning models in high stakes spaces such as these (Cuccaro-Alamin et al 2017).

In many ways, this logic continues the more quantified approach to risk and action found in the wide array of managerialist tools and practices associated with New Public Management. These have long had an algorithmic flavour, including performance measures and indicators, targets, and audits. Researchers have also emphasized that while these transformations are often justified as straightforward steps towards greater efficiency and effectiveness, in practice they represent core changes in expectations and in accountability (Burton & van den Broek 2009).

---

[3] Very rarely do those calling for this consider whether, were systems to be in place using such information, the number of false positives would be small enough to effectively enable identification of particular tragic cases.

Particularly in areas where professional judgement plays a key role in service delivery, such as social work, augmentation tools monitor and structure work to render individuals countable and accountable in new ways, taking organizations to new and more extreme bureaucratic heights of predictability, calculability, and control.

Recently, these modern forms of automation and augmentation tools have also received criticism from an emerging interdisciplinary field consisting of computer scientists, lawyers, sociologists of data, and more. It is to this that we turn next.

4. Scholarly Interest in Socio-Algorithmic Issues

Scholars in the field of 'critical data studies' initially were fuelled by the belief that decisions made through the processing of large volumes of data have gained a veneer of neutrality (boyd 2016; boyd & Crawford 2012). Until recently, in high profile legal cases, the 'algorithmic neutrality' argument was commonly employed by large technology platforms to attempt to absolve themselves of responsibility (Kohl 2013). A plethora of studies have demonstrated how systems in areas such as natural language processing (Bolukbasi et al 2016; Caliskan et al 2017), policing (Ensign et al 2018), justice (Chouldechova 2017), and online content moderation (Binns et al 2017), among others, are *far* from neutral. At a narrow level, they display detectable instances of unfairness between the way different groups are allocated results or represented in such systems (Crawford 2017). At a broader level, they raise deeper questions of whom the technology empowers or disempowers over time through its framing, context, purpose, and use.

These concerns of algorithmic bias or discrimination (Barocas & Selbst 2016) have generated widespread interest in technical fields. In the computer science literature, it has spurred debate on how to mathematically specify fairness in such a way that it can be audited or placed as a statistical constraint during the training of a machine learning system (Kamiran et al 2012). Such debate has spread from niche venues and conferences into the public eye (Courtland 2018), and is now a commonplace topic at the world's top research fora for machine learning, conferences such as the International Conference on Machine Learning (ICML) and Advances in Neural Information Processing Systems (NIPS).[4]

Given that both automation and augmentation systems are seen as political, and at times, problematic, a range of speculative and analytical work has been undertaken around how systems can be held to account. This includes how assurance can be provided that the models actually used are the ones claimed to be used (Kilbertus et al 2018; Kroll et al 2016) or how the logic of systems can be inspected

---

[4] At the time of writing, the NIPS conference is under consultation to be renamed amidst heavy accusations of problematic and discriminatory sexist culture in its own community.

and explained (Edwards & Veale 2017) or how users feel about such explanations (Binns et al 2018). Some argue that the potential for pervasive and adaptive deployment of these systems challenges the potential for them ever to be legitimate or meaningfully accountable (Yeung 2017a).

As questions of discrimination, power, and accountability rise, there is a clear need to map both the problems and proposed means of managing them to institutions and practices in the public sector. Only a limited array of work has specifically focused on administrative practices around these value-laden issues and technologies (eg Veale et al 2018). In the following section, drawing on current and emerging policy initiatives, we will attempt to make this link.

5. Emerging Management of Public Sector Machine Learning

We now outline and comment on the challenges of these systems that concern administrative structures at three different levels of public management and delivery. Firstly, the 'macro' scale, where governments play a strategic role in steering the implementation of this technology across public functions, and perform a duty to balance their benefits with their unintended consequences. Secondly, the 'meso' scale, where the delivery of individual public functions and policies is actualized in part through algorithmic systems and where the design, monitoring, and evaluation of algorithmic systems is considered. Lastly, the 'micro' scale, looking at where specific frontline decisions affecting individuals, communities, and other entities are made and navigated by or with machine learning systems.

5.1 Macro: Government Strategy and Best Practices

At the highest level, governments have been discussing how to deal with machine learning and 'artificial intelligence' across many functions, including how to manage and promote innovation in the business environment, how to drive best practice and regulate misuse, and, most importantly, how to fit them into the day-to-day work of government. Here, we identify several domains where the integration of machine learning in the public sector appears to be occurring: the creation of new coordination mechanisms; new cross-cutting rights and obligations, and new capacities.

5.1.1 New Coordination Mechanisms
One way that governments have reacted to this change is by creating and strengthening coordinating bodies, codes, and best practices that deal with algorithmic systems in the public sector.

New bodies and actors designed to take a cross-cutting role in data processing and analysis are emerging. Following a report from the Royal Society and British Academy suggesting a 'data stewardship body' (The Royal Society and the British Academy 2017), the UK government is establishing a 'Centre for Data Ethics and Innovation' as an arms-length body (or 'quango') from the Department for Digital, Culture, Media and Sport. The exact terms of this body are, at the time of writing, out for consultation, but it is proposed that this centre will 'support the government to enable safe and ethical innovation in the use of data and AI' through (i) identifying steps to ensure that the law, regulation, and guidance keep pace with developments in data-driven and artificial intelligence (AI)-based technologies; (ii) publishing recommendations to government on how it can support safe and ethical innovation in data and AI; and (iii) providing expert advice and support to regulators (including eg the Information Commissioner's Office, Competition and Markets Authority, and sector regulators) on the implications of data and AI uses and areas of potential harm. It is also proposed that such a body has a statutory footing (Department for Digital, Culture, Media and Sport 2018a). Bodies with comparable cross-cutting competencies can be found emerging elsewhere, such as the French National Digital Council (*Conseil national du numérique*) and the recent German Data Ethics Commission (*Datenethikkommission*), designed to 'develop ethical guidelines for the protection of individuals, the preservation of the structure of social life and the safeguarding of prosperity in the information age' (Bundesministerium des Innern, für Bau und Heimat 2018).

Alongside these bodies are emerging guidance documents and codes designed to inform the development of algorithmic systems across public functions. Perhaps the most complete at the time of writing is the UK government's Data Ethics Framework (Department for Digital, Culture, Media and Sport 2018b), currently in its second iteration. This document is intended to guide 'the design of appropriate data use in government and the wider public sector', and is 'aimed at anyone working directly or indirectly with data in the public sector, including data practitioners (statisticians, analysts and data scientists), policymakers, operational staff and those helping produce data-informed insight'. Other countries are working on similar documents: for example, the Treasury Board of Canada is currently finalizing a 'Directive on Automated Decision-Making' and further documentation on 'Responsible AI for the Government of Canada'. The city government of New York has legislated for a temporary 'task force' to produce a guidance report of a similar flavour.

While the documents above lack the binding force of law (although their use may be referenced as evidence of meeting broader obligations, such as the UK's public sector equality duty[5]), a few more binding documents have also been

---

[5] Equality Act 2010, s 149.

proposed. In the UK's Data Protection Bill 2018, a 'Framework for Data Processing in Government' was added by government amendment, which 'contains guidance about the processing of personal data' for the exercise of public functions. A person carrying out such a function must have regard to such a document when in force, as, controversially, should the independent Information Commissioner, if it appears 'relevant' to her. Such a document has not yet been published. It is also worth noting that the GDPR supports the creation and adoption of codes of conduct on a sectoral level, which may include codes of conduct relating to data management and public functions.

These documents and bodies may be useful to some of the low-stakes machine learning systems that are being built and implemented, to do tasks such as filter comments or triage parliamentary questions,[6] but may be less compelling for times where the stakes are higher or involve fundamental rights, liberties, or 'taboo trade-offs' that are difficult to apply principles to (Fiske & Tetlock 1997). The persistently non-binding nature of these strategic documents and bodies, as well as the lack of resource of statutory obligation to consider their opinion or guidance, may seriously limit their impact. Experience from the wing-clipping of other digital cross-cutting bodies such as the UK's Government Digital Service (GDS) (Hill 2018) would indicate that any binding effort in this area would be subject to bureaucratic competition and 'turf wars' between government departments (Bannister 2005), particularly exacerbated if data becomes the central force in government that many strategy documents hope.

5.1.2 New Cross-Cutting Rights and Obligations

Cross-cutting individual rights have been positioned as a proportionate counterbalance to public sector algorithmic systems. Fully automated decisions in many parts of government have been under the remit of data protection law across Europe since 1995, yet the requirement under these provision for decisions to be *solely* based on automated processing before requirements or safeguard triggers has limited their application to augmentation systems, which typically have a human mediating between the computer system and the decision, even nominally (Edwards & Veale 2017).[7]

In France, where the automated decision-making rights in data protection law originate from (Bygrave 2001), 2016 legislation provided for further individual rights concerning cross-cutting government decisions based on an 'algorithmic

---

[6] See eg the UK Ministry of Justice's parliamentary questions tool <https://github.com/moj-analytical-services/pq-tool> or the Government Digital Service's comment clustering tool <https://dataingovernment.blog.gov.uk/2016/11/09/understanding-more-from-user-feedback/> accessed 7 October 2018.

[7] Whether augmentation systems produce *solely* automated decisions, and what organizational means might result in meaningful human oversight in individual cases, are discussed below in the section on the 'micro' scale of administration.

treatment'. These provisions, placed into the French Administrative Code in early 2017, specify that upon request, individuals are provided with:

1. the degree and the mode of contribution of the algorithmic processing to the decision-making;
2. the data processed and its source;
3. the treatment parameters and, where appropriate, their weighting, applied to the situation of the person concerned; and
4. the operations carried out by the treatment

(following the translation in Edwards & Veale 2018).

All EU countries must lay down safeguards relating to fully automated, significant decisions taken on the basis of national law (Article 22, GDPR), but these will not necessarily include decision support systems within their remit, as these are not 'solely' automated. Of interest in the French provision is that only a 'degree' of contribution of the algorithm is required, bringing a range of systems, and potentially even information sources we would traditionally consider 'evidence', within scope (Edwards & Veale 2018).

Explanation rights seem popular, but there is a tension between explanation (that computer scientists may favour) and justification, which is a more classic feature of administrative decisions. While the 'treatment parameters' in French law seem clearly connected to a model, provisions elsewhere, such as the common law *duty to give reasons* in England and Wales, may only require some justification (potentially post-hoc) for an algorithmic decision rather than inspection mechanisms at play (Oswald 2018).[8] It could be argued this is more appropriate—there is a difference between *explanation* in law and *justification*, and tracing back why a decision occurred (eg treatment parameters) may not serve to justify it (Hildebrandt 2017). On the other hand, justification does not allow analysis of errors within a system, which may be systematic or distributed in discriminatory ways across a population, and these errors cause real harm and time wasted, even if a court or dispute resolution service may overturn them.

5.1.3 New Capacities
Another cross-cutting response has been to build capacities, training, and career pathways in order to support machine learning in the public sector. The UK government has created the 'Government Data Science Partnership', which is a collaboration between the GDS, Office for National Statistics (ONS), and the Government Office for Science. Under this brand, initiatives such as new career

---

[8] The scope of this duty is limited however: 'courts [in England and Wales] have consistently avoided imposing any general duty in administrative law to give reasons for decisions' (Oswald 2018: 5).

paths for civil servant 'data scientists', new capacity building schemes such as the 'Data Science Accelerator', where civil servants work on public sector projects with mentors, and a new national framework of skills for the roles falling within the 'Digital, Data and Technology' profession, have been proposed. In different parts of government, new capacity centres have been set up, such as the Home Office's Data Analytics Competency Centre (DACC, formerly HODAC) and the ONS's Data Science Campus.

Technology strategy and translation capabilities are also being introduced inside other parts of the public sector. Organizations such as the Centre for Data Ethics and Innovation, described above, also intend to hold capacity and capacity building functions according to the released consultation documents. The Information Commissioner's Office has launched a technology strategy with a specific focus on AI, machine learning and algorithmic systems, indicating its intention to hire post-doctoral fellows, establish technology sandboxes, administer collaborative research grant programmes to build knowledge, and engage specialist expertise in new ways (Information Commissioner's Office 2018).

Whether these will be sufficient to be effective is yet to be seen. In particular, capacities that are not deeply woven within the day-to-day policy process, or accessible to different projects, directorates, or functions, may fail to help shape and define algorithmic interventions, particularly when decisions or engagement around vendors, project scoping, and public procurement are made in different places and with different timescales and involvement. Furthermore, it is an open question as to whether these individuals, and their skills, remain in the public sector, particularly at a time of great demand for quantitative talent in all areas of economy and society.

5.2 Meso: From High Level Policy to Practice

The macro level described above attempts to make a horizontal, facilitating environment for algorithmic design, deployment, and maintenance in the public sector. Zooming in towards specific policy instances provides a different view on the challenges and practices as they are developing on the ground. The 'meso' level, as we describe it, concerns the practices of implementing high-level policy intentions with algorithmic components into a deployable and deployed system. At this meso level of public programme design and implementation, one of the main challenges is how to best balance bureaucratic control over the quality of the algorithmic system with measurement, monitoring, and reporting practices that show how decisions made about and by algorithmic systems meet the high-level guidelines and requirements specified in binding or soft laws. Thus, the implementation of models and machine learning tools in the design and delivery of public programmes raises important questions about how public sector performance and the 'explicit outcomes of government action' are measured and evaluated, in line with the continued relevance of New Public Management in the public sector (Heinrich 2003; Behn 2003).

Implementation is an old theme in public administration. A canonical model, and one that has drawn the focus of much implementation research, assumes that policy intentions (eg the goals of an algorithm-assisted policy) are formulated at a high level, for example, in a policy document, and that these are then 'implemented' on the ground (see discussion in Hupe et al 2014). Such implementation may be more or less faithful—or 'congruent'—to the higher-level intentions (Hupe 2011). Bureaucrats between high-level policy-makers and the citizens may influence this congruence in a variety of ways (Bowen 1982).

Algorithmic systems clearly shake this classic notion of implementation with its focus on success and failure, as this assumes there is a vision of what 'the policy' looks like (Hupe et al 2014). In practice, ambiguity is often inherent in policy, leaving lower levels to define it or further specify it, in ways which can be considerably political and value-laden (Knoepfel & Weidner 1982; Matland 1995). Ministers and senior civil servants do not specify the training parameters or data sources of algorithmic systems, and so ambiguity is practically unavoidable. Where are decisions for acceptable performance of fraud detection systems made—around false positives, false negatives, performance on demographics, interpretability of decisions, or so on? Many of these cannot even be made until a pilot system has been developed, implying (in an ideal world, perhaps) a ping-ponging process between implementation and 'political' decision-making which may not resemble current programme performance measurement and management practices. This is made even more difficult by statistical properties of these systems: some notions of fairness, for example, may be statistically incompatible with each other, even though they seem simultaneously desirable (Chouldechova 2017).

This situation gives significant discretionary, or at the very least agenda-setting power, to what Bovens and Zouridis (2002) call 'system-level' bureaucrats. Here, we contrast their roles to both higher level decision-makers such as ministers, as well as their contrasting point, the 'street-level' bureaucrats of Lipsky (Lipsky 2010: 12) (who we come to below in the 'micro' section).

5.2.1 Balancing Quality Assurance and Accountability

The challenges of algorithmic systems within government still retain a frame of quality, rather than considering the subjectivity of the deployed systems. In the UK, the failure of a computational model resulted in the mis-awarding of a rail franchise (Comptroller and Auditor General 2012), and led to a new guidance handbook, the *Aqua Book* (HM Treasury 2015) which sets out standards for analytical modelling in terms of assuring 'quality analysis'. Other erratic algorithmic systems which have triggered policy failure can be viewed through this frame. The Australian *Centrelink* welfare system made headlines and was subject to several parliamentary investigations when it sent thousands of individuals incorrect debt notices (Karp & Knaus 2018), leaving its own automated system far from compliant with the law (Carney 2018).

The guidance prescribed by the *Aqua Book* describes institutional quality assurance processes which increase in rigour and burden as models increase both in complexity and in business risk (Figure 6.1). These range from, at a basic level, ensuring version control, testing, and the following of guidelines, to periodic internal and external peer review or audit. Peer review for models is also emphasized within other documents, such the UK Government Data Ethics Framework, which states that '[p]eer review is an essential part of quality assurance. Get feedback from your own team or organisation's data science function. If you're working alone, you may need to look elsewhere to receive appropriate scrutiny.'

Yet a focus on peer review however risks omitting what the recent critical algorithmic literature has been so vocal about—that even when a model seems to 'work', it may not 'work' for everyone. The Dutch civil service *does* have a similar set of guidelines which do recognize this issue, albeit not as explicitly as might be possible. In the late 1990s, a senior statistician in the Netherlands National Institute for Public Health and the Environment (Rijksinstituut voor Volksgezondheid en Milieu, RIVM) published a national op-ed criticizing the environmental assessment branch for relying too heavily on models rather than measurements, cautioning that this was a dangerous 'imaginary world' (Petersen 2012: 1–2). For what might be considered quite an arcane issue of policy analysis, this led to a great media outcry in the Netherlands, with headlines including 'Environmental

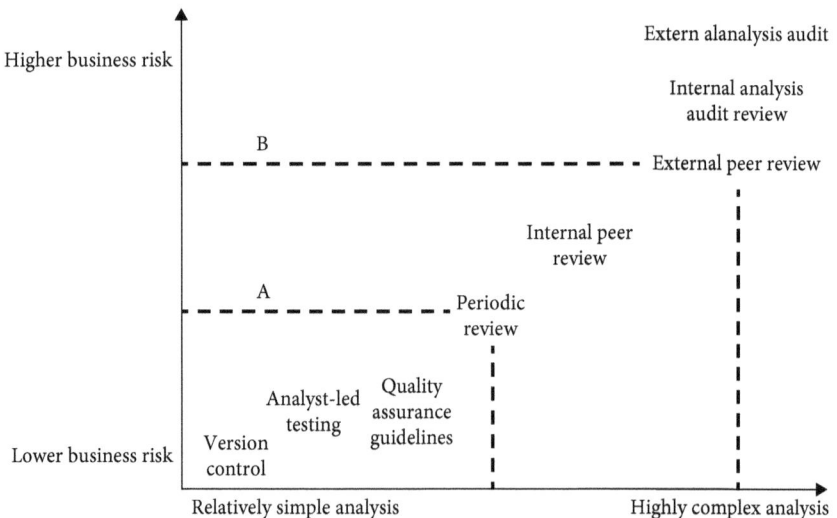

Figure 6.1 Institutional quality assurance processes. Adapted from HM Treasury (2015).

institute lies and deceits', 'Kafka and the environmental numbers', 'Credibility crisis surrounding environmental numbers' and 'Society has a right to fair information, RIVM does not provide it' (Van der Sluijs 2002). The issue was debated on the floor of the Parliament within a matter of days. As a result of this, guidance on the assessment and communication of uncertainty during modelling was drawn up (Petersen et al 2013), designed for use by civil servants and modellers. It breaks down uncertainty by quality and location, explicitly including uncertainty that is rooted in values or value-laden outcomes, with complementary tools made available within the civil service for the undertaking of this analysis.

The approach taken in the Netherlands (which in practice is still used primarily for models of natural phenomena rather than models based on personal data, such as for social policy) is connected to ideas in 'post-normal science' regarding 'extended peer review', where the 'peer community is … extended beyond the direct producers, sponsors and users of the research, to include all with a stake in the product, the process, and its implications both local and global. This extension of the peer community may include investigative journalists, lawyers and pressure groups' (Funtowicz & Ravetz 1993). Where the value-laden stakes are high, and affected communities are found widely, then narrow peer review may not be suited for ensuring the legitimacy of public sector models (Van der Sluijs 2002).

This notion of extended peer review is yet to gain traction in algorithmic practices within government, but seems more promising for the types of issues identified in the critical algorithm studies literature than the highly technical assumptions made by the *Aqua Book*. There are, however, movements in policy initiatives and proposals towards infrastructure which would enable such extended peer review. The UK Government Data Ethics Framework (Department for Digital, Culture, Media and Sport 2018b) states that

> Developed data science tools should be made available for scrutiny wherever possible … Even if the model cannot be released publicly, you may be able to release metadata about the model on a continual basis, like its performance on certain datasets. If your data science application is very sensitive, you could arrange for selected external bodies, approved by your organisation, to examine the model itself in a controlled context to provide feedback. This could be expertise from another government department, academia or public body.

The UK House of Commons Science and Technology Committee, in its report on algorithms in decision-making, has stated similar intentions to open up algorithmic systems to third party actors, writing that 'the Government should produce, publish, and maintain a list of where algorithms with significant impacts are being used within Central Government' and make them available for analysis, or if there are intellectual property issues, in a 'suitably de-sensitised format' (House of Commons Science and Technology Committee 2018). While un-credited in the

Lords' report, a similar recommendation was present in the UK government's review of quality assurance of analytic models in 2013 (HM Treasury 2013). This led to a published list of the models used in government, although the list primarily focuses on models of phenomena and policies rather than system that, for example, assess risk at the level of individuals or entities.[9] Third sector proposals for public sector organizations have similar aims. These include the Code of Standards for Public Sector Algorithmic Decision-Making proposed by Copeland (2018) ('Public sector organisations should publish details describing the data on which an algorithm was (or is continuously) trained, and the assumptions used in its creation, together with a risk assessment for mitigating potential biases') and the proposals around public sector machine learning from the AI Now Institute at NYU (Reisman et al 2018), which states that there should be a 'comprehensive plan for giving external researchers and auditors meaningful, ongoing access to examine specific systems, to gain a fuller account of their workings, and to engage the public and affected communities in the process'. There have also been attempts by universities to establish a list of of 'newsworthy' algorithmic systems in a US context, which bears similarities to the UK government's internal inventory effort described above.[10]

These proposals are promising, however they typically focus narrowly on the models rather than the broader process. Extended peer review mechanisms that are limited to the software alone may be insufficient. While public sector organizations might be able to provide general information about the data used or model built in a transparent manner, either to the public or to third parties (Edwards & Veale 2018), it is unlikely that they will be able to transparently evidence the broader process, of which machine learning is only a part, through which policy options or prediction mechanisms were supported. Proposals for 'algorithmic transparency' often go beyond explaining individual actions of a model to call for information about intentions of the individuals and teams involved, and the environment a system was trained and tested in (Edwards & Veale 2017; Selbst & Barocas 2018). This seems sensible in a technical sense, as it is hard to detect issues such as bias and discrimination in models for both statistical as well as practical reasons (Veale & Binns 2017).

5.2.2 Monitoring Algorithmic Systems Performance

One mode of achieving transparency that has been proposed is through the publication of broad and relevant algorithmic metadata. The idea of metadata for data with a social focus, considering issues such as bias and sampling, has already been

---

[9] See Annex D of HM Treasury (2013) at <https://assets.publishing.service.gov.uk/government/uploads/system/uploads/attachment_data/file/206948/review_of_govt_models_annex_d_table_of_returns.pdf> accessed 1 June 2019.

[10] See eg <http://algorithmtips.org/> and <https://www.muckrock.com/project/uncovering-algorithms-84/> accessed 1 June 2019.

proposed in the form of 'datasheets' (Gebru et al 2018), which cover procedural elements as well as substantive features of the data sets themselves. As proposed, these would include answers to questions such as why the data set was created; who funded it; what preprocessing or cleaning was undertaken (eg, discretization or bucketing, tokenization, part-of-speech tagging, SIFT feature extraction, removal of instances); aspects concerning its collection (eg presence of consent and ability to revoke); and information on updating and maintenance.

Translating these sheets to models is more of a challenge. How exactly models should be tested is still a matter of debate, and is likely to be highly context specific. In some cases, it may be worth considering how well they perform compared to human judgement (both in terms of the quantity and quality of the errors made). In other situations, it might be more important to see how they perform on different subsets of the population, and the segments concerned will in turn vary strongly. Given that models can fail in unexpected ways (such as being 'fooled', as the domain of adversarial machine learning shows; see Nguyen et al (2014)), it is unlikely that all potential aspects of salience and interest could be pre-empted in any set of metadata. Furthermore, as the growth of algorithmic systems in the public sector continues, it may be the interaction effects of these systems in tandem with each other, rather than metadata in isolation, which becomes important in practice. Incorporating all the relevant features of the model is enough of a challenge; considering the myriad ways it will be trained, used, and deployed in enough detail to judge for the purposes of responsibility or accountability appears more daunting still.

Interestingly, if transparency *were* meaningfully introduced into the broader processes surrounding algorithmic conception and implementation, this would shine considerably more light on policy development than implementation processes generally get. As more policy development involves algorithmic systems, this could even change the way that decisions in government are scrutinized more broadly. Freedom of Information law, at least in the UK, contains a notable exemption for the 'formulation or development of government policy', which is often engaged to provide a 'safe space' for decisions and trade-offs, and transparency rights extending to process are likely to push against this safe space.[11] Time will tell whether transparency provisions related to algorithmic systems substantially change the way governments deal with internal decision-making; we use this space to present the considerable possibility that they might.

Finally, whether this additional transparency would result in more public trust around these systems is questionable. Some research has shown that the effect of

---

[11] This should be caveated by noting that the Information Commissioner states that this exemption does not apply to implementation, and it will 'therefore be important to identify where policy formulation or development ends and implementation begins' (Information Commissioner's Office 2016: para 34). However, as we have seen, algorithmic systems make this difficult in practice.

transparency on public legitimacy is moderated by policy area. In particular, decisions involving 'taboo trade-offs' (Fiske & Tetlock 1997; Tetlock et al 2000), where, for example, human well-being is traded off against economic considerations, may be made to appear less legitimate when transparency is applied, at least in part due to greater salience placed on these trade-offs by doing so (de Fine Licht 2014). Examples of these might be in areas such as algorithmic detection of child abuse (see eg Chouldechova et al 2018), where the social perception of the cost of false negatives is so high that it is likely to make discussion of appropriate levels of invasiveness, accuracy, cost difficult. Such transparency might seem positive, but in effect, might end up bringing unintended consequences at this meso level of algorithmic system design and monitoring. This is compounded by the quantitative nature of the deployed systems. While it might be possible to stomach that an office of humans could fail to spot a specific case of child abuse without knowing the crystallized details of the office's success rate, it seems somehow less palatable that a bureaucracy has decided to deploy a system with a 15 per cent rate of false negatives; that is to say, there is an *expectation* that 15 per cent of cases which turn out to merit investigation or intervention will not be noticed.

5.3 Micro: Frontline Service Delivery

After these systems are designed, with the specific practices at the meso level and the support from the macro level, they are deployed day-to-day at the micro level. The purposes these systems can be put to are varied. Current public sector machine learning applications include tax fraud detection; a range of uses in policing from detecting geographic areas, potential victims, or required staffing levels; the risk scoring of prisoners to deliver appropriate rehabilitative courses; and the use of pre-emptive tools for child protection (Veale et al 2018). The use of a similar flavour of technologies, sometimes using rudimentary forms of machine learning (such as regression methods) for decision-making in government is far from new (Griffiths 2017). Much service delivery now works around more advanced 'risk-based frameworks' (Yeung 2017b), where 'the development of decision-making frameworks and procedures to prioritise regulatory activities and the deployment of resources, principally inspection and enforcement activities, [are] organised around an assessment of the risks that regulated firms pose to the regulator's objectives' (Black 2005: 514). Regulators have long been overburdened: those managing inspections, for example, have rarely had the resources to meaningfully audit more than a fraction of the organizations governed. A risk-based approach historically promised more effective uses of limited resources, while also serving to manage the operational risk of the organization: that it will not meet its own goals.

5.3.1 Automated Processing and the Rights of the Data Subject

At this level—the level where individual decisions are made concerning citizens and entities—legal regimes and scholars have been concerned about the threats of such automation to procedural justice in both its substance (Crawford & Schultz 2014; Keats Citron & Pasquale 2014) and the perception of it by citizens (Binns et al 2018). There are emerging legal norms and regimes which attempt to manage this by envisaging significant gatekeeping and oversight roles for frontline decision-makers. As we will describe, these appear in some ways to be in tension with the logics of New Public Management. We argue that this tension highlights dimensions and lessons of importance that have been considered in emerging public sector practices that some scholars have called 'New Public Service' (RB Denhardt & Denhardt 2000).

The emerging legal regimes we are discussing largely only trigger when decisions impact directly on individuals.[12] Intrinsic concerns around automation of decisions have been of particular concern in European law for decades, as some have argued that in contrast to the United States, Europe has treated automated decisions of many flavours as an inherent threat to human dignity (Jones 2017). Administrative law, particularly in France, included provisions as early as 1978 forbidding automated decisions by default in the public sector, and giving individuals information rights when automated treatments were lawfully applied (Bygrave 2001). These were 'uploaded' to European level through Article 15 of the Data Protection Directive 1995 and Article 22 of the GDPR 2016, both similar provisions which forbid significant, automated decisions without a specific lawful basis (Edwards & Veale 2017). The decisions explicitly envisaged by these provisions include 'automatic refusal of an online credit application or e-recruiting practices without any human intervention'; however, outside the law enforcement domain, and without explicit member state derogations in national law, this provision applies across the public sector, as well as to contractors that in practice are often engaged to manage systems such as welfare assessment and provision.

Similar to the provisions that preceded it in the 1995 Data Protection Directive, all such decisions require a legal basis before they are taken, one of explicit consent of the decision subject; necessity for the performance of a contract with the subject; or authorization by national law. For the public sector, the latter will apply. In the UK, section 14 of the Data Protection Act 2018 mandates that the public body must 'as soon as reasonably practicable, notify the data subject in writing that a decision has been taken based solely on automated processing', and that 'the data subject may, before the end of the period of 1 month beginning with receipt of the

---

[12] An ongoing debate exists around the extent to which such provisions do or should take into account the impact upon *groups*, rather than just individuals (Edwards & Veale 2017).

notification, request the controller to— (i) reconsider the decision, or (ii) take a new decision that is not based solely on automated processing'.

For our purposes, it is important to note that whether these provisions apply depends on whether a decision is considered to be 'solely' based on automated processing. The group of data protection regulators that interpret the law across Europe, the Article 29 Working Party (now superseded by a new European body, the European Data Protection Board, which has vouched for this former guidance), state that for a decision to be considered 'not based solely on automated processing' as section 14(4)(b)(ii) requires, the individual using a system as decision-support must (Veale & Edwards 2018):

(i) have authority and competence to challenge the decision, and
(ii) routinely express disagreement with any decision-support tool they might be using, rather than just apply a generated profile.

Without these characteristics, such a decision will collapse into being considered solely automated, and require notification to the individual, an ability to challenge a decision (though a simple written request, rather than through an expensive and largely inaccessible route of judicial review), and meaningful information to be provided surrounding the logic of processing (Edwards & Veale 2017). In some cases, these may be seen as proportionate safeguards that should always be provided. Yet to provide these safeguards in all cases where decision-support systems are used seems extensive, and public sectors may also consider it a burden they do not wish to engage with. If government *is* to become more 'data-driven', it will inevitably want to avoid a situation where the use of any routine decision-support system triggers Article 22 of the GDPR.

5.3.2 Algorithmic Decisions, Legitimacy, and Frontline Discretion

To avoid the triggering of this provision however presents an organizational challenge which pushes against some of the logics behind New Public Management. New Public Management emphasizes the need for standardized procedures that can be easily evaluated across inputs, processes, outputs, outcomes, and impacts, informed predominantly by market values of efficiency and tailored allocation of resources (Heinrich 2003). The Article 29 Working Party guidance, and this direction of law more generally, emphasizes what scholars have called *organizational humanism*, a characteristic that would align more closely with the assumption of 'citizen engagement in the conduct of public administration' that the 'New Public Service' literature proposes. Those focused on this approach have sought to replace the traditional top-down approach to authority in administrative structures with structures more attentive to the needs and concerns of a variety of internal and external actors, in part to 'supplement or even replace the authority of role or status with the authority of knowledge or competence' (JV Denhardt & Denhardt 2007: 36–37). Without imbuing the frontline of an organization with the authority to challenge or change the systems imposed by higher levels, a great number of systems will be considered, legally, solely automated.

Yet organizational humanism presents certain accountability tensions. In particular, there is a tricky balance between the professional responsibility that this organizational structure promotes and the legitimacy of a more standardized approach.

While at the meso-level modelling process, as discussed, developers' value-laden decisions can be overseen through mechanisms such as extended peer review, at the micro-level decisions are too numerous and granular to augment accountability through third party oversight. Where this high level of autonomy is present, internal accountability mechanisms have usually emphasized professionalism—the practices and norms accepted by a domain (Romzek & Ingraham 2000). Yet in these 'decision factories' of service delivery (Bovens & Zouridis 2002), New Public Management has taken the trend away from professionalism and towards measurable standards amenable to market-based instruments of monitoring and incentivization. Even in domains where professionalism remains, such as social work, New Public Management has led to a far greater standardization of decisions through guides, codes, and the like (Ponnert & Svensson 2016). Such standardization might help at building legitimacy and accountability in other ways (such as treating similar individuals similarly), but also risks turning decision-support systems back into what would legally be considered 'solely' automated ones.

While it is early days for advanced, granular decision-support systems within frontline public entities, we should expect them to catalyse new hybrid forms of accountability within these decision factories. For example, might individual 'authority and competence', which brings with it risks of problematic or arbitrary discretion if not undertaken with expensive care and professionalism, be supplemented by low-cost group oversight, such as second opinions given by peers? How might the practices of individuals disagreeing with decisions be documented, and how will these lower-level choices interact with hierarchies that are likely to want to monitor and assess them? Some scholars have argued that decision-support systems can effectively hide discretionary activities from those seeking to monitor them (Jorna & Wagenaar 2007); even if managers feel they understand how discretionary authority is being used, limitations of monitoring systems in practice can serve to make these grey areas invisible on the ground (Buffat 2011; 2015). These issues may well create new approaches to monitoring and oversight which differ from those we see today, with their own transformative effects on frontline service delivery.

6. Concluding Remarks

The use of machine learning in the public sector appears to be growing in preva-lence. Entities at all levels of government are increasingly using automation and augmentation systems to either increase the efficiency of public sector operations or to support public decision-making for complicated or complex policy issues and programmes. While, at this stage, the discussion about the use of algorithmic sys-tems in the public sector is framed around the dichotomy between 'transformation' and 'dynamic conservatism' that Hood (2008) outlined with regard to most infor-mation and communication technologies used in and by government, algorithmic systems raise new concerns that are not captured in the e-government literature or, indeed, in the practice of New Public Management that governments still adhere to. Many of these concerns are highly political and value-laden, and thus deserve particular attention as these technologies expand the range of roles and domains they touch upon.

In this chapter, we reviewed and analysed the latest developments and chal-lenges that governments who promote and deploy machine learning in the public sector are facing. Looking at the macro level of government strategy and guide-lines, at the meso level of public programme design, monitoring, and evaluation, and at the micro level of implementation in frontline service delivery, we argue that the deployment of machine learning in the public sector challenges established in-stitutions and administrative practices. Above, we outline three main challenges:

(a) *Macro level*: The creation of new cross-cutting individual rights and obliga-tions that require new skills and administrative capacities in order to fully assess the intended and unintended consequences of machine learning on established public values of accuracy, fairness, transparency, and equity;

(b) *Meso level*: The development of more dynamic ways to measure, monitor, and evaluate the inputs, process information, outputs, outcomes, and im-pacts of public programmes using machine learning, which challenge estab-lished measures of public sector performance, quality, and risk assessment;

(c) *Micro level*: The emergence of new tensions between the legitimacy of algo-rithmic decisions used in frontline service delivery, the discretion of street-level bureaucrats when employing, assessing, or overriding automated decisions, and the rights of the data subjects when these processes are used to inform the allocation of public goods and services, and the discretion that street-level bureaucrats.

Scholars of public administration and management should place themselves at the heart of debates around the deployment and strategies of these technolo-gies at all levels. This requires a heightened connection, as we have drawn, be-tween the emerging scholarship on the socio-technical challenges of algorithmic systems and the work around digital technologies in the public sector. In this period of rapid change—not so much in technology as the coping strategies and structures of administrators at all levels—studying these emerging processes alongside the computer scientists, sociologists, technology lawyers, and anthropologists doing the same is likely to bring new questions to the fore that will be difficult for any single field to answer alone. Public management and public administration scholars can impart important contributions to this debate, but only in close collaboration and when being open to issues and challenges, particularly around discrimination and fairness, that may currently be more salient in other fields than they traditionally have been in the study of topics such as risk regulation or e-Government.

Bibliography

Andrews L, 'Public Administration, Public Leadership and the Construction of Public Value in the Age of the Algorithm and "Big Data"' (2018) 36 Public Administration 397 doi: 10.1111/padm.12534.

Atkinson K, Bench-Capon T, and Modgil S, 'Argumentation for Decision Support' Database and Expert Systems Applications Springer Berlin Heidelberg 822 (2006) doi: 10.1007/11827405_80.

Bamberger KA and Mulligan DK, *Privacy on the Ground: Driving Corporate Behavior in the United States and Europe* (MIT Press 2015).

Bannister F, 'E-Government and Administrative Power: The One-Stop-Shop Meets the Turf War' (2005) 2(2) Electronic Government doi: 10.1504/EG.2005.007092.

Barocas S, and Selbst AD, 'Big Data's Disparate Impact' (2016) 104 California Law Review 671 doi: 10.15779/Z38BG31.

Behn RD, 'Why Measure Performance? Different Purposes Require Different Measures' (2003) 63(5) Public Administration Review 586 doi: 10.1111/1540-6210.00322.

Bench-Capon T and Sergot MJ, 'Towards a Rule-Based Representation of Open Texture in Law' in C Walter (ed), *Computer Power and Legal Language* (Quorum Books 1988).

Bevan G and Hood C, 'What's Measured Is What Matters: Targets and Gaming in the English Public Health Care System' (2006) 84(3) Public Administration 517 doi: 10.1111/j.1467-9299.2006.00600.x.

Binns R, 'Fairness in Machine Learning: Lessons from Political Philosophy' Proceedings of the First Conference on Fairness, Accountability and Transparency (FAT*) (2018).

Binns R, Veale M, Van Kleek M, et al, 'Like Trainer Like Bot? Inheritance of Bias in Algorithmic Content Moderation' in GL Ciampaglia, A Mashhadi, and T Yasseri (eds), *Social Informatics: 9th International Conference, SocInfo 2017, Oxford, UK, September 13-15 2017 Proceedings Part II* (Springer International Publishing 2017) doi: 10.1007/978-3-319-67256-4_32.

Binns R, Van Kleek M, Veale M, et al, '"It's Reducing a Human Being to a Percentage"; Perceptions of Justice in Algorithmic Decisions' Proceedings of the ACM SIGCHI Conference on Human Factors in Computing Systems (CHI'18) (2018) doi: 10.1145/3173574.3173951.

Black J, 'The Emergence of Risk-Based Regulation and the New Public Risk Management in the United Kingdom' (2005) Public Law 512.

Bolukbasi T, Chang K-W, Zou JY, et al, 'Man is to Computer Programmer as Woman is to Homemaker? Debiasing Word Embeddings' in DD Lee, M Sugiyama, UV Luxburg, I Guyon, and R Garnett (eds), *Advances in Neural Information Processing Systems 29* (NIPS 2016).

Bovens M, and Zouridis S, 'From Street-Level to System-Level Bureaucracies: How Information and Communication Technology is Transforming Administrative Discretion and Constitutional Control' (2002) 62(2) Public Administration Review 174 doi: 10.1111/0033-3352.00168.

Bowen ER, 'The Pressman-Wildavsky Paradox: Four Addenda or Why Models Based on Probability Theory Can Predict Implementation Success and Suggest Useful Tactical Advice for Implementers' (1982) 2(1) Journal of Public Policy 1 doi: 10.1017/S0143814X0000176.

boyd d, 'Undoing the Neutrality of Big Data' (2016) 16 Florida Law Review Forum 226.

boyd d and Crawford K, 'Critical Questions for Big Data: Provocations for a Cultural Technological and Scholarly Phenomenon' (2012) 15(5) Information, Communication and Society 662 doi: 10.1080/1369118X.2012.678878.

Buffat A, 'Pouvoir discrétionnaire et redevabilité de la bureaucratie de guichet: Les taxateurs d'une caisse de chômage comme acteurs de mise en oeuvre' Université de Lausanne Switzerland (2011).

Buffat A, 'Street-Level Bureaucracy and E-government' (2015) 17(1) Public Management Review 149 doi: 10.1080/14719037.2013.771699.

Bundesministerium des Innern, für Bau und Heimat, 'Datenethikkommission' (German Federal Ministry of Interior, Construction and Homeland Affairs 2018) <https://www.bmi.bund.de/DE/themen/it-und-digitalpolitik/datenethikkommission/datenethikkommission-node.html> accessed 4 August 2018.

Burrell J, 'How the Machine 'Thinks': Understanding Opacity in Machine Learning Algorithms' (2016) 3(1) Big Data & Society doi: 10.1177/2053951715622512.

Burton J and van den Broek D, 'Accountable and Countable: Information Management Systems and the Bureaucratization of Social Work' (2009) 39(7) British Journal of Social Work 1326 doi: 10.1093/bjsw/bcn027.

Bygrave LA, 'Automated Profiling: Minding the Machine: Article 15 of the EC Data Protection Directive and Automated Profiling' (2001) 17(1) Computer Law & Security Review 17 doi: 10.1016/S0267-3649(01)00104-2.

Caliskan A, Bryson JJ, and Narayanan A, 'Semantics Derived Automatically from Language Corpora Contain Human-Like Biases' (2017) 356(6334) Science 183 doi: 10.1126/science.aal4230.

Carney T, 'The New Digital Future for Welfare: Debts Without Legal Proofs or Moral Authority?' UNSW Law Journal Forum Sydney Law School Research Paper No. 18/15 (2018).

Chouldechova A, 'Fair Prediction with Disparate Impact: A Study of Bias in Recidivism Prediction Instruments' (2017) 5(2) Big Data 153 doi: 10.1089/big.2016.0047.

Chouldechova A, Benavides-Prado D, Fialko O, et al, 'A Case Study of Algorithm-Assisted Decision Making in Child Maltreatment Hotline Screening Decisions' in SA Friedler and C Wilson (eds), Proceedings of the 1st Conference on Fairness, Accountability and Transparency, Proceedings of Machine Learning Research Vol 81 New York NY, USA (2018).

Christie GC, 'An Essay on Discretion' (1986) Duke Law Journal HeinOnline.

Comptroller and Auditor General, *Lessons from Cancelling the InterCity West Coast Franchise Competition* (National Audit Office 2012).

Copland E, '10 Principles for Public Sector Use of Algorithmic Decision Making' (Nesta 2018) <https://www.nesta.org.uk/blog/10-principles-for-public-sector-use-of-algorithmic-decision-making/> accessed 1 June 2019.

Courtland R, 'Bias Detectives: The Researchers Striving to Make Algorithms Fair' (2018) 558(7710) Nature 357 doi: 10.1038/d41586-018-05469-3.

Crawford K, 'The Trouble with Bias' NIPS 2017 (Keynote).

Crawford K and Schultz J, 'Big Data and Due Process: Toward a Framework to Redress Predictive Privacy Harms' (2014) 55 Boston College Law Review 93.

Cuccaro-Alamin S, Foust R, Vaithianathan R, et al, 'Risk Assessment and Decision Making in Child Protective Services: Predictive Risk Modeling in Context' (2017) 79 Children and Youth Services Review 291 doi: 10.1016/j.childyouth.2017.06.027.

Dahlström C, Lapuente V, and Teorell J, 'The Merit of Meritocratization: Politics Bureaucracy and the Institutional Deterrents of Corruption' (2011) 65(3) Political Research Quarterly 656 doi: 10.1177/1065912911408109.

Denhardt JV, 'The New Public Service Revisited' (2015) 75(5) Public Administration Review 664 doi: 10.1111/puar.12347.

Denhardt JV and Denhardt RB, The New Public Service: Serving Not Steering (M.E. Sharpe 2007).

Denhardt RB and Denhardt JV, 'The New Public Service: Serving Rather than Steering' (2000) 60(6) Public Administration Review 549 doi: 10.1111/0033-3352.00117.

Department for Digital, Culture, Media and Sport, 'Centre for Data Ethics and Innovation Consultation' (HM Government 2018a) <https://www.gov.uk/government/consultations/consultation-on-the-centre-for-data-ethics-and-innovation/centre-for-data-ethics-and-innovation-consultation> accessed 8 April 2018.

Department for Digital Culture Media and Sport, 'Data Ethics Framework' (HM Government 2018b) <https://www.gov.uk/government/publications/data-ethics-framework> accessed 22 June 2018.

Downs A, 'A Realistic Look at the Final Payoffs from Urban Data Systems' (1967) 27(3) Public Administration Review 204 doi: 10.2307/973283.

Dunleavy P and Hood C, 'From Old Public Administration to New Public Management' (1994) 14(3) Public Money & Management 9 doi: 10.1080/09540969409387823.

Dunleavy P, Margetts H, Bastow S, et al, Digital Era Governance: IT Corporations, the State and e-Government (Oxford University Press 2006) doi: 10.1093/acprof:oso/9780199296194.001.0001.

Dzindolet MT, Peterson SA, Pomranky RA, et al, 'The Role of Trust in Automation Reliance' (2003) 58(6) International Journal of Human-Computer Studies 697 doi: 10.1016/S1071-5819(03)00038-7.

Edwards L and Veale M, 'Slave to the Algorithm? Why a "Right to an Explanation" is Probably Not the Remedy You Are Looking For' (2017) 16(1) Duke Law and Technology Review 18 doi: 10.2139/ssrn.2972855.

Edwards L and Veale M, 'Enslaving the Algorithm: From a "Right to an Explanation" to a "Right to Better Decisions"?' (2018) 16(3) IEEE Security & Privacy 46 doi: 10.2139/ssrn.3052831.

Ensign D, Friedler SA, Neville S, et al, 'Runaway Feedback Loops in Predictive Policing' Proceedings of the 1st Conference on Fairness, Accountability and Transparency (FAT*) (2018).

Erickson P, Klein JL, Daston L, et al, How Reason Almost Lost Its Mind: The Strange Career of Cold War Rationality (University of Chicago Press 2013).

de Fine Licht J, 'Policy Area as a Potential Moderator of Transparency Effects: An Experiment' (2014) 74(3) Public Administration Review 361 doi: 10.1111/puar.12194.

Fiske AP and Tetlock PE, 'Taboo Trade-offs: Reactions to Transactions That Transgress the Spheres of Justice' (1997) 18(2) Political Psychology 255 doi: 10.1111/0162-895X.00058.

Funtowicz SO and Ravetz JR, 'Science for the Post-Normal Age' (1993) 25(7) Futures 739 doi: 10.1016/0016-3287(93)90022-L.

Gama J, Žliobaitė I, Bifet A, et al, 'A Survey on Concept Drift Adaptation' (2013) 1(1) ACM Computing Surveys doi: 10.1145/2523813.

Gebru T, Morgenstern J, Vecchione B, et al, 'Datasheets for Datasets' Presented at the 5th Workshop on Fairness, Accountability, and Transparency in Machine Learning (FAT/ML), Stockholm, Sweden (2018).

Grgić-Hlača N, Zafar MB, Gummadi KP, et al, 'On Fairness, Diversity and Randomness in Algorithmic Decision Making' (2017) arXiv [stat.ML] Retrieved from arXiv.

Griffiths A, 'Forecasting Failure: Assessing Risks to Quality Assurance in Higher Education Using Machine Learning' (PhD, King's College London 2017).

Heinrich CJ, 'Measuring Public Sector Performance and Effectiveness' in BG Peters and J Pierre (eds), The SAGE Handbook of Public Administration (SAGE 2003).

Hood C, 'The Tools of Government in the Information Age' in RE Goodin, M Moran, and M Rein (eds), The Oxford Handbook of Public Policy (Oxford University Press 2008).

Hood C, The Art of the State: Culture Rhetoric and Public Management (Oxford University Press 2000).

Hoppe R, The Governance of Problems: Puzzling, Powering and Participation (Policy Press 2010).

House of Commons Science and Technology Committee, Algorithms in Decision-Making (HC 351) (UK Parliament 2018).

Hildebrandt M, Smart Technologies and the End(s) of Law (Edward Elgar 2015).

Hidlebrandt M, 'Privacy as Protection of the Incomputable Self: From Agnostic to Agonistic Machine Learning' (2017) doi: 10.2139/ssrn.3081776.

Hill R, ' "Toxic" Whitehall Power Culture Fingered for GDS's Fall from Grace' The Register (2018) <https://www.theregister.co.uk/2018/07/06/government_digital_service_fall_from_grace_it_was_toxic_whitehall_power_culture_what_done_it/> accessed 13 August 2018.

HM Treasury, Review of Quality Assurance of Government Models (HM Government 2013).

HM Treasury, The Aqua Book: Guidance on Producing Quality Analysis for Government (HM Government 2015).

Hood C, 'A Public Management for All Seasons?' (03/1991) 69(1) Public Administration 3 doi: 10/bdwbfj.

Hood C and Peters G, 'The Middle Aging of New Public Management: Into the Age of Paradox?' (2004) 14(3) Journal of Public Administration Research and Theory 267 doi: 10.1093/jopart/muh019.

Hupe PL, 'The Thesis of Incongruent Implementation: Revisiting Pressman and Wildavsky' (2011) 26(1) Public Policy and Administration 63 doi: 10/dp9xr9.

Hupe PL, Hill M, and Nangia M, 'Studying Implementation Beyond Deficit Analysis: The Top-Down View Reconsidered' (2014) 29(2) Public Policy and Administration 145 doi: 10.1177/0952076713517520.

Information Commissioner's Office, Government Policy (Section 35): Freedom of Information Act (ICO 2016).

Information Commissioner's Office, Technology Strategy 2018–2021 (ICO 2018).

Jones ML, 'The Right to a Human in the Loop: Political Constructions of Computer Automation and Personhood' (2017) 47(2) Social Studies of Science 216 doi: 10.1177/0306312717699716.

Jorna F and Wagenaar P, 'The 'Iron Cage' Strengthened? Discretion and Digital Discipline' (2007) 85(1) Public Administration 189 doi: 10.1111/j.1467-9299.2007.00640.x.

Kamarinou D, Millard C, and Singh J, 'Machine Learning with Personal Data' (2016) Queen Mary School of Law Legal Studies Research Paper No 247/2016. <https://papers.ssrn.com/sol3/papers.cfm?abstract_id=2865811>.

Kamiran F, Calders T, and Pechenizkiy M, 'Techniques for Discrimination-Free Predictive Models' in B Custers, T Calders, B Schermer, and T Zarsky (eds), *Discrimination and Privacy in the Information Society* (Springer 2012).

Karp P and Knaus C, 'Centrelink Robo-Debt Program Accused of Enforcing "Illegal" Debts' *The Guardian* (4 April 2018).

Kearney RC and Sinha C, 'Professionalism and Bureaucratic Responsiveness: Conflict or Compatibility?' (1988) Public Administration Review 571 JSTOR.

Keats Citron D and Pasquale F, 'The Scored Society: Due Process for Automated Predictions' (2014) 89(1) Washington Law Review 1.

Kilbertus N, Gascon A, Kusner M, et al, 'Blind Justice: Fairness with Encrypted Sensitive Attributes' Proceedings of the 35th International Conference on Machine Learning, ICML 2018, International Machine Learning Society (IMLS) (2018).

Knoepfel P and Weidner H, 'Formulation and Implementation of Air Quality Control Programmes: Patterns of Interest Consideration' (1982) 10(1) Policy & Politics 85 doi: 10.1332/030557382782628914.

Kohl U, 'Google: The Rise and Rise of Online Intermediaries in the Governance of the Internet and Beyond (Part 2)' (2013) 21(2) International Journal of Law and Information Technology 187 doi: 10.1093/ijlit/eat004.

Kroll JA, Huey J, Barocas S, et al, 'Accountable Algorithms' (2016) University of Pennsylvania Law Review 165.

Lipsky M, *Street-Level Bureaucracy: Dilemmas of the Individual in Public Services* (Russell Sage Foundation 2010).

Lapsley I, 'New Public Management: The Cruellest Invention of the Human Spirit? 1' (2009) 45(1) Abacus 1 Wiley Online Library doi: 10.1111/j.1467-6281.2009.00275.x.

Lember V, Kattel R, and Tõnurist P, 'Technological Capacity in the Public Sector: The Case of Estonia' IIPP Working Paper Series 2017-03.

Lodge M and Wegrich K, *The Problem-Solving Capacity of the Modern State: Governance Challenges and Administrative Capacities* (Oxford University Press 2014).

Manzoni J, 'Big Data in Government: the Challenges and Opportunities' (*GOV.UK* 2017) <https://perma.cc/GF7B-5A2R> accessed 4 October 2018.

Margetts H, *Information Technology in Government: Britain and America* (Routledge(1999).

Martinho-Truswell E, 'How AI Could Help the Public Sector' (2018) (Jan) Harvard Business Review <https://hbr.org/2018/01/how-ai-could-help-the-public-sector> accessed 1 June 2019.

Matland RE, 'Synthesizing the Implementation Literature: The Ambiguity-Conflict Model of Policy Implementation' (1995) 5(2) Journal of Public Administration Research and Theory 145 doi: 10.1093/oxfordjournals.jpart.a037242.

Milner C and Berg B, *Tax Analytics: Artificial Intelligence and Machine Learning* (PwC Advanced Tax Analytics & Innovation 2017).

Mitchell TM, *Machine Learning* (McGraw Hill 1997).

Nguyen A, Yosinski J, and Clune J, 'Deep Neural Networks are Easily Fooled: High Confidence Predictions for Unrecognizable Images' (2014) arXiv:1412.1897 [cs].

Northrop A, Kraemer KL, Dunkle D, and King JL, 'Payoffs from Computerization: Lessons over Time' (1990) 50(5) Public Administration Review 505 doi: 10.2307/976781.

Oswald M, 'Algorithm-Assisted Decision-Making in the Public Sector: Framing the Issues Using Administrative Law Rules Governing Discretionary Power' (2018) 376(2128) Philosophical Transactions of the Royal Society of London. Series A: Mathematical and Physical Sciences 20170359 doi: 10.1098/rsta.2017.0359.

Petersen AC, *Simulating Nature: A Philosophical Study of Computer-Simulation Uncertainties and their Role in Climate Science and Policy Advice* (CRC Press 2012).

Petersen AC, Janssen PHM, van der Sluijs JP, et al, *Guidance for Uncertainty Assessment and Communication* (PBL Netherlands Environmental Assessment Bureau 2013).

Ponnert L and Svensson K, 'Standardisation—The End of Professional Discretion?' (2016) 19(3–4) European Journal of Social Work 586 doi: 10.1080/13691457.2015.1074551.

Prakken H, *Logical Tools for Modelling Legal Argument* (Kluwer 1997).

Reisman D, Schultz J, Crawford K, et al. *Algorithmic Impact Assessments: A Practical Framework for Public Agency Accountability* (AI NOW Institute 2018).

Romzek BS and Ingraham PW, 'Cross Pressures of Accountability: Initiative, Command, and Failure in the Ron Brown Plane Crash' (2000) 60(3) Public Administration Review 240 doi: 10.1111/0033-3352.00084.

Seaver N, 'Knowing Algorithms' Paper presented at Media in Transition 8, Cambridge, MA (2013).

Seaver N, 'Algorithms as Culture: Some Tactics for the Ethnography of Algorithmic Systems' (2017) 4(2) Big Data & Society doi: 10.1177/2053951717738104.

Selbst A and Barocas S, 'The Intuitive Appeal of Explainable Machines'(2018) draft available on SSRN.

Skitka LJ, Mosier KL, and Burdick M, 'Does Automation Bias Decision-Making?' (1999) 51 International Journal of Human-Computer Studies 991 doi: 10.1006/ijhc.1999.0252.

van der Sluijs JP, 'A Way Out of the Credibility Crisis of Models Used in Integrated Environmental Assessment' (2002) 34(2) Futures 133 doi: 10.1016/S0016-3287(01)00051-9.

Smith ML, Noorman ME, and Martin AK, 'Automating the Public Sector and Organizing Accountabilities' (2010) 26(1) Communications of the Association for Information Systems 1.

Snellen I, 'Electronic Governance: Implications for Citizens, Politicians and Public Servants' (2002) 68(2) International Review of Administrative Sciences 183 doi: 10.1177/0020852302682002.

Statistics New Zealand, 'Integrated Data Infrastructure' (Government of New Zealand 2016) <https:// perma.cc/9RXL-SV7P> accessed 4 October 2018.

Stivers C, 'The Listening Bureaucrat: Responsiveness in Public Administration' (1994) 54 Public Administration Review 364.

Sunstein CR, *Risk and Reason: Safety, Law, and the Environment* (Cambridge University Press 2002).

Tetlock PE, Kristel OV, Elson SB, et al, 'The Psychology of the Unthinkable: Taboo Trade-Offs Forbidden Base Rates and Heretical Counterfactuals' (2000) 78(5) Journal of Personality and Social Psychology 853.

The Royal Society and the British Academy, *Data Management and Use: Governance in the 21st Century* (The Royal Society and the British Academy 2017).

Veale M and Binns R, 'Fairer Machine Learning in the Real World: Mitigating Discrimination without Collecting Sensitive Data' (2017) 4/2 Big Data & Society doi: 10.1177/2053951717743530.

Veale M and Edwards L, 'Clarity, Surprises, and Further Questions in the Article 29 Working Party Draft Guidance on Automated Decision-Making and Profiling' (2018) 34(2) Computer Law & Security Review 398 doi: 10.1016/j.clsr.2017.12.002.

Veale M, Van Kleek M, and Binns R, 'Fairness and Accountability Design Needs for Algorithmic Support in High-Stakes Public Sector Decision-Making' Proceedings of the ACM SIGCHI Conference on Human Factors in Computing Systems (CHI'18) (2018) doi: 10.1145/3173574.3174014.

Willcocks LP and Lacity M, *Service Automation Robots and the Future of Work* (SB Publishing 2016).

Woollard M, 'Administrative Data: Problems and Benefits. A Perspective from the United Kingdom' in A Duşa, D Nelle, G Stock, and GG Wagner (eds), *Facing the Future: European Research Infrastructures for the Humanities and Social Sciences* (SCIVERO Verlag 2014).

Yeung K, '"Hypernudge": Big Data as a Mode of Regulation by Design' (2017a) 20(1) Information, Communication and Society 118 doi: 10.1080/1369118X.2016.1186713.

Yeung K, 'Algorithmic Regulation: A Critical Interrogation' (2017b) 347 Regulation & Governance 509 doi: 10.1111/rego.12158.

Zeleznikow J, 'The Split-Up Project: Induction, Context and Knowledge Discovery in Law' (2004) 3(2) Law, Probability and Risk 147 doi: 10.1093/lpr/3.2.147.

Žliobaitė I, Pechenizkiy M, and Gama J, 'An Overview of Concept Drift Applications' in N Japkowicz and J Stefanowski. (eds), *Big Data Analysis: New Algorithms for a New Society* Studies in Big Data (Springer International Publishing 2016) doi: 10.1007/978-3-319-26989-4_4.

7

The Practical Challenges of Implementing Algorithmic Regulation for Public Services

*Alex Griffiths**

1. Introduction

Big data, and the algorithms that make sense of it, potentially offer huge bene-fits for the regulation of public services. Ever-growing volumes of data de-tailing their performance, including their financial health, who uses the services when, and for what reason, provide the opportunity for advanced analytics to better target regulatory interventions. In theory, algorithmic monitoring of the wealth of data available can not only better identify poorly performing serv-ices and automatically trigger interventions, but also rapidly identify and ar-rest changes in the quality of service provision before they become too severe. Successfully realizing the potential of 'algorithmic regulation' is, however, far from straightforward.

Although the phrase 'algorithmic regulation' only came into existence in 2013, the goal of using data to deliver effective and efficient regulation is not a new one (Yeung 2016). Since the start of this millennium, with the rise of 'risk-based' ap-proaches, regulators have assiduously proclaimed their intention to 'make better use of data' to decide where they should focus their efforts (Ofsted 2017; CQC 2016). There is good reason to be optimistic given the wealth of data available concerning public service provision. To take the case of an individual injured in a traffic accident and treated by the English National Health Service (NHS), we know: how long the ambulance takes to reach them, which hospital it takes them to, how quickly they were treated at the hospital, by whom, how much this cost, how long the care lasted, what other health conditions the patient had, any medication they were prescribed, and there is a good chance we will know whether they would recommend the hospital to their friends and family seeking similar treatment.

* The author gratefully acknowledges the financial support provided by the Economic and Social Research Council (Grant Ref: ES/N018869/1) under the Open Research Area Scheme (Project Title: QUAD—Quantification, Administrative Capacity and Democracy). QUAD is an inter-national project co-funded by the Agence Nationale de la Recherche (ANR, France), Deutsche Forschungsgemeinschaft (DFG, Germany), Economic and Social Research Council (ESRC, UK), and the Nederlands Organisatie voor Wetenschappelijk Onderzoek (NWO, Netherlands).

Furthermore, we know the number, qualifications, and absence rate of staff, how satisfied both those staff and patients are at the hospital, its financial health, its performance against a range of key government targets including waiting times and readmission and mortality rates, and how inspectors judged the hospital to be performing on their last visit. With all this data available, why shouldn't regulators be able to quickly identify quality concerns and act accordingly?

This chapter begins by identifying and exploring three different ways public service regulators can use data to target their interventions. Simple, rules-based methods place regulatees into prioritization groups based on a small number of often contextual metrics selected a priori. Data-informed approaches present and aggregate numerous, wide-ranging metrics selected a priori to inform prioritization decisions by one or more experts. Algorithmic approaches use machine learning techniques to determine the most accurate prioritization model from the available data.

The specifics of data-informed and algorithmic approaches are then explored further in two case studies. To begin with we examine the Care Quality Commission (CQC), the independent quality regulator for 30,000 diverse health and social care providers throughout England, and its data-informed 'Intelligent Monitoring' approach to prioritizing hospital inspections. CQC's 'Intelligent Monitoring' provides an excellent case study for two reasons. First, as a nationalized, centralized, and target-driven system, the NHS is arguably the most data-rich healthcare system in the world; if algorithmic regulation cannot work in the NHS, it is likely it will struggle elsewhere. Second, not only has CQC published the outcomes of inspections—as most regulators do—it has also, unusually, published its pre-inspection risk ratings of hospitals allowing us to evaluate the relationship between Intelligent Monitoring's risk ratings and the subsequent inspection outcomes.

Following the examination of CQC's data-informed approach, we assess attempts to develop an algorithmic approach for the Quality Assurance Agency for Higher Education (QAA)—the body responsible for assuring the quality of UK higher education. QAA were selected as the second case study as, in addition to having a wealth of data and a long, steady history of comparable review (inspection) outcomes, they allowed the author privileged access to their data to examine the possibility of developing an algorithmic model.

The two case studies show the data-informed and algorithmic approaches were unsuccessful. The chapter subsequently discusses the reasons for the failure identified in the case studies and concludes that there are significant practical challenges to implementing a successful, algorithmic approach to the regulation of quality in the public sector. Most notably, data are not sufficiently accurate, timely, or granular, and, due to the nature of public services, there are too few regulatory outcomes with which to develop an effective model. What's more, even where the obstacles with the data can be overcome, an algorithmic approach will only be successful if the outcome the model is trying to predict is unambiguous and consistently judged.

2. The Role of Data in Regulation

Regulators often have more to do than their resources permit (Black 2005). Accordingly, regulators need to prioritize their limited resource. The Office for Standards in Education (Ofsted), for example is responsible for inspecting almost 22,000 schools, over 80,000 childcare providers, and almost 3,000 providers of children's social care in England (2016–17). This need to prioritize regulatory resource is nothing new; however, the way it is done, using a 'risk-based' approach, is (Pontell 1978). Risk-based regulation replaces the implicit prioritization of resource previously conducted behind closed doors with the explicit, *ex ante* determination of risk through assessment frameworks (Black 2005).

Risk-based regulation is an approach practised by regulators in which their resources are allocated in proportion to the risks posed to the standards they are charged with upholding (Rothstein et al 2006). Risk-based regulation ostensibly provides practitioners with a means with which to 'maximise the benefits of regulation while minimising the burdens on regulatees by offering "targeted" and "proportionate" interventions' (Rothstein, Huber, & Gaskell 2006). In the public sector, this can be understood to mean the ability to lighten or eliminate inspections for low-risk providers—that is those providers that regulators believe to be performing well—leaving them free to prosper, whilst using the resource saved to conduct reviews of high-risk providers—that is those providers that regulators believe to be performing poorly—and quickly eliminate or prevent any poor practice, all at the same or reduced cost to the taxpayer.

Risk-based approaches would not have become so popular had they not satisfied, or at least been perceived to have satisfied, the key regulatory requirements of their time. First and foremost, risk-based approaches promised a more efficient use of resource. To use the UK's Quality Assurance Agency (QAA) as an example, until the recent introduction of their *Higher Education Review* approach in 2013 all universities were reviewed (inspected) every six years regardless of their prior review outcomes or current performance data. Investing resource in reviewing a university that always demonstrated the highest standards and current data suggests is continuing to do so whilst waiting six years to re-review a poorly performing university that is showing no obvious signs of improvement is arguably a poor use of resource. By prioritizing these universities according to the risk posed to the QAA's objectives, the high-performing universities will be rewarded for their efforts by a reduced burden from review whilst the poorly performing universities will receive the attention they warrant, and the support they need, to improve, all with the same amount of overall resource as before.

Second, regulators cannot and do not prevent all harms. This can be easily exemplified: major healthcare failings at Bristol Royal Infirmary and Mid-Staffordshire hospital saw the unnecessary deaths of hundreds of patients (2009); confidence in food safety has been harmed by the BSE, Foot and Mouth disease, and e-coli crises; and train crashes at Potters Bar, Ladbroke Grove, and Hatfield killed 42 and injured 634 people in a 30-month period (Cullen 2002; *Rail Safety & Standards Board* 2005; ORR 2006). The seemingly continuous stream of failures and a decline in confidence over what regulation can achieve at the same time as the adoption of New Public Management practices has seen increased oversight and accountability for regulators (Löfstedt 2008). Conceiving of harms, both to those they are charged with protecting and to themselves, in terms of risks to be managed allows regulators to demonstrate a rational defence for their actions (Rothstein et al 2006). The ostensibly objective risk assessments underpinning the risk-based approaches promised regulators a defensible rationale for their prioritization activity (Sunstein 2002). Where low-level 'probabilistic' risks have a high public salience, or where the regulator failed to prevent an incident of which the available data contained no forewarning, a demonstrable defence for inaction in the form of a risk assessment is highly desirable and has the further benefit of providing transparency in an era of heightened public accountability (Lodge & Wegrich 2012; Demeritt et al 2015).

Third, the adoption of *en vogue* methodologies provides regulators with legitimacy and aids bureaucratic survival (Meyer & Rowan 1977). Risk-based approaches promised regulators not only the ability to rationalize, manage, and control the notoriously complex challenges of regulation, but the ability to do so whilst appearing forward-thinking in a period of political enamourment with private-sector practices (Hunter 2005; Baldwin et al 2012).

The appeal of risk-based approaches is clear: practitioners make rational and efficient use of their resource, they do so in a readily defensible manner, appear favourable to government, and allow compliant actors to prosper whilst affording non-compliant actors the attention they require. As always, however, the devil is in the detail of the regulator's risk assessment tools and the technical, legal, and political implementation of their approach. Most importantly, a risk-based approach cannot be successfully operated if a regulator cannot successfully identify risk. So how are risks identified, and what role do algorithms play?

3. Determining Risk

Modern regulatory strategy documents frequently extol the virtues of risk-based approaches and claim that the better use of data will lead to improved performance, however, they rarely detail *how* their data will be used as part of a risk-based (CQC 2015; Australian Skills Quality Authority Bar 2016; Ofsted 2015; SRA 2014; TEQSA 2012/5). Despite regulators' limited disclosure of the specifics of their risk-based approaches, they can generally be placed into one of three broad categories devised by the author: rules-based, data informed, and algorithmic approaches. These three broad categories are explored below.

3.1 Rules-Based Approaches

Far simpler than modern, data-science and big-data driven approaches, simple rules-based approaches are typically utilized by regulators developing their first risk-assessment methodology. Regulatees can be assigned one of a small number of risk categories by means of a simple, and often contextual, rules-based assessment. This is exemplified by the Maritime and Coastguard Agency's simple, rules-based approach based on ship type, age, and inspection history (NAO 2009). Similarly, inspectors from the Food Standards Agency score businesses on the hazards present and how willing and able they are to manage them, and then use that score to calculate the suitable length of time until the next inspection (FSA 2016).

Such contextual, rules-based approaches have clear advantages. The simplicity of the approach means little data collection, processing, or analysis is required saving on staffing and infrastructure costs. The use of contextual data over performance data also makes such systems hard to game: one cannot readily change a fishing trawler into a canal boat, or amend the result of a past inspection, to avoid additional oversight.

The simplicity of such approaches does create a number of issues however. First, they are not very discerning and, arguably, unfairly discriminatory. For example, being a small, countryside school may put you in a category of school more likely to be non-compliant with educational standards than a large, urban school, but the property of being a small countryside school cannot be changed nor does it make an individual school inherently risky. Second, the rules are more likely to be based on flawed assumptions than data-led models. The simple criteria are based on an a priori selection of measures rather than a statistical analysis of what best predicts regulatory findings. Third, rules-based approaches do not fully resolve issues of prioritization. Once regulatees have been divided into a small number of risk categories, how then are they prioritized within their categories? Finally, regulators leave themselves open to challenge when a regulatee deemed 'low-risk' is shown to be performing poorly and it transpires that performance data not included in the simplistic model indicated as much.

Simple, rules-based approaches utilizing contextual data are therefore transparent and inexpensive, but do not accurately identify individual regulatees of concern and can discriminate unfairly. The remaining, and more popular, prioritization techniques rely heavily on the use of metrics to target individual regulatees. The key difference between these data-reliant processes is how the metrics are selected and the use of 'expert interpretation' in the prioritization decisions.

3.2 Data-Informed Approaches

Data-informed prioritization tools aggregate a large number of a priori metrics to generate a risk rating and/or report used to inform, but not replace, expert judgement within a regulator. A pioneer in the field, Financial Services Authority's Advanced Risk Responsive Operating Framework (ARROW) tool saw forty-five 'elements', irreducible areas of risk, rated on a four-point scale, either subjectively or automatically depending on the element, and mapped to seven 'risks to objectives'. The ARROW tool automated the weighted aggregation of the forty-five elements and sent the result to a supervisor who had the ability to override any risk rating. The final report was then sent with others to a panel to prioritize regulatory action (FSA 2002–03). Likewise, from 2010 to 2013, CQC operated 'Quality and Risk Profiles' (QRPs) which contained approximately 800 metrics for each NHS trust. Each metric was mapped to one of sixteen 'outcomes' related to the quality of care. Each metric was automatically scored on a seven-point scale based on each provider's deviation from the national average and then all individual metric scores were aggregated, based on three weighting factors, to form an 'outcome risk estimate' on an eight-point scale for each of the sixteen 'outcomes' (CQC 2013a). Rather than a panel, an individual inspector would prioritize their own activity based on the QRPs for each of their sixty or so health and social care providers in their varied portfolio (Griffiths 2012).

Prioritizing inspections using such 'data-informed' approaches overcome a number of the issues associated with a simple, rules-based approach. Data-informed approaches allow regulators to target individual regulatees, present themselves as monitoring all aspects of performance, and provide a rational defence when regulatory failings occur. Risk assessments considering large quantities of data are also difficult for regulatees to game; simply shuffling resource to improve performance on one metric will likely result in worsening performance on another of the large number of metrics. Finally, the attraction of adding a layer of expert interpretation is clear. Taking higher education as an example, universities vary tremendously and knowing that, for example, Oxford University has fewer contact hours than most due to their system of individual tuition rather than a lack of attention being paid to students, could improve the use of data to target those universities not meeting quality standards. The expert interpretation of the risk scores means regulators are not beholden to the data. Tacit knowledge, notoriously difficult to capture in large-scale quantitative models, can be employed when the data is misleading.

'Data-informed' approaches can suffer from two significant failings however. First, the numerous and wide-ranging metrics that comprise data-informed risk tools are selected on the a priori basis of what parties *believe*, rather than *know empirically*, to predict non-compliance, or they are pressured to include for political purposes. This may lead to biases being ingrained and useful information being overlooked at the expense of misleading data.

Second, even when there are fewer risk assessments to consider, the well-established empirical literature tells us that the consistency, and accuracy, of expert decisions will be highly problematic. Meehl (1954) reviewed some twenty studies evaluating the performance of expert decision-making and prediction against simple regression models in diverse fields including higher education, parole violation, pilot training, and clinical recidivism and found the models outperformed or equalled experts in every study. The finding that simple models are superior, or at worst equal, to expert judgements has been assiduously confirmed in fields as diverse as business bankruptcy (Libby 1976; Beaver 1966; Deakin 1972), survival times (Einhorn 1978), the outcome sports events (Song et al 2007; Forrest 2005), police disciplinary matters (Inwald 1988), military training success (Bloom & Brundage 1947), heart attacks (Lee et al 1986; Goldman et al 1988), psychiatric and neuropsychological diagnosis (Wedding 1983; Goldberg 1965; Leli & Filskov 1984), auditing (Brown 1983), wine prices (Ashenfelter 2008), and violence (Werner & Rose 1983). Moreover, Grove et al's (2000) meta-analysis of 136 studies of clinical judgement versus statistical prediction concluded that 'superiority for [statistical]-prediction techniques was consistent, regardless of the judgment task, type of judge, judges' amounts of experience, or the types of data being combined'. It has even been demonstrated that models outperform clinicians when the clinicians have the output of the model available to assist their judgement (see eg Goldberg 1968; Montier 2009).

Over 200 robust studies into the performance of expert decision-making versus simple statistical models have been performed. No convincing exception has been reported (Kahneman 2011). Decades after his original findings and following their repeated confirmation, Meehl (1986) has concluded 'There is no controversy in social science that shows such a large body of qualitatively diverse studies coming out so uniformly in the same direction as this one.'

'Data informed' approaches therefore tend to comprise a large number of metrics selected a priori without statistical assessment and aggregated to provide a risk report and overall risk score for consideration by experts. They allow regulators to consider, and be seen to consider, a wide range of performance measures and incorporate tacit knowledge. These advantages however may be outweighed by the incorrect a priori selection of metrics which the tool uses, and the fact that numerous studies have assiduously demonstrated expert interpretation to be worse than simple models.

3.3 Algorithmic Approaches

Algorithmic approaches make use of machine learning techniques to identify useful metrics and develop optimal statistical models. Machine learning techniques enable computers to analyse vast data sets that would be far too large and complex for any conventional statistical tool to assess or human to comprehend (Raschka 2015). The use of machine learning is ubiquitous in the modern world. For example, Amazon and Netflix tailor recommendations to individual customers based on their purchasing habits and those of millions of other customers; credit companies assess their ever-growing databases of transactions to identify patterns of fraudulent spending to freeze accounts, and optical recognition tools continue to learn and identify handwriting (Coglianese & Lehr 2016).

The use of machine learning techniques has spread to the regulatory environment and promises substantial benefits (Yeung 2016). With advances in machine learning, it is now possible in principle to examine vast historic data sets and determine precisely which collection of metrics best prioritize inspections, excluding imperfect 'expert' judgement. In contrast with risk assessment tools that aggregate metrics selected a priori, machine learning is non-parametric; the algorithms 'allow the data to dictate how information contained in input variables is put together to forecast the value of an output variable' (Coglianese 2016; Berk 2008). With the algorithm objectively determining the best possible combination and weighting of metrics to predict outcomes, expert interpretation is unnecessary, often impossible given the size of the regulated sector and complexity of the model, and, as explored above, actively harmful to the accuracy of predictions. In algorithmic approaches, risk assessment models will not only be more accurate than their predecessors developed by a priori belief, intuition, and consensus, they will not suffer from the biases that lead to poor expert judgement.

Purely algorithmic approaches have been adopted by a number of government bodies. In 2004, the US General Accountability Office (2004) identified over fifty federal agencies engaged in 'data mining' activities. The US Environmental Protection Agency (EPA) has developed a machine learning tool to prioritize a subset of the tens of thousands of new chemicals developed each year for comprehensive testing (Kavlock et al 2012). The US Internal Revenue Service (IRS) uses machine learning algorithms to prioritize tax collection from self-employed individuals and small business most at risk of not paying, and tax returns for review (DeBarr & Harwood 2004; Martin & Stephenson 2005).

Further to removing the requirement for a priori metric selection and weighting, and problematic expert interpretation, purely algorithmic approaches have a number of other advantages. First, eliminating expert interpretation and, usually, the more automated processes that accompany algorithmic approaches both reduce costs. Second, the machine learning algorithms can constantly learn and improve themselves, and be continuously monitored and updated with new data. Third, the risk assessments are empirically derived and hence provide a robust defence of prioritization decisions in the face of political or media scrutiny.

These advanced algorithmic approaches, however, also have their limitations. Depending on the machine learning approach selected, prioritization models can be incredibly complex, which can make it hard to justify why an individual regulatee has been prioritized for inspection. In practice, the more complex approaches, such as neural networks, are not used in regulatory environments where there is a requirement to fully understand the model (Schutt & O'Neil 2013). Furthermore, in environments where data has to be manually processed and loaded into any risk assessment tool, rather than being automatically monitored, the volume of information which can be analysed is limited by the human effort which is necessarily constrained in a system promoted as an efficient use of resources. Purely algorithmic approaches also face difficulties trying to incorporate tacit knowledge that is not easily or readily quantified. Furthermore, the relationships identified between the data and outcomes can only be regarded as correlations, rather than causal inferences. If an algorithm tends to predict that larger schools are more likely to fail their Ofsted inspection than smaller schools, one cannot claim that increasing the size of a school will increase its probability of failing its next Ofsted inspection.

Algorithmic approaches, therefore, use machine learning techniques to objectively determine what collection and weighting of metrics best prioritize inspections. Such approaches are not reliant on the a priori selection of metrics based on intuition and consensus, but offer an evidence-based and objective model not hampered by flawed expert interpretation that can be continuously monitored and updated. More complex machine learning models can, however, prove challenging to explain and maintain and, as with all quantitative models, will struggle to incorporate tacit information that cannot easily be quantified or categorized.

In summary, risk-based approaches for prioritizing inspections can be broadly grouped into three categories. *First*, simple, rules-based methods place regulatees into prioritization groups based on a small number of often contextual metrics selected a priori. *Second*, data-informed approaches present and aggregate numerous, wide-ranging metrics selected a priori to inform prioritization decisions by one or more experts. *Third*, algorithmic approaches use machine learning techniques to determine the most accurate prioritization model from the available data. The first case study below looks at an example of a prioritization tool designed as part of a data-informed approach and explores what lessons can be learned from this. This in turn is followed by the second case study which examines an attempt to develop an algorithmic approach.

4. Case Study I: 'Intelligent Monitoring' and the Care Quality Commission

The CQC is the independent regulator responsible for ensuring the quality of over 30,000 health and social care providers in England. From 2013 to 2016, CQC operated it's 'leading edge' 'Intelligent Monitoring' system to support the prioritization if its limited inspection resource (Care Quality Commission Enquiry 2015). This case study examines the relationship between the risk scores generated by the 'Intelligent Monitoring' tool for NHS Acute trusts—administrative groupings of one or more hospitals in a geographical region that provide the majority of hospital-based care for the NHS—and the outcome of their inspections (CQC 2013b).

The CQC underwent a strategic overhaul in 2013 that introduced a new inspection and ratings system, and the new 'Intelligent Monitoring' tool to help prioritize the new inspections (Walshe & Phipps 2013). The now defunct 'Intelligent Monitoring' tool comprised approximately 150 equally weighted indicators chosen following a consultation process to identify those indicators that are 'most important for monitoring risks to the quality of care' (CQC 2013b). These indicators included mortality rates, waiting times, whistleblower reports, staff and patient surveys, and 'Healthcare Worker Flu vaccination uptake' amongst others (CQC 2015). Each indicator was scored as either 'No evidence of risk', 'Risk', or 'Elevated Risk' and assigned a value of zero, one or two respectively. The overall risk score was then calculated by adding up the resultant indicator values and dividing it by the maximum possible score, that is, two (the score for 'Elevated Risk') multiplied by the number of indicators that are relevant to the trust. For ease, CQC also classified Trusts into one of six ordinal risk bands according to their risk score. The 'Intelligent Monitoring' tool was updated simultaneously for all 150 Trusts every four or five months.

Overall quality ratings based on inspections are awarded on a four-point scale, with the worst Trusts being rated 'Inadequate', with improving ratings of 'Requires improvement', 'Good', and the best possible outcome 'Outstanding'. The comprehensive inspections comprise multi-day onsite visits where professional inspectors, staff, including clinicians, from other Trusts, analysts and 'experts by experience' (people who have personal experience of using or caring for someone who uses similar health services) (CQC 2018) interview staff and patients, and review evidence of compliance with regulatory standards.

The CQC committed to establishing a baseline view on performance across the NHS under its new system and subsequently set out to inspect all Trusts regardless of the risk it believed they posed. Accordingly, in scheduling this initial round of inspections, CQC senior management considered a host of factors in addition to the risk score, including the time since the last inspection, the geographical availability of expert inspection team members, and the need to evaluate the new inspection methodology. This provided the grounds for an insightful natural experiment as NHS Trusts which posed varying degrees of risk were inspected, and both the 'Intelligent Monitoring' risk score and the inspection outcomes were published (CQC 2013c).

The study looked at all the new-style inspections between 17 October 2013, when they were first put in to practice, and 29 September 2015. During this period CQC completed and published the quality ratings resulting from 103 inspections of ninety different NHS hospital trusts. This provided a representative sample of 55 per cent of all NHS hospital trusts in England. To assess the effectiveness of the tool, the most recent 'Intelligent Monitoring' risk estimates prior to each of the 103 inspections were paired with the quality rating resulting from that inspection. The relationship between these pairings was then examined in a series of less demanding tests.

4.1 How Did 'Intelligent Monitoring' Perform?

First, the relationship between the 'Intelligent Monitoring' risk score and the four ordinal rating categories was assessed using an ordinal regression analysis. This ability to predict the probability of an inspection resulting in each of the four possible ratings represents the ideal for a fully risk-based approach to prioritization. Were CQC able to predict the specific quality ratings, it would then be able to set differentiated thresholds for triggering inspections that reflect its tolerance for false positive errors (inspecting trusts performing well) and false negative errors (not inspecting trusts performing badly).

Second, the relationship between the 'Intelligent Monitoring' risk score and the Trusts that were 'performing well', that is were rated 'Good' or 'Outstanding' and Trust that were 'performing poorly', that is were rated 'Requires improvement' or 'Inadequate', was assessed. Whilst such an approach is not as optimal as being able to predict specific ratings, it would still prove useful for CQC. Third, the relationship between the 'Intelligent Monitoring' risk score and the Trusts that were 'inadequate' or 'Not Inadequate' was assessed. This test is the least strict of the three and represents the minimum one would hope to achieve from a risk-based tool.

For the first test, the 'Intelligent Monitoring' risk scores failed to predict the outcome of inspections. Not only were the risk scores not a statistically significant predictor of the subsequent inspection ratings, but the median risk score preceding a 'Good' inspection was higher—indicating a greater risk of poor-quality provision—than the median risk score preceding a 'Requires improvement' inspection. For the second test, the 'Intelligent Monitoring' risk scores failed to predict the less stringent measure of whether trusts were 'performing well' or 'performing poorly'. Again, not only were the risk scores not a statistically significant predictor of the grouped inspection outcomes, but the median risk score preceding a 'performing well' inspection was higher than the median risk score preceding a 'performing poorly' inspection.

For the third test, the risk scores again were not a statistically significant predictor of inspection outcomes, indeed there was so much variation between the risk scores and subsequent inspection outcome, only a very poor logistic regression model could be fitted. The median risk score preceding an 'Inadequate' inspection was higher than the median risk estimate preceding all other inspections; however, there was no possible risk score threshold for triggering an inspection that did not result in either a significant number of false positives—that is 'Not Inadequate' trusts being inspected—or a significant number of 'Inadequate' trusts not being inspected. When the risk and rating groupings used by both CQC and the National Audit Office were used, 'Intelligent Monitoring' was wrong more often than it was right.

The results of the analysis reveal that CQC's 'Intelligent Monitoring' tool was unable to predict which providers were at greatest risk of performing poorly so that it could prioritize them for inspection and improvement. It may be the case that expert interpretation could have improved the performance of 'Intelligent Monitoring'; however, CQC abandoned it in 2016 after it had completed its planned inspections of all providers to form a baseline view on quality so this cannot be tested. Given the evidence presented earlier it is unlikely that expert judgement would have significantly improved CQC's prioritization decisions.

4.2 Why Did 'Intelligent Monitoring' Perform Poorly?

Why then might it be the case that 'Intelligent Monitoring' performed so poorly? 'Intelligent Monitoring' may have been too simplistic. It could have been the case that some of the indicators within the tool were good predictors of poor quality care, but the equal weighting of all 150 indicators meant that the signal from those useful indicators went undetected, drowned out by other less insightful indicators. Likewise, it could be the case that limiting the tool to 150 indicators meant that some insightful indicators were left out of the tool altogether.

Another possible explanation is that the data, or the indicators made up of the data, are inadequate. One reason may be that the majority of data available to CQC is at Trust-level. These data may be too coarse in scale to discern the localized pockets of poor quality care detected by skilled inspectors. It may also be the case that the data is not timely enough. Much of the data available to CQC at the time was annual, and once it had been submitted to the central reporting body, cleaned, published, obtained, and processed by CQC, and then the next update of 'Intelligent Monitoring' came around, some of the data contained within the annual data collection could be eighteen months old. Any issues flagged by the data could have been rectified by the Trust already, or conversely, any indicated good performance could have deteriorated.

Another explanation may be that 'Intelligent Monitoring' was effective at identifying poor quality care, but that the inspection ratings were unreliable (Walshe et al 2014). This is always a possibility; however, it is hard to realistically imagine more comprehensive inspections than those practised by CQC—with widespread support from the sector (Health Select Committee 2013; NAO 2015; CQC 2013d)—involving teams of professional inspectors, analysts, clinicians, and experts by experience visiting the site over multiple days. Alternatively, it may be that data-driven statistical surveillance systems and inspectors are simply assessing different things. There are substantial challenges to comprehensively assessing the quality of care provided by large, complex, multi-site NHS hospital trusts and their highly skilled workforce. Moreover, judgements of care quality are subjective, in-tangible, and difficult to capture by indicators alone. Indeed, if it were simple, there would be little need for inspection.

Despite undertaking a comprehensive consultation with experts from across the world of healthcare to decide on the indicators best suited to effectively priori-tize regulatory interventions, CQC and 'Intelligent Monitoring' comprehensively failed. In simple terms, the tool was wrong more often than it was right. One pos-sible reason for this is the selection and weighting of indicators used to identify poor quality care. This is a problem that could potentially be solved by taking a machine-learning led, algorithmic approach. Whether such an approach worked in the UK higher education sector is the subject of the second case study.

5. Case Study II: Prioritizing Quality Assurance Agency Reviews

The QAA is 'the independent body entrusted with monitoring, and advising on, standards and quality in UK higher education' (QAA 2015). Up until 2013, over-seeing a sector comprising a near-fixed number of well-established universities, QAA operated a cyclical review system, visiting all providers every six years re-gardless of their reivew history of current performance against national metrics. This approach had its benefits: providers could not rest on their laurels knowing that they would be subject to another review, little resource was needed to monitor data, and regular reviews of all providers allowed for the sharing of novel and best practice.

The cause of QAA's shift in approach was a significant change in the UK higher education landscape. New undergraduate students would be the first to face fees of up to £9,000 a year, students attending new, for-profit 'alternative providers' would be allowed access to government-backed student loans, and the restrictions on the use of the protected term 'university' were being lessened. A sector which had been relatively stable, albeit expanding, for many years faced unprecedented change and 'marketisation' (Brown & Caradsso 2013). To keep pace with these developments and remain fit for purpose, the regulation of higher education also needed to change. The 2011 White Paper Students at the Heart of the System called for the QAA to adopt a new:

> … genuinely risk-based approach, focusing QAA effort where it will have most impact and giving students power to hold universities to account. All providers must continue to be part of a single assurance framework. But we would explore options in which the frequency—and perhaps need—for a full, scheduled institutional review will depend on an objective assessment of a basket of data, monitored continually but at arm's length. (BIS 2011)

This case study examines attempts to devise an algorithmic approach for QAA. At the time of the decree to prioritize reviews based on an objective assessment of a basket of data, QAA had been conducting reviews comparable to its then approach for a period of seven years. With a significant volume of historic performance data available, it was possible to pair each review outcome with the most up-to-date version of each indicator prior to that particular review, and then determine the best possible, algorithmic model for prioritizing reviews.

The higher education sector can be divided into three clear subsectors: universities, further education colleges (FECs) that provide higher education, and new 'alternative providers' which are responsible for a small but growing proportion of UK higher education and can be run for a profit. Each subsector had different volumes and types of data available with little overlap, requiring separate models be developed for each subsector. For universities there were over 800 indicators available including: applications data, the Destinations of Leavers from higher education (DLHE) Survey, research statistics, unit expenditure statistics, Higher Education Statistics Agency (HESA) performance indicators, staffing indicators, student indicators, staff–student ratios, finance indicators, details of students studying overseas for a UK HE qualification, the National Student Survey (NSS), previous QAA review outcomes, and student complaints to QAA known as 'QAA Concerns'. Far less data were available for FECs. As with universities, student characteristics data, financial information, previous QAA review outcomes, and 'QAA Concerns' were available. Furthermore, the outcome of Ofsted inspections were available for FECs. For alternative providers, more independent from government than universities and FECs, the only information available was the outcome of previous QAA reviews and QAA 'Concerns'. To supplement these data the past two sets of financial accounts of each provider were purchased from Companies House where available.

Despite the differences in the available data, the data preparation was the same for developing the three models. First, missing data was addressed. Where data were not missing for structural reasons—for example an indicator detailing the percentage of postgraduate students that are female at an undergraduate-only provider can have no legitimate value—the missing values were imputed (statistically estimated) using a weighted average of the indicator values for the five most similar universities across the data set. None of the imputed indicators had coverage below 85 per cent, a high value meaning the imputation was more likely to be accurate and the analysis robust (Harrell 2001; McKnight et al 2007; Van Buuren 2012).

One- and two-year absolute and percentage change-over-time variants were then calculated for each indicator collected annually. This meant each provider's 'direction of travel' could be modelled in addition to its current performance at the time of its review. Next, a small number of anomalous providers, with missing data for a significant number of indicators that were complete for nearly all others, were removed from the data set. Finally, invariant and highly correlated indicators that could increase the probability of a chance meaningless relationship between an indicator and the outcome of QAA reviews being identified resulting in a misleading model were removed from the data set (Zhao 2013).

As noted in the earlier discussion on algorithmic regulation, not all cutting-edge data science methods can be practically implemented by public sector regulators. QAA is no exception. For the algorithmic approach to fulfil the central tenet of risk-based approaches, it should be both effective and efficient. As the data could not be automatically retrieved and processed any ongoing tool would need to use a subset of the available data—to use all data would require significant analyst resource and might also lead to constantly changing risk estimates as new data sources are regularly loaded, making it difficult for QAA to determine which reviews to prioritize. The prioritization tool could not be a 'black box', those using the tool would need to understand *why* a provider's risk had changed, and also be able to explain this to the provider themselves who would question any assertion that they were high risk. Based on these requirements an *elastic net* approach was used to determine the optimal model for predicting the outcome of QAA reviews, and hence prioritizing future reviews. The *elastic net* approach, in effect, tries every combination of indicators and weightings to find the best possible model (James et al 2013). The resultant model predicted the probability of each provider being judged 'unsatisfactory' based on their contemporary data.

5.1 How Effective was the Algorithmic Approach?

Having gathered all this data and, in effect, tried every possible combination of indicators, how effective were the predictive models? For universities, having analysed all those metrics that could feasibly form part of a cost-effective, data-driven, risk-based approach, not just in their absolute form but multiple change-over-time variants, in their natural, imputed, standardized and benchmarked form, no possible combination of metrics effectively predicted the outcome of previous QAA reviews of universities, even with perfect hindsight.

The best possible model comprised three indicators concerning the one-year change in the proportion of successful applicants aged twenty-five and over, the proportion of research income spent on research, and the one-year change in the proportion of full-time equivalent staff who are financed by the institution, rather than by research grants or other sources. The model was only able to produce a very narrow range of predicted probabilities with the university deemed most likely to receive an 'unsatisfactory' review outcome having less than a 25 per cent chance of doing so, whilst the university deemed least likely to receive an 'unsatisfactory' review outcome has a 10 per cent chance of doing so. Had QAA conducted the reviews in order of the predicted likelihood of the review outcome being 'unsatis-factory', they would have needed to have conducted 174 out of the 191 actually per-formed to identify all 'unsatisfactory' reviews, 163 of which would have resulted in a 'satisfactory' outcome. This represents an error rate of 92.5 per cent. There is no effective relationship between the metrics and the outcome of QAA reviews of universities.

For further education colleges delivering higher education, the study again con-sidered all metrics with a feasible link to quality assurance that could form part of a cost-effective, data-driven, risk-based approach, not just in their absolute state but also modified to account for changes over time, both in percentage and absolute terms. The best predictive model again contained three indicators: the outcome of a previous comparable QAA review, the amount of income the college generated from non-educational streams, and the one-year change in the college's reliance on reserve funds.

To have prioritized all 'unsatisfactory' reviews based on the best possible model, QAA would have been required to carry out over 80 per cent of all the reviews they conducted under their cyclical approach, over 80 per cent of which would have re-sulted in a 'satisfactory' outcome. Moreover, when the model was applied to new data resulting from QAA reviews that occurred while the original analysis took place, the model performed even worse. Indeed, QAA would have successfully pri-oritized more 'unsatisfactory' new reviews by focusing on those predicted as being *least* likely to be 'satisfactory'.

For alternative providers, the best model was based on previous review per-formance and the age and size of the provider. The model was more promising than the models for universities or FECs: the predictions based on the held-back testing data demonstrated that the model was picking up on genuine underlying patterns in the data and the metrics themselves make intuitive sense.

These genuine patterns however were weak, with the characteristics shared by most 'unsatisfactory' providers also shared by a far greater number of 'satisfac-tory' providers. The result was that, as with the university and FEC models, a sub-stantial number of 'satisfactory' reviews would have to be prioritized in order to successfully identify all the 'unsatisfactory' providers. Even with perfect hindsight, over 80 per cent of the reviews undertaken would still have been required to identify all 'unsatisfactory' provision. If we were to accept some 'unsatisfactory' provision not being prioritized however the model did a reasonable job: combining the training and testing data sets, thirty-four out of forty-one 'unsatisfactory' providers were in the riskiest 50 per cent of providers.

Whether or not a model can be deemed a success is subjective. The success of the models can in part be determined by the proportion of 'satisfactory' providers prioritized for review (the error rate), and how many reviews were conducted in total before all 'unsatisfactory' provision had been detected. With such a narrow range of predicted probabilities and high error rate, the alternative provider models would be unlikely to win much support from the providers themselves, a significant number of which would suffer the burden of a review, a burden which their competitors may well be spared, knowing they have been singled out by a prioritization system that is wrong more than 80 per cent of the time. Further to the additional burden, the provider may also suffer reputational damage after being selected as a high-risk provider.

In summary, despite the varying volumes of data and an approach which, in effect, tried every possible combination of indicators, the best algorithmic models that could be obtained still performed very poorly. Of the three models, the model for alternative providers performed best despite, or perhaps because of, its smaller, simpler data set.

5.2 Why Did the Algorithmic Approach Fail?

The results of this case study demonstrate that an algorithmic approach was not feasible for QAA. But why, given the wealth of data available, is this the case? It is not unreasonable to assume students will be less willing to apply to, less satisfied at, and earn less on graduating from 'unsatisfactory' providers. Moreover, it is easy to imagine that providers in poor financial health, producing little research of note, and with high staff turnover may be more likely to be 'unsatisfactory'.

There are three logical assumptions underpinning the use of a predictive risk model for prioritizing QAA activity: available metrics measure, or act as a proxy for, the quality of a university's higher education provision; the outcome of QAA reviews is a measure of a university's quality; and that quality can be objectively defined or measured. Given the findings of the study it is clear that at least one of these three assumptions do not hold true.

As with healthcare quality in the first case study, the metrics used in the model are subject to criticism. Most higher education metrics relate to an academic year and are reported once that year is complete. The data then needs to be centralized and cleaned before publication, meaning that by the time it is available, it is already out of date. As with hospitals, a higher education provider's improvement may have significantly changed by the time the regulator can act on the data. Regardless of their timeliness, metrics are also subject to natural variability. Whilst teaching on a course may remain identical, scores will fluctuate year on year. Measures such as student satisfaction and employability assume teaching to be a one-way process divorced from the need for student engagement and effort. Metrics are subject to gaming, from the low-level additional focus on students' well-being prior to their completion of the NSS, through to the more questionable reminding students that the reputational value of their degree is influenced by their answers to the NSS, to the outright fraudulent misreporting of earnings data (*The Guardian* 2013). As the BIS Select Committee's inquiry into 'Assessing Quality in Higher Education' was told 'Academics are a clever bunch of people. They will optimise behaviours to achieve the best possible outcomes against the indicators that are being used to measure them' (Wilsdon 2015). Most metrics are also reported at the institutional level, as are QAA reviews, which likely masks the variable performance across a university. Finally, whilst metrics aren't inherently good or bad, their misuse poses clear problems. Satisfaction is important, but satisfied students are not necessarily satisfied as they have received a good quality education. A student who leaves with a first having not been challenged for three years may be satisfied with what they have got, but it may not be a quality education. Likewise, students who go on to earn more have not necessarily had a better quality education, or every nurse's degree would be lower quality than every investment banker's. Unlike the first case study though, we know it is not the selection or weighting of individual indicators that is the problem as, in effect, all possible options were explored.

Second, available metrics may not measure, or act as a proxy for, the quality of a university's higher education provision. Gibbs' (2010) review of metrics and their relation to quality in higher education identifies three types of metric: inputs, those that are in place before students arrive at a university such as funding, research performance, and reputations; environmental, those relevant to a student during the course of their study such as class size, the levels of student effort and engagement, and the quality of feedback; and outputs, the result of the student's study such as grades and employability. Gibbs' comprehensive study shows that input measures serve as excellent predictors of output measures as the best students compete for the best funded institutions. Likewise, output measures are strongly influenced by input measures. Those students arriving with the best A-levels tend to get the best jobs regardless of what they learn at university for a host of societal reasons, such as social capital, that we cannot standardize for. Gibbs therefore argues the only meaningful way to measure quality is to assess 'learning gain', the value added to a student during their time at university, and this is best measured by environment variables. Environmental variables are, however, incredibly difficult to quantify and convert to a metric. So, in an extension of Bevan and Hood's (2006) mantra that 'what's measured is what matters', what's measured is what is used to judge quality.

Also highlighted as an issue in our first case study, it may be the case that the regulator's judgements are not a true measure of quality. QAA reviews are based on assuring providers have the necessary processes in place to ensure quality. This is in part driven by the belief that processes lead to quality outcomes as Peter Williams, former Chief Executive of QAA, stated to the Innovation, Universities, Science and Skills Select Committee, in 2009:

> Processes and outcomes are very strongly linked. It is not an accident. It is because things are done that other things happen. Because teachers plan their teaching, then students will learn. Because students are guided in their learning, they will learn. (IUSSC 2009)

Further, the focus on processes is seen as necessary given the insurmountable challenges of making robust judgements about the comparative quality of different institutions—an issue not faced by regulators of healthcare or even lower-level education. As Roger Brown, former Chief Executive of the Higher Education Quality Council, stated, to do so would require, *inter alia:* degree programmes to be comparable in aims, design, structure, content, learning outcomes, delivery, support, learning environment, resourcing, mission, ethos, etc; the associated awards to involve comparable assessment methods, criteria, procedures, outcomes; the assessment judgments to be valid, reliable, consistent and fair; and the students to have comparable starting attainments, aspirations, motivations, learning objectives, etc (Brown 2015). In addition, attempts to assess academic outcomes have been rigorously opposed and in 2001 led to the academic board of LSE announce its plans to 'secede from [its] engagements with the QAA' which it believed had 'infringed academic freedom, imposed its own bureaucratic and pedagogical agenda, neglected students' intellectual development and used incompetent and unprofessional reviewers' (THE 2001).

The QAA therefore necessarily focuses on processes, but why might its assessment of whether these processes are in place not be a measure of quality? Ostensibly all new courses are internally validated by universities, then subject to annual monitoring and assessed against a nationally agreed framework every five years. Throughout this time external examiners check course aims, objectives, and marking standards. The QAA (2012) checks that these processes are in place. Power (1997), however, cites such quality audits as an epitome of the 'audit society'. In response to external quality oversight, universities have established quality assurance units which serve as a buffer between QAA and frontline staff. These units produce the required paper work and complete the QAA's 'ritual of verification' yet, Power argues, the process is decoupled from reality and, rather than genuinely assuring quality, serves only to satisfy the need to be seen to be holding universities to account. Thus, one possibility is that the processes being assured by the QAA are divorced from reality and hence their assessment will not serve as a measure of quality. A second, more straightforward option is that processes do not necessarily equate to outcomes. Being able to demonstrate to reviewers a written policy stating that 'feedback should be prompt and constructive' does not mean that it will be in practice. Conversely, the absence of such a written policy does not mean feedback cannot be prompt and constructive.

There are therefore challenges with both the assertion that QAA reviews and metrics are a measure of quality. There is also the third challenge that the concept of 'quality' itself is contested; if we cannot agree what quality is, how can any model measure and predict it? Pirsig (1974) suggests that quality is in the eye of the beholder and there is no objective measure that everyone, with their different experiences and interpretations, will agree on. Harvey and Green's (1993) review of quality in higher education identifies in excess of twenty different definitions of quality, foremost amongst which are the ideas of quality being defined in either absolute terms or as 'fitness-for-purpose'. One could argue that Oxbridge are of a higher quality than other institutions with less prestigious research, fewer alumni of world-renown, and fewer of the brightest students competing for entry. However, does such well-resourced universities taking the brightest students and seeing them prosper make them of greater quality than an institution which takes struggling students and, with limited resource, sees half of them go on to be the first in their families ever to graduate or gain professional employment? Gibbs' (2010) argument for quality to be seen in terms of 'learning gain' strikes a similar 'relative' view of quality although it, along with the fitness-for-purpose definition, may be seen to be unfair on those taking the brightest students who have less value to be added and high expectations. To these definitions we can also add that, from a regulatory perspective, quality is often seen through the lens of 'what went wrong last time' adding ever more standards to the quality 'layer cake' [7] (Beaussier et al 2016). Finally, QAA's Quality Code (2011) defines quality in terms of nineteen standards categorized as academics standards, teaching and learning, the provision of information, and enhancement. Quality therefore can be absolute or relative, it can be a measure of inputs, environmental variables, outcomes, or a combination of all three. In addition, it can include a university's enhancement activities and their provision of information and all of this can be relative to the assessor.

Given these three challenges outlined above, it is clear that there are significant obstacles to successfully operating an algorithmic approach to quality assurance in higher education. Furthermore, many of the possible explanations as to why a predictive risk model cannot work in higher education are clearly applicable to other sectors including health and social care, primary and secondary education, and rehabilitation services where quality is contested and difficult to measure. The final section below therefore explores the conditions necessary for an algorithmic approach to be successful.

6. The Conditions Necessary for Algorithmic Regulation to Succeed

Both case studies suggest common reasons for the failure of risk tools to effectively prioritize regulatory interventions, and, coupled with wider research, indicate the conditions necessary for algorithmic regulation to succeed. First, the data used to prioritize activity needs to meet a number of criteria. Data must be of satisfactory quality, timeliness, and of sufficient granularity. Healthcare and teaching quality are difficult to measure, and key performance indicators, like patient waiting times or NSS scores, are liable to gaming by regulatees. Indicator sets were often based on annual data collections and compiled at NHS trust or university-level. As such indicator data lagged behind current performance and failed to reflect significant variation in quality within the large, complex organizations. Interestingly, the simpler nature of indicators for alternative providers of higher education led to the most successful, albeit still very much wanting, model suggesting indicators that are too 'narrow' miss the bigger quality picture.

An additional data challenge is posed by the nature of the regulated sectors. Algorithmic techniques work best when there is a large number of data-rich cases so that statistical associations can be found between the outcomes of regulatory interest (eg 'Inadequate' Trusts or 'unsatisfactory' higher education providers) and various independent indicators on which the probability of those outcomes statistically depend. In the case of public services, the number of organizations or other units being regulated is often quite small; universities and hospitals need to be of a certain size to be viable and to accommodate various specialities. However, the ability to develop effective models, algorithmic or otherwise, will always be limited by this small number of regulatees and inspection outcomes available for use in training algorithms and correctly identifying rare events with low base rates. This problem is further exacerbated by regulators frequently changing their assessment criteria, meaning it is not possible to build up a sizeable history of previous results than can be used to develop an effective model. One area which is more likely to achieve a successful approach is public schools. There are approximately 22,000 public schools in the UK meaning there is a significant number of past inspections from which to help develop a model. Moreover, there is a large volume of standardized, and most importantly, objective data available, including national testing of all children at various ages. Hospitals, universities, and prisons however will always find it harder to gather sufficient volumes of past inspection to derive effective algorithmic models.

A further condition necessary for successful data-driven regulation is clear, uncontested outcomes for any model to predict. In the NHS successive governments have struggled to agree on the relative priority that should be given to cost efficiency, safety, waiting times, and patient satisfaction or to acknowledge the trade-offs between those different measures of healthcare quality. Likewise, in higher education should university quality be assessed in terms of student employability, satisfaction, retention, widening participation, or A-level tariffs? Conversely, Her Majesty's Revenue and Customs (HMRC), responsible for tax collection in the UK, has had the consistent goal of identifying those not paying the tax that they owe, and the amount of tax that should be paid, since its inception. This, coupled with objective data (the majority of tax disputes are agreed upon by both parties and settled after the first meeting) and millions of tax returns each year has allowed HMRC to implement an effective algorithmic approach (Lord & Culling 2016).

Beyond the two case studies presented here, three secondary barriers to effective algorithmic regulation have been identified that render the potential benefits of the approach difficult to achieve in practice. First, data protection rules often limit the ability of public sector bodies to link and share data sets or use them for purposes beyond those for which they were originally collected. This may of course be for an entirely valid reason, but the ideal of using individual patient or student records, for example, faces significant legal challenges. Second, leadership must be willing both to support potentially risky innovation and also mindful of the limitations and caveats about the use of algorithmic decision-making tools. It is easy for the heads of regulators to champion tools of which they have limited understanding as cutting-edge, world-leading, or similar, but such over-hyping of tools only serves to build expectations that cannot be met, and ultimately leads to trouble and dis-illusionment with such approaches. Third, despite the expense, regulators must be willing and able to hire staff with the relevant data science skills to understand the issues and deliver the desired outcomes.

7. Conclusion

The potential benefits of algorithmic regulation are clear to see. Making use of ever-growing volumes of administrative and performance data to make regulation more responsive, effective, and efficient, all while reducing the burden on well-performing or compliant regulatees, is win-win for all parties. Regulators are understandably reticent over the details of their risk tools, but those risk tools that have been studied academically and detailed above do not realize the potential benefits of algorithmic regulation in practice.

Multiple possibilities have been identified for why the algorithmic approaches in the case studies above did not work. For all sectors, not just health and higher education, data needs to be timely, robust, granular in terms of the unit being assessed (eg a hospital ward or department rather than a collection of hospitals), possibly not too specific (eg the budget shortfall or surplus of a hospital, rather than spending on a specific type of catheter), and of sufficient volume so that an effective model can be developed based on underlying patterns in the data set. Even with these stringent data criteria, an algorithmic approach will only be successful if the outcome the model is trying to predict is unambiguous and consistently scored. If different inspectors reach different decisions about the same quality of provision, any data-driven model will struggle. If the data meets the stringent criteria—it is a timely and effective measure of what is intended to be measured, and what is measured is done consistently—then practitioners may still need to overcome legal obstacles and make sure they have the necessary expertise and whole-hearted support of the organization. Only then is it likely the promised benefits of algorithmic regulation will be revealed in practice.

Achieving more timely, granular, and accurate data is challenging for health and higher education regulation, and indeed for the regulators of many public services. Taking the timeliness of data collections as an example, more frequent data returns often make little sense for universities as they operate on annual cycles. These problems may not be impossible to at least partially overcome however. Research has shown that previously untapped data sources, such as patient and student feedback via social media, can overcome the problems of granularity and gaming, and do so in a near-real time alongside more traditional performance measures (Griffiths & Leaver 2017).

What may prove impossible to overcome for the regulators of public services are the challenges of the low number of negative findings and the consistency of those negative findings. The volume of negative findings can be helped by regulators maintaining a consistent approach over the years in order to establish a larger set of historic inspections, but this may still get nowhere near the number of cases required to develop a robust model identifying genuine patterns in the data. Furthermore, obtaining consistent judgements of 'quality' of large, complex, and varied service providers will always be challenging. Indeed, even the definition of 'quality' in healthcare or higher education is highly contested (Beaussier et al 2016; Green 1994). Until the challenges of the low number of negative findings and the consistency of those negative findings are overcome, the algorithmic regulation of public services will remain impossible.

Bibliography

Ashenfelter O, 'Predicting the Quality and Prices of Bordeaux Wine' (2008) 118(529) The Economic Journal F174.

Australian Skills Quality Authority, 'Risk-Based Regulation' (2016) <http://www.asqa.gov.au/about/risk-based-regulation/risk-based-regulation.html> accessed 24 August 2016.

Baldwin R, Cave M, and Lodge M, *Understanding Regulation: Theory, Strategy, and Practice* (Oxford University Press 2012).

Bar Standards Board, 'Our Risk-Based Approach' (2016) <https://www.barstandardsboard.org.uk/about-bar-standards-board/how-we-do-it/our-risk-based-approach/> accessed 22 August 2016.

Beaussier A-L, Demeritt D, Griffiths A, et al, 'Accounting for Failure: Risk-based Regulation and the Problems of Ensuring Healthcare Quality in the NHS' (2016) 18 Health, Risk & Society 18.

Beaver WH, 'Financial Ratios as Predictors of Failure' (1966) 4 Journal of Accounting Research 71.

Berk RA, *Statistical Learning from a Regression Perspective* (Springer Science & Business Media 2008).

Bevan G and Hood C, 'What's Measured is What Matters: Targets and Gaming in the English Public Health Care System' (2006) 84(3) Public Administration 517.

BIS, *Students at the Heart of the System* (BIS 2011).

Black J, 'The Emergence of Risk-based Regulation and the New Public Risk Management in the United Kingdom' (2005) 3 Public Law 512.

Bloom RF and Brundage EG, *Predictions of Success in Elementary School for Enlisted Personnel*: Personnel Research and Test Development in the Naval Bureau of Personnel (Princeton University Press 1947).

Brown PR, 'Independent Auditor Judgment in the Evaluation of Internal Audit Functions' (1983) 21 Journal of Accounting Research 444.

Brown R and Carasso H, *Everything for Sale? The Marketisation of UK Higher Education* (Routledge 2013).

Brown R, 'Reflections on the Green Paper', Council for the Defence of British Universities (22 November 2015) <http://cdbu.org.uk/reflections-on-the-green-paper-tef/> accessed 30 July 2019.

Coglianese C. and Lehr D, 'Regulating by Robot: Administrative Decision Making in the Machine-Learning Era' (2016) 105 Georgetown Law Journal 1147.

CQC, 'A New Start: Responses to our Consultation on Changes to the Way CQC Regulates, Inspects and Monitors Care Services' (2013) <http://www.cqc.org.uk/sites/default/files/documents/cqc_newstartresponse_2013_14_tagged_sent_to_web.pdf> accessed 08 January 2013.

CQC, 'Building on Strong Foundations: CQC' (2015) <http://www.cqc.org.uk/sites/default/files/20151030_building_strong_foundations_FINAL.pdf> accessed 13 November 2015.

CQC, 'Chief Executive's Report to the Board (October 2015)' (2015) <http://www.cqc.org.uk/sites/default/files/CM101504%20Item%204%20Chief%20Executive%20report%20to%20Public%20Board.pdf> accessed 30 October 2015.

CQC, 'Experts by Experience' (2018) <https://www.cqc.org.uk/about us/jobs/experts-experience> accessed 14 June 2018.

CQC, 'Hospital Intelligent Monitoring' (2013c) <http://www.cqc.org.uk/public/hospital-intelligent-monitoring> accessed 12 July 2014.

CQC, 'Intelligent Monitoring: NHS Acute Hospitals Indicators and Methodology—May 2015: Care Quality Commission' (2015) <http://www.cqc.org.uk/sites/default/files/20150526_acute_im_v5_indicators_methodology_guidance.pdf> accessed 21 July 2015.

CQC, 'Proposed Model for Intelligent Monitoring and Expert Judgement in Acute NHS Trusts (Annex to the Consultation: Changes to the Way CQC Regulates, Inspects and Monitors Care Services): CQC' (2013b) <http://www.cqc.org.uk/sites/default/files/documents/cqc_consultationannex_2013_tagged.pdf> accessed 13 November 2015.

CQC, 'Quality and Risk Profiles: Statistical Guidance, Outcome-Based Risk Estimates in QRPs Produced for NHS Providers' (2013a) <http://www.cqc.org.uk/sites/default/files/documents/20130314_nhs_statistical_guidance_march_2013_for_publication.pdf> accessed 12 July 2014.

CQC, 'Raising Standards, Putting People First: Our Strategy for 2013 to 2016' (2013d) <https://www.cqc.org.uk/sites/default/files/documents/20130503_cqc_strategy_2013_final_cm_tagged.pdf> accessed 15 June 2014.

CQC, 'Shaping the Future: CQC's Strategy for 2016 to 2021' (2016). <http://www.cqc.org.uk/sites/default/files/20160523_strategy_16-21_strategy_final_web_01.pdf> accessed 04 May 2017.

Cullen WD, *The Ladbroke Grove Rail Inquiry* (HSC 2002).

Deakin EB, 'A Discriminant Analysis of Predictors of Business Failure' (1972) 10 Journal of Accounting Research 167.

DeBarr D and Harwood M, 'Relational Mining for Compliance Risk' Internal Revenue Service Research Conference (2004).

Demeritt D, Rothstein H, Beaussier A-L, et al, 'Mobilizing Risk: Explaining Policy Transfer in Food and Occupational Safety Regulation in the UK' (2015) 47(2) Environment and Planning A 373.

Einhorn HJ and Hogarth RM, 'Confidence in Judgment: Persistence of the Illusion of Validity' (1978) 85(5) Psychological Review 395.

Forrest D, Goddard J, and Simmons R, 'Odds-Setters as Forecasters: The Case of English Football' (2005) 21(3) International Journal of Forecasting 551.

Foundation Trust 2009 [cited 2014 13/08/2014] Healthcare Commission, 'Investigation into Mid Staffordshire NHS' http://www.midstaffspublicinquiry.com/sites/default/files/Healthcare_Commission_report_on_Mid_Staffs.pdf accessed 13/08/2014 2014.

FSA, 'Food Law Code of Practice: Chapter 5—Organisation of Official Controls: FSA' (2016) <https://www.food.gov.uk/enforcement/codes-of-practice/food-law-code-of-practice-2015/5-3-frequency-of-controls-and-the-requirements-of-a-risk-based-approach> accessed 03 July 2016.

FSA, *Building the New Regulator: Progress Report 2* (FSA 2002).

FSA, *The Firm Risk Assessment Framework* (FSA 2003).

General Accountability Office, Data Mining: Federal Efforts Cover a Wide Range of Uses (Report No GAO-04-548) (2004).

Gibbs G, *Dimensions of Quality* (Higher Education Academy York 2010).

Goldberg LR, 'Diagnosticians vs. Diagnostic Signs: The Diagnosis of Psychosis vs. Neurosis from the MMPI' (1965) 79(9) Psychological Monographs: General and Applied 1.

Goldberg LR, 'Simple Models or Simple Processes? Some Research on Clinical Judgments' (1968) 23(7) American Psychologist 483.

Goldman L, Cook EF, Brand DA, et al, 'A Computer Protocol to Predict Myocardial Infarction in Emergency Department Patients with Chest Pain' (1988) 318(13) New England Journal of Medicine 797.

Green D, *What is Quality in Higher Education?* (ERIC 1994).

Griffiths A and Leaver MP, 'Wisdom of Patients: Predicting the Quality of Care Using Aggregated Patient Feedback' (2017) 27(2) BMJ Quality & Safety doi: 10.1136/bmjqs-2017-006847.

Griffiths A, *In Theory & in Practice: Can Risk-based Approaches to Regulation Work in the Care Quality Domain?* (King's College London 2012).

Grove WM, Zald DH, Lebow BS, et al, 'Clinical versus Mechanical Prediction: A Meta-Analysis' (2000) 12(1) Psychological Assessment 19.

Harrell FE, *Regression Modeling Strategies: With Applications to Linear Models, Logistic Regression, and Survival Analysis* (Springer 2001).

Harvey L and Green D, 'Defining Quality' (1993) 18(1) Assessment & Evaluation in Higher Education 9 doi: 10.1080/0260293930180102.

Health Select Committee, 'Accountability Hearing with the Care Quality Commission' Health Select Committee, House of Commons (2013) <http://www.publications.parliament.uk/pa/cm201314/cmselect/cmhealth/761/761.pdf> accessed 23 April 2019.

Healthcare Commission, 'Investigation into Mid Staffordshire NHS'.

Hutter BM, 'The Attractions of Risk-Based Regulation: Accounting for the Emergence of Risk Ideas in Regulation' (2005) <http://www.lse.ac.uk/collections/CARR/pdf/Disspaper33.pdf>. Accessed 06 September 2013.

Hutter BM, 'The Attractions of Risk-Based Regulation: Accounting for the Emergence of Risk Ideas in Regulation' (2005) <http://www.lse.ac.uk/collections/CARR/pdf/Disspaper33.pdf> accessed 16 May 2013.

Inwald RE, 'Five-Year Follow-Up Study of Departmental Terminations as Predicted by 16 Preemployment Psychological Indicators' (1988) 73(4) Journal of Applied Psychology 703.

IUSSC, *Students and Universities: Eleventh Report of Session 2008–09* (HMSO 2009).

James G, Witten D, Hastie T, et al, *An Introduction to Statistical Learning* (Springer 2013).

Kahneman D, *Thinking, Fast and Slow* (Macmillan 2011).

Kavlock R, Chandler K, Houck K, et al, 'Update on EPA's ToxCast Program: Providing High Throughput Decision Support Tools for Chemical Risk Management' (2012) 25(7) Chemical Research in Toxicology 1287.

Lee KL, Pryor DB, Harrell Jr FE, et al, 'Predicting Outcome in Coronary Disease Statistical Models versus Expert Clinicians' (1986) 80(4) The American Journal of Medicine 553.

Leli DA and Filskov SB, 'Clinical Detection of Intellectual Deterioration Associated with Brain Damage' (1984) 40(6) Journal of Clinical Psychology 1435.

Libby R, 'Man versus Model of Man: Some Conflicting Evidence' (1976) 16(1) Organizational Behavior and Human Performance 1.

Lodge M and Wegrich K, *Managing Regulation: Regulatory Analysis, Politics and Policy* (Palgrave Macmillan 2012).

Löfstedt R, *Risk Management in Post-Trust Societies* (Earthscan 2008).

Lord J and Culling A, 'O.R. IN HM REVENUE & CUSTOMS. Impact' (Autumn 2016). https://www.amazon.co.uk/Clinical-Versus-Statistical-Prediction-Theoretical/dp/0816600961/ref=sr_1_2?keywords=Clinical+versus+statistical+prediction%3A+A+theoretical+analysis+and+a+review+of+the+evidence+meehl&qid=1560256679&s=gateway&sr=8-2.

Martin J and Stephenson R, 'Risk-based Collection Model Development and Testing' Internal Revenue Service Research Conference (2005).

McKnight PE, McKnight KM, Sidani S, et al, *Missing Data: A Gentle Introduction* (Guilford Press 2007).

Meehl PE, 'Causes and Effects of My Disturbing Little Book' (1986) 50(3) Journal of Personality Assessment 370.

Meehl PE, *Clinical versus Statistical Prediction: A Theoretical Analysis and a Review of the Evidence* (University of Minnesota Press 1954).

Meyer JW and Rowan B, 'The Structure of Educational Organizations' in JH Ballantine and JZ Spade (eds), *Schools and Society: A Sociological Approach to Education* (Sage Publications 1977).

Miller M and Morris N, 'Predictions of Dangerousness: An Argument for Limited Use' (1988) 3(4) Violence and Victims 263.

Montier J, *Behavioural Investing: a Practitioners Guide to Applying Behavioural Finance* (John Wiley & Sons 2009).

NAO, 'Care Quality Commission: Capacity and Capability to Regulate the Quality and Safety of Health and Adult Social Care' (2015) <https://www.nao.org.uk/wp-content/uploads/2015/07/Capacity-and-capability-to-regulate-the-quality-and-safety-of-health-and-adult-social-care.pdf> accessed 06 November 2015.

NAO, *The Maritime and Coastguard Agency's Response to Growth in the UK Merchant Fleet* (The Stationer's Office 2009).

Ofsted, 'Children's Social Care Data in England 2016: Key Findings 2016' (updated 24 June 2016) <https://www.gov.uk/government/statistics/childrens-social-care-data-in-england-2016> accessed 09 February 2018.

Ofsted, 'Official Statistics: Childcare Providers and Inspections as at 31 December 2017 2018' (updated 14 June 2018) <https://www.gov.uk/government/publications/childcare-providers-and-inspections-as-at-31-december-2017/childcare-providers-and-inspections-as-at-31-december-2017-main-findings#number-of-providers> accessed 15 June 2018.

OfSted, 'Ofsted Strategy 2017–22' (2017) <https://assets.publishing.service.gov.uk/government/uploads/system/uploads/attachment_data/file/648212/Ofsted_strategy_2017-22.pdf> accessed 12 February 2018.

Ofsted, 'The Framework for School Inspection' (2015) <https://www.gov.uk/government/uploads/system/uploads/attachment_data/file/389974/The_framework_for_school_inspection.pdf> accessed 16 May 2015.

ORR, *Train Derailment at Hatfield: A Final Report by the Independent Investigation Board* (ORR 2006).

PAC, 'Oral Evidence to HC501—Care Quality Commission Inquiry' (2015).

Pirsig RM, *Zen and the Art of Motorcycle Maintenance* (William Morrow and Company 1974).

Pontell HN, 'Deterrence Theory versus Practice' (1978) 16(1) Criminology 3.

Power M, *The Audit Society: Rituals of Verification* (Oxford University Press 1997).

QAA (2012a). How Is Quality Assured? [Online]. Available: https://www.youtube.com/watch?v=smnVysMigfY accessed 14 December 2015.

QAA (2013). Higher Education Review: A Handbook for Providers <http://www.qaa.ac.uk/Publications/InformationAndGuidance/Documents/HER-handbook-13.pdf> accessed 17 December 2013.

QAA, 'About Us' (2015) <http://www.qaa.ac.uk/about-us> accessed 14 December 2015.

QAA, 'The UK Quality Code for Higher Education' (2011) <http://www.qaa.ac.uk/AssuringStandardsAndQuality/quality-code/Pages/default.aspx> accessed 26 May 2014.

Rail Safety and Standards Board, 'Formal Inquiry: Derailment of Train 1T60, 1245 hrs Kings Cross to Kings Lynn at Potters Bar on 10 May 2002 (FI2013/F)' (2005).

Raschka S, *Python Machine Learning* (Packt Publishing Ltd 2015).

Ratcliffe R and Adams R, 'Derby University Accused of Falsifying Data on Graduate Employment Rate' *The Guardian* (1 October 2013).

Rothstein H, Huber M, and Gaskell G, 'A Theory of Risk Colonization: The Spiralling Regulatory Logics of Societal and Institutional Risk' (2006) 35(1) Economy and Society 91 doi: 10.1080/03085140500465865.

Rothstein H, Irving P, Walden T, et al, 'The Risks of Risk-based Regulation: Insights from the Environmental Policy Domain' (2006) 32(8) Environment International 1056 doi: http://dx.doi.org/10.1016/j.envint.2006.06.008.

Schutt R and O'Neil C, *Doing Data Science: Straight Talk from the Frontline* (O'Reilly Media, Inc 2013).

Song C, Boulier BL, Stekler HO, 'The Comparative Accuracy of Judgmental and Model Forecasts of American Football Games' (2007) 23(3) International Journal of Forecasting 405.

SRA, 'SRA Regulatory Risk Framework' (2014) <https://www.sra.org.uk/documents/solicitors/freedom-in-practice/risk-framework.pdf> accessed 17 December 2015.

Sunstein CR, *Risk and Reason: Safety, Law, and the Environment* (Cambridge University Press 2002).

TEQSA, 'A Risk and Standards Based Approach to Quality Assurance in Australia's Diverse Higher Education Sector' (2015) <http://www.teqsa.gov.au/sites/default/files/publication-documents/RiskStandardsSectorPaperFeb2015.pdf> accessed 04 June 2016.

TEQSA, 'Regulatory Risk Framework' (2012) <http://teqsa.gov.au/sites/default/files/TEQSARegulatoryRiskFramework_0.pdf> accessed 02 March 2014.

THE, *LSE Leads Revolt against QAA* (THE 2001).

Van Buuren S, *Flexible Imputation of Missing Data* (CRC Press 2012).

Walshe K and Phipps D, *Developing a Strategic Framework to Guide the Care Quality Commission's Programme of Evaluation* (CQC 2013).

Walshe K, Addicott R, Boyd A, et al, *Evaluating the Care Quality Commission's Acute Hospital Regulatory Model: Final Report* King'Fund (CM/07/14/06) (2014).

Wedding D, 'Clinical and Statistical Prediction in Neuropsychology' (1983) 5(2) Clinical Neuropsychology 49.

Werner PD, Rose TL, and Yesavage JA, 'Reliability, Accuracy, and Decision-Making Strategy in Clinical Predictions of Imminent Dangerousness' (1983) 51(6) Journal of Consulting and Clinical Psychology 815.

Wilsdon J, *Oral Evidence to the BIS Select Committee 'Assessing Quality in Higher Education' Inquiry* (The Stationary Office Ltd 2015).

Yeung K, 'Algorithmic Regulation and Intelligent Enforcement' LSE CARR Workshop: 'Regulatory Scholarship in Crisis' London (2016).

Zhao Y and Cen Y, *Data Mining Applications with R* (Academic Press 2013).

8

Reflecting on Public Service Regulation by Algorithm

Martin Lodge and Andrea Mennicken*

1. Introduction

Regulatory bodies across sectors and countries are paying increasing attention to the potential of 'big data' for the purposes of regulation. Algorithmic regulation, as noted by Tim O'Reilly (2013), is said to offer the promise of a move towards outcome-focused regulation; real-time measurement to determine if outcomes are being achieved; and algorithms (ie a set of rules) that make adjustments based on new data (O'Reilly 2013: 289–90). Furthermore, successful algorithmic regulation requires periodic, deeper analysis of whether the algorithms themselves are correct and performing as expected (O'Reilly 2013: 290).

The prospect of algorithmic regulation has attracted considerable enthusiasm in the world of regulatory practice. This is not surprising given that outcome- and risk-based regulation have been long-held goals. The prospect of moving to 'real time' measurement is alluring, as is algorithmic regulation's potential for prediction, for example with regards to the prediction of failure (eg operational and financial failure in hospitals, schools, universities, prisons, and other regulated entities). Put differently, algorithmic regulation offers scope for advancing risk-based regulation (Yeung 2017: 7–8): a better, more efficient and accurate, identification of sites that require regulatory attention. In this context, there has also been a growing interest in using algorithmic regulation for the forecasting of future events. Thanks to the combination of algorithms, superior computing power, unprecedented volumes of digital data, and 'the cloud' regulatory oversight can be complemented with simulations of the future that previously remained outside regulatory capacity (and imagination). Thus, the ability to draw

* The authors gratefully acknowledge the financial support provided for this study by the Economic and Social Research Council (Grant Ref: ES/N018869/1) under the Open Research Area Scheme (Project Title: QUAD—Quantification, Administrative Capacity and Democracy). QUAD is an international project co-funded by the Agence Nationale de la Recherche (ANR, France), Deutsche Forschungsgemeinschaft (DFG, Germany), Economic and Social Research Council (ESRC, UK), and the Nederlands Organisatie voor Wetenschappelijk Onderzoek (NWO, Netherlands).

on 'facts' and extrapolated 'futures' adds to knowledge about potential regulatory futures.[1]

Furthermore, algorithmic regulation promises an answer to frustrations with existing regulatory practice: regulatory regimes are often criticised for too much overlap or 'underlap'; failings in information exchange; too many opportunities for gaming; inconsistencies in the regulatory approach (eg human-led inspections are seen as open to arbitrary judgements); and too much focus on process rather than outcomes (eg Hood et al 1999; Koop & Lodge 2014; Lodge & Wegrich 2012: Chapter 10; see also O'Reilly 2013).

This chapter considers ways in which algorithmic regulation challenges regulatory practices building on insights from regulation scholarship. Following Julia Black, we define regulation as 'the sustained and focused attempt to alter the behaviour of others according to defined standards and purposes with the intention of producing a broadly identified outcome or outcomes, which may involve mechanisms of standard-setting, information-gathering and behaviour-modification' (Black 2002a: 26; Koop & Lodge 2017). Algorithmic regulation, in this context, can be referred to as regulation that relies, to varying degrees, on the 'computational generation of knowledge by systematically collecting data (in real time on a continuous basis)' (Yeung 2017: 1). Such data are 'emitted directly from numerous dynamic components pertaining to the regulated environment in order to identify and, if necessary, automatically refine (or prompt refinement of) the system's operations to attain a pre-specified goal' (Yeung 2017: 1).

As Yeung (2017: 2) cautions, the term 'algorithm' may be variously understood. Our concern here is with the computational generation of knowledge involving 'machine learning'. Machine learning algorithms depart from traditional techniques of statistical modelling, as they do not require a priori specification of functional relationships between variables (Yeung 2017: 2). Machine learning algorithms draw on vast and unstructured sources of data to identify patterns and correlations between the data which cannot be detected by human cognition. Through iterative adaptation and the utilization of ever more data, machine learning promises the identification of predictive relationships between certain factors (inputs) and outputs (Yeung 2017: 2, 1).

This chapter focuses on potentials and challenges posed by the utilization of machine learning algorithms in the regulation of public services. Public services are those that are supplied by or on behalf of government to a particular jurisdiction's community, including such services as healthcare, education, or the correctional services. These services can be delivered by public or private providers (eg private or public universities, private or public hospitals, public or private prisons), yet the government holds the ultimate responsibility for ensuring sustained availability

---

[1] An earlier attempt at such a system was Stafford Beer's cybernetic application for the Allende regime in Chile in the early 1970s, the 'Cybersen' (Medina 2015).

and quality of such services. In contrast to private services which, in theory at least, individuals may be able to opt out from, public services usually do not come with the same kind of choice options (we cannot easily elect to live without water or electricity, even if we might be able to change supplier). How, then, public services are being regulated matters, partly because the actual delivery of public services matters, partly because (usually unelected) regulators carry specific requirements in terms of accountability and legitimacy. The delivery of public services often involves different types of professions (doctors, accountants, nurses, teachers, policemen, prison officers, etc), which deal with diverse constituencies, including vulnerable individuals. For the purposes of this chapter, we concentrate on the use of algorithmic regulation by regulatory bodies in the exercise of oversight over hospitals, care homes, schools, universities, or prisons, rather than the regulation of the use of big data and machine learning algorithms by (public or private) public service providers themselves.

We highlight that algorithmic regulation that utilizes machine learning in the context of public service regulation represents an *extension* to existing systems of processing and storing information that support regulatory decision-making, but is *qualitatively* different, given its reliance on machine learning in particular, and it is potentially *distinct* as it can rely on often hidden forms of observation. These particular properties offer scope for enhancing regulatory capacity, but they also introduce distinct side effects.

In view of the initial promise of algorithmic regulation as suggested by O'Reilly (2013), this chapter argues first that the widespread enthusiasm for algorithmic regulation hides much deeper differences in worldviews about regulatory approaches, and that advancing the utilization of algorithmic regulation potentially transforms existing mixes of regulatory approaches in non-anticipated ways. Second, we argue that regulating through algorithmic regulation presents distinct administrative problems in terms of knowledge creation, coordination, and integration, as well as ambiguity over objectives. Finally, we argue that these challenges for the use of machine learning algorithms in public service algorithmic regulation require renewed attention to questions of the 'regulation of regulators'. In developing these arguments, this chapter does not offer systematic testing of particular research questions, but draws on different examples from regulatory practice, especially in the UK, in order to contribute to emerging debates in the worlds of research and practice.[2]

---

[2] We use an expansive definition of regulators, including statutory agencies subordinate to, but formally independent of ministerial departments, professional oversight bodies, and self-regulatory organizations. More specifically, this chapter builds on joint comparative work on 'quantification, administrative capacity and democracy' (QUAD, see footnote *). The research involved both documentary as well as (non-attributable) interview research in the domains of health, higher education, and prisons.

2. Regulatory Capacity and Algorithmic Regulation

The promise of using unconnected data sets and novel sources (such as social media rather than complaints or records of weighting times in the case of hospitals) and their processing with the help of machine learning algorithms are underlying the very promise of more pinpointed and accurate detection (eg detection with regards to hospitals or universities at risk of breaching quality standards). In addition, it also comes with the promise of additional knowledge gained through advanced simulations; in the absence of being able to experiment with 'trial and error' in many regulatory settings (such as disasters or pandemics), relying on machine learning algorithms offers scope to explore potential futures beyond the kind of risk scenario planning that has so far occupied regulatory planners.

There is hardly a regulator who is not attracted to exploiting machine learning algorithms to reform regulatory regimes, especially in terms of finding ways of identifying troubling trends. In the UK, regulators have sought to expand their 'intelligence' on the basis of analysing complex data-points. For example, the UK regulator for care quality in areas such as nursing homes and hospitals (the Care Quality Commission) has used machine learning to refine its 'risk-based' approach to regulation.[3] Similarly, the regulators for higher education (formerly Hefce, now OfS) have used such techniques to identify potential 'problems' among higher education providers without, however, claiming that such analysis would offer 'predictions'. The UK Food Standards Agency uses social media analysis to monitor potential outbreaks of foodborne diseases (Oldroyd et al 2018).[4]

Algorithmic regulation offers the promise not just of identifying potential (emerging) problems, it also suggests the potential for targeted and bespoke interventions, thereby providing efficiency gains and reduced potential for failure (and therefore blame) for regulators in terms of either 'missing' failure or in terms of being 'over-bearing' in terms of inspection intensity. What unites these perspectives is the enthusiasm about the possibilities for better informed decision-making by being able to draw on vast amounts of data to exploit the information-processing capacities of new machine learning technologies. For example, in the UK, the Better Regulation Executive is seeking to develop so-called GovTech approaches to address overlapping regulatory requirements and to analyse the effectiveness of regulatory regimes.[5]

The seemingly shared view on the potential of algorithmic regulation hides underlying differences in fundamental worldviews about regulatory

---

[3] <https://www.cqc.org.uk/guidance-providers/independent-healthcare/cqc-insight-independent-healthcare> accessed 29 October 2018.

[4] 'Tweet when you vomit, it is your duty' BBC website (13 December 2016) <https://www.bbc.co.uk/news/blogs-trending-38227094> accessed 21 October 2018.

[5] See <https://gds.blog.gov.uk/2018/09/06/second-round-of-govtech-catalyst-challenges-revealed/> accessed 20 October 2018.

approaches—what regulation should deliver and how. Drawing on Christopher Hood's grid-group cultural theory inspired framework for different control styles (Hood 1998; Hood et al 1999; Lodge & Wegrich 2012; Lodge et al 2010), one can distinguish between four distinct worldviews that have different implications for regulatory approaches and therefore regard algorithmic regulation as a natural extension of their preferred way of regulation. According to this approach, worldviews can be distinguished according to different degrees of social integration ('group') and rule-boundedness ('grid') (see also Douglas & Wildavsky 1982). On this basis four distinct and rival worldviews can be diagnosed, ranging from the hierarchist (emphasizing rule-boundedness and social differentiation), egalitarian-mutualist (emphasizing the importance of social norms), individualist (emphasizing the importance of loose individual ties towards groups and rules), and so-called fatalists (emphasizing the inherent fallibility of all intended interventions) views.

How we regulate, hold organizations and individuals responsible, is fundamentally affected by these different worldviews which can be associated with different control styles (Hood 1998; Hood et al 2004; Lodge et al 2010) and information biases (Wildavsky and Thompson 1986).[6] These questions affect all regulatory approaches and are therefore also central for developing understanding about the rationale of using machine learning algorithms in public service regulation. In other words, understanding why particular actors advocate the use of machine learning algorithms for the regulation of public services matters: it reveals inherent preferences about the ultimate objective of using a particular regulatory approach.

A hierarchist worldview would propagate a control style based on oversight which works by monitoring and direction of individuals from a central point of authority. An egalitarian-mutualist view would support mutuality as control style which works by exposing individuals to horizontal influence from other individuals (eg the pairing of police officers on patrol). An individualist view puts emphasis on competition, which works by fostering rivalry among individuals or organizations (see eg league tables of better and worse performers). Fatalists would regard contrived randomness as preferred control style, which works by unpredictable processes or combinations of people to deter corruption or anti-system behaviour (see here the examples of selection by lot, rotation of staff around institutions) (Hood 1998; Hood et al 2004).

For some ('hierarchists'), therefore, regulating by algorithm would be regarded as offering scope for increased oversight by being able to draw on 'big data' and smart information processing power. Data-driven machine learning is seen as superior to human inspection regimes that are regarded as flawed given human 'variation'. Individual inspectors or inspection teams have for example different views

---

[6] More generally, this perspective challenges the notion of a 'scientific' and 'objective' form of algorithmic regulation and highlights the biases that emerge from a reliance on machine learning based on 'big data' (see boyd & Crawford 2011).

as to what is regarded as 'acceptable'. They also have different propensities to report on potential warning signs. This, in turn, makes risk-based allocation of regulatory attention rather problematic. Backed by machine learning, it is said to be possible to advance the identification of problem areas in more targeted and preemptive ways (thereby reducing false negatives and positives). For others ('mutualists'), the greater ability to contrast and interrogate patterns offers the opportunity for enhanced deliberation and informed engagement (Hildebrandt 2018). Thus, a more extensive use of algorithmic regulation might allow for enhancing informed 'regulatory conversations' (Black 2002b). 'Individualist' worldviews would point to algorithmic regulation's potential for more comparative information, therefore enabling enhanced use of benchmarking and, potentially, informed choice by public service users. Seeing in 'real time' how different hospitals (or schools or universities) compare in terms of social media word clouds, for example, might place additional pressure on providers to improve customer 'experience', especially when such information is made available to users. Finally, for 'fatalists', algorithmic regulation offers scope for introducing elements of surprise (contrived randomness) into systems of control. As there is a movement away from consistent 'governing by numbers' (governing by pre-defined targets), there is less scope for managers to massage the underlying numbers in order to game systems. Adaptive 'creative compliance' is less feasible in systems that rely on diverse data sources and where data-gathering is non-reactive (ie does not require a response by regulated organizations), especially also when the underlying algorithms are not accessible and therefore not prone to re-engineering.

At the margins, there is potential for agreement across different worldviews about the uses of algorithmic regulation. For example, contrasting patterns might be seen as both a device for deliberation and conversation as well as for generating comparative pressures via directly monitorable dashboards. However, ultimately, there will always be, as with all systems of regulation, conflict over the underlying purpose of algorithmic regulation.[7]

It is not just in terms of advocacy of particular regulatory approaches where underlying worldviews reveal fundamental differences about the appeal of algorithmic regulation. The utilization of algorithmic regulation within regulatory settings interacts with existing approaches. As a result, algorithmic regulation can be seen to be either advancing existing regulatory approaches, shifting patterns of oversight, or even undermining established systems of regulatory oversight. To illustrate, the potential emphasis of a particular worldview's preferred use of algorithmic regulation is likely to increase side-effects and criticism from actors

---

[7] In view of the example on utilizing comparative information, the difference is between encouraging conversations about differences in 'performance' that encourage learning for enhanced professional and regulatory practice, and those who assume that competitive pressure will lead to adaptation, based on the observed patterns alone.

associated with other worldviews. Thus, an ever-growing emphasis on utilizing algorithmic regulation for 'hierarchist' purposes in terms of greater surveillance and less 'human' intervention brings with it a concern over expanding ('mission creep') surveillance powers and intrusive state oversight over the activities of public service professionals.

Similarly, there is a concern that a regime supposed to support regulatory conversations (on 'mutualist' lines) will only be short-lived, as the knowledge 'created' through algorithmic regulation clashes with existing sources of expertise. Initiatives to advance automation in regulation are feared to inevitably lead to a deskilling of regulatory staff as human judgement will be disregarded when contradicting machine-based findings. At minimum, given the complexity of algorithmic regulation, it is likely that such regulatory conversations will mostly involve data scientists with only limited (informed) input from other actors, especially those attached to more 'human' forms of inspection.

Utilizing algorithmic regulation for purposes of incentivizing competitive 'spirits' via league-tabling and benchmarking might encourage gaming if not outright corruption, for example via bots and malware software. Whilst illegal, it is doubtful whether regulators would detect such behaviours easily, given also the low-cost nature of such attempts aimed at corrupting the data generation.

Also, an emphasis on elements of unpredictability and surprise via algorithmic regulation brings distinct concerns. A lack of consistency and openness (eg it is not visible which indicators the algorithm identifies as critical) reduces the possibility for regulators and regulated institutions to 'learn' as it is not clear on what basis certain public services are being 'condemned' or singled out for being 'at risk'. Given limited resources within organizations and inherent ambiguity (ie 'garbage can decision-making', Cohen et al 1972), it is questionable whether, according to this view, algorithmic regulation not simply adds to the complexity and fluidity of regulatory decision-making. At the very least, it is not unlikely that a greater reliance on machine-learning algorithms will accentuate conflicts between different units within regulatory organizations. As noted by Miller et al (2017), for algorithmic regulation to gain acceptance by target populations, it requires 'explainable artificial intelligence' that builds on existing regulatory knowledge rather than on programmers' preferences (Miller et al, eg, highlight the risks of 'inmates running the asylum') (see also Danaher 2016). Similarly, by making 'algorithms' open to external scrutiny, one is also exposing vulnerabilities, therefore providing additional scope for exploiting diagnosed weaknesses. Table 8.1 below summarizes this discussion.

We started out by highlighting the supposed advantages of algorithmic regulation, as noted for instance by one of the earliest enthusiasts and advocates, O'Reilly (2013). Table 8.1 highlights the pluralities of ways in which machine learning algorithmic regulation might impact on the regulation of public services. In this section we stressed that the promises of, and enthusiasm for, algorithmic regulation needs

Table 8.1 Algorithmic regulation, regulation and contrasting worldviews

Increased contrived randomness + Makes gaming and corruption less feasible as regulators can process vast information flows rather than rely on key indicators – Complex and vast information reduces possibilities of detecting essential information/non-transparency of algorithms means lack of understanding of patterns	**Increased oversight** + Enhances risk-based assessments due to more fine-grained analysis and possibility of bespoke oversight – Considerable increases in intrusiveness and surveillance powers
Increased rivalry + Enhances possibility for ranking and benchmarking – Enhances vulnerability to gaming and corruption by bots and malware attacks	**Increased mutuality** + Enhances information for informed engagement – Increases dominance of data analyst over other kinds of professional (and other) knowledge

'+' denotes strengths and '-' denotes weaknesses

to be explored in the context of contrasting worldviews about the ways in which regulation is to be conducted. Such views include views about the preferred ways of organizing social relationships (in our case, relationships between regulatory and regulated actors). For regulatory agencies to develop a better understanding of the challenges of enhancing the adoption of algorithmic regulation, it is therefore essential to consider the underlying rationale(s) of regulating in the first place. To develop this argument further, the next section considers some of the central challenges of applying machine learning algorithms to the regulation of public services. We then turn to questions as to how to regulate regulators themselves.

3. Regulating Public Services *by* Algorithm

The potential for enhanced regulatory knowledge that enables more targeted regulation offers the prospect of a move away from 'governing by numbers' on the basis of predefined targets, concentration on assumed key factors, usually collected at set deadlines (P Miller 2001; Supiot 2015) to continuous 'governance by data' (Roberts-Holmes & Bradbury 2016). A reliance on 'big data'—the use of different databases built from tax returns, complaints data, social media commentary, and such like—offers the opportunity to move away from a reliance on predefined performance metrics towards bringing together different types of data. In other words, a future of machine learning algorithmic regulation seems to promise a world less preoccupied by 'hitting targets' (as noted by Bevan & Hood 2006), partly as monitoring is continuous and incorporating multiple data sources. This potentially reduces the scope for creative compliance-driven behaviours by individual organizations (as illustrated by Hood 2006). Furthermore, in an age of publicly available administrative data, the move towards machine learning algorithmic regulation might also imply a future of decentred regulators: rather than relying on regulatory agencies to assess performance, any programmer can draw on openly available data to develop performance scores (which in turn raises questions regarding certification and the role of 'public regulation').

In the following, we concentrate on three central administrative challenges affecting all regulatory approaches and all regulators: those of knowledge creation, of coordination and integration, and of ambiguity of objectives (ie desired outcomes). While by no means unique to algorithmic regulation, these three administrative problems are generic to algorithmic regulation and incorporate O'Reilly's (2013) enthusiasm for real time measurement, adjustment, and review of algorithms' performance, as well as desired clarity of outcomes. We consider each of the three administrative problems in turn, concentrating, again, on the context of regulating public services.

3.1 Knowledge Creation

Knowledge creation points to critical aspects that support the way in which algorithmic regulation can support enhanced 'intelligence'. Algorithms are said to introduce a particular 'knowledge logic', with its very own understandings of what knowledge is and what its most relevant components are (see eg Gillespie 2014). This concern with the 'knowledge logic' reflects on questions concerning the nature of the underlying data, and the ways in which the algorithm 'processes' these data and adjusts itself. For the practice of regulation, algorithmic regulation has particular attraction due to particular key properties of machine learning algorithms: they are self-executing on the basis of data, building on vast processing and storage capacities that facilitate new forms of comparison and knowledge creation. Machine learning algorithms learn from patterns emerging from different data sets, enabling, under certain conditions, prediction (we can guess which public service providers fail in one way or another), and allowing for imputation (we can infer missing data points from similar units).

In addition, 'governance by data' has the advantage of utilizing a number of different data sets, for example data drawn from social media platforms. As noted by Griffiths in this volume (Chapter 7), regulators can utilize unsolicited, open feedback from public service users, generated through social media, such as patient feedback voiced on twitter (see also Griffiths & Leaver 2018). Monitoring such unsolicited feedback is said to offer many advantages over administrative data: it is real-time, it reflects on many aspects of the service 'experience' along the 'production chain' (eg in hospitals, from car park, to hospital ward and operation theatre to morgue), and it bypasses the service providers' administrative processes, thereby also their ability to directly game the data. Indeed, studies have suggested that the analysis of social media commentary can successfully predict subsequent actual in-depth inspections in hospitals (Griffiths & Leaver 2018). Similarly, in the case of UK higher education, Griffiths and colleagues noted that an analysis of different forms of social media commentary, summarized in a 'collective judgement score', predicted the relative teaching quality classification of the various higher education providers (in terms of bronze, silver, and gold).[8]

In view of such extensions of regulatory oversight (and future imagining), critical issues apply to questions of the underlying data infrastructure: the quality of the data, the way in which machine learning algorithms operate, and the ways in which outputs of such calculations are utilized (see Yeung 2017; Kirkpatrick 2016). In other words, for machine algorithmic regulation to provide for meaningful regulatory oversight, a better understanding is required about the underlying data, their biases, the ways in which the underlying data are made 'algorithm-ready', and what data may, as a result, be 'excluded' from the analysis. It also involves an understanding of the underlying assumptions of the regulators about the regulated organizations, an understanding of the ways in which algorithms identify as 'relevant' certain factors rather than others (and therefore display potential bias), and then, finally, the ways in which regulators and regulated organizations respond to an increased reliance on regulation by algorithm.

The debate about algorithmic regulation has exhibited increasing concern with the quality of the data (see also Chapter 4 on digital discrimination in this volume), including potential biases. One challenge is that often data are missing as certain activities, individuals, organizations, or business models may not be covered by existing data-gathering activities (or where legal restrictions exist). There are also issues about what kind of data is obtainable and how in the process of 'making data algorithm ready', certain information is filtered out (see also Gillespie 2014).

As widely known, including certain crime data can lead to racially biased predictions, given the racial biases in the original data.[9] To mitigate racial or other biases, therefore, algorithms may require biased inputs so as to avoid highly undesirable and divisive outcomes in terms of regulatory interventions. However, reliance on 'discrimination-aware' data mining is in itself problematic, as suppressing certain biases might be regarded as insufficient (or might be criticized for being politically motivated).

---

[8] See <https://www.qaa.ac.uk/docs/qaa/about-us/the-wisdom-of-students-monitoring-quality-through-student-reviews.pdf> accessed 4 June 2019.

[9] For example, in the context of predictive policing it has been suggested that including certain crime data would encourage biased prediction, given the racial biases in the original data. Even where race-related indicators were removed, algorithms quickly identified proxies for race and therefore displayed similar biased outcomes <https://www.technologyreview.com/s/602933/how-to-hold-algorithms-accountable/> accessed 21 October 2018. See also Kirkpatrick (2017) and Feller et al (2016).

Even if technical fixes to deal with 'biases' were available, it is nevertheless a question to what extent regulators can and should legitimately use them. As (usually) non-majoritarian bodies, regulators face the challenge of how to choose what data to 'scrub', how to compensate for under-representation of the 'weak' and over-representation of the 'powerful', especially in terms of defining what type of distribution should be defined as 'desirable'. Such challenges are not new to regulators, for example, in terms of school league-tabling where there have been moves away from measuring pure exam grade outcomes to 'relative performance' given certain student profiles. Such choices are inherently political choices, and it is therefore questionable whether regulators should be engaged in such choices in the first place (or let non-transparent algorithms make the choice for them). The challenge for regulators is not only to identify biases in the data, but to decide whether and how to address these biases, especially as data or algorithms are likely to be biased in some way or another. Hence, what might be seen as essential are models that highlight such discriminatory or biased patterns so as to encourage discussion and learning (Berendt & Preibusch 2014; Hajian et al 2016; Hajian & Domingo-Ferrer 2013; Zemel et al 2013). Indeed, such an approach is arguably more suitable for the context of regulation than simply stripping out sensitive features from data. Such stripping is neither desirable nor always feasible, if alone because of the tendency of organizations (and individuals) to over-estimate their levels of openness (ie transparency) vis-a-vis others (Weller 2017: 60).

An overlapping challenge with regards to knowledge creation relates to understanding the workings of the algorithm itself.[10] As noted in studies on predictive policing and sentencing (Starr 2014), no algorithm is 'unbiased' (Bozdag 2013; Friedman & Nissenbaum 1996; Noble 2018). Initial default settings matter and, as noted, so do the sources of information available for updating. The unique— and therefore distinct—feature of machine learning algorithmic regulation is 'learning': within the constraints of a model, these algorithms update themselves in light of incoming data, and they also update the underlying assumptions on the basis of knowledge created by the algorithms themselves. As these algorithms are no longer strictly rule-based, the task for regulators (and other organizations) is how to understand the ways in which algorithms 'learn' within these models. As Burrell highlights,

> there are certain challenges of scale and complexity that are distinctive to machine learning algorithms. These challenges relate not simply to total number of lines or pages of code, the number of team members on the engineering team, and the multitude of interlinkages between modules or subroutines. These are

---

[10] Usually the problem of inappropriate 'training data' combines biases emerging from both the data from which the algorithm learns and the statistical rules applied by the algorithm itself.

challenges not just of reading and comprehending code, but being able to understand the algorithm in action, operating on data. (Burrell 2016: 5)

Understanding 'the algorithm in action', in particular its updating, is often not immediately accessible to observers, including those that created the initial codes. Thus, machine learning models are accused of being opaque, non-intuitive, and therefore difficult to comprehend, especially to those on the receiving end of regulatory decision-making. To address these concerns (accentuated by the EU's General Data Protection Regulation), 'explainable' algorithms have been put forward, namely in the form of decision trees or requirements that the logic of the algorithm's decision-making can be traced back in terms of broad decision-making parameters. At minimum, this might require transparency of the initial programme (in terms of 'traceability' also to the programmer), the types of data that the algorithm has been exposed to, and over-time performance (see Miller et al 2017; Holzinger et al 2017).

A reliance on such 'explainable' machine learning algorithms is particularly critical for regulators in a legal context of a right to an explanation, as regulated organizations are (understandably) prone to challenging particular regulatory decisions and it is unlikely that they will easily consent to decisions made by an algorithm, even on the basis of 'decision trees': Explainable approaches are one thing, they also need to be accompanied by acceptable levels of explanation, namely a type of explanation that is comprehensible to those at the receiving end of regulatory activity and not just to those (usually male) professional programmers who built the models underpinning machine learning algorithmic regulation (see also Yeung, Chapter 2 in this volume).

Whether explanations based on broad logics of the algorithm's decision-making are sufficient in case of controversies with regulated organizations is also debatable and raises questions as to what the consequences are of particular algorithmic decision-making. For regulators, such issues regarding algorithms are central to questions about accountability and legitimacy. Using algorithmic regulation points to certain limits on conditions of 'transparency'. At best, traceability implies that 'explainable artificial intelligence' can offer *ex post* rationalizations of decisions taken or recommended.

The challenge for regulators is not just that they should understand how their own systems are working, but that their decisions (based on algorithmic decision-making) are accepted by target populations and that explanations can be made available for external scrutiny (see also Weller 2017). However, as replication is problematic, it is questionable who can be held accountable for regulatory outputs and outcomes, especially as a transparent initial code cannot be seen as 'programmed' to make decisions down the line. It also makes the task of continued updating, in terms of 'debugging' and ensuring continued relevance, problematic as responsibilities are not clearly defined. This is particularly challenging in the organizational context of regulators where particular views of a 'situation' will be inevitably affected by confirmation bias and therefore discount challenges to the ongoing validity of the algorithm. One response is to rely on varying algorithms to 'check' on each other—either by running them in parallel or in hierarchical relationship to each other. However, such a system reduces the goal of obtaining unique 'predictive' regulatory forecasting and therefore is likely to destabilize regulatory organizations' internal learning functions. The broader question of explanation and evaluation of algorithms where 'numerical data' need to be turned back into 'meaning facts' (Kelly & McGoey 2018) therefore accentuates an existing regulatory challenge, namely ambivalence about the actual degree to which regulatory interventions contribute to achieving certain outcomes.

In sum, we do not argue that questions of quality and bias in the data or the opaque nature of the algorithm are unknown to practitioners and students of algorithmic regulation. We argue, however, that an agenda that puts an emphasis on 'debiasing' and 'explainable' approaches places particular challenges on regulatory organizations in view of their mandate of overseeing *public* services and their nature of (usually) being unelected bodies.

3.2 Coordination and Integration

One further key challenge in contemporary regulation is information exchange and coordination. As regulators are increasingly interested in exploiting diverse data sets, created by other agencies, questions about how to arrange for coordination of data exchange are likely to become ever more pertinent. Examples of such data-sharing do exist, but ultimately also highlighted the limited degree to which the scope for such cross-agency coordination has been exploited so far (see also Office for Statistics Regulation 2018). While for some the prospect of algorithmic regulation points to a future of limited regulatory 'bureaucracy', the way in which algorithmic regulation is being introduced into existing regulatory regimes requires not just working together across regulatory and other organizations, but also integration within regulatory organizations.

First of all, joining up data sets (such as legal transactions and complaints data) from different regulatory bodies encounters considerable problems (even if these agencies are in friendly, non-rivalrous relations with each other).[11] One problem is that the information gathered might not be aligned time-wise, or that they are recorded in different ways, therefore making comparability challenging. Such issues about different types of data gathering by regulated institutions apply, for example,

---

[11] The problem of coordination across regulatory bodies is therefore somewhat different to the problem of obtaining data from third parties by machine learning algorithm programmers where the initial basis of the data collection is not transparent.

to healthcare.[12] In the English NHS, healthcare providers report differently on aspects of their operation, therefore, making comparison and data analysis problematic. In addition, there are also concerns about the need to write highly legalistic memorandums of understandings so as to ensure that one set of regulators do not use data from another regulator that the latter may not feel comfortable with (as it may, eg, disturb its relationship with its target population of regulated organizations) (see also Laurie & Stevens 2016). For the regulatory use of algorithmic regulation this raises the challenge of resisting the temptation of throwing together incompatible sets of data or of underestimating the legal minefield associated with an exchange of data across regulators.

Second, integrating algorithmic regulation within existing regulatory regimes is not just about establishing memorandums of understanding over access and use of data, it is also about managing internal organizational challenges. The rise of algorithmic regulation gives rise to a new type of regulatory analyst. This is, arguably, the age of the forensic data analyst and programmer rather than the age of the lawyer, economist, or accountant. Apart from specifying what exactly the competency profile of a data forensic regulatory analyst might be, altering regulatory capacities by emphasizing one set of professional competencies over another is never unproblematic as it challenges existing role understandings and power structures.

Furthermore, data-driven predictive analysis clashes with the logic of human-led inspection styles that suggest that insights can mostly be gained from 'getting a feel' for a regulated organization. There is the organizational challenge of bringing together different sources of information and styles of control, and ensuring coordination of these when exercising oversight. In other words, coordination capacities are required to bring together data from different organizations, while delivery capacity (ie the exercise of regulatory activity) needs to be linked to data analysis in order to support the running of regulatory infrastructures. In such an organizational environment, there is the risk of either insulating algorithm-driven data analysis from other regulatory activities, or that algorithms come to dominate conversations within regulatory organizations, thereby potentially undermining alternative sources of knowledge and expertise. This is particularly problematic for regulatory enforcement, regardless of the promises of 'quantitative regulatory prediction'. For one, regulatory inspection of smaller providers has been widely recognized not to be of a 'detection' but of an advisory kind (Fairman & Yapp 2005). Small providers do not have the capacities to formally learn the latest regulatory requirements. As a result, human inspection regimes are not so much about the detection of actualized risk, it is about learning and advice, thereby also generating the knowledge base for emerging risks (such as new business models). It is questionable whether pure reliance on 'big data' would offer such educational benefits

[12] <https://www.mobihealthnews.com/content/interoperability-challenges-slow-down-machine-learning-healthcare> accessed 21 October 2018.

to small (low risk) providers and whether emerging risks would be detected given that these risks emerge in areas where data (intentionally or non-intentionally) are not 'algorithm-ready' (eg due to lack of registration or licensing).

A third, related coordination and integration challenge for regulators is what to do with the results produced by algorithms. A reliance on algorithmic regulation may aggravate tensions within regulatory bodies and between regulators and the regulated as 'letting the data speak for themselves' does not offer an explanation as to why such patterns necessarily may lead to observed effects, as noted above. A reliance on 'letting the data speak for themselves' is also seen as risking a decline in professionalism. Although it usually is suggested that reliance on 'algorithmic regulation' (and the promise of more refined detection and prediction) is supposed to enable humans to concentrate on the 'important' issues and objectives, the more likely outcome is that organizations will focus on the 'results' proposed by the algorithm itself, that is, even where humans are supposed to make a final evaluative choice based on the information provided by algorithmic calculations, the bias within organizations will be to encourage acceptance of machine-learnt recommendations rather than reflection. Indeed, it is likely that 'objecting' to such results will be actively discouraged. Therefore, even where algorithmic decision-making is subject to final human judgement, it is questionable whether such 'judging' will not simply accept the 'recommendations' of the supposedly superior technology. Such 'automation bias' has been widely diagnosed in the context of humans operating in systems characterized by a large degree of automated decision-making. It applies however more broadly to regulatory decision-making, for example in the context of Regulatory Impact Assessments: Discussions focus on the 'conclusion' or 'result' of a calculation, rather than the process in which this number or conclusion has been derived.

To illustrate, in the context of regulating public services, the emergence of a 'raw risk score' on the basis of machine learning (or any other technique) produces a probability of a forthcoming inspection revealing problems. In doing so, it provides regulators with the belief that such scoring systems enhance their capacity to identify performance problems in a timely and precise manner. However, such raw risk scores usually come with a reliability specified in percentage terms ('With 63% certainty, it can be predicted that a set number of schools identified as being a risk of decline are actually found to be in decline during an inspection'). For regulators, the question arises whether such reliability measures are sufficient or require improvement, especially also in view of their accountability to different audiences. Furthermore, it raises questions, as noted earlier, about the quality of the underlying data, on the one hand, and the quality of actual inspection on the other. Such scores also impact on actual inspections: once officials are aware of such raw risk scores, this awareness introduces biases into the actual inspection. In addition, relying on such scores brings with it the risk of excluding the actual participants from the regulatory process. Such exclusion is particularly problematic in public services where 'high performing' public services are associated with high levels of individual professional responsibility and engagement, such as in healthcare.

Finally, regulating by algorithm raises issues about internal risk management within regulatory organizations (and organizations more generally). In particular, it raises the question at what level decisions are being 'automated' (ie left to machine learning computers) and where humans are being left in charge, whether it is by individual assessment or by requiring machine learning systems to offer 'recommendations' for final human decision-making. Students of organizational behaviour would suggest that such decisions will be shaped by an institution's concerns about its core mission, reputation, and legal liability (see Wilson 1989). Accordingly, algorithms would be put in the driving seat for issues of perceived secondary importance (as individual error is seen as being reversible and of limited risk to the organization itself), whereas humans will grant themselves authority over issues deemed of primary importance.[13] In the context of a regulated organization, this would mean, for example, that higher education institutions would solely rely on algorithms to select undergraduate students, but would require humans to make choices when it came to the selection of research-level/PhD-level applications. Such bifurcated treatments might be explained away in terms of administrative feasibility and efficacy, but they introduce their own discriminatory biases (that are inherent in all human decision-making as well). For regulators, such decisions become even more complex as 'predictive quality' regarding the 'best option' not necessarily overlaps with perceptions of public legitimacy and concerns about the need for deliberation.

3.3 Ambiguity over Objectives

One of the promises of algorithmic regulation is said to lie in its capacity to facilitate more outcome-focused regulation. However, public services are rarely 'production-type agencies' with well-defined and measurable outputs and outcomes (as defined by Wilson 1989) where clear or at least persuasive causal relationships between inputs and outcomes exist. Institutions such as hospitals and educational organizations are complex. They are based on multiple parallel processes (some tightly, other loosely coupled), based on ambiguous understandings of what 'safety' and 'quality' entail. Here, regulators are confronted, in many cases, with 'wicked problems'—problems that relate to value choices, where their solution inherently means having to trade one set of interests and concerns off for the interests of others (Rittel & Webber 1973). It also means that certain key outcomes are not associated with single indicators. Such concerns have, for example, been

---

[13] Ironically, given the claim that algorithms eliminate human error, the reverse order may be more appropriate with machines dealing with the 'important' issues.

raised by debates about 'quality' as a regulatory outcome goal. Measuring 'customer satisfaction' as an indicator of 'quality' in the context of health or education cannot therefore merely rely on individual users' views about their current experience, it has to be placed in the context of much wider and long-term effects,[14] leading to difficult choices as to how to select data.

Finally, there are questions about the impact of algorithmic regulation on the identity and reputation of regulators and regulated organizations. Both sides will inevitably be in tension between the permanent wish for 'more' and 'better' data by regulators and the concern among regulated organizations, first, not to be exposed to continuous data collection, and, second, not to suddenly be identified as an outlier as additional data has been added. This, in turn, is likely to affect the underlying understandings of what 'quality' (for example) might mean, shifting it to understandings that appear 'verifiable' through algorithmic regulation.

In conclusion, the promise of algorithm regulation, as formulated by O'Reilly (2013), encounters distinct challenges for regulators that fundamentally affect understandings about their appropriate role in legitimate governing and therefore concern also questions about the possibility of account-giving when the account-holder is ill-defined. Concerns about knowledge creation highlight questions about data, real-time measurement and updating by algorithms as well as evaluation, whereas ambiguity over public service objectives stands in the way of the advocated promise of 'clarity' over outcomes. Moreover, discussions of algorithmic regulation have, as yet, paid only limited attention to questions of coordination and integration. In other words, the challenges for regulation by algorithm are not about 'better technology' and 'more data', they are about developing appropriate ways of regulating, integrating, and coordinating machine learning algorithms within the broader context of the organization of regulation, given dispersion of regulatory functions and data. Ultimately, this is about the assurance of legitimacy in governing.

4. Who Regulates the Algorithms?

Much interest has been paid to regulating algorithmic regulation in the context of private parties as well as in the context of administrative data. Less attention has been paid to the ways in which the regulators themselves should be regulated. Such a 'who guards the guardians' discussion is, of course, well established in the context of (usually legal) discussions about the role of supposedly independent regulatory bodies that are outside of immediate channels of parliamentary accountability. In the context of algorithmic regulation, however, it offers an opportunity to bring

---

[14] In health, it might be about future complications or 'quality of life' indicators; in education, it is, in a narrow sense, about opportunities in contributing to society, not just in the labour market.

together debates about 'laws of robotics' with traditional regulation debates about 'quis custodiet ipsos custodes?' (Balkin 2017; Pasquale 2017).

Given the growing ubiquity of algorithmic regulation in the context of regulators' activities, the challenge for regulators is to establish understandings for some of the key questions noted above. These relate to questions of bias, perceived fairness of decision-making, explainability of machine learning algorithms, both in terms of transparency and presumed causality, reliability of the decision-making based on such algorithms, and continued external 'debugging' so as to ensure the algorithms remain 'in control' and uncorrupted.[15]

In the context of regulatory activity, some of these well-known concerns are arguably more problematic than in other settings. As noted, one concern relates to the transparency of the way in which algorithms 'learn' and about the ways in which information is gathered, especially given the often insidious nature in which information (administrative and private data) is collected as users consent to highly complex 'conditions of service' that reduce their capacity to control the way 'their' data is being used and connected. At what point this concern translates into ways in which regulators are able to draw on and utilize information (such as social media communication, administrative, or private data) has received less attention in view of the much larger concern about the power of private networks utilizing algorithmic regulation for commercial purposes. Nevertheless, the boundary lines between privately provided services, public services, and regulatory interest are inherently blurred, whether it is about accessing private information about communication flows, or questions concerning national security. Furthermore, in the context of data protection laws, there is also the question about what happens once regulators have obtained data—are they to be used for clearly defined purposes only to be deleted immediately afterwards, or are data going to be stored for potential future uses?

So, what can be done about 'regulating the regulators' use of algorithmic regulation'? Without seeking to offer a fully exhaustive set of options, we consider four in particular (drawing also on accounts discussed above, such as 'explainable AI'):

One is the creation of centralised oversight that seeks to develop professional standards specifically for algorithmic regulation by regulatory bodies and that seeks to regulate their actual practice. This might involve the direct auditing of algorithms used by regulatory bodies or simply the checking on internal testing exercises to deal with bias concerns. Recent debates about regulating algorithmic regulation have advocated the creation of such bodies more generally, usually in view of the use of data by public sector bodies. For example, the House of Commons Science and Technology Select Committee supported in its *Algorithms in Decision-Making* report (House of Commons 2018) the creation of an advisory 'Centre for Data Ethics

---

[15] See also Copeland (2018).

& Innovation', largely however dealing with the activities of service providers than regulators themselves (appointments to this body began in 2018).

A second way of regulating regulators' use of algorithmic regulation would be to create procedures (on the lines of the UK Cabinet Office's 'Data Science Ethics Framework'[16]): requiring specific ways of dealing with bias as well as 'explainable' algorithms as well as prescribing ways to 'de-discriminate' algorithmic regulation. This would support the idea that regulators are bound by certain minimum conditions on which they can be held to account and through which they make their activities somewhat open for external scrutiny.

Somewhat overlapping is a third option, namely to prescribe maximum transparency on the operations of algorithmic regulation. This making open to external scrutiny would potentially encourage competition between different algorithms (from private and regulatory sources) and therefore highlight areas of potential bias. It would also require an emphasis on making algorithms 'explainable' (eg Miller et al 2017).

A fourth, and final, way is to rely on disciplinary standards. As other professions, regulatory data forensics staff may be difficult to regulate in terms of 'procedure' or '*ex post*' as their activities (and those of the algorithms they have programmed) are difficult to monitor. Traditional inspectors have 'fiduciary duties' and it might therefore be also required to impose such fiduciary obligations on programmers of algorithms. This therefore might be a case for '*ex ante*' regulation in the forms of training and the development of professional norms (see House of Commons 2018: Chapter 3).

5. Implications

The rise of the 'regulatory state' has been associated with the appeal of regulatory organizations and technologies in terms of promising greater expertise, consistency, regularity, and, therefore, predictability (see Moran 2003). Regulating via algorithmic regulation offers an extension of the very same promises. Regulating by algorithm promises the 'magic' technological solutionist way of regularizing regulation, in view of the existing uncertainty about the appropriateness of regulatory standards for achieving desired outcomes, concern about existing information-gathering, and criticism about the under- and over-inclusiveness of enforcement activities. Whether such a rise of 'quantitative regulatory prediction' offers such a future is, however, doubtful, especially in the 'wicked issue' world of regulation of public services.

Who beyond the world of rent-seeking consultancies, then, benefits from a future of regulatory use of algorithmic regulation? This chapter points to the organizational

---

[16] <https://www.gov.uk/government/publications/data-ethics-framework/data-ethics-framework> accessed 11 September 2018.

and relational effects of regulators using machine learning algorithms to inform their oversight functions, thereby moving beyond the more extensive interest in the impact of algorithmic regulation by private and public bodies on individuals. The move from 'governing by numbers' to 'governance by data' points to a future where regulators have access to additional capacities to inform their practices, but they also face a future where alternative providers might use publicly available data to perform similar league-tabling and benchmarking activities.

This chapter has used existing debates surrounding algorithmic regulation to focus on implications for regulators. Questions of bias and 'explanation' cannot merely be answered by a reliance on technical solutions, but need to be understood in the context of understandings of legitimate use of state power. Whether the technical ambition for 'more data' and 'better algorithms' can also be contained within the constraints of constitutional orders, in terms of protecting individual-level data, administrative-legal constraints, and competing understandings regarding appropriate enforcement styles is questionable and requires further attention in the worlds of practice and research.

For regulated organizations, a future of being overseen by algorithmic regulation promises a future of less inconsistent inspection regimes. However, at the same time, the risk of stigmatization exists if the award of a 'bad' score is not associated with recourse to transparent standards, appropriate explanation, and potential reversal. The more algorithmic regulation seeks to move into the direction of greater transparency and explainability, the more vulnerable the algorithm becomes to exploitation and gaming. In addition, the more regulators consent to such openness, the more they lose the reputational gains of relying on an 'impartial' quantitative predicting tool.

A standard response to emerging policy problems associated with technologies is to call for enhanced ethics, sustained oversight, and appropriate legal frameworks to establish procedural standards and prescribe degrees of scrutiny (as noted in the previous section). The field of algorithmic regulation in general lacks all of these. To advance the agenda to deal with ethical, legal, and oversight challenges within the regulation of public services is highly demanding as legal powers of the analogue world are stretched into the cyberworld, where short-term commercial and disciplinary incentives stand in the way of long-term ethical self-restraint, and where adequate jurisdictional boundaries are difficult to define.

Bibliography

Balkin J, The Three Laws of Robotics in the Age of Big Data' (2017) 78 Ohio State Law Journal 1217.

Berendt B and Preibusch S, 'Better Decision Support through Exploratory Discrimination-Aware Data Mining: Foundations and Empirical Evidence' (2014) 22(2) Artificial Intelligence and Law 175.

Bevan G and Hood C, 'What's Measured is what Matters: Targets and Gaming in the English Public Health Care System' (2006) 84(3) Public Administration 517.

Black J, 'Critical Reflections on Regulation' (2002a) 27 Australian Journal of Legal Philosophy 1.

Black J, 'Regulatory Conversations' (2002b) 29(1) Journal of Law and Society 163.

boyd d and Crawford K, 'Critical Questions for Big Data' (2011) 15(5) Information, Communication & Society 662.

Bozdag E, 'Bias in Algorithmic Filtering and Personalization' (2013) 15(3) Ethics of Information Technology 209.

Burrell J, 'How the Machine 'Thinks': Understanding Opacity in Machine Learning Algorithms' (2016) January–June 2016 Big Data and Society 1.

Cohen MD, March JG, and Olsen JP, 'A Garbage Can Model of Organizational Choice' (1972) 17(1) Administrative Science Quarterly 1.

Copeland E, '10 Principles for Public Sector Use of Algorithmic Decision Making' (2018) <https://www.nesta.org.uk/blog/10-principles-for-public-sector-use-of-algorithmic-decision-making/> accessed 31 October 2018.

Danaher J, 'The Threat of Algocracy' (2016) 29 Philosophy and Technology 245.

Douglas M and Wildavsky A, *Risk and Culture* (University of California Press 1982).

Fairman R and Yapp C, 'Enforced Self-Regulation, Prescription, and Conceptions of Compliance within Small Businesses: The Impact of Enforcement' (2005) 27(4) Law & Policy 491.

Feller A, Pierson E, Corbett-Davies S, et al, 'A Computer Program Used for Bail and Sentencing Decisions was Labeled Biased against Blacks. It's Actually Not that Clear' *Washington Post* (17 October 2016) <http://www.cs.yale.edu/homes/jf/Feller.pdf> accessed 31 October 2018.

Friedman B and Nissenbaum HF, 'Bias in Computer Systems' (1996) 14(3) ACM Transactions on Information Systems (TOIS) 330.

Gillespie T, 'The Relevance of Algorithms' in T Gillespie, P Boczkowski, and K Foot (eds), *Media Technologies* (MIT Press 2014).

Griffiths A and Leaver M, 'Wisdom of Patients: Predicting the Quality of Care Using Aggregated Patient Feedback' (2018) 27 British Medical Journal: Quality and Safety 110.

Hajian S and Domingo-Ferrer J, 'A Methodology for Direct and Indirect Discrimination Prevention in Data Mining' Paper presented at the IEEE Transactions on Knowledge and Data Engineering (2013).

Hajian S, Bonchi F, and Castillo C, 'Algorithmic Bias: From Discrimination Discovery to Fairness-Aware Data Mining' Paper presented at the Proceedings of the 22nd ACM SIGKDD International Conference on Knowledge Discovery and Data Mining (2016).

Hildebrandt M, 'Algorithmic Regulation and the Rule of Law' (2018) Philosophical Transactions A doi: 10.1098/rsta.2017.0355.

Holzinger A, Biemann C, Pattichis C, et al, 'What Do We Need to Build Explainable AI Systems for the Medical Domain' (2017) arXiv:1712.09923 accessed 21 October 2018.

Hood C, *The Art of the State: Culture, Rhetoric, and Public Management* (Clarendon Press 1998).

Hood C, 'Gaming in Targetworld' (2006) 66(4) Public Administration Review 515.

Hood C, Scott C, James O, et al, *Regulation inside Government* (Oxford University Press 1999).

Hood C, James O, Peters GB, et al (eds), *Controlling Modern Government: Variety, Commonality and Change* (Edward Elgar 2004).

House of Commons, *Science and Technology Select Committee—Algorithms in Decision-making* (HC 351 2018).

Kelly AH and McGoey L, 'Facts, Power and Global Evidence: A New Empire of Truth' (2018) 47(1) Economy and Society 1.

Kirkpatrick K, 'Battling Algorithmic Bias' (2016) 59(10) Communications of the ACM doi: 10.1145/2983270.

Kirkpatrick K, 'It's Not the Algorithm, It's the Data' (2017) 60(2) Communications of the ACM 21.

Koop C and Lodge M, 'Exploring the Co-ordination of Economic Regulation' (2014) 21(9) Journal of European Public Policy 1311.

Koop C and Lodge M, 'What is Regulation? An Interdisciplinary Concept Analysis' (2017) 11 Regulation and Governance 95.

Laurie G and Stevens L, 'Developing a Public Interest Mandate for the Governance and Use of Administrative Data in the United Kingdom' (2016) 43(4) Journal of Law and Society 360.

Lodge M and Wegrich K, *Managing Regulation: Regulatory Analysis, Politics and Policy* (Palgrave Macmillan 2012).

Lodge M, Wegrich K, and McElroy G, 'Dodgy Kebabs Everywhere? Variety of Worldviews And Regulatory Change' (2010) 88(1) Public Administration 247.

Medina E, 'Rethinking Algorithmic Regulation' (2015) 44(6/7) Kybernetes 1005.

Miller P, 'Governing by Numbers: Why Calculative Practices Matter' (2001) 68(2) Social Research 379.

Miller T, Howe P, and Sonenberg L, 'Explainable AI: Beware of Inmates Running the Asylum' Paper presented at the Workshop on Explainable AI (XAI) Vol 36 (2017).

Moran M, *The British Regulatory State* (Oxford University Press 2003).

Noble SU, *Algorithms of Oppression: How Search Engines Reinforce Racism* (New York University Press 2018).

Office for Statistics Regulation, 'Joining Up Data for Better Decisions' (September 2018) <https://www.statisticsauthority.gov.uk/wp-content/uploads/2018/09/Data-Linkage-Joining-Up-Data.pdf> accessed 23 October 2018.

Oldroyd RA, Morris MA, and Birkin M, 'Identifying Methods for Monitoring Foodborne Illness' (2018) JMIR Public Health Surveillance doi: 10.2196/publichealth.8218.

O'Reilly T, 'Open Data and Algorithmic Regulation' in B Goldstein and L Dyson (eds), *Beyond Transparency: Open Data and the Future of Civic Innovation* (Code for America 2013).

Pasquale F, 'Towards a Fourth Law of Robotics: Preserving Attribution, Responsibility, and Explainability in an Algorithmic Society' (2017) 78 Ohio State Law Journal 1243.

Rittel H and Webber M, 'Dilemmas in a General Theory of Planning' (1973) 4(2) Policy Sciences 155.

Roberts-Holmes G and Bradbury A, 'Governance, Accountability and the Datafication of Early Years Education in England' (2016) 42(4) British Educational Research Journal 600.

Starr S, 'The Risk Assessment Era: An Overdue Debate' (2014) 27(4) Federal Sentencing Reporter 205.

Supiot A, *La Gouvernance par les nombres* (Fayard 2015).

Weller A, 'Challenges for Transparency' (2017) <https://arxiv.org/abs/1708.01870> accessed 14 September 2018.

Wildavsky A and Thompson M, 'A Cultural Theory of Information Bias in Organizations' (1986) 23(3) Journal of Management Studies 273.

Wilson JQ, *Bureaucracy* (Basic Books 1989).

Yeung K, Algorithmic Regulation: A Critical Interrogation' (2017) Regulation and Governance doi:10.1111/rego.12158.

Zemel R, Wu Y, Swersky K, et al, 'Learning Fair Representations' Paper presented at the International Conference on Machine Learning (2013).

PART III
GOVERNING ALGORITHMIC SYSTEMS

9

Algorithms, Regulation, and Governance Readiness

Leighton Andrews

1. Introduction

Algorithmic accountability—embracing such issues as artificial intelligence (AI), cloud computing, 'big data', and machine learning—has risen up the public agenda in recent years, with a range of reports and inquiries emanating from international agencies, government scientists and government departments, legislative committees, think-tanks, and academic bodies (Cath et al 2018; Council of Europe 2017; Data and Society 2018; Executive Office of the President 2016; House of Commons 2018; House of Lords 2018; Mulgan 2016; Royal Society and British Academy 2017; Walport 2013 and 2016. As Amoore (2017) suggests, two factors have largely driven these issues into the public domain: the availability of 'big data' has transformed the ways algorithms can be designed, trained, and executed; and the 'exponential' rise in the use of algorithms with an element of automation or machine learning. Proposals have been made for a variety of technical, governance, regulatory, legislative, and institutional approaches or solutions (House of Commons 2017; Andrews 2017). Ethical factors have been prominent in discussions (Mittelstadt et al 2016). Governments, local, regional, and national, have made use of algorithms in regulatory governance systems, not least for 'risk-based prioritization' for agency resource allocation purposes, as has been systematically documented and analysed (Yeung 2018). Veale et al (2018) point out that public sector practitioners deploying these systems 'are facing immediate, value laden challenges'. Algorithmic decision-making and AI are often discussed together. Wachter says 'The most important thing is to recognise the similarities between algorithms, AI and robotics' (Turing 2017): indeed, the recent House of Commons report on 'Algorithms in Decision-Making' often moves seamlessly between discussions of algorithms and AI (House of Commons 2018a).

The potential benefits of algorithmic analysis are frequently raised, sometimes uncritically, in media reports of their use in a variety of domains. Few would challenge the potential benefits of using algorithmic analysis to identify patterns in medical data which might lead to an assessment of likely preponderance for risk of dementia, provided privacy is protected and premature decision avoided

(Lay 2018), but there are algorithmic failures, such as that identified by the UK Secretary of State for Health, which resulted in failures to call women for breast cancer screening who should have been flagged as at risk (Hansard 2018). The undoubted but limited success of training a computer to beat chess or Go champions, in which moves undertaken by the machine seemed counter-intuitive to human experts, and whose rationale may have been obvious only to the machine itself (House of Commons 2018a), has reinforced fears of an apocalyptic world in which human decision-making is overridden by superior machine decision-making, which may be something of a deflection from the real concerns about corporate and state misuse of these technologies in the here and now (Chollet 2018; House of Lords 2018).

Two broad concerns have begun to be articulated by researchers, policy-makers, and others: the first set of concerns relates to the existing use of algorithmically based systems developed by corporations or governments. Evidence is regularly being surfaced that many such systems may raise significant ethical challenges, or even undermine existing laws, including laws on human rights, equality, and discrimination, either consciously or unconsciously, or that they may be used by hostile foreign actors to undermine democracy or state security. The second set of concerns relates to future developments: that the advent of machine learning, with the development of algorithms which train on massive inputs of data, and develop their own rules for determining their decisions and judgements subsequently, could lead to a dystopian future in which human intelligence and human life will be undermined or controlled by intelligent, decision-making machines who set their own rules and codes of behaviour.

Implicit in much of the political, policy, and media commentary about these issues are questions of power and the ability of government and civic society to shape policies and rules in respect of algorithms. As well as governments themselves, powerful private actors are in the business of creating algorithms and developing AI. There is an asymmetrical balance of information, resource, and power creating an environment in which these powerful private actors are able to determine the discourse around these issues. So, for example, Google has announced its own ethical framework for the development of AI (Pichai 2018). Meanwhile, a senior executive of Facebook has been actively involved in the shaping of UK government policy responses to AI (DBEIS/DDCMS 2018). (It should be stated that he was working for a different company when his original work for the UK government was published: Hall and Pesenti 2017.) Facebook also presented at 'a private, introductory seminar on algorithms' for the House of Commons Science and Technology Committee (House of Commons 2018).

This chapter takes the UK as its subject of analysis, and asks how prepared are public administrators and political leaders for the challenges of algorithmic decision-making and AI: in other words, what is the state of governance readiness? These challenges are now being encountered at multiple levels of government: internationally, at national, devolved nation or English regional level, and at the local government level. The challenges in each domain may overlap or may be different. This is a new and emergent field, raising novel questions for public administrators and political leaders. Ethical considerations are proceeding even as algorithmic systems are being utilized. Yet some of the issues raised may have a longer pedigree, bound up in older questions which pre-date the emergence of the newer technologies of cloud computing, big data, and machine learning. Concerns about biases in computer systems for judgements on employment offers, for example, are at least thirty years old. Indeed, the British Medical Journal published an article in 1988 about how a computer program for evaluating potential applicants to St George's Hospital Medical School in London discriminated against women and those with non-European sounding names, and had been found guilty of so doing by the then Commission for Racial Equality (CRE). The CRE recommendations then could have come from evidence to any relevant political enquiry today:

> It is emphasised that where a computer program is used as part of the selection process all members of staff taking part have a responsibility to find out what it contains. A major criticism of the staff at St George's was that many had no idea of the contents of the program and those who did failed to report the bias. All staff participating in selection should be trained so that they are aware of the risk of discrimination and try to eliminate it. (BMJ 1988)

More and more examples of algorithmic bias are coming to light (Pasquale 2015; O'Neil 2016; Noble 2018). The scale and speed of modern systems may simply be amplifying older questions on the one hand and rearticulating fears culturally embedded in science fiction narratives on the other.

The chapter begins by examining the literature on governance readiness and administrative capacity. It considers whether this literature is adequate to the task of identifying such capacity issues in a context where the discourse is dominated by the larger technology companies—collectively often described as 'Big Tech'—and raises the question of whether 'discursive capacity' is a requirement for governance readiness in this area. It then sets out evidence gathered from empirical research on algorithmic harms and the consideration that has been given to these issues in the political sphere. The chapter then discusses the state of administrative capacity at multiple levels of governance in the UK and concludes by setting out questions which might guide further research.

2. Governance Readiness

Lodge and Wegrich (2014a) examine issues of administrative capacity and identify the challenge of *governance readiness*. They define governance as 'the interdependent co-production of policies among state and non-state actors across different levels'. Governance readiness, they say, 'requires the presence of agreed goals and objectives that inform the identification of problems and the type of responses to address these problems, the presence of appropriate tools to identify challenges and problems, and the presence of a range of resources to address these problems'. They highlight four governance capacities—'the kind of actual competencies we expect bureaucracies to have': delivery, regulatory, coordination, and analytical. They explain these further: 'delivery capacities deal with affecting the front-line of policy ... regulatory capacities are required to conduct oversight over activities ... coordination capacities are required to bring dispersed constituencies together; and analytical capacities address demands on forecasting and intelligence that inform policy making'.

They note that contemporary governance challenges are often said to be 'wicked problems' which are 'characterised by contestation over the definition of the actual problem and over solutions' which may themselves create new problems. The specificity of the problem means that learning is difficult and solutions hard to replicate (Lodge and Wegrich 2014a). They do not consider leadership, though they are emphatic in their recognition of the political dimension to public administration, whereas Carr (2016) has suggested that political leadership in the 'information age' requires understanding that politics can shape technology. Assessing governance readiness in the context of algorithmic decision-making requires us to consider what will this mean for public leaders, public bodies, and regulatory authorities. For Head and Alford (2015) decisions on problem definition and solution identification also depend on stakeholder perspectives—in other words, technical issues are only part of the discussion. There are not only 'cognitive-analytical challenges but also communicative, political and institutional challenges'. Separately they have argued that the term 'wicked problem' is 'inflated and over-used', leading to pressure for 'a dramatic transformative intervention' rather than incrementalist approaches (Alford and Head 2017).

There is a missing dimension in Lodge and Wegrich's account of 'governance readiness'. As well as the necessary delivery, regulatory, coordination, and analytical capacities, governance readiness also requires 'discursive capacity'. 'Big Tech'—defined by the House of Lords Select Committee on Artificial Intelligence (2018) as 'large technology corporations, headquartered in the United States but with a global reach'—influences discussions around policy options for new technology. The House of Lords Select Committee calls them 'data monopolies'—I have elsewhere (Andrews 2018) called them 'information utilities'. These companies have discursive power, influencing both cognitive and normative views—debates on the practicalities of political action and on the principles of political action. They shape the 'master discourse' underpinning political programmes. The UK Information Commissioner has called their dominance 'a vexing problem' (House of Lords 2018). In Carstensen and Schmidt's terms

(2016), they have power *through, over,* and *in* ideas. They are able to influence understanding of practical policy solutions; they have the power to impose certain ideas through the use of proprietorial code and algorithms; and they have had the opportunity over time to structure what is allowed in discussions on technology policy at elite level. They provide what Gandy (1982) has called 'information subsidies' to the media:

> An information subsidy is an attempt to produce influence over the actions of others by controlling their access to and use of information relevant to those actions. The information is characterized as a subsidy because the source of that information causes it to be made available at something less than the cost a user would face in the absence of that subsidy.

Information subsidies can include advertising, material provided through corporate public relations, speeches etc. Big Tech's information subsidies significantly influence the reporting of debates on new technologies—but they also influence law-makers and policy-makers. As Gandy (1992) notes 'the notion of information subsidies is based on the recognition that access to information represents genuine costs to decision makers'. He particularly emphasizes the role of information subsidies in helping to create a positive image of the 'information society'. Gandy's warnings a quarter of a century ago about issues of surveillance and privacy sound highly contemporary today:

> The information systems that make possible the collection, processing, and sharing of information about individuals allow organizations to restrict, reward, invite, ignore, prod, and probe almost at will.

Sometimes these Big Tech interventions tend to reinforce the stereotypical tropes of science fiction, confirming established public fears of anthropomorphic forms of AI rebelling against humanity or (seeking to) control it (Winner 1977, 1986), evidenced in a range of audiovisual and written fiction, rather than enabling critical public discussion of some of the real underlying issues connected to power and political choices, a concern expressed by several witnesses in evidence to the House of Lords (2018).

Driessens (2013), following Bourdieu's field theory (1984), has defined celebrity capital as: *accumulated media visibility through recurrent media representations, or broadly as recognizability.* To sustain their celebrity capital, 'celebrities' have to play the game of celebrity, reinforcing their status by playing to the rules: there has to be recognition of their status by the media and indeed by the public. In the summer of 2017 TESLA founder Elon Musk and Facebook founder Mark Zuckerberg had a public spat over the dangers of AI, with Musk fearful, and Zuckerberg optimistic. It has been suggested that their real focus was not AI but rather 'their individual and corporate hopes, dreams, and strategies' in order to 'lay the groundwork for future support among investors, policymakers, and the general public' (Bogost 2017).

Governments, and regulators, in response, need effective discursive capacity. Parrado's essay on analytical capacity (2014) briefly touches on discursive capacity in reference to one narrow area, that of the role of the 'spin doctor': Lodge and Wegrich (2014a) refer to 'sage-type advice on political tactics and scheming'. However, discursive capacity is far broader than that. I develop the concept of 'discursive capacity' from the writings of Schmidt (2008, 2010, 2011) on discursive institutionalism. Schmidt (2008) argues that 'ideas and discourse matter'. Her concept of discursive institutionalism argues that political ideas have a central role in constituting political action, stressing the power of persuasion in political debate, the centrality of deliberation for democratic legitimation, the construction and reconstruction of political interests and values, and underpinning the dynamics of change. Discourse is not just about ideas but is the interactive process through which ideas are conveyed. Discursive process helps explain why some ideas succeed. Discourse may include the development of ideas at several levels—detailed policy, a broader political programme, or the underlying philosophy. Discourse will include types of ideas—cognitive, which illustrate how to do things, or normative, the underpinning values which guide action; but discourse can also include form: narratives, myths, frames, collective memories, stories, scripts, scenarios, images, and more. Schmidt also considers two kinds of discursive public sphere: the policy sphere—coordinative discourse about policy construction, and the political sphere where communicative discourse about effect of policies takes place:

> In the policy sphere, the coordinative discourse consists of the individuals and groups at the center of policy construction who are involved in the creation, elaboration, and justification of policy and programmatic ideas. These are the policy actors—the civil servants, elected officials, experts, organized interests, and activists, amongst others—who seek to coordinate agreement among themselves on policy ideas.

The political sphere is where the communicative discourse takes place and includes political leaders, governments, parties, the opposition, media pundits, academics, activists etc: in other words, informed publics, strong publics, and civil society. These elites may 'interweave the coordinative and communicative discourses into a master discourse that presents an at least seemingly coherent' programme. Discourse involves—'discussion, deliberation, negotiation and contestation' (Schmidt 2011). In respect of algorithms and AI, it requires identifying and seeking to shape the 'public narratives' (House of Lords 2018) around specific policy challenges.

In the development of policy on algorithms in high-frequency trading in the UK, for example, we can trace a discursive process of both coordinative and communicative aspects over a period of time, whose development is represented in the policy-making process through deliberative exchanges of views between regulatory bodies, parliamentary select committees, government departments, including their specialist advisors such as the Government Office of Science, European institutions, academics, and other specialists. The Foresight Report on the Future of Computer Trading in Financial Markets developed by the Government Office for Science (GOS) alone involved '150 leading experts from more than 20 countries': sponsored by the Treasury, guided by a high level stakeholder group and a lead group of experts, over fifty 'driver reviews', working papers, economic impact assessments, and surveys informed the final report (GOS 2012).

Discursive capacity, then, refers to government's ability to frame problems in terms that are capable of a recognized public or political consensus, requiring discussion, deliberation, and negotiation. The *discursive* capacity of governments includes the very important function of *convening* capacity. Governments will use that convening capacity to draw in specialist expertise, but they may also choose to allow external bodies, such as think-tanks or professional bodies, to undertake processes of developing information in new areas of policy. Sometimes this thinking may be done by Select Committees of either House of Parliament, whose role is not only there as a process of scrutiny of government departments, but may also, in areas of development around new technologies, act to establish both cognitive understanding and a normative consensus. So the recent report by the House of Lords Committee on AI states that AI raises issues which 'challenge existing ideological questions which have defined politics in the UK', arguing 'AI policy must be committed to for the long-term, agreed by consensus and informed by views on all sides' (House of Lords 2018). Some may argue whether discursive capacity is a legitimate matter for administrative, rather than political, capacity: however, Hartley, Alford, and others have identified 'political astuteness' as a necessary capacity for public managers (Hartley and Fletcher 2008; Manzie and Hartley 2013; Hartley et al 2013, 2105a and b; Alford et al 2017).

Governmental 'discursive capacity', including 'convening capacity' is essential to the deliberative process of problem-sensing, problem-definition, and problem-solving (Schoen 1983; Grint 2010; Hoppe 2011). This is a necessary task at a time when governments—at whatever level—may not themselves possess all of the information or understanding internally, and where technology companies may have disproportionate access to resources for shaping discourse on these issues. This in itself is not a new problem—technological pioneers have often over time been able to set the terms of discourse around new technologies, their governance, and regulation (Marvin 1988; Spar 2001). But it is noteworthy how little the public administration literature has had to say about digital technologies (Dunleavy 2009; Pollitt 2010, 2012).

3. Algorithmic Harms and their Governance Challenges

The documentation of algorithmic harms and risks by researchers proceeds apace. Amoore (2017) says the overriding risks are 'the introduction of forms of discrimination, injustice, prejudice, exclusion and even violence that are inadequately addressed by all current forms of oversight, law, human and civil rights'. These 'algorithms of oppression' (Noble 2018) may give rise to 'technological red-lining' on the basis of race, gender, to access to capital: so we have well-documented examples of *algorithmic bias*, in which judgements on individual futures—employment, eligibility for loans, likelihood of imprisonment—are determined by algorithmic choices which have in-built human errors or conscious or unconscious biases (Angwin 2016, Buolamwini 2017; Datta et al 2015; Lum and Isaac 2016; O'Neil 2017a and b; Sweeney 2013; Tatman 2016). However, as Amoore told the House of Commons Select Committee, bias is 'intrinsic to the algorithm': in other words, its primary purpose is to select (House of Commons 2018a).

Second, we have clear examples of *algorithmic manipulation*, in which judgements about, for example, news, information, or advertising, are constructed on the basis of data collected on individuals and used to channel what is presented according to inferred preferences, as with Facebook's News Feed algorithm (Luckerson 2015; Tambini 2017; Thompson 2018).

Thirdly, we have perceived or actual *algorithmic law-breaking*, in which algorithms are apparently deliberately constructed to deceive law-makers and regulators, for example, in terms of Volkswagen's evasion of emissions controls (Congressional Research Service 2016; Environmental Protection Agency 2017), Uber's resistance to enforcement of local traffic management laws (Isaac 2017) or algorithmic price-fixing, which the Royal Statistical Society (RSS) told the House of Commons Science and Technology Committee should be the subject of a Competition and Markets Authority inquiry (House of Commons 2018a). (Other potential examples of algorithmic crimes are set out in King et al 2018.)

Fourth, we have growing evidence of algorithm usage in propaganda, from disinformation campaigns by unfriendly countries to election campaign bots, sometimes exploiting the algorithms of major social media platforms like Facebook or YouTube (Cadwalladr 2017; Grassegger and Krogerus 2017; Keter 2017; Office of the Director of National Intelligence 2017; Solon and Siddiqui 2017).

Fifth, there is *algorithmic brand contamination* where through programmatic advertising (IAB 2014) major brands have found their advertising placed alongside hate speech or terrorist material (Mostrous & Dean 2017; Solon 2017; Vizard 2017).

Sixth, there is what I call *algorithmic unknowns*—the question of how machine learning means algorithms are becoming too complicated for humans to understand or unpick, a situation well described by the evidence from the Information Commissioner's Office to the House of Commons Science and Technology Committee (2018a). Pasquale (2015) has noted that algorithms may be seen as inscrutable 'black boxes'—while this may be true of many proprietorial algorithms, it may be particularly true of algorithms developed through machine learning.

While I cite six broad examples of algorithmic challenges for public policy, others have broken these down even further into nine 'categories of risk' (see Saurwein et al 2015). My intention is illustrative: it indicates the broad algorithmic challenges facing public leaders at local, national, and international levels in order to demonstrate the widespread necessity of building administrative capacity in this field. However, while these examples illustrate the problem, many of them are based on US examples and it is necessary to consider whether the same issues apply in the UK, though given the ubiquity of 'Big Tech', the scope is certainly there for that to happen.

Therefore, algorithms are becoming challenges for multiple levels of government. We need to turn to questions of governance and accountability. As the House of Lords Select Committee noted, trust in these new systems will depend on governments providing a governance framework or frameworks that offers the public reassurance. These kinds of potential harms arise at a number of levels of government, and require us to assess a number of the elements of governance readiness outlined by Lodge and Wegrich. So, for example, the range of algorithmic judgements made about individuals may arise in respect of local or devolved government, or UK government, or by agencies such as the police—county or regional level ordinarily in England and Wales, national that is devolved level in Scotland; in health, at a number of different levels, sometimes on a national (Wales, England or Scotland, or Northern Ireland) basis, but possibly at regional or more local levels. Were algorithms to be deployed in the UK for decisions on school teacher accountability or performance, as O'Neil cites in the US case (O'Neil 2017a) then the level of governance would vary—in England, possibly at individual academy, or academy chain level; in Wales or Scotland, at school or at local authority level: where discrimination is involved on the basis of the protected characteristics, then the Equality and Human Rights Commission would become involved at UK level, and data breaches would engage the Information Commissioner's Office at UK level.

In the case of the second examples, these are likely to be UK-wide level, though under current UK law and regulation there is a regulatory lacuna, and this is under consideration in current inquiries in both the House of Commons and House of Lords (House of Commons 2018a; House of Lords 2018). Algorithmic law-breaking could become an issue for authorities at national, devolved, and local levels: for example, if Uber, or Airbnb were to operate in ways which breached local planning or traffic management laws, then this could be an issue for local and devolved governments; Volkswagen's breaches of emissions controls have become an issue for the Mayor of London; price-fixing issues could be matters for the Financial Conduct Authority (FCA) or Competition and Markets Authority. In respect of propaganda and disinformation, then the police, the UK's intelligence agencies, and the National Cyber Security Centre would be engaged, but as we know from recent UK experience, so are the Electoral Commission (2018) in respect of referendum spending and the Information Commissioner's Office (2018) in respect of data breaches. The policing of advertising next to abusive media content could engage the advertising regulator, the ASA, but also the media regulator, OFCOM. In respect of algorithmic unknowns, then the new Centre for Data Ethics and Innovation would have a lead role.

The House of Lords Select Committee has identified a number of areas where there is legislative, regulatory, or governance uncertainty. It has called on the Law Commission to consider the adequacy of existing legislation on liability. It has questioned whether the recent spate of UK policy announcements on new institutions, including the Centre for Data Ethics and Innovation, the Government Office for AI, and the UK AI Council, and the designation of the Alan Turing Institute as the national research centre for AI, have been 'produced in concert with one another', and with existing policy, calling for a national policy framework for AI, and for clearly designated ministerial leadership at Cabinet level, saying that the public and the technology industry need to be clear about who is responsible for what kind of 'authoritative advice' on AI. It also says that the new bodies need to 'take heed' of the work of longer-established bodies such as the Information Commissioner's Office and the Competition and Markets Authority. It argues that the work programmes of the new bodies should be subject to quarterly agreement with one another, and should take into account work taking place across government as well as recommendations from Parliament, regulators, and 'the work of the devolved assemblies and governments'. It identifies capacity issues which need to be addressed, notably in terms of staffing but also in terms of support for research posts and studentships in AI.

Some have argued for a specific AI Watchdog or Machine Intelligence Commission (see evidence from the Oxford Internet Institute to the House of Lords 2018; also Mulgan 2016). The House of Commons Science and Technology Select Committee, in its report on algorithms in decision-making, believed that the Centre for Data Ethics and Innovation and the Information Commissioner (ICO) 'should review the extent of algorithm oversight by each of the main sector-specific regulators'. (House of Commons 2018a). The Committee also urged the Centre and the ICO to consider whether the European General Data Protection Regulation (GDPR)legislation in respect of 'data protection impact assessments' provided sufficient guarantees: others have urged the undertaking of algorithmic impact assessments (see eg Reisman et al 2018). The House of Lords Select Committee also looked at regulatory responsibility, ruling out proposals for general AI-specific regulation in favour of existing sector-specific regulation, but noting that there could be a substantial 'additional burden' on existing regulators, who would have to identify gaps in legislation and regulation and give consideration to the impact of AI in their sectors. They urged the development of 'a cross-sector ethical code of conduct' to be drawn up by the Centre for Data Ethics and Innovation, which could, if necessary, in future 'provide the basis for statutory regulation'.

There is a significant international dimension to the issues of governance readiness. The European Parliament's Legal Affairs Committee suggested a European Agency for Robotics and AI (EP 2016). Cath et al (2018) argued for an 'international, independent, multi-stakeholder Council on AI and Data Ethics', stating:

> AI is not merely another utility that needs to be regulated only once it is mature; it is a powerful force that is reshaping our lives, our interactions and our environments. It is part of a profound transformation of our habitat into an infosphere.

They suggest that the concept of human dignity assumed in the GDPR, which draws on the 1948 Universal Declaration of Human Rights, should be the pivotal concept for the 'good AI society'. The House of Lords Select Committee urged the UK government to convene a global summit in London in 2019 'to develop a common framework for the ethical development and deployment of artificial intelligence systems'.

It is striking, however, how little consideration is given to multi-level governance in either the House of Commons or House of Lords Select Committee reports. The same is true of the Royal Society and British Academy's 2017 report on Data Governance. Some of the issues outlined above are likely to affect law-makers and policy-makers at local and devolved levels of government as well as at UK level, and these may not be captured through the work of existing regulators.

4. Assessing Governance Readiness

Both the House of Lords and House of Commons Select Committees have identified potential resource implications for regulators in respect of the emergent new issues being raised by algorithms and AI. What does this mean for governance readiness across the UK? The two Select Committee reports are part of a process of ensuring that *discursive capacity* exists at a UK level for governance of algorithms in decision-making, and can be allied to previous work undertaken by the Royal Society and British Academy on data governance, and the ICO in preparation for the introduction of GDPR (Royal Society and British Academy 2017; ICO 2017). However, if we turn to the areas of administrative capacity identified by Lodge and Wegrich as being necessary for governance readiness, and ask also about the existence of discursive capacity at local or devolved levels of government, then the picture becomes more cloudy. As they have argued, while much is said about the transformative character of Big Data and associated technologies, 'much less has been said about the capacities required by public bureaucracies to regulate, organise, and finance such "breakthrough" technologies, let alone understand their effects' (Lodge & Wegrich 2014a).

Beginning with delivery capacity, Lodge and Wegrich define this as 'the exercise of mediated authority, regardless of whether delivery activity involved services or coercive activities'. On both counts, it is questionable whether sufficient delivery capacity exists. Police forces using algorithmic devices for facial identification of terrorists have found their systems to be wanting (Burgess 2018). The English National Health Service's recent challenges with regard to cancer screening are illustrative of a different kind of selection problem dedicated to the delivery (or not) of a service. Sometimes delivery capacity may be constrained or criticized with reference to a different kind of discursive narrative: so when the Mayor of London followed the advice of Transport for London in banning Uber in 2017, he immediately came under fire from the UK government's Minister for Innovation for undermining 'business and innovation' (Schomberg 2017). The RSS in evidence suggested that public sector authorities, including in the NHS, did not always understand the value of their data, and the House of Commons Science and Technology Committee therefore made suggestions for a standard procurement model (2018). Would every relevant local authority in the UK have the capacity to challenge Uber or, for the sake of argument, Airbnb, if they were felt to be in breach of relevant by-laws or planning rules? It seems unlikely, given the variable scale of different local authorities. With an estimated significant shortfall of data scientists in Europe by 2020 (EU 2015), skills issues are likely to remain an inhibitor of delivery capacity.

Regulatory capacity is defined by Lodge and Wegrich as 'the way in which coercive powers of the state are used to constrain economic and social activities'. They note that frequently, self-regulation of or by firms is preferred, that there has been an emphasis on risk-based regulation, and also that regulatory capacity can depend on the recruitment of expertise. It is notable that only a limited range of regulators gave evidence to the House of Commons Select Committee inquiry. Both the House of Lords and House of Commons Select Committees have identified potential weaknesses in delivery capacity for regulators as they attempt to get to grips with these new challenges. However, both have expressed a preference for sector-specific regulation. Without conducting a formal audit of regulatory capacity in this field, it is possible to identify that certain regulators, such as the FCA, have been in the business of addressing issues of algorithmic regulation for some years, and have deep experience in this field, giving practical examples of their work in their evidence (House of Commons 2018a). Following the Cambridge Analytica case, the regulatory powers of the Information Commissioner are being upgraded in the recent Data Protection Act (House of Commons 2018b), and certain requirements are being imposed for data controllers to inform individuals when decisions about them were essentially determined by algorithms, though the House of Commons Select Committee questioned whether this should be expanded to include a wider range of algorithmic decisions than those simply 'required or authorised by law'. The Electoral Commission meanwhile has identified areas where it believes that the law needs to be strengthened to take account of digital developments, and has clearly found it difficult to address the challenges thrown up during the Brexit referendum under existing law. Ofgem gave a comprehensive overview of where algorithmic judgements were made within the energy sector. Ofsted, the English education inspectorate, explained how algorithms were used to prioritize school inspections. Ofcom suggested in evidence to the House of Commons Select Committee that it did not have 'a direct regulatory role in overseeing the use of algorithms' but said it could use existing powers where algorithms resulted in consumer detriment (House of Commons 2018a). The House of Lords Select Committee (2018) recommended that the government and Ofcom research the impact of AI on conventional and social media outlets, specifically in respect of attempts to 'mislead or distort' public opinion.

In terms of coordinative capacity, Lodge and Wegrich identify that coordination has become ever more important as states delegate powers to agencies and to 'subnational' and 'supranational' levels of government: they also identify the need for 'boundary-spanners' in public services who can lead this work. I have already dealt above with proposals for international coordination. Coordinative capacity in the space of algorithmic regulation is identified as a necessary role for the UK government itself, by the House of Lords Select Committee on AI, which is urged to ensure that the Government Office for AI develop 'a national policy framework for AI, to be in lockstep with the Industrial Strategy, and to be overseen by the AI Council', as well as establishing a ministerial lead on this subject. Coordination amongst regulators is suggested by the House of Commons Science and Technology Select Committee to be a matter that should be led by the ICO and the new Centre for Data Ethics and Innovation, as I set out above. It is clear that some of the issues raised by big data, algorithms, and AI may cross regulatory boundaries: the regulation of political advertising, based on personalized advertisements targeted through data analysis, to take one example, could engage electoral regulators, media regulators, advertising regulators, and data protection authorities, requiring cross-organizational attention. However, these are intra-Whitehall and inter-regulator roles. No consideration has been given to the need for coordination across the devolved administrations, or with local government or through the NHS in each of the UK's four nations, or through the UK's forty-plus police forces, for example, though potentially the UK government's Date Ethics Framework (DDCMS 2018) which recently replaced the Government Digital Service's *Data Science Ethical Framework* (GDS 2016), could provide a coordinating framework for discussions across multiple levels of government and public services and regulators.

Analytical capacity, say Lodge and Wegrich, requires both on-the-job experience and subject knowledge, and is bound up with both understanding current performance and identifying future need. Contemporary governments, they say, need to be intelligent consumers of different sources of expertise both inside and outside government itself. Foresight, as Cath et al (2018) propose, needs a key element of what is now to be called the Centre for Data Ethics and Innovation, though this work clearly needs to be connected to existing Foresight operations such as that in the Government Office for Science which along with the Council for Science and Technology has taken the lead in promoting issues to do with algorithms and AI in recent years (Walport 2013 and 2016). Contemporary UK regulatory discussions have identified specific policy solutions advocated for future regulation of algorithms and big data, which include technical, governance, regulatory, legislative, and institutional solutions (for a fuller summary, see Andrews 2017). The DDCMS gave a summary of existing UK government initiatives (House of Commons 2018), with significant sums being invested in the creation of data trusts, for example. Some regulators, notably the ICO, with its responsibilities under GDPR for which it has been preparing for some time, and the FCA, with a longstanding commitment to address abuse through its market surveillance activities and its deployment of a 'Regulatory Sandbox' where companies can test innovative ideas for their implications for consumers. Parrado (2014) notes that austerity policies have had an impact on analytical capacity within UK government: the singular focus on Brexit since 2016 has had an impact on the analytical capacity of the UK government in other policy domains, with the Brexit process absorbing an increasing number of civil servants (Owen et al 2018). The immediacy of some of the algorithmic challenges may not be sufficiently apparent to underpin investment in analytical capacity in these areas. The impact of austerity on other levels of government, including the budgets of the devolved governments and local government, will have had a direct impact on analytical capacity in particular. Regulators have also been urged 'to do more with less' since 2010.

Finally, discursive capacity. The exchanges around the Select Committee reports, and the prior work by the Royal Society and the Information Commissioner, indicate that at UK level discursive capacity does exist. But is there space or scope for the effective development of discursive capacity on these issues at devolved or local levels? The Welsh government has commenced a review of digital innovation, including AI (Welsh Government 2018) led by a senior academic from Cardiff University. The Scottish government has identified AI and robotics as growth sectors (Heriot-Watt University 2017). It is not clear that any branch of UK local government has gone as far as New York in creating an Automated Decision Systems Task Force, including individuals from academic and legal communities, experts in data and technology, and leaders of non-profits and think-tanks to address how its own administration uses algorithms (NYC Mayor 2018).

5. Conclusion

This chapter has considered current developments within the UK, seeking to take a preliminary snapshot of the state of governance readiness in respect of algorithmic decision-making. It is evident from the documentary material surveyed that this is an emergent field of governance, but that certain regulators, notably the FCA and ICO, have significant experience. The documentary evidence suggests that at this stage little account has been taken of multi-level governance, whether at devolved or local government level. The chapter has also sought to expand our understanding of the nature of the necessary administrative capacities required for governance readiness, adding the dimension of discursive capacity to those areas of capacity previously identified by Lodge and Wegrich and their collaborators (Lodge & Wegrich 2014a and b), which is felt to be especially important given the dominant position of the 'Big Tech' companies, as noted by the House of Lords Select Committee. Further research could be undertaken by an audit of the algorithmic governance readiness of individual sectoral regulators and inspectorates, or of different levels of government within the UK, including through surveys or elite interviews, and deeper analysis of documentary materials. The conclusions in this chapter must necessarily remain preliminary, as policy is developing at national and international levels and public and media awareness of the issues is largely restricted to elite audiences at the present time.

Bibliography

Alford J and Head BW, 'Wicked and Less Wicked Problems: A Typology and a Contingency Framework' (2017) 36(3) Policy and Society 397.

Alford J, Hartley J, Yates S, et al, 'Into the Purple Zone: Deconstructing the Politics/Administration Distinction' (2017) 47(7) The American Review of Public Administration 752.

Amoore L, 'Written Evidence (ALG0042), House of Commons Science and Technology Committee' (2017) <http://data.parliament.uk/writtenevidence/committeeevidence. svc/evidencedocument/science-and-technology-committee/algorithms-in-decisionmaking/written/69065.html> accessed 1 June 2019.

Andrews L, 'Algorithms, Governance and Regulation: Beyond "the Necessary Hashtags"' in L Andrews, B Benbouzid, J Brice, LA Bygrave, D Demortain, A Griffiths, M Lodge, A Mennicken, and K Yeung (eds), Algorithmic Regulation, LSE Discusison Paper 85 (September 2017).

Andrews L, 'Written Evidence (IRN0041), House of Lords Communications Committee' (2018) <http://data.parliament.uk/writtenevidence/committeeevidence.svc/evidencedocument/ communications-committee/the-internet-to-regulate-or-not-to-regulate/written/82663. html> accessed 1 June 2019.

Angwin J, 'Make Algorithms Accountable' New York Times (1 August 2016) <https://mobile. nytimes.com/2016/08/01/opinion/make-algorithms-accountable.html?referer=&_r=0> accessed 1 June 2019.

BMJ, 'A Blot on the Profession' (5 March 1988) <http://europepmc.org/backend/ptpmcrender.fcgi?accid=PMC2545288&blobtype=pdf> accessed 1 June 2019.

Bogost I, 'Why Zuckerberg and Musk are Fighting about the Robot Future' *The Atlantic* (27 July 2017).

Bourdieu P, *Distinction* (Routledge 1984).

Buolamwini J, 'When Algorithms Are Racist' *Observer* (28 May 2017). <https://www.theguardian.com/technology/2017/may/28/joy-buolamwini-when-algorithms-are-racist-facial-recognition-bias> accessed 1 June 2019.

Burgess M, 'Facial Recognition Tech Used by UK Police Is Making a Ton of Mistakes' *WIRED* (4 May 2018) <https://www.wired.co.uk/article/face-recognition-police-uk-south-wales-met-notting-hill-carnival> accessed 1 June 2019.

Cadwalladr C, 'The Great British Brexit Robbery: How our Democracy Was Hijacked' *Observer* (7 May 2017).

Carr M, *US Power and the Internet in International Relations—the Irony of the Information Age* (Palgrave MacMillan 2016).

Carstensen MB and Schmidt VA, 'Power through, over and in Ideas: Conceptualizing Ideational Power in Discursive Institutionalism' (2016) 23(3) Journal of European Public Policy 318.

Cath CJN, Wachter S, Mittelstadt B, et al, 'Artificial Intelligence and the "Good Society": The US, EU, and UK Approach' (2018) 24(2) Science and Engineering Ethics 505.

Chollet F, 'What Worries Me about AI' *Medium* (28 March 2018) <https://medium.com/@francois.chollet/what-worries-me-about-ai-ed9df072b704> accessed 1 June 2019.

Congressional Research Service, 'Volkswagen, Defeat Devices, and the Clean Air Act: Frequently Asked Questions' (1 September 2016) <https://fas.org/sgp/crs/misc/R44372.pdf> accessed 1 June 2019.

Council of Europe, 'Revised Version of the Study on the Human Rights Dimensions of Algorithms' (March 2017) <https://rm.coe.int/168070b74f> accessed 1 June 2019.

Data and Society, 'Algorithmic Accountability: A Primer' Document prepared for the Congressional Progressive Caucus's Tech Algorithm Briefing: How Algorithms Perpetuate Racial Bias and Inequality (18 April 2018) <https://datasociety.net/output/algorithmic-accountability-a-primer/> accessed 1 June 2019.

Datta A, Tschantz MC, and Datta A, 'Automated Experiments on Ad Privacy Settings' (2015) 1 Proceedings on Privacy Enhancing Technologies 92.

DBEIS/DCMS [Department for Business, Energy and Industrial Strategy/Department of Digital, Culture, Media and Sport], 'AI Sector Deal' (26 April 2018) <https://www.gov.uk/government/publications/artificial-intelligence-sector-deal/ai-sector-deal#foreword> accessed 1 June 2019.

DBIS [Department for Business, Innovation and Science], 'Plans for World Class Research Centre in the UK' (19 March 2014) <https://www.gov.uk/government/news/plans-for-world-class-research-centre-in-the-uk> accessed 1 June 2019.

DCMS [Department of Digital, Culture, Media and Sport], *Data Ethics Framework* (13 June 2018) <https://www.gov.uk/government/publications/data-ethics-framework> accessed 1 June 2019.

Driessens O, 'Celebrity Capital: Redefining Celebrity Using Field Theory' (2013) 42(5) Theory and Society 543.

Dunleavy P, 'Governance and State Organization in the Digital Era' in C Avgerou, R Mansell, D Quah, and R Silverstone (eds), *The Oxford Handbook of Information and Communication Technologies* (Oxford University Press 2009).

Electoral Commission, 'Electoral Commission Statement on Investigation into Leave. EU' (21 April 2018) <https://www.electoralcommission.org.uk/i-am-a/journalist/electoral-commission-media-centre/news-releases-referendums/electoral-commission-statement-on-investigation-into-leave.eu> accessed 1 June 2019.

Environmental Protection Agency, 'Volkswagen Clean Air Act Civil Settlement' (2017) <http://www.epaarchive.cc/enforcement/volkswagen-clean-air-act-partial-settlement.html> accessed 1 June 2019.

European Parliament (EP), 'Draft Report with Recommendations to the Commission on Civil Law Rules on Robotics' (2015/2103(INL)) Committee on Legal Affairs (31 May 2016) <http://www.europarl.europa.eu/sides/getDoc.do?pubRef=-//EP//NONSGML%2BCOMPARL%2BPE-582.443%2B01%2BDOC%2BPDF%2BV0//EN> accessed 1 June 2019.

European Union, Blog by A Ansip, Digital Market Commissioner, 'Digital Skills, Jobs and the Need to Get More Europeans Online' (2015) <https://ec.europa.eu/commission/commissioners/2014-2019/ansip/blog/digital-skills-jobs and-need-get-more-europeans-online_en> accessed 1 June 2019.

Executive Office of the President, 'Artificial Intelligence, Automation and the Economy' (2016) <https://obamawhitehouse.archives.gov/blog/2016/12/20/artificial-intelligence-automation-and-economy> accessed 1 June 2019.

Gandy O, *Beyond Agenda Setting* (Ablex 1982).

Gandy O, 'Public Relations and Public Policy: The Structuration of Dominance in the Information Age' in EL Toth and RL Heath (eds), *Rhetorical and Critical Approaches to Public Relations* (Lawrence Erlbaum Associates 1992).

Government Digital Service, 'Data Science Ethics Framework' (2016) <https://www.gov.uk/government/publications/data-science-ethical-framework> accessed 1 June 2019.

Government Office of Science (GOS), 'Future of Computer Trading in Financial Markets: Final Report' (2012) <https://www.gov.uk/government/publications/future-of-computer-trading-in-financial-markets-an-international-perspective> accessed 1 June 2019.

Grassegger H and Krogerus M, 'The Data that Turned the World Upside Down' Motherboard, Vice.com (28 January 2017). <https://motherboard.vice.com/en_us/article/mg9vvn/how-our-likes-helped-trump-win> accessed 1 June 2019.

Grint K, 'Wicked Problems and Clumsy Solutions: The Role of Leadership' in S Brookes and K Grint (eds), *The new Public Leadership Challenge* (Palgrave MacMillan 2010).

Hall W and Pesenti J, 'Growing the Artificial Intelligence Industry in the United Kingdom' (15 October 2017) <https://www.gov.uk/government/publications/growing-the-artificial-intelligence-industry-in-the-uk> accessed 1 June 2019.

Hansard, House of Commons Oral Statement: 'Breast Cancer Screening' (2018) <https://hansard.parliament.uk/commons/2018-05-02/debates/BE9DB48A-C9FF-401B-AC54-FF53BC5BD83E/BreastCancerScreening> accessed 1 June 2019.

Hartley J and Fletcher C, 'Leading with Political Awareness: Leadership across Diverse Interests Inside and Outside the Organisation' in KT James and J Collins (eds), *Leadership Perspectives* (Springer 2008).

Hartley J, Alford J, and Hughes O, 'Political Astuteness as an Aid to Discerning and Creating Public Value' in JA Bryson, BC Crosby, and L Bloomberg (eds), *Public Value and Public Administration* (Georgetown University Press 2015a).

Hartley J, Alford J, Hughes O, et al, *Leading with Political Astuteness: A Study of Public Managers in Australia, New Zealand and the United Kingdom* (Australia and New Zealand School of Government and the Chartered Management Institute, UK 2013).

Hartley J, Alford J, Hughes O, et al, 'Public Value and Political Astuteness in the Work of Public Managers: The Art of the Possible' (2015b) 93(1) Public Administration 195.

Head BW and Alford J, 'Wicked problems: implications for public policy and management' (2015) 47(6) Administration and Society 711.

Heriot-Watt University, 'Minister Given Insight into the Future of AI' (14 December 2017) <https://www.hw.ac.uk/about/news/minister-given-insight-into-the-future-of-ai.htm> accessed 1 June 2019.

Hoppe R, *The Governance of Problems* (Policy Press 2011).

House of Commons, Select Committee on Science and Technology, 'Algorithms in Decision-Making Inquiry' (2017) <https://www.parliament.uk/business/committees/committees-a-z/commons-select/science-and-technology-committee/inquiries/parliament-2015/inquiry9/> accessed 1 June 2019.

House of Commons, Select Committee on Science and Technology, 'Algorithms in Decision-Making Inquiry' Oral Evidence (23 January 2018a) <http://data.parliament.uk/writtenevidence/committeeevidence.svc/evidencedocument/science-and-technology-committee/algorithms-in-decisionmaking/oral/77536.html> accessed 1 June 2019.

House of Commons, 'Notices of Amendments' (27 April 2018b) <https://publications.parliament.uk/pa/bills/cbill/2017-2019/0190/amend/data_rm_rep_0427.1-7.html> accessed 1 June 2019.

House of Lords, Select Committee on Artificial Intelligence, 'AI in the UK: Ready, Willing and Able?' (HL Paper 100, 16 April 2018) <https://publications.parliament.uk/pa/ld201719/ldselect/ldai/100/10002.htm> accessed 1 June 2019.

Information Commissioner's Office (ICO), 'ICO Statement: Investigation into Data Analytics for Political Purposes' (2018) <https://ico.org.uk/about-the-ico/news-and-events/news-and-blogs/2018/05/ico-statement-investigation-into-data-analytics-for-political-purposes/> accessed 1 June 2019.

Interactive Advertising Bureau (IAB), *The Programmatic Handbook* (2014) <https://iabuk.net/sites/default/files/The%20Programmatic%20Handbook.pdf> accessed 1 June 2019.

Isaac M, 'How Uber Deceived the Authorities Worldwide' *New York Times* (3 March 2017) <https://www.nytimes.com/2017/03/03/technology/uber-greyball-program-evade-authorities.html?_r=0> accessed 1 June 2019.

Keter G, 'Uhuru Hires Firm behind Trump, Brexit Victories' *The Star*, Kenya (10 May 2017) <http://www.the-star.co.ke/news/2017/05/10/uhuru-hires-data-firm-behind-trump-brexit-victories_c1557720> accessed 1 June 2019.

King TC, Aggarwall N, Taddeo M, et al, 'Artificial Intelligence Crime: An Interdisciplinary Analysis of Foreseeable Threats and Solutions' (2018) <https://ssrn.com/abstract=3183238> or <http://dx.doi.org/10.2139/ssrn.3183238> accessed 1 June 2019.

Lay K, 'Algorithm Spots Dementia from GP Records' *The Times* (13 June 2018) <https://www.thetimes.co.uk/article/algorithm-spots-dementia-from-gp-records-3qzld6xfv> accessed 1 June 2019.

Lodge M and Wegrich K, 'Setting the Scene: Challenges to the State, Governance Readiness, and Administrative Capacities' in M Lodge and K Wegrich (eds), *The Governance Report* Hertie School of Governance (Oxford University Press 2014a).

Lodge M and Wegrich K, *The Problem-Solving Capacity of the Modern State* (Oxford University Press 2014b).

Luckerson V, 'Here's how Facebook's News Feed Really Works' (9 July 2015) <http://time.com/collection-post/3950525/facebook-news-feed-algorithm/> accessed 1 June 2019.

Lum K and Issac W, 'To Predict and Serve?' (2016) 13(5) Significance 14.

Manzie S and Hartley J, 'Dancing on Ice: Leadership with Political Astuteness by Senior Public Servants in the UK' (Open University Business School 2013).

Marvin C, *When Old Technologies Were New* (Oxford University Press 1988).

Mittelstadt BD, Allo P, Taddeo M, et al, 'The Ethics of Algorithms: Mapping the Debate' (July–December 2016) Big Data and Society 1.

Moore M, *Creating Public Value* (Harvard University Press 1995).

Mostrous A and Dean J, 'Top Brands Pull Google Adverts in Protest at Hate Video Links' *The Times* (23 March 2017).

Mulgan G, 'A Machine Intelligence Commission for the UK: How to Grow Informed Public Trust and Maximise the Positive Impact of Smart Machines' (2016) <http://www.nesta. org.uk/sites/default/files/a_machine_intelligence_commission_for_the_uk_-_geoff_ mulgan.pdf> accessed 1 June 2019.

Noble SU, *Algorithms of Oppression: How Search Engines Reinforce Racism* (New York University Press 2018).

NYC Mayor, 'Mayor de Blasio Announces First-In-Nation Task Force to Examine Automated Decision Systems Used by the City' (16 May 2018) <http://www1.nyc.gov/ office-of-the-mayor/news/251-18/mayor-de-blasio-first-in-nation-task-force-examine- automated-decision-systems-used-by> accessed 1 June 2019.

Office of the Director of National Intelligence, 'Background to "Assessing Russian Activities and Intentions in Recent US Elections": The Analytic Process and Cyber Incident Attribution' (2017) <https://www.intelligence.senate.gov/sites/default/files/documents/ ICA_2017_01.pdf> accessed 1 June 2019.

O'Neil C, *Weapons of Math Destruction* (Crown Random House 2016).

O'Neil C, 'The Math Whizzes Who Nearly Brought Down Wall Street' *Saturday Evening Post* (March/April 2017a) <http://www.saturdayeveningpost.com/2017/04/03/in-the- magazine/weapons-math-destruction.html> accessed 1 June 2019.

O'Neil C, 'Don't Grade Teachers With a Bad Algorithm' *Bloomberg View* (15 May 2017b) <https://www.bloomberg.com/view/articles/2017-05-15/don-t-grade-teachers-with- a-bad-algorithm?utm_content=view&utm_campaign=socialflow-organic&utm_ source=twitter&utm_medium=social&cmpid%3D=socialflow-twitter-view> accessed 1 June 2019.

Owen J, Lloyd L, and Rutter J, 'Preparing Brexit: How Ready is Whitehall?' (Institute for Government 2018) <https://www.instituteforgovernment.org.uk/publications/ preparing-brexit-how-ready-whitehall?inf_contact_key=70083cb2eb06d6cd73cb71555 69b0e469d7d68f3f5a27ae84abff4f99e80c401> accessed 1 June 2019.

Parrado S, 'Analytical Capacity' in M Lodge and K Wegrich (eds), *The Problem-Solving Capacity of the Modern State* (Oxford University Press 2014).

Pasquale F, *The Black Box Society* (Harvard University Press 2015).

Pichai S, 'AI at Google: Our Principles' (7 June 2018) <https://blog.google/topics/ai/ai- principles/> accessed 1 June 2019.

Pollitt C, 'Technological Change: A Central yet Neglected Feature of Public Administration' (2010) 3(2) NISPAcee Journal of Public Administration and Policy 31.

Pollitt C, *Time, Policy, Management—Governing with the Past* (Oxford University Press 2012).

Reisman D, Schultz J, Crawford K, et al, 'Algorithmic Impact Assessments: A Practical Framework for Public Agency Accountability' AINow Institute (9 April 2018) <https:// ainowinstitute.org/reports.html> accessed 1 June 2019.

Royal Society and British Academy, 'Data Management and Use: Governance in the 21st Century' (2017) <https://royalsociety.org/topics-policy/projects/data-governance/> ac- cessed 1 June 2019.

Saurwein F, Just N, and Latzer M, 'Governance of Algorithms: Options and Limitations' (2015) 17(6) Info 35.

Schmidt VA, 'Discursive Institutionalism: The Explanatory Power of Ideas and Discourse' (2008) 11 Annual Review of Political Science 303.

Schmidt VA, 'Taking Ideas and Discourse Seriously: Explaining Change through Discursive Institutionalism as the Fourth 'New Institutionalism' (2010) 2(1) European Political Science Review 1.

Schmidt VA, 'Speaking of Change: Why Discourse is the Key to the Dynamics of Policy Transformation' (2011) 5(2) Critical Policy Studies 106.

Schoen D, *The Reflective Practitioner* (Basic Books 1983).

Schomberg W, 'Minister for London Greg Hands Criticises Blanket Ban on Europe' *Business Insider* (23 September 2017) <http://uk.businessinsider.com/minister-for-london-greg-hands-criticised-the-blanket-ban-on-uber-2017-9?r=US&IR=T> accessed 1 June 2019.

Solon O, 'Google's Bad Week: YouTube Loses Millions as Advertising Row Reaches US' *Observer* (25 March 2017).

Solon O and Laughland O, 'Cambridge Analytica Closing after Facebook Data Harvesting Scandal' *Guardian* (2 May 2018) <https://www.theguardian.com/uk-news/2018/may/02/cambridge-analytica-closing-down-after-facebook-row-reports-say> accessed 1 June 2019.

Solon O and Siddiqui S, 'Russia-backed Facebook Posts "Reached 126m Americans" during US Election' *Guardian* (31 October 2017) <https://www.theguardian.com/technology/2017/oct/30/facebook-russia-fake-accounts-126-million> accessed 1 June 2019.

Spar D, *Ruling the Waves* (Harcourt 2001).

Sweeney L, Discrimination in Online Ad Delivery' (2013) 11(3) Queue <http://dl.acm.org/citation.cfm?id=2460276&picked=prox&cfid=777433242&cftoken=41783991> accessed 1 June 2019.

Tambini D, 'How Advertising Fuels Fake News' *Inforrm Blog* (26 February 2017) <https://inforrm.wordpress.com/2017/02/26/how-advertising-fuels-fake-news-damian-tambini/> accessed 1 June 2019.

Tatman R, 'Google's Speech Recognition Has a Gender Bias' (2016) <https://makingnoiseandhearingthings.com/2016/07/12/googles-speech-recognition-has-a-gender-bias/> accessed 1 June 2019.

Thompson M, 'Journalism, Free Speech and the Search and Social Giants' Speech to the Open Markets Institute' *New York Times* (12 June 2018) <https://www.nytco.com/wp-content/uploads/sites/3/MARK-THOMPSON-OPEN-MARKETS-INSTITUTE-.pdf> accessed 1 June 2019.

Turing, 'How Can We Design Fair, Transparent, and Accountable AI and Robotics?' *Alan Turing Institute Blog* (2017) <https://www.turing.ac.uk/blog/can-design-fair-transparent-accountable-ai-robotics/> accessed 1 June 2019.

Veale M, van Kleek M, and Binns R, 'Fairness and Accountability Design Needs for Algorithmic Support in High-Stakes Public Sector Decision-Making' Chi 2018 paper (April 2018) <https://arxiv.org/pdf/1802.01029.pdf> accessed 1 June 2019.

Vizard S, 'Vodafone Blocks Ads from Appearing on Sites that Promote Hate Speech or Fake News' *Marketing Week* (6 June 2017).

Walport M, Letter to the Prime Minister 'The Age of Algorithms' Council for Science and Technology (2013) <https://www.gov.uk/government/uploads/system/uploads/attachment_data/file/224953/13-923-age-of-algorithms-letter-to-prime-minister__1_.pdf> accessed 1 June 2019.

Walport M, Letter to the Prime Minister 'Robotics, Automation and Artificial Intelligence (RAAI)' Council for Science and Technology (2016) <https://www.gov.uk/government/uploads/system/uploads/attachment_data/file/592423/Robotics_automation_and_artificial_intelligence_-_cst_letter.pdf> accessed 1 June 2019.

Welsh Government, Written Statement by Ken Skates, Cabinet Secretary for Economy and Transport, Review of Digital Innovation 'Artificial Intelligence and Automation in Wales' (28 March 2018) <https://gov.wales/about/cabinet/cabinetstatements/2018/innovation/?lang=en> accessed 1 June 2019.

Winner L, *Autonomous Technology* (MIT Press 1977).

Winner L, 'Do Artefacts Have Politics?' in L Winner (ed), *The Whale and the Reactor: A Search for Limits in an Age of High Technology* (University of Chicago Press 1986).

Yeung K, 'Algorithmic Regulation: A Critical Interrogation' (2018) 12(4) Regulation & Governance 505.

10

Legal Practitioners' Approach to Regulating AI Risks

Jason D Lohr, Winston J Maxwell, and Peter Watts

1. Introduction

Many firms, including those that do not regard of themselves as traditional 'tech' firms, consider the prospect of artificial intelligence (AI) both an intriguing possibility and a potential new area of risk for their businesses. They want to make sure they can seize the new opportunities and manage the new risks that AI promises. Yet achieving these objectives can be particularly challenging, given that firms face uncertainties concerning the current and future state of AI technology and when and how it will significantly impact them. The term 'AI' is used generally to refer to several different types of technology, which contributes to some of the uncertainty and is apt to confuse. Artificial intelligence in its purest form would involve machines being able to think for themselves, essentially operating as sentient beings, a technology called Artificial General Intelligence, or 'AGI'. While advances in AI research mean that we are closer to achieving AGI, we are still (depending on who you talk to) decades away from this being available and widely adopted (Knight 2017). However, we are already seeing the deployment of many computational systems which are capable of undertaking more than simple mechanical tasks, performing decision-making functions and predictive analysis. These are starting to permeate the operations of businesses and institutions across a wide swathe of the economy.

The application of existing AI technologies raises significant new issues in some of the most fundamental areas of law, including: ownership and property rights; the creation, allocation, and sharing of value; misuse, errors, and responsibility for resulting harm; individual liberty and personal privacy; economic collusion and monopolies.

This chapter first examines how businesses are already managing some of these risks through contract. We will then examine some of the considerations involved in public regulation of AI-related risks. We will conclude by proposing a four-layer model for thinking about AI regulation in the broad sense: the foundational layer consists of existing laws on liability, property, and contracts, permitting parties to allocate risks, responsibilities, and economic value through contract. The second

Legal Practitioners' Approach to Regulating AI Risks. Jason D Lohr, Winston J Maxwell, and Peter Watts. © Jason D Lohr, Winston J Maxwell, and Peter Watts, 2019. Published 2019 by Oxford University Press.

layer is corporate governance to ensure that decision-making bodies exercise effective controls over AI systems. The third layer is sector-specific regulation, such as banking or automobile safety regulation, to address specific risks arising from AI use cases. The last layer is a light-touch regulatory framework for observing and measuring more diffuse horizontal harms to society that sector-specific regulators would not be in a position to detect and regulate.

Before starting this analysis, we present a short introduction to machine learning and some of the unique legal issues it generates.

2. Machine Learning and the Law

2.1 Machine Learning is a Subset of AI

Falling short of pure or 'general' AI, today's AI technology is largely based on machine learning. Without going into detail that is well described elsewhere,[1] machine learning is more of an 'augmented' or 'arranged' intelligence than true artificial intelligence. Machine learning models can generally be trained to 'learn' specific relationships or skills. As a result they can be used to classify data input to those models or make decisions or 'predictions' on the basis of that data. An important point to bear in mind is that the data we are concerned with is not limited to purely numerical data of the type many business people are most familiar with. Of course machine learning can be applied to numerical data—like the information which generates a credit score. But increasingly the technology reaches much further than this. For example, a machine learning algorithm might be provided with a set of 'training data'[2] that includes thousands of images of vehicles and thousands of images of pedestrians, which are all labelled as such, and can 'learn' to recognize (or classify) whether an object is a vehicle or a pedestrian, even though the model has not previously encountered that object. The recognition is based on patterns or relationships learned through the training on labelled data. The results generated by the model, particularly once determined to be correct or incorrect, can also be used as additional training data to further train the model for continued learning and improvement. With sufficient training, the results produced by models of this type can be very accurate, and can be obtained without the significant additional processing or programming that would be required under conventional rule-based approaches. The accuracy and speed of analysis of these models can provide many benefits across industries.

---

[1] For a bibliography on machine learning, see Wikipedia Machine Learning article: https://en.wikipedia.org/wiki/Machine_learning

[2] 'Training data' is the information which a machine learning system absorbs in order to 'learn' patterns and so acquire its 'intelligence'.

The remainder of this chapter will focus on machine learning. Machine learning can be treated in many respects the same way as various existing processes that perform similar tasks. Many companies presume therefore that little needs to change in their current legal approach. The nature of the training and usage of machine learning, however, is different from the development and use of conventional rule-based algorithms, requiring a new approach to contract risk allocation, and perhaps even to regulation due to several properties associated with the way in which machine learning algorithms operate. Some of these unique problems are examined below.

2.2 Lack of Explainability

As mentioned above, training for machine learning typically involves providing the machine learning models or networks (eg convolutional or deep neural networks) with a large amount of data that the models can use to 'learn' a classification, identification, or prediction based on relationships determined from the input data. In many instances, the output may generate extraordinarily high rates of accuracy, but it may not be possible to determine 'how' the model arrived at its determinations. Even if a technologist might be able to provide a technical explanation, the normal user of the technology is unlikely to have an accessible explanation available. This is currently one of the main issues with machine learning that is preventing it from being more widely adopted, and is a significant area of current research in the machine learning industry (*The Economist* 2018; see also, Wachter et al 2017). For example, a doctor may want (or need) to be able to understand the logic underpinning a clinical diagnosis generated by an AI-driven decision-support system before recommending a treatment option. That the machine-generated diagnosis may not be easily explicable to the doctor is potentially a matter of real concern. The need for explanations is particularly important if harm arises. For example, if an autonomous vehicle decides to take an action that results in injury, the vehicle manufacturer, the insurer, courts, and safety regulators will want to understand the logic used to choose the given action. This is not simply a matter of intellectual curiosity. Even if it appears that a decision-making process usually reaches the correct conclusion, without understanding how a decision has been reached it is difficult to evaluate whether the system overlooked a factor which might occasionally be critical to achieving the correct decision, for example a highly unusual weather condition. A machine learning financial trading platform might operate with remarkable success in 'normal' conditions but, without understanding how it makes decisions, it will be difficult to assess how the platform may function in abnormal market conditions.

Currently, decision-making systems that rely on machine learning are in many ways opaque, lacking adequate explainability in many instances. Engineers may solve certain aspects of the problem in the next few years (Gunning 2017). The ability to audit and understand AI decisions *ex post* will facilitate wider uptake of machine learning. However, the explainability problem is unlikely to disappear entirely, meaning that contracts and law will need to find ways to address what Frank Pasquale (2015) calls the 'black box' phenomenon of AI decisions.

2.3 New Types of Rogue Errors

If well designed, machine learning models will generally result in highly accurate outcomes most of the time. However, as we have described above, even apparently well-functioning models may yield grossly inaccurate or incorrect decisions on rare occasions. A chatbot may insult a customer with a racial slur, or an AI system may erroneously answer 'Toronto' when asked to name a major US city having certain characteristics (Tutt 2017: 88).

High quality machine learning, while much more accurate than human analysis in the vast majority of cases, can occasionally make outlier mistakes that will seem incomprehensibly stupid to human observers. The error may be one that no human would make. These errors may cause harm directly—the insulted customer may be amongst the least harmful. They may also be compounded because other systems, or even human beings, rely on the outputs in which those errors appear. This creates a new kind of liability paradigm. While courts, companies, insurers, and regulators are accustomed to managing risks associated with human error (eg a driver falling asleep), or traditional manufacturing or programming errors, risks associated with rare but bizarre machine learning outcomes will require new thinking about negligence principles. Where machines make mistakes, courts will have to determine the standard of liability. Where liability is based on the traditional negligence standard, courts may have to refer to the 'reasonable computer' as opposed to the 'reasonable person' level of care (Abbott 2018). Submitting AI to product liability rules will raise questions as to what constitutes an unsafe or defective product. For example, is an AI system that is 10, or 100, times safer than a human driver nevertheless unsafe or defective because it causes injury on exceedingly rare occasions in circumstances where a human driver almost certainly would not? (Abbott 2018: 18) How safe is safe enough? One commentator observed that: 'The critical issue is not whether computers are perfect (they are not), but whether they are safer than people (they are)' (Abbott 2018: 18). But this may not be a complete answer if computers cause harm in ways humans would not.

If a hospital comes to believe that the use of a machine learning tool can render a procedure sufficiently routine thereby justifying the dispensation of clinicians with particular medical expertise, who is responsible when a member of staff without the relevant clinical expertise using the tool fails to spot an outlier error which a properly trained clinician could reasonably be expected to have identified—the staff member, the hospital, or the system developer? As noted in our discussion below, liability rules are flexible, and have adapted to many new technologies over the years. Nevertheless, regulatory intervention may be necessary in some cases, particularly to set safety standards, and/or provide liability caps or safe harbours for AI system providers in the event liability risks are so large as to prevent AI systems that bring net benefits to society from being deployed.

2.4 Human Automation Bias

Decision support systems (DSS) can help doctors, lawyers, judges, pilots, and others make better decisions. But an increasing body of evidence shows that humans suffer from automation bias and automation-induced complacency (Goddard et al 2012). Humans have a tendency to rely too much on the machine's decision, lowering their own vigilance and critical analysis, potential rendering DSS a direct 'cause' of negligence. This leads to errors, including situations where the human decision would have been correct at the outset but was reversed by the human to align with the computer's erroneous recommendation. A number of researchers are studying this phenomenon in order to better design DSS, and provide appropriate training, so that DSS make human users smarter, not more complacent.

As DSS become more commonplace, they may influence professional liability standards. If a physician or lawyer makes a mistake, how would his or her use, or failure to use, DSS affect liability? A judge's use of DSS to help evaluate a criminal defendant's likelihood of committing another crime was scrutinized by the Wisconsin Supreme Court in *State v Loomis*.[3] The Wisconsin Supreme Court found that the sentencing judge's use of the DSS tool did not violate the defendant's due process rights because the judge made an independent decision, using the DSS tool only as a source of information. However critics argue that the *Loomis* decision did not adequately address the risks associated with judges' increasing reliance on AI tools, including the risk that humans will give undue weight to the recommendations issued by the AI systems (Pasquale 2017).

2.5 New Challenges for Corporate Responsibilities and Governance

Machine learning is already starting to make or influence decisions at all levels of organizations—a trend which will only accelerate. As these systems proliferate, the

---

[3] *State v Loomis*, 881 N.W.2d 749 (Wis. 2016).

outputs from one system will increasingly generate inputs into another, leading to decisional chain reactions. Companies and other organizations have been built around legal concepts defining how decisions will be taken and where responsibility for those decisions should lie. Companies will typically have responsibility for the actions of their employees—a concept called 'vicarious liability'. Boards of directors will generally be responsible for ensuring that proper decision-making processes are in place throughout the organization. These measures are part of corporate governance.

AI will challenge the application of these established principles. If a machine learning tool rather than an individual makes a decision, will the company which deploys the system be vicariously liable in the same way as if that tool were an employee, or will the rules need to be subtly different? What will the board of director's responsibility be to understand how machine learning tools make decisions for their company and to ensure they exercise effective control over those decisions? Much of the regulation emerging after the 2001 Enron and 2008 Lehman Brothers bankruptcies is aimed at ensuring that companies have effective controls in place to prevent complex accounting and financial systems from running amok without the full knowledge and control of the board. Some of the accountability provisions in the European General Data Protection Regulation (GDPR) strive to achieve the same objective, by ensuring that major data protection risks are identified and escalated to senior management. AI risks will likely require similar oversight measures.

A more fundamental question is whether corporate board decisions must necessarily be human, or whether robots and code might one day supplant human boardroom decisions (Möslein 2017). A team of economists suggest that AI will make prediction cheap, but that prediction is not the same as judgement, and that judgement will necessarily remain human. As the cost of prediction plummets, the value of its complement, human judgement, will increase (Agrawal et al 2016). Boards will want to design corporate governance frameworks that carefully separate prediction, which can usefully use AI tools, and judgement, which must remain squarely on the shoulders of human institutions.

2.6 New Market Distortions

A key role the law plays in a market economy is to maintain a level playing field. Abusive use of inside information, mergers which create monopolistic power, and collusive behaviour between competitors are just three examples of areas in which the law has intervened to protect the integrity of a functioning market. Machine learning provokes consideration of an entirely novel set of questions for securities and competition law. For example, the power of AI enables it to make predictions that can achieve a high degree of accuracy. The law will have to determine when those predictions might become 'inside information' for the purposes of insider trading laws. The use of alternative data can create new uniquely insightful information offering those with access to it benefits that are potentially unfair compared to the information available to ordinary investors. The law will need to decide whether to treat these insights as inside information for purposes of securities laws (*Integrity Research Associates* 2018). In a similar vein, AI may combine competitor data sets or provide insights to competitors which encourage them, even if not consciously, to follow similar pricing strategies. Once again, the law will need to decide whether and when this should be treated as unlawful anti-competitive collusion between competitors (McSweeny & O'Dea 2017). AI tools may offer new opportunities to derive value from different data sets to create unique market opportunities, including highly granular marketing or price discrimination strategies (Townley et al 2017). Once again, the law will need to decide when price discrimination becomes an unfair consumer practice, and when the merging of data should be subjected to anti-trust or competition law controls on anti-competitive transactions.

2.7 Diffuse Social Harms

One of the most difficult kinds of harms to measure and mitigate is the longer-term risk for our human-based institutions—what Professor Karen Yeung (2017: 30) refers to as our democratic commons:

> core legal and constitutional principles that are ultimately rooted in the liberal commitment to treat individuals with fairness and dignity, and which, in liberal democratic societies, include principles of transparency and accountability, due process and the rule of law.

Like global warming, erosion of the democratic commons would not result from any single AI system, but from an accumulation of algorithm-based decisions increasingly replacing human-based decision-making in different contexts, whether in the field of music recommendations, news editing, or prison sentencing. The law has always had an important role in managing risks to our social structures and norms, although its capacity to intervene is limited by the extent to which the law's focus is on resolving specific conflicts in individual cases—for example, balancing freedom of speech against malicious falsehood in the context of a specific conflict between parties. AI recasts those risks in both specific ways, such as a machine learning tool that generates outcomes that undermine the concept of 'truth' and more generally by breaking down the connection between democratic institutions and the making of social decisions (*World Wide Web Foundation* 2017). A view of risk that ignores social impacts or focuses only on individual machine learning applications and overlooks the cumulative impact on society will fall short, which is why we see a benefit to a regulatory institution—which could be a multi-stakeholder organization similar to those that govern the internet—to monitor different forms of social harm that may escape the attention of sector-specific regulators.

3. The Role of Data in AI

Data is the raw material of machine learning. Data can be distilled, processed, combined, and transferred for many purposes and in many places. But, as with any raw material, data can be valuable, may be misused, or can become contaminated. Anything which is valuable or can cause damage will inevitably raise legal questions.

3.1 Input Data May Be Subject to Restrictions

For many industries, the data used to train the machine learning models (or networks) will include at least some amount of data about private individuals (eg customers), confidential company data, or other sensitive data (eg data that should not be exposed, whether publicly, to competitors, or otherwise). This data is commonly subject to regulatory restrictions under privacy or other laws and is often tightly controlled contractually by the respective companies, and/or under data protection laws. Those using the data, and those using machine learning solutions which utilize the data, must satisfy themselves that the use is legitimate and will not expose them to potential liabilities.

3.2 Input Data Will Influence Outcomes

'Rubbish in, rubbish out' is an eternal truth of computing. It is no less true of machine learning, but the consequences in the AI field are potentially more severe. As we have already explained above, data is not simply used to generate individual outputs; it is also used to train AI systems. Accordingly, poor quality or 'bad' data does not simply undermine tool performance, it also risks creating a tool which may generate poor quality or erroneous decisions in future uses, and these can have serious consequences. The digital economy increasingly resembles production lines and complex supply chains in other sectors of the economy where harmful impacts of contaminated raw materials can quickly spread far and wide.

For example, a detection system for a driverless car developed using data from an inner city may be badly suited for use in rural environments. Equally, using a credit worthiness analysis tool which has been trained using data drawn from a wealthy suburb may be worse than useless if used to manage customers from a less wealthy district; and if the outputs from the latter are used to train a tool for use in another district the errors are likely to grow further. The reliance on AI tools on the quality of the underlying training data and the appropriate use of that tool in a given context have far-reaching implications for anyone wanting to use an AI tool. How do you satisfy yourself that the tool is not only built correctly but that the data used to train it is of the right quality, has not been contaminated, is not artificially skewed and is going to produce suitable results?

3.3 Input Data May Make the Algorithm More Valuable

Algorithms developed by a firm are typically treated as the intellectual property of that firm for use as it sees fit. The algorithms are used and licensed accordingly— just like other software. The use of customer data to train machine learning models results in a new type of 'information' or 'object' that would typically not be covered by a traditional software-like approach. Even though a third party may have developed the machine learning models, it may not be appropriate for the developer to retain full ownership of a version of that model that has been trained using data of another entity. Reasons for restricting use of the trained machine learning models include the fact that the trained models may have some insight or learning that was derived from sensitive data of another company, such as the customer data or confidential commercial data that was used in the training data set.

As an example, Bank A might hire a Provider to analyse its customer data using machine learning. A machine learning model trained on Bank A's customer data might be used by Bank A to classify customers into different risk categories, or determine the terms that should be offered to different types of customers. The Provider does not retain any of Bank A's customer data after the training. The Provider may, however, retain at least a copy of the trained model. Bank B, who is a competitor of Bank A, might also contact the Provider to perform a similar analysis. Can the Provider use the model, whose capabilities have been built around Bank A's data, to analyse the customer data of Bank B?

As noted, none of the confidential data of Bank A will be exposed to Bank B, and the models were developed by the Provider. It may be difficult, however, to determine the extent to which aspects of the customer data of Bank A might be discoverable through the application of the trained model—for example, might the performance of the model enable Bank B to assess how many of Bank A's customers are high income customers? Equally there may be situations where Bank B might benefit from knowledge learned through the training that would not have been learned if only customer data of Bank B were used for the training. For example, how high income customers might behave in a situation even though

Bank B only has a small number of such customers? And if the data involved was confidential corporate data of Bank A, could the use of that trained model to process the data of Bank B expose trade secrets of Bank A, or at least enable Bank B to take advantage of knowledge learned through the training on the corporate data of Bank A?

In essence, the use of input data to train the model is creating value for the model and its future users. Companies, like Bank A in our example, should already be considering contractual provisions to share in this value or protect their data in these scenarios. More fundamentally the law will need to determine whether it needs to develop new confidentiality-like principles to address how the value created in trained models should be shared.

3.4 Identity Data May Be Reverse Engineered

The issue is further complicated when dealing with individual customer data. A company might believe that as long as the customer data is de-identified (eg spend behaviour is tagged to an anonymized customer number rather than a named individual) that there is no harm in the trained machine learning models being used for other purposes. It is possible, however, that models trained using de-identified customer data may include learning that would enable those customers to be singled out and tracked based on data or aspects that are independent of conventional identifying data. It is also possible that machine learning tools might be developed with that specific aim in mind.

For example, various behaviours or types of action taken by a user over time may correspond to a pattern that can be used to single out and monitor a specific user, even if the person's name, appearance, or other identifying information is not known—this might be a particular risk if the individual belongs to a relatively small group such as high net worth customers. These behaviours and actions can also be used to classify groups of users along aspects such as gender, age, race, or other types of classifications, which can lead to discrimination, unintentional bias, or other such issues.

European standards for anonymizing personal data require data to be de-identified to the extent that re-identification is impossible using 'all the means reasonably likely to be used' (Recital 26, GDPR). By seeing correlations between unrelated data sets, machine learning may make re-identification increasingly easy, thereby continuously raising the bar on what constitutes anonymization under EU data protection law and potentially similar laws elsewhere. What is adequately anonymized today may become identifiable tomorrow thanks to machine learning. This may require law-makers, in Europe and elsewhere, to adopt an evolutionary approach. It also means that advances in AI tools may cause businesses to start to breach laws in the future with which they currently comply.

4. Using Contracts to Manage AI Risk

The preceding discussion has outlined a number of challenges which AI raises for the law, and the resulting legal uncertainty facing enterprises. In principle, many of AI-related risks should be capable of being managed through legally binding contracts—for example, between the business providing an AI tool and its enterprise customers who use the tool, between the enterprise user and its insurers, and between the enterprise user and its customers. But in practice, businesses (and insurers, investors, and consumers) are faced with the need to develop new approaches to contracts to address these developing risks whilst those risks continue to evolve.

In addition, as we will see in the following sections, there is a need for a broader discussion of underlying legal principles and whether they remain fit for purpose in a networked digital age in which AI tools are commonly employed. For example, does the law need to develop new liability principles? Do consumers need special protection? Does public policy require new regulatory frameworks to address AI-related market failures or broader social or economic impacts?

AI systems involve at least three stakeholders in the vertical value chain: the developer of the AI system, the enterprise customer, and the end-user (which may be the customer's customer). The contracts between the AI system developer and the enterprise customer will be the first important risk mitigator.

4.1 Protecting the Value of a Trained AI Model

Development of machine learning tools is a significant investment. Developers (and their investors) will want to ensure that they secure the value in their tools. The discussion in this section identifies various ways in which contractual risk management techniques can be adopted in order to protect the value of this investment, from the perspective of developers and their investors. Like other software tools, most trained machine learning models will contain elements which are capable of protection as copyright, patent, or other intellectual property. Those concerned to protect their investment in these models should ensure that ownership or usage is clearly specified in agreements and licences, with pricing set accordingly.

The enterprise whose data is teaching the model will wish to protect the value of its data through appropriate contractual restrictions. While the intellectual property rights associated with raw data are not always clear, enterprises holding data generally have the right to restrict usage. Where personal data are involved, imposing contractual restrictions on use is an obligation in some legal systems (Article 28, GDPR).

The legal treatment of any models trained by using that data (in particular whether a trained model will be protected as intellectual property) is less clear.

Nonetheless, enterprise users wishing to retain rights to those models regardless of the entity doing the training could attempt to do so via contract. Even for enterprise users not seeking to retain ownership of trained models, it may be wise for them at least to define or restrict the usage of the trained model, at least for certain industries or with respect to other competitors. If the training will involve data from multiple entities, as in the case of big data consortium projects for example, this may include specifying the scope for which each of the consortium members may utilize the trained models, or results produced by those models.

In addition to these protective provisions concerned with protecting the value of a firm's investment in AI tools, firms at each stage of the chain of origination, development, and use of machine learning tools, including data providers and technology developers, should consider the way in which their relationships are legally structured. For example, should their relationships be based on a royalty type model (eg percentage of revenues generated) rather than a flat fee? If so, what provisions need to be included to ensure that the revenues used as the basis for the royalty calculation reflect all of the value generated? Should the relationship be structured as a consortium or joint venture? Should there be co-ownership in the trained model or results? Should a separate entity be created to conduct the analysis and control access to the results?

4.2 Contractual Use Restrictions to Avoid Revealing Trade Secrets

The training of the machine learning algorithms may enable others to learn trade secrets or patentable technology. To prevent this, it might be appropriate to restrict the usage of the machine learning model to prevent use for any application or entity that might gain advantage from such trade secrets or technology. It might also be possible to restrict certain types of decisions from being made using the trained machine learning algorithms, where those decisions may relate to the defined intellectual property. The training data, trained models, and usage thereof should also be analysed to determine whether they themselves constitute trade secrets or patentable subject matter requiring legal protection. Specific provisions may also be included in commercial agreements to indicate the ownership of any inventions utilizing, or resulting from usage of, the trained machine learning models or results.

4.3 Allocating Liability if Things Go Wrong

A key contractual question will be the allocation of liability for decisions made using machine learning. This might be anything from harm caused to a patient who is wrongfully diagnosed by a tool, to injury to a pedestrian who is not accurately identified by an autonomous driving system, to a wide range of financial losses which businesses might suffer from 'errors' made by AI tools. The various businesses involved in the development and deployment of machine learning tools (and their insurers) will want to allocate liability risks so that it is clear who is responsible if something goes wrong. The law has a well-established framework for identifying when civil liability arises. For example, the law of negligence generates obligations of compensation if proper care has not been taken. The main tools available for that allocation between businesses will be contractual promises by which one party agrees to assume liability to another (typically warranties and indemnities) and agreements to limit the liability of one party to another. Firms exposed to potential civil liability associated with the use of AI tools will understandably wish to employ contractual risk management approaches to allocate liability to the entity in the best position to prevent the harm in the first place. They will also wish to ensure that the ways they have traditionally used contractual risk management will function as intended when faced with new scenarios.

One example of a new scenario in which machine learning will generate potential liabilities which will need to be addressed is where one entity provides training data to enable development of a tool. That entity may be liable for the accuracy of that training data, including any labelling or classification data that is relied upon, so that if use of the trained model 'harms' someone the provider of the data could have legal responsibility for that harm. This potentially generates a need for indemnification to make clear who will bear the costs arising from any inaccurate or improper training data. Similarly, if an entity provides a trained model for a specific purpose (eg distinguishing a human from a shadow on the road), that entity may need to provide indemnification for decisions made by the trained model where those decisions are utilized to perform an action that results in injury to person or property (such as a pedestrian struck by an autonomous vehicle equipped with that tool). Equally, they will want to seek an indemnity from anyone purchasing the tool against the consequences of it being used other than for the purposes for which it has been designed.

Firms may also wish to make provision requiring some type of auditing to enable them to verify the provenance of the tool. This might require that information as to the process or logic used to make specific decisions will be available and maintained for at least a minimum period of time. Provisions of this type might also include determining the type of information to be made available for auditors.

As discussed above, in some instances machine learning models may learn relationships that are not easily explainable in human terms, but produce very accurate results. A consideration may be made as to whether to specify that the machine learning should be limited to explainable decisions or relationships only, even though it may result in somewhat less accurate decisions or results, specifically where there are significant liability or regulatory issues that require a full audit trail.

5. Contractual Provisions to Ensure Compliance with Regulatory Requirements

5.1 Avoiding Issues Related to Profiling or Bias

In order to avoid risks associated with the use of AI tools which may make decisions that could unlawfully discriminate, or which might violate the requirements of data protection laws, those involved in building these tools may wish to utilize contractual provisions that delineate the scope of permitted use of a trained model in order to attempt to avoid any issues with data privacy or bias. For example, customer data might train a machine learning model to recommend types of music to provide to customers of a music streaming service based on their past listening behaviour. While the data may be identity-agnostic, a sufficient amount of data can enable a specific user to be identified based on their current streaming selections. This can bring about issues of data privacy, as the model has learned customer-specific knowledge that can be used to track a given user. Under EU data protection legislation, the ability to single out an individual, even without identifying him or her, is sufficient to trigger application of data protection rules. Even in jurisdictions where this legislation does not have direct impact, the 'singling out' and 'tracking' criteria may align with public expectations, meaning that businesses globally will be considering the more restrictive EU rules as a potential benchmark for best practices in other territories.

AI-created profiles can also bring about potential issues of bias if the model can relatively accurately predict the race, gender, age, income, or other such aspects of the person, which can then potentially be used to make decisions based on that information, such as whether to provide a service to the person, determine a risk level for a person, etc. Wherever personal data of EU citizens is involved, the 'purpose limitation' principle of EU data protection legislation will likely require that explicit restrictions be placed on the scope of use but, even where those specific rules do not apply there are likely to be broader concerns to prevent 'abuses' of this kind. Profiling that leads to a 'legal effect' or similar significant effect on individuals will trigger additional obligations under EU law, including the obligation to inform the individual of the underlying logic involved in making the relevant profiling decision (Articles 13 and 22 GDPR).

To address these issues, firms might wish to consider defining the permissible scope of use and specifically prohibiting any usage in ways which enable re-identification or where decisions might be made that could exploit or be unfairly influenced by this information. These fears again highlight the danger of using machine learning without adequate transparency and explicability, because much of the bias or privacy aspects may be unable to be readily determined simply by analysing the results. This reinforces the desirability of including audit provisions in contracts.

5.2 Sector-Specific Compliance Responsibilities

Most businesses that use, or come to rely on, machine learning tools will be subject to a range of existing regulations regarding their activities. Depending on their line of business and the nature of the AI tool, regulation which is relevant might cover anything from composition of products or integrity of services to workplace safety or fair advertising. Business users will need to ensure that the use of machine learning tools, whose developers may have a limited understanding of the subtleties of the user's regulatory environment, does not compromise their compliance with these various legal requirements. To achieve this, users should consider either requiring contractual undertakings or selecting providers (whether of the tools or of training data) that will ensure compliance or consider securing rights to audit the steps taken to ensure legal compliance.

5.3 Geographic Restrictions Linked to Export Controls and Data Localization Requirements

There will be situations in which the use of tools could infringe legal controls which are designed to ensure national sovereignty and geographical integrity. One example will be where the machine learning models have been trained by data covered by data export controls. If an entity is licensing usage of a trained machine learning model, it might be worth considering where the model will be used and what the resulting output data will be. If the models might be considered to include data that would be subject to export control (or other geographic restrictions, including under privacy or data localization laws) thought should be given to the locations where the models themselves can be utilized. For example, the servers using the models might be restricted to a specific country or region, even though the result data might be able to be transmitted to, and utilized in, other locations.

5.4 Data Security

Data security policies should be re-evaluated in light of machine learning, even if the machine learning models and resulting data are only for internal use. Access to certain data used for training might be restricted to specific users or groups within the company. It is possible that the models trained using this data may expose, directly or indirectly, the relevant data to others who might otherwise not have permission to access the underlying data.

Internal policies or access controls may need to be updated or put in place to specify the usage of, or access to, the trained models, as well as the output of the trained models. Model users should take care to understand the extent to which the developers will continue to train the models by reference to the data handled by the model in ongoing use (ie will the user's input and output data also be training data?) and the need for contractual protections that may be necessary to ensure data security in that scenario.

5.5 Respecting Data Privacy Obligations

Any business that provides data for a machine learning tool will need to ensure that doing so does not breach obligations it may have under the ever expanding range of data privacy laws worldwide that are concerned with maintaining the integrity and controlling the use of personal data, whether in general, or in specific contexts such as health-related information. Equally, those laws increasingly create risks not simply for the originator of the data but also for others who might use that data in ways not permitted by law (or by the individual to whom that data relates).

Where customer data is utilized for training, firms should ensure that their terms of use and privacy policies explain that data will be used for such training, and where required, seek consent. Data analytics are often covered in existing privacy policies, and can be covered under EU law by either a 'legitimate interest' or 'consent' legal basis (Article 6 GDPR). However, existing privacy policies seldom envisage the case where individual user data is used to train an algorithm that would then be used to analyse data in other contexts.

A question might arise whether a provider's trained model continues to process indirectly the original personal data from which it learned, even when the algorithm is performing an unrelated task on unrelated data. In other words, does the trained model retain a phantom version of the original personal data, a 'ghost in the machine?' If that were the case, the use of a trained model might be prohibited under personal data legislation, and would have to be purged of all its previous learning experience in order not to be indirectly processing any of the old data. Such an extreme outcome would hinder AI research. It will behove AI providers to be able to demonstrate that the model's residual intelligence contains no information permitting an individual to be singled out.

Tool developers, who may be involved in processing the data in question, and even potentially other users of the tool, will want to consider ensuring they put in place sufficient contractual protections to satisfy themselves that proper consents have been obtained, or other legal grounds secured, from end users whose data are being used.

6. Corporate Governance Requires Human Decision-Making

For corporations, which make up the vast majority of significant businesses globally, responsibility for commercial decisions ultimately rests with the board of directors. It is the board that will be responsible for ensuring that their business grasps the opportunities, and manages the risks, associated with machine learning tools some of which we have outlined in this chapter. However, those tools provide a new kind of challenge for boards—how to effectively govern an organization in which an increasing number of decisions of increasing significance are taken by machines?

Boards of directors will need to ensure that the use by their businesses of machine learning tools does not undermine fulfilment of their obligations to exercise effective control over those businesses in order to ensure that they discharge their legal obligations of care and diligence as company directors. This will require them to review their corporate governance frameworks and internal reporting lines to ensure that 'machine driven decisions' do not go beyond established frameworks for the delegation of decision-making and that the board of directors always has an adequate understanding of frameworks within which those decisions are being made.

Corporate boards will also need to consider updating other legal policies and procedures to ensure corporate compliance with regulatory requirements throughout the organization. For example, many companies maintain policies regarding competition or antitrust law. Given the potential risks that the use of AI tools might result in anti-competitive collusive behaviour, internal training and policies will need to be updated. Similarly, publicly listed companies will need to consider updating their policies on inside information to ensure continuing compliance with securities laws in the age of alternative data.

7. Models for Regulation

7.1 Do We Need Specific AI Regulation at All?

While internal governance and contractual agreements between commercial parties can manage many of the foreseeable and unforeseeable risks associated with machine learning, there may be instances where these measures are insufficient due to externalities, that is risks affecting third parties that none of the contracting parties has any reason to care about. Companies deploying AI systems will internalize most AI-associated risks because they know that in the event of an AI-related accident, the reputational and liability risks will likely fall on the company that deployed the system.

For example, where Bank A uses an AI provider's algorithm to classify bank customers, a mistake in the output will almost inevitably result in liability and/or reputational damage for Bank A, leading Bank A to internalize the risk and adopt appropriate mitigation measures through contracts, audits, and governance mechanisms. In most situations, the company deploying the system—Bank A in our example—will have the right economic incentives to make sure the system is safe, and that its contracts with the AI provider and insurers cover all possible contingencies. Where incentives are aligned in the right direction, regulation is generally unnecessary.

A market failure might occur where the risk is so large that insurance becomes unavailable, or companies over-react to liability risks by reducing their AI-related activity below levels that are optimal for society. According to the economic analysis of law, liability rules can be understood as seeking to encourage both the optimal level of care and the optimal level of activity so that social welfare is maximized (Coase 1960; Shavell 2004: 199).[4] Current liability rules—no doubt with refinement through case law—would appear to achieve this twin objective for AI. However, if entire fields of AI activity are blocked or inhibited because of fears of excessive liability, regulatory intervention might be required to provide liability safe harbours.[5]

A market failure might also occur where existing liability rules do not sufficiently protect potential victims from AI-related damage. One concern on the liability front is that it will be difficult in most cases for the victim of an AI-caused harm to prove negligence, in part because of the lack of transparency of the systems, and because of the multiple suppliers involved. Consequently, some form of reversal of the burden of proof will likely be necessary, as is already the case for liability for defective products or for data protection violations under European data protection legislation.[6] Reversal of the burden of proof will motivate companies to make sure AI systems are tested, and potential harms evaluated and mitigated, consistent with the state of the art before the systems go into operation. Risk assessment is commonplace for product safety and for risky forms of data processing.[7] Evaluating the safety of AI systems should in theory be no different from evaluating the safety of other complex systems. Integrating machine learning into

[4] 'The measure of social welfare will be taken to be the utility that victims and injurers derive from their activities less their costs of care and expected accident losses.'

[5] The liability safe harbours provided by the European E-Commerce Directive and the United States Communication Decency Act are examples of legislation aimed at encouraging the activities of internet intermediaries that otherwise would have been inhibited by liability fears. For an examination of how tort liability may cause ISPs to adopt preventive strategies that create broader social costs, see Katyal (2003).

[6] Art 24(1) of the GDPR requires that data controllers demonstrate compliance. To escape liability, the data controller must prove that it was not in any way responsible for the event giving rise to the damage. Art 82(3) GDPR.

[7] Art 35 of the GDPR requires data protection impact assessments for processing that is likely to result in a high risk to the rights and freedoms of natural persons.

existing risk assessment frameworks is already underway, for example in the context of automobile safety standards (Salay et al 2017).

Some have suggested that autonomous systems should have some form of legal personality in order to ensure the proper functioning of liability rules.[8] However this seems merely to displace the problem towards a new form of AI legal entity which would have many of the drawbacks of existing corporate structures. The AI entity would have to be adequately capitalized and insured in order for liability rules to have teeth. AI legal entities would be similar to special-purpose companies created to own ships or aircraft, and which often have inadequate capitalization to indemnify accident victims. This is why courts sometimes 'pierce the corporate veil' to assign liability to entities with sufficiently deep pockets. Sufficient insurance is also required for some forms of activity, and that is likely to be the case for AI systems integrated into products that could cause significant harm. A new form of legal entity for AI systems would not add anything to the current liability approaches.

7.2 AI Risks Should Be Regulated Using a Sector Approach

One of the biggest debates is whether AI regulation should be developed organically within different regulatory bodies responsible for different industries and risks (transport regulation, banking regulation, securities regulation, health regulation), or whether there would be benefit to an overarching AI regulator and regulatory framework. This debate involves considerations that go beyond the scope of this chapter. However, from a legal practitioner's viewpoint, the costs of an overarching AI framework seem to outweigh the benefits, for four reasons:

First, an AI regulatory framework would require defining what systems would fall within the new regulatory category. What exactly is being regulated? Forms of machine learning have been around since the 1950s, and as we saw in the introduction, AI is a broad category that encompasses different forms of technology that evolve every day. Defining AI for purposes of regulation would itself be a daunting task. Most definitions would be over inclusive or under inclusive, and run the risk of becoming obsolete due to technological change.

A second obstacle would be that any AI legal principles would have to be drafted in highly general terms in order to cover the multiple contexts in which AI systems are used: from medical diagnoses to autonomous vehicles, through to music recommender systems. Detailed rules governing specific AI activity run the risk of missing their mark and becoming quickly outdated. Drafters would have to revert

---

[8] See, eg Resolution of the European Parliament dated 16 February 2017, with recommendations to the Commission on Civil Law Rules on Robotics, s 59(f).

to general principles which would largely repeat existing legal principles, for example the requirement to market 'safe' products.[9]

Third, a general AI regulator would be ill-equipped to conduct risk analyses for the different kinds of AI applications that could potentially cause harm. One of the most important functions of regulators is to help define an appropriate level of safety and consumer protection. Data protection regulators, and to some extent the Federal Trade Commission in the United States, are responsible for evaluating the adequacy of data protection and consumer protection in a wide variety of industries. An AI regulator could potentially be modelled on this horizontal, multi-industry, approach.

However, the harms associated with AI systems seem much more diverse than the harms associated with data protection violations. In many instances human life is at stake, such as in the case of medical devices or autonomous vehicles. In other cases, the harms may relate to systemic risks to the banking system, or protection of criminal defendants against unfair sentencing.[10] The analysis of these risks is extremely different, and should be left to industry specialists: health regulators, transport regulators, banking regulators, and the like.

Fourth, a general AI regulator would likely issue rules and recommendations that create friction with sector-specific rules. Institutional rivalry could even emerge as two regulatory authorities, one sector-specific and one general, both try to stay ahead of new AI developments. This has occurred in the field of data security, for example, where banking regulations, cyber-security regulations, and data protection regulations all impose their own layer of overlapping data security obligations, creating needless complexity and uncertainty for those trying to comply. The urge to regulate platforms in Europe has run into the same difficulty: online platforms are already subject to multiple existing regulations depending on their sector of activity (transport, lodging, insurance) and the political desire to create an overarching platform regulation has run into two kinds of difficulties. First, how to define a platform, and second, what would a new regulation of platforms add compared to existing competition law, consumer protection law and sector-specific regulation? (Maxwell & Pénard 2015).

7.3 A Regulatory Role Observing and Measuring Diffuse AI Harms

One area where an overarching regulator for AI may be appropriate is to keep track of the broader social risks associated with AI, and ring alarm bells when regulatory

---

[9] On the benefits and drawbacks of general principles compared to detailed rules, see Breyer (1984) and Kaplow (1992).
[10] For a discussion of AI in the criminal justice system, see case note *State v Loomis* (2017).

intervention appears necessary. As mentioned above, AI can have a cumulative adverse effect on the broader social ecosystem or democratic commons. Advocates of regulation point out that multi-sourced harms can erode the democratic commons before we realize what has happened. At that point it may be too late to prevent at least some of the harm (Yeung 2011). Applying a precautionary principle to AI applications[11] would in most cases do more harm than good, by stifling innovation and many of the social benefits associated with AI.

A regulator or multi-stakeholder body whose job is to define, observe, and measure possible harms to broader social values and institutions might have a role as an early warning system, a form of canary in the AI coal mine. This role naturally dovetails with the field of AI ethics, where a number of firms and international organizations are already devoting considerable resources (IEEE 2019). Harms to society flowing from disinformation illustrate the kind of effects that need to be observed and measured before appropriate regulatory remedies can be designed and implemented. Perhaps as a precursor to thinking of this kind, the European Commission has recommended a progressive regulatory approach to disinformation: self and co-regulatory solutions accompanied by key performance indicators (KPIs), observation, and then (and only then) more prescriptive regulatory obligations if self and co-regulation are not sufficient.[12] Developing KPIs for measuring societal harms from AI is itself a daunting and important exercise. As technology profoundly transforms society, there will be a combination of positive and negative effects, some of which will be hard to define, let alone measure. If regulation is to hit its mark, the precise harms that regulation is intended to address must be defined and measured, so that the regulatory cure is adapted to the disease, and its effectiveness can be monitored.[13]

7.4 High-Level Guiding Principles

In addition to observing and measuring social harms caused by AI, a regulator or multi-stakeholder body might define guiding principles that would help courts and sector-specific regulators do their job. For example, one could imagine a rule that each AI application should always specify the person or entity that is responsible for the system, and that the responsible person or entity must have liability insurance. The level of insurance, and the existence of other minimum qualifications

---

[11] For a description of the precautionary principle and when it should be used, see European Commission Future Brief, 'The precautionary principle: decision-making under uncertainty' September 2017; see also Sunstein (2003).

[12] European Commission Communication, 'Tackling online disinformation: a European Approach' 26 April 2018, COM(2018) 236 final.

[13] On the adverse side effects of regulation, particularly of fast-moving technology, see Breyer (1984) and Maxwell (2017); see also, European Commission Better Regulation Toolbox https://ec.europa.eu/info/better-regulation-toolbox_en (accessed 20 June 2019).

for the responsible person, would naturally depend on the type of AI system and would be left to the sector-specific regulator. Another high-level principle may be that any AI-based decision-making process must be transparent and auditable on request from a court or regulator.

7.5 Who Will Take the Initiative?

A range of governmental, international and policy-based entities and groups have already started to explore the issues raised by machine learning and AI. However, the challenges to developing a coherent approach are immense. These are issues which raise complex and multi-faceted questions, which are truly international and which impact every type of business and human activity. Over recent years we have seen how challenging institutions have found it to address what is, relatively, a narrow set of questions regarding regulation of platforms and online content—issues which have risen to a high level of public concern with regulators seemingly still unable to find a coherent answer. This begs the question whether legislators and regulators will be able effectively to take the initiative when it comes to AI.

Large users and providers of AI systems will be looking for principles—including ethical principles—that can guide their AI deployment internationally. The first examples of international AI regulation may therefore come from corporate boardrooms that are developing company-specific AI ethics and governance principles. International organizations, such as ISO and IEEE,[14] are also developing norms for AI ethics and safety that companies will be able to refer to in the not-too-distant future.

8. Conclusion

The purpose of this chapter is to show how legal practitioners are already using contracts to address some of the legal risks associated with machine learning. In addition to allocating risks for system errors, contracts must consider the role of data used to train the models. These data add value to the model, but they may also create future errors. Parties to contracts must consider to what extent the trained model may reveal trade secrets derived from the use of old training data, or whether the trained model might even retain knowledge permitting individuals whose old training data was used to be singled out in violation of data protection laws. Audit provisions, and mechanisms to ensure that machine learning decisions

[14] IEEE (2019).

can be understood by courts and regulators, will be critical for AI to be used in regulated industries such as banking or transport.

In addition to contracts, enterprise users of machine learning tools will have to update their internal governance mechanisms to make sure that the board of directors maintains sufficient controls over AI-based decisions.

On the regulatory front, we argue that most AI-related risks can and should be addressed through sector-specific regulation. The banking regulator should address AI risks in the banking sector, the transport regulator should address AI risks in autonomous driving, the health regulator should address AI risks in medical devices, and so on. Creating a separate regulatory framework for AI would be counterproductive because of the great diversity of AI applications and risks.

The one area where a separate regulatory authority or multi-stakeholder organization would be useful is to monitor broad social harms caused by AI that may go unnoticed by sector-specific regulators. These social harms may emerge in unforeseen places, as we have seen in connection with fake news and the potential impact on democratic institutions. One of the most important tasks for the monitoring institution would be to develop KPIs relating to social harms that may be adversely affected by AI. When KPIs hit dangerous levels, the institution would ring alarm bells.

In summary, we recommend using a four-layer model to think about regulation of AI. The foundational layer consists of existing liability, property, and contract law, which can go a long way to allocating risks and value-sharing for AI projects in a socially optimal manner. The second layer consists of corporate governance measures, to ensure that AI systems do not escape human controls and decision-making. The third layer consists of sector-specific regulation to deal with risks arising in particular AI use cases, for example in medical devices or bank trading platforms. The last layer consists of a high-level monitoring body to watch for broader social harms that may emerge from AI-related applications, and ring alarm bells if the KPIs evolve in the wrong direction.

Bibliography

Abbott R, 'The Reasonable Computer: Disrupting the Paradigm of Tort Liability' (2018) 86 George Washington Law Review 1.

Agrawal A, Gans J, and Goldfarb A, 'The Simple Economics of Machine Intelligence' *Harvard Business Review* (17 November 2016).

Breyer S, *Regulation and its Reform* (Harvard University Press 1984).

Coase R, 'The Problem of Social Cost' (1960) 3 Journal of Law and Economics 1.

Goddard K, Roudsary A, and Wyatt J, 'Automation Bias: A Systematic Review of Frequency, Effect Mediators, and Mitigators' (2012) 19 Journal of the American Medical Informatics Association 121.

Gunning D, 'Explainable Artificial Intelligence (XAI) Program Update' (November 2017) <https://www.darpa.mil/attachments/XAIProgramUpdate.pdf> (accessed 20 June 2019).

IEEE, 'Ethically Aligned Design: A Vision for Prioritizing Human Well-being with Autonomous and Intelligent Systems', First Edition (2019) <https://ethicsinaction.ieee.org> accessed 28 July 2019.

Integrity Research Associates, 'Mitigating Risks Associated With Alternative Data' (January 2018).

Kaplow L, 'Rules versus Standards: An Economic Analysis' (1992) 42 Duke LJ 557.

Katyal NK, 'Criminal Law in Cyberspace' (2003) 149 U Pa L Rev 1003, 1100.

Knight W, 'Progress in AI Isn't as Impressive as You Might Think' *MIT Technology Review* (30 November 2017); see also Artificial Intelligence Index, '2017 Annual Report' (November 2017) <aindex.org>.

Maxwell W, *Smart(er) Internet Regulation Through Cost-Benefit Analysis* (Presses des Mines 2017).

Maxwell W and Pénard T, 'Regulating Digital Platforms in Europe—A White Paper' (December 2015) <https://ssrn.com/abstract=2584873> or <http://dx.doi.org/10.2139/ssrn.2584873>.

McSweeny T and O'Dea B, 'The Implications of Algorithmic Pricing for Coordinated Effects Analysis and Price Discrimination Markets in Antitrust Enforcement' (2017) 32 Antitrust 75.

Möslein F, 'Robots in the Boardroom: Artificial Intelligence and Corporate Law' in W Barfield and U Pagallo (eds), *Research Handbook on the Law of Artificial Intelligence* (Edward Elgar 2018) <https://ssrn.com/abstract=3037403> or <http://dx.doi.org/10.2139/ssrn.3037403>.

Pasquale F, *The Black Box Society* (Harvard University Press 2015).

Pasquale F, 'Secret Algorithms Threaten the Rule of Law' MIT Technology Review (2017); see also, case note *State v Loomis* (2017) 130 Harvard Law Review 1530.

Salay R, Queiroz R, and Czarnecki K (2017), 'An Analysis of ISO 26262: Using Machine Learning Safely in Automotive Software' eprint arXiv:1709.02435.

Shavell S, *Foundations of Economic Analysis of Law* (Harvard University Press 2004).

Sunstein CN, 'Beyond the Precautionary Principle' (2003) 151 U Pa L Rev 1003. The Economist, 'For Artificial Intelligence to Thrive, it Must Explain Itself' *The Economist* (15 February 2018).

Tutt A, 'An FDA for Algorithms' (2017) 69 Administrative Law Review 83.

Wachter S, Mittelstadt B, and Floridi L, 'Transparent, Explainable, and Accountable AI for Robotics' (2017) 2(6) Service Robotics doi: 10.1126/scirobotics.aan6080.

World Wide Web Foundation, 'Algorithmic Accountability: Applying the Concept to Different Country Contexts' (July 2017).

Yeung K, 'Can We Employ Design-Based Regulation While Avoiding Brave New World' (2011) 3(1) Law, Innovation and Technology 1.

Yeung K, 'Algorithmic Regulation: A Critical Interrogation' King's College London Dickson Poon School of Law, Legal Studies Research Paper Series: Paper No 2017-27.

11

Minding the Machine v2.0

The EU General Data Protection Regulation and Automated Decision-Making

Lee A Bygrave*

1. Introduction

Just under two decades ago, I published a paper with the title 'Minding the Machine: Article 15 of the EC Data Protection Directive and Automated Profiling' (Bygrave 2001). The paper provided an analysis of Article 15 of the former Data Protection Directive (Directive 95/46 (DPD)) adopted by the then European Community in 1995. Article 15 gave individual persons a qualified right not to be subject to fully automated decisions based on profiling. For this right to apply, the decision concerned must have, firstly, had legal or otherwise significant effects on the person whom the decision targeted and, secondly, been based solely on auto-mated data processing that was intended to evaluate certain personal aspects of that person. The right in Article 15 was complemented by a right to knowledge of the logic involved in such decisions (Article 12(a) DPD). Although innovative and intriguing, these rights remained largely dormant throughout their lifespan under the DPD—as elaborated in section 2 below.

Their essence has been reproduced, with some modifications, in the European Union (EU) General Data Protection Regulation (Regulation 2016/679 (GDPR)), which recently repealed and replaced the DPD. Article 22 GDPR (set out in full in section 3 below) provides a similar right to that provided by Article 15 DPD, while Article 15(1)(h) GDPR provides a similar right to that provided by Article 12(a) DPD. These rights are supplemented by new duties of disclosure imposed on data controllers that engage in fully automated decision-making (Articles 13(2)(f) and 14(2)(g)) GDPR, elaborated in section 3 below). Also new are provisions on 'data

* Work on this chapter has been conducted under the aegis of the research project 'Security in Internet Governance and Networks: Analysing the Law' (SIGNAL), funded by the Norwegian Research Council and UNINETT Norid AS. Thanks go to these institutions and the SIGNAL research team—particularly Luca Tosoni, Worku Gedefa Urgessa, and Tobias Mahler—for support. Thanks go also to the friendly hospitality of the 3A Institute at the Australian National University where the chapter was finalized. The usual disclaimer nonetheless applies. References to legal instruments are to their amended state as of 1 June 2019.

protection by design and by default', which require controllers to implement technical and organizational measures so that the processing of personal data will meet the Regulation's requirements and otherwise ensure protection of the data subject's rights (Article 25 GDPR, set out in greater detail in section 4 below). These provisions are directed at information systems development, with the aim of ensuring that privacy-related interests be taken into due account throughout the lifecycle of such development. Thus, the GDPR is aimed not just at 'minding the machine' but also at moulding it. Part and parcel of this agenda is to tame the potentially deleterious impact of algorithmic regulation (in the sense used by this volume) on the rights and freedoms of individual persons.

Given experience with the DPD, it is pertinent to ask whether this aim is likely to succeed. It is with this question that the chapter is broadly concerned. A definitive and complete treatment of the question is beyond the bounds of the chapter. Rather, what follows is a concise critique of Articles 22 and 25 GDPR, building on recent and more extensive analyses of these provisions (particularly Edwards & Veale 2017; Wachter et al 2017; Bygrave 2017a; Bygrave 2017b; Mendoza & Bygrave 2017; Brkan 2019), supplemented by relatively superficial observations of the EU data protection regime in general. These limits notwithstanding, the chapter manages to highlight significant deficiencies in the ability of EU data protection law to ensure that algorithmic regulation does not unduly impinge on human rights and freedoms.

2. Minding the Machine v1.0

Article 15 of the Data Protection Directive was the first pan-European legislative norm aimed directly at regulating purely machine-based decisions in a data protection context. Although enacted in the 1990s, its roots reached back at least to the 1970s. An important source of its inspiration was France's 1978 Act on data processing, files and individual liberties (*Loi no. 78-17 du 6. janvier 1978 relative à l'informatique, aux fichiers et aux libertés*), which prohibited judicial, administrative, or personal decisions involving assessment of human behaviour insofar as these were based solely on automatic data processing which defined the profile or personality of the individual concerned.

Animating both Article 15 and its French antecedents was fear for the future of human dignity in the face of machine determinism. Their rationale was grounded in a concern to ensure that humans maintain ultimate control of, and responsibility for decisional processes that significantly affect other humans, and that they thereby maintain the primary role in 'constituting' themselves (Bygrave 2001: 18). The result of this concern was a norm that was rather special compared to other data protection norms in that it sought primarily to subject a type of decision, rather than the processing of personal data, to particular quality controls. It thus bore strong similarities with rules on due process and 'natural justice' in administrative and criminal law.

In practice, Article 15 DPD ended up being a second-class right in the EU data protection framework. It never figured centrally in litigation before the Court of Justice of the EU (CJEU) or any national courts, with one exception. In the latter case, the contested decision-making system was deemed to fall outside the scope of the national rules transposing Article 15 because it was not fully automated.[1] Article 15 also failed to figure prominently in enforcement actions by national data protection authorities (DPAs), bar that of France.[2] Further, it played a marginal role in assessments of the adequacy of third countries' data protection regimes with a view to regulating the flow of personal data to those countries. In this context, the former Working Party on the Protection of Individuals with regard to the Processing of Personal Data established pursuant to Article 29 DPD (WP29) took the view that Article 15 did not establish a 'basic' principle but rather an 'additional principle to be applied to specific types of processing' (WP29 1998: 6–7). Not surprisingly, Article 15 was rarely replicated in legal regimes outside Europe. This is not to say that it was basically a 'dead letter'. It lives on, albeit in a somewhat different form, not just in the new EU data protection framework, but also in the modernized Council of Europe Convention on data protection of 2018.[3] Nonetheless, it had scant practical bite on information systems development during the time of its life under the DPD. Concomitantly, it did little to heighten the accountability of algorithmic regulation.

Several features of Article 15 undermined its traction. First, it only applied if multiple cumulative conditions were met, which raised the bar for its application

---

[1] See judgment of the German Federal Court of Justice (Bundesgerichtshof) in the so-called SCHUFA case concerning the use of automated credit-scoring systems: judgment of 28 January 2014, VI ZR 156/13. The court held that the credit-scoring system fell outside the scope of the German rules that transposed Article 15 DPD because the decisions to provide credit were ultimately made by a person. Also noteworthy is an earlier judgment of the French Supreme Court (Cour de cassation) concerning, inter alia, judges' utilization, in the course of criminal court proceedings, of statistical analysis of the activities of masseur-physiotherapists by means of computer systems: Cour de Cassation, Chambre criminelle, Audience publique du 24 septembre 1998, No de pourvoi 97-81.748, Publié au bulletin. The Court held that the statistics usage was not affected by the French rules restricting automated judicial decision making as the statistics had not been generated and used in such a way as to define the profile or personality of the person concerned. This case formally did not turn on French transposition of Article 15 DPD but on application of Article 2 of France's 1978 Act on data processing, files and individual liberties. As noted above, Article 2 was an antecedent to Article 15 DPD and prohibited, inter alia, judicial decisions involving assessment of human behaviour when these were based solely on automatic data processing which defined the profile or personality of the targeted person. The provisions of Article 2 were later reformulated and moved to Article 10 of the French legislation to align better with Article 15 DPD.
[2] See eg Commission Nationale de l'Informatique et des Libertés (CNIL) Decision No 2017-053 of 30 August 2017 in which an automated system for determining admission to French universities was found to violate the French rules transposing Article 15 DPD.
[3] See Article 9(1)(a) of the Modernised Convention for the Protection of Individuals with regard to the Processing of Personal Data (consolidated text), adopted by the 128th Session of the Committee of Ministers, 17–18 May 2018.

significantly. Secondly, a considerable degree of ambiguity inhered in these conditions and this ambiguity was exacerbated by a lack of authoritative guidance on how they were to be understood. Thirdly, even if all of the conditions for its exercise were met, the right was subject to fairly broad and nebulous derogations. One derogation allowed a fully automated decision based on profiling where the decision was taken in the course of entering into or executing a contract at the request of the data subject, and either the request had been fulfilled, or provision was made for 'suitable measures' to safeguard the data subject's 'legitimate interests' (Article 15(2)(a)). The derogation was duly criticized for fallaciously assuming that fulfilling a person's request to enter into or execute a contract is never problematic for that person (Bygrave 2001: 21). Additionally, Article 9 DPD required derogations from Article 15(1) in the interests of freedom of expression, but this seems to have had little practical effect, probably because Article 15 was rarely invoked.

3. Article 22 GDPR

The baton held by Article 15 DPD has been reshaped and handed to Article 22 of the GDPR. A similar baton has been passed also to Article 11 of the Law Enforcement Directive (Directive 2016/680), which applies to law enforcement authorities' processing of personal data. The following analysis, however, focuses on the GDPR which has a much broader field of application than the Law Enforcement Directive.

The provisions of Article 22 GDPR are long, complex, and best set out in full if the subsequent assessment of them is to make sense. They read as follows:

Article 22 Automated individual decision-making, including profiling
1. The data subject shall have the right not to be subject to a decision based solely on automated processing, including profiling, which produces legal effects concerning him or her or similarly significantly affects him or her.
2. Paragraph 1 shall not apply if the decision: (a) is necessary for entering into, or performance of, a contract between the data subject and a data controller; (b) is authorised by Union or Member State law to which the controller is subject and which also lays down suitable measures to safeguard the data subject's rights and freedoms and legitimate interests; or (c) is based on the data subject's explicit consent.
3. In the cases referred to in points (a) and (c) of paragraph 2, the data controller shall implement suitable measures to safeguard the data subject's rights and freedoms and legitimate interests, at least the right to obtain human intervention on the part of the controller, to express his or her point of view and to contest the decision.
4. Decisions referred to in paragraph 2 shall not be based on special categories of personal data referred to in Article 9(1), unless point (a) or (g) of Article 9(2) apply and suitable measures to safeguard the data subject's rights and freedoms and legitimate interests are in place.

The preparatory works for Article 22 provide scant information on its rationale but it is likely animated by much the same fears as animated its predecessors over two decades ago (Mendoza & Bygrave 2017: 83–84). Additionally, Recital 71 of the preamble to the GDPR highlights concerns about the potential for machine error and unfair discrimination in the context of automated decision-making and pro-filing. While these concerns were implicit in the legislative deliberations for the DPD, profiling per se received far more explicit attention in the deliberations for the GDPR (Mendoza & Bygrave 2017: 84) and ended up being directly addressed in Article 22 and defined in Article 4(4) (ie as 'any form of automated processing of personal data consisting of the use of personal data to evaluate certain personal aspects relating to a natural person, in particular to analyse or predict aspects concerning that natural person's performance at work, economic situation, health, personal preferences, interests, reliability, behaviour, location or movements').

Another difference between the respective legislative deliberations for the DPD and GDPR concerns children. The protection of children as data subjects was never expressly addressed in the DPD but figures prominently in the GDPR, also with respect to profiling. Thus, Recital 38 in the preamble to the GDPR states that 'specific protection' of personal data on children 'should, in particular, apply to the use of ... [such data] for the purposes of ... creating personality or user profiles', while Recital 71 states that a measure involving the making of an automated decision based on profiling 'should not concern a child'.

Turning to a comparison of the provisions of Article 22 GDPR with those of Article 15 DPD, the scope of application of the former is wider than the latter. Whereas decisions caught by the latter had to be based, in effect, on profiling, this appears not to be so under Article 22(1) GDPR, which states that the decision must be based on 'automated processing, including profiling' and thereby indicates—at least on a conventional reading—that profiling is one of two alternative baseline criteria of application (the other being 'automated processing'). DPAs have generally embraced this line of interpretation (WP29 2018), yet it has not been embraced by all. Mendoza and Bygrave (2017: 90–91) argue that this interpretation runs counter to the provisions' rationale and background, and that the use of 'including' must accordingly be read as equivalent to 'involving'. Brkan (2019: 97) seems to agree, but their argument is tenuous. In any case, many if not most types of decisions caught by Article 22 will likely involve profiling (see too Brkan 2019: 97).

A further difference in scope of application occurs with respect to especially sensitive categories of personal data (as listed in Article 9—eg data on health or sexual orientation). Article 22(4) prohibits automated decisions based on these data types, unless there is explicit consent (Article 9(2)(a)) or statutory permission grounded in 'reasons of substantial public interest' (Article 9(2)(g)). Article 15 DPD did not contain such a prohibition.

A salient point of contention concerns the very nature of the rule laid down by Article 22(1): does it lay down a right to be exercised by a data subject or is it really laying down a qualified prohibition on a particular type of decisional process, independently of a data subject's objections? Article 15(1) DPD was operationalized by some member states as a right and by other member states as a prohibition. Article 11 of the Law Enforcement Directive expressly takes the latter form. As for Article 22(1) GDPR, some commentators view it as a form of prohibition (WP29 2018; Mendoza & Bygrave 2017; Brkan 2019); others view it as a right (Schartum 2018a; Tosoni 2019). On the one hand, viewing Article 22(1) as a qualified prohibition gives it more bite and thus does greater justice to the Regulation's overarching aim of strengthening data protection (Mendoza & Bygrave 2017: 87). This approach also preserves the operational functionality of the safeguard of 'human involvement' laid down in Article 22(3) (Mendoza & Bygrave 2017: 87), and it aligns the GDPR with the Law Enforcement Directive, thus making the EU's broader data protection framework more coherent (Brkan 2019: 99). On the other hand, an interpretation of Article 22(1) as a right to be exercised by the data subject is consistent with its actual wording and makes sense in light of other GDPR provisions which seem to assume the existence of the decisional processes caught by the rule (see Article 13(2)(f); see further Tosoni 2019). It would also recognize the fact that these decisional processes are already used extensively in both private and government sectors where digitalization is advanced (further on actual use of these processes, see eg Pasquale 2015; Edwards & Veale 2017. Moreover, it would arguably do better justice to the fact that these decisional processes can have socially justifiable benefits (not just potential disbenefits).

Regardless of whether Article 22(1) is a right or a prohibition masquerading as a right, it is heavily encumbered by qualifications. Thus, the house of cards metaphor used to characterize its predecessor (Bygrave 2001: 21) applies equally well to it. In particular, the requirement that a decision be based 'solely' on an automated process will continue to hinder application of Article 22(1) to systems of algorithmic regulation that function, in effect, as decisional *support*—and here it is assumed that the human decision-maker does not blindly follow the thrust of the algorithm but considers its merits. If the criterion of 'solely' is read as necessitating that the initial input of the data utilized in the decisional process is also automated (eg through use of sensor devices)—as Schartum (2018a: 6; cf 2018b: 395) argues—this raises the bar for application even higher. At the same time, the criterion of 'solely', while crucial, is not the only hurdle: significant difficulties exist in determining precisely when a decision has been made and whether it has the requisite effect on the data subject, not least in machine learning contexts (Edwards & Veale 2017: 46–48; Mendoza & Bygrave 2017: 89, 93).

The criteria laid down in Article 22(1), though, are just one layer of qualifications. Another layer inheres in Article 22(2), which essentially states that the 'right' in Article 22(1) does not exist in three alternative sets of circumstances (consent, statutory authority, and contract). Yet another layer inheres in Article 22(3) which basically states that, regardless of the exemptions of contract and consent in Article 22(2), 'at least' three further rights apply, but only when the decision-making is pursuant to contract or consent. On top of all these layers comes that of Article 22(4), which introduces further complex qualifications involving cross-referencing beyond the provisions of Article 22. This clumsy structuring of Article 22 does little to promote clarity and understanding of its import, particularly for laypersons.

Elaborating on the derogations to Article 22(1), these are, in one sense, broadened relative to the derogations under Article 15 DPD. This means, for example, that automated decisions that were potentially hit by Article 15 DPD might be permitted under the new exception for consent. This exception is likely to lower the *de facto* level of protection for individuals, particularly given the relative strength of most individuals vis-à-vis banks, insurance companies, online service providers, and many other businesses. However, the Regulation elsewhere tightens the assessment of what is a *freely given* consent and what automated decisions are *necessary* for the purpose of entering into or performance of a contract (see Article 7(4) and Recital 43). The traction of this tightening will rest on how strictly the necessity criterion is interpreted.

The level of protection under Article 22 will also depend on what safeguards the data controller is obliged to put in place under Article 22(3). At the outset, it is important to highlight that aspects of Article 22(3) offer a higher level of protection than under the DPD. Unlike the latter, a data subject will *always* have the right to demand human review of a fully automated decision, except where the decision is pursuant to statute. Even if statutory authority kicks in, this might well also allow for a right of review—as part of the requisite 'suitable measures to safeguard the data subject's rights and freedoms and legitimate interests' (Article 22(2)(b)).

The list of rights laid down by Article 22(3) is the bare minimum required, and accordingly not exhaustive. Which other rights it encompasses is contested. In particular, debate has ignited over whether data subjects are to be provided with a right to *ex post* explanation of automated decisions affecting them—debate that also afflicts interpretation of some of the other provisions in the Regulation (Articles 13(2)(f), 14(2)(g), and 15(1)(h)—elaborated below). While the preamble to the GDPR explicitly references such a right (Recital 71), the operative provisions of the Regulation do not—leading some scholars to claim that the right does not exist under the Regulation, at least in a legally enforceable form (Wachter et al 2017). However, most other scholars who have addressed the issue disagree (eg Selbst & Powles 2017; Mendoza & Bygrave 2017; Kaminski 2018; Brkan 2019)—and for good reasons. One such reason is that the right inheres in those provisions of the Regulation that provide a right to 'meaningful information about the logic involved, as well as the significance and envisaged consequences' of automated decision-making (Articles 13(2)(f), 14(2)(g), and 15(1)(h)) (eg Selbst & Powes 2017; Brkan 2019: 113–14). Moreover, the right to *ex post* explanation ensures the efficacy of other GDPR rights, such as the right to contest a decision (Article 22(3)) (Mendoza & Bygrave 2017: 93–94; Brkan 2019: 114), and it arguably inheres in the GDPR's overarching requirement that personal data be processed 'fairly and in a transparent manner' (Article 5(1)(a)) (Mendoza & Bygrave 2017: 94). Further, the right to *ex post* explanation arguably follows from the general requirements for controller accountability in Articles 5(2) and 24.

The level of protection under Article 22 will additionally depend on the specifics of member state legislation, in light of the derogations provided in Articles 22(2)(b) and 22(4). Indeed, national legislation will be decisive in determining how Article 22 is operationalized. EU member states have been given relatively broad latitude in this regard. As a result, it will not be surprising if significant differences emerge between national regulatory frameworks for automated decision-making, thus undermining the harmonization aims of the Regulation. We see signs of this potential for divergence in the recent decision by the Italian legislature to extend the scope of application of Article 22 to encompass data on deceased persons (Article 2 terdecies of the Personal Data Protection Code of 2003 (*Decreto legislativo 30 giugno 2003, n. 196: Codice in Materia di Protezione dei Dati Personali*), as amended by Legislative Decree 101/2018). This extension permits—with some qualifications—the estate of a deceased person (data subject) to utilize the 'right' in Article 22(1). The GDPR applies only to processing of data on living persons, but permits member states to enact rules on the processing of data on deceased persons as well (Recital 27 GDPR). Few member states have taken the latter step.

This potential for divergence notwithstanding, we can expect national legislators across Europe to arrive at fairly similar solutions around particular issue sets. One such issue set concerns the protection of children, which, as elaborated above, is flagged for special attention in Recitals 71 and 38 of the preamble to the GDPR. While these Recitals do not create on their own a legally binding prohibition on automated decisions or profiling directed at children, they will likely increase the stringency with which the provisions of Article 22 are nationally operationalized in respect of such processes (eg in the interpretation of what decisions may qualify as having a 'significant' effect (Article 22(1)), in disfavour of controllers.

4. Moulding the Machine v1.0

One of the most striking features of the recent reform of EU law on the protection of personal data is the introduction of explicit and expansive requirements concerning data protection by design and by default. These requirements inhere principally in the first two paragraphs of Article 25 GDPR which read as follows:

Article 25 Data protection by design and by default
1. Taking into account the state of the art, the cost of implementation and the nature, scope, context and purposes of processing as well as the risks of varying likelihood

and severity for rights and freedoms of natural persons posed by the processing, the controller shall, both at the time of the determination of the means for processing and at the time of the processing itself, implement appropriate technical and organisational measures, such as pseudonymisation, which are designed to implement data-protection principles, such as data minimisation, in an effective manner and to integrate the necessary safeguards into the processing in order to meet the requirements of this Regulation and protect the rights of data subjects.

2. The controller shall implement appropriate technical and organisational measures for ensuring that, by default, only personal data which are necessary for each specific purpose of the processing are processed. That obligation applies to the amount of personal data collected, the extent of their processing, the period of their storage and their accessibility. In particular, such measures shall ensure that by default personal data are not made accessible without the individual's intervention to an indefinite number of natural persons.

Expressed more concisely, Article 25 imposes a qualified duty on controllers of personal data to implement technical and organizational measures that are designed to ensure that the processing of personal data meets the Regulation's requirements and otherwise to ensure protection of data subjects' rights. The duty extends to ensuring default application of particular data protection principles—namely, the principles of minimization and proportionality—and default limits on data accessibility. In short, personal data shall be kept 'lean and locked up' (Bygrave 2017b: 116). The duty applies not just to the design of software or hardware; it extends to business strategies and other organizational practices as well. A similar (though not identical) duty is laid down in Article 20 of the Law Enforcement Directive. While the DPD contained provisions with a similar thrust as Article 25, they were focused more narrowly on maintaining information security.

Article 25 manifests the increased salience of an overarching accountability principle in EU data protection law—a principle requiring that data controllers be accountable for their processing of personal data—particularly visible in Articles 5(2) and 24. The ideological roots of Article 25, though, are mainly to be found in older policy discourses on 'Privacy by Design' (Cavoukian 2009) and 'Privacy-Enhancing Technologies' (PETs)— technological mechanisms that promote respect for privacy-related interests (Hes & Borking 1995). These discourses are in turn part of a larger interdisciplinary effort aimed at embedding key human values—particularly those central to virtue ethics—in the technology design process (Wiener 1954; Friedman 1997; Spiekermann 2016). In this perspective, Article 25 may be regarded as an attempt to embed the values of EU data protection law in information systems architecture such that the resultant 'lex informatica' (Reidenberg 1997) or 'ambient law' (Hildebrandt & Koops 2010) renders the GDPR largely self-executing. Animating this endeavour is a belief that information systems architecture can often shape human behaviour more effectively than traditional law (Bygrave 2017a).

The requirements of Article 25 are pinned primarily on controllers of personal data—the entities that determine or co-determine the purposes, conditions, and means of processing personal data (Article 4(7) GDPR). Yet, the requirements are also pinned on mere processors of personal data—the entities that carry out processing on behalf of controllers (Article 4(8) GDPR)—since controllers may only use processors that 'provid[e] sufficient guarantees to implement appropriate technical and organisational measures' (Article 28(1) GDPR; see too Recital 81 GDPR). Thus, Article 25 concerns not just the technology foundations for information systems development, but also its market foundations. In the latter regard, Article 25 is indirectly aimed at breathing life into the market for PETs and privacy-friendly business systems—a market that has traditionally struggled (Bygrave 2017a: 765). This becomes apparent also from the preamble to the GDPR which states that 'producers' of products, services, and applications that involve processing of personal data 'should be encouraged' to take on board Article 25 ideals (Recital 78).

Although the aspirations behind Article 25 are difficult to fault, they face an uphill struggle in their implementation, not least in terms of their potential purchase on algorithmic regulation. One problem is the vagueness of Article 25 requirements, particularly the 'by design' duty in Article 25(1). Not only is this duty heavily qualified, it is pitched at a high level of abstraction that provides little clarity over the parameters and methodologies for achieving its aims (see also Tamò-Larrieux 2018: 209). A scarcity of external guidance on such methodologies, particularly amongst information systems engineers (ENISA 2014), exacerbates the problem.

Another difficulty concerns the actors to whom Article 25 requirements are pinned. The fact that Article 25 is directed primarily at controllers only, with indirect obligations placed also on processors, is a basic design flaw that afflicts data protection law generally. Many of the fundamental decisions governing design of information systems—including the architecture of algorithmic regulation—are not made by entities working in the role of controllers or processors of personal data, as defined by the GDPR. The Institute of Electrical and Electronics Engineers Standards Association (IEEE-SA) is one example in point; the Internet Engineering Task Force (IETF) another. Although the GDPR exhorts 'producers' of data-processing systems to respect Article 25 ideals, this exhortation is tucked away in a densely packed preamble that is not in itself legally binding. Even with respect to controllers and processors of personal data, the GDPR provides few real incentives for them to engage deeply with Article 25. The threat of punitive sanctions in the event of non-compliance is, of course, one such incentive, but the fluffy formulation of Article 25 undermines the ability to wield a 'big stick'.

The surrounding environment in which Article 25 is rolled out presents additional difficulties. For various reasons, a burgeoning market for PETs does not exist (Mayer & Narayanan 2013: 94–95), and the ideals of Article 25 have been largely peripheral to the traditionally more technocratic concerns of the engineering community (Bygrave 2017a: 764–65). Further, any attempt to introduce strong hardwiring of privacy and data protection safeguards will collide with powerful business and state interests that prefer to maintain weak or merely symbolic forms of such protection (Bygrave 2017a: 766).

5. Taming the Machine?

So how are we to view the prospects of EU data protection law—more particularly, the norms laid down in Articles 22 and 25 GDPR—in ensuring that automated decisional systems respect human rights and freedoms? Arriving at a firm and definitive conclusion at this point in time is well-nigh impossible; we do not yet have extensive experience with how these norms are implemented. For example, the practical effect of Article 22 will depend considerably on national legislation which, in many countries, is still being drafted or amended to take account of GDPR demands. Case law, particularly from the CJEU, will also play a role, and so far there is a paucity of judicial pronouncements on how Article 22 is to be construed. The same goes for interpretation of Article 25, although there is case law suggesting that the ideals of 'data protection by design' inhere in the EU constitutional fabric (Bygrave 2017b: 112–13). If they do inhere, this will likely strengthen the stringency of Article 25 requirements.

Even so, the foregoing analysis evidences a variety of factors that are likely to impede the ability of Articles 22 and 25 to 'tame the machine'. These include poor formulation and syntax in their wording, a complex multiplicity of qualifications that narrow the scope of the rights and duties at stake, lack of clarity over the parameters and methodologies for hardwiring data protection, and a paucity of incentives (other than the vague threat of punitive sanctions) to spur the sought-after shaping of information systems development. On top of these 'GDPR-internal' factors comes a range of well-documented external impediments, including fickleness of consumer concern for privacy, the basic logic of the 'internet economy', and the growing complexity and opacity of decisional systems driven by machine learning.

How some of these factors play out depends on multiple 'ifs'. For example, if persons only rarely utilize their rights under Article 22(3), the overall effect of Article 22 on the automation of decisional processes might well end up being negligible—just as it was with Article 15 DPD. At the same time, it is important to bear in mind that even if a right of review is exercised, Article 22 will not guarantee that a decision will end up having a different or better outcome for the data subject. Moreover, other provisions in the GDPR—and data protection law generally—provide poor controls over the quality of decisional outcomes and of the inferences that controllers draw from the data they utilize (Wachter & Mittelstadt 2019).

To take another example, the problem of a lack of guidance on methodologies for achieving 'data protection by design' will lessen in the long term if DPAs issue guidance notes, if technical standards on point are established, or if the engineering community warms to the message of Article 25. The first listed possibility is bound to happen, but the prospects of the second and third listed 'ifs' are less certain (Kamara 2017). A basic difficulty in respect of the latter is that Article 25 communicates poorly with the wider world, including the engineering community. The same can be said of Article 22: its message is muddied by clumsy structure and syntax to a far greater degree than was the case with its predecessor. Numerous other provisions in the GDPR are afflicted by similar communicative difficulties. Indeed, in this respect, the entire Regulation may be seen as a form of 'black box' decision-making.

On a more positive note, it is remarkable to see the difference in noise levels generated by discussion on Articles 22 and 25 compared with discussion on predecessor provisions in the DPD. Whereas Article 15 DPD was, in a sense, ahead of its time and thus left slumbering for years with only an occasional poke from scholars and practitioners, Article 22 GDPR has generated an immense amount of discussion in just a short period, and already been the subject of extensive guidance from the WP29 (now European Data Protection Board). Discussion on Article 25 GDPR is also burgeoning. This suggests that both provisions are very much in synchronicity (though not necessarily conformity) with current technological-organizational developments and associated discourse. Further, data protection more generally is now on many organizations' agendas to an unprecedented degree—thanks largely to the beefed-up clout of the GDPR's sanctions regime. This hopefully means that, at the very least, we will not go sleepwalking into a machine-driven future.

Yet, it is perhaps unfortunate that much of the noise surrounding that possible future has emanated from debate around whether or not Article 22 and other parts of the Regulation provide for a right to *ex post* explanation of automated decisions. The long-term health of human rights and freedoms will not depend simply or even largely on the availability of such a right. Transparency is not a silver bullet that will necessarily keep algorithmic regulation 'honest' (Annany & Crawford 2018). As Edwards & Veale (2017: 22–23) aptly observe:

> there is some danger of research and legislative efforts being devoted to creating rights to a form of transparency that may not be feasible, and may not match user needs. As the history of industries like finance and credit shows, rights to transparency do not necessarily secure substantive justice or effective remedies. We are in danger of creating a 'meaningless transparency' paradigm to match the already well known 'meaningless consent' trope.

Edwards and Veale go on to argue that provisions on data protection by design, data protection impact assessments, and certification may be more useful in the long term in countering the challenges of algorithmic regulation, although they properly note as a caveat that these provisions 'bring with them a real danger of formalistic bureaucratic overkill alongside a lack of substantive change: a happy vision for more form-filling jobs and ticked boxes, but a sad one for a world where algorithms do their jobs quietly without imperilling human rights and freedoms' (Edwards & Veale 2017: 80). To this may be added the qualms expressed in this chapter and elsewhere (Bygrave 2017a) over the stunted 'regulatory conversation' (Black 2002) that the GDPR initiates with the broader world, particularly the community of engineers.

Although Articles 22 and 25 GDPR constitute important normative cornerstones for securing human rights and freedoms in the face of algorithmic regulation, they are by no means the only such cornerstones. Numerous other provisions in the GDPR may also play a useful role. Edwards and Veale (2017) point to provisions on data protection impact assessment (Article 35), data portability (Article 20), certification (Article 42), and data erasure (Article 17) as eligible candidates. To this list I add the principle that personal data be processed 'fairly and in a transparent manner' (Article 5(1)(a))—a principle that both encompasses and generates other data protection principles (Bygrave 2014a: 146) and has, at the same time, work to do over and above them. The principle's breadth of scope and open texture, gives data protection law a powerfully flexible norm with which to hold automated decisional systems to account. While its open texture offers little upfront prescriptive guidance and there is otherwise as yet little research explicating in detail the notion of fairness in the data protection context (Clifford & Ausloos 2018), the principle has clear potential to help provide a basis for developing *new* legal norms. An example in point is the 'right to reasonable inferences' which Wachter and Mittelstadt (2019) call to be introduced into data protection law with the aim of better controlling the way in which personal data is evaluated. In making their case, Wachter and Mittelstadt do not rely on the fairness principle but it is an eminent candidate for normatively grounding (at least partially) this sort of right.

Finally, we must remember that data protection law generally is, and ought to be, but one of many points of departure for taming the machine, not the legal end-point for this endeavour. This follows partly from the general limitation in the scope of data protection law to the processing of *personal* data. Although this limitation is being stretched as the practical and legal ambit of the personal data concept expands (Purtova 2018), it still hinders the applicability of data protection law to automated decisional systems across the board—and rightly so, if we are to minimize potential for 'normative disconnection' (Brownsword 2008: 166) or 'regulatory overreaching' (Bygrave 2014b: 261–62). Moreover, algorithmic regulation now features in so many different contexts that it must engage a variety of legal rules beyond the data protection sphere: administrative law, criminal law, intellectual property law, contract law, and competition law are obvious cases in point. In the field of competition law, for example, the use of algorithms to coordinate price collusion or to enable differentiated charging of various groups of consumers is becoming a concern. Ezrachi and Stucke (2016) accordingly raise the prospect of the 'digital Hand' replacing the 'invisible Hand'. How and whether these challenges are adequately met by traditional competition law rules are urgent questions.

Similar sorts of algorithm-related questions are replicated across numerous fields of law. Scholars, practitioners, and policy entrepreneurs who are expert in these various fields need to be addressing them *now*. At the same time, they need to be cognizant of the fact that these respective areas of law are not discrete regulatory frameworks operating independently of other such frameworks. Strong operational and ideological ties exist, for instance, between data protection law and many of the areas of law listed above. Efforts to address the challenges thrown up by algorithmic regulation in one area of law must take into account, and leverage off, equivalent efforts in other areas. Such processes of regulatory cross-fertilization are a *sine qua non* for any true taming of the machine.

Bibliography

Annany M and Crawford K, 'Seeing without Knowing: Limitations of the Transparency Ideal and Its Application to Algorithmic Accountability' (2018) 20(3) New Media & Society 973.

Article 29 Working Party, 'Transfers of Personal Data to Third Countries: Applying Articles 25 and 26 of the EU Data Protection Directive' (WP 12, 24 July 1998).

Article 29 Working Party, 'Guidelines on Automated Individual Decision- Making and Profiling for the Purposes of Regulation 2016/679' (WP 251rev.01, 6 February 2018).

Black J, 'Regulatory Conversations' (2002) 29(1) Journal of Law and Society 163.

Brkan M, 'Do Algorithms Rule the World? Algorithmic Decision Making and Data Protection in the Framework of the GDPR and Beyond' (2019) 27(2) International Journal of Law and Information Technology 91.

Brownsword R, *Rights, Regulation, and the Technological Revolution* (Oxford University Press 2008).

Bygrave LA, 'Minding the Machine: Article 15 of the EC Data Protection Directive and Automated Profiling' (2001) 17(1) Computer Law & Security Review 17.

Bygrave LA, 'Hardwiring Privacy' in R Brownsword, E Scotford, and K Yeung (eds), *The Oxford Handbook of Law, Regulation, and Technology* (Oxford University Press 2017a).

Bygrave LA, 'Data Protection by Design and by Default: Deciphering the EU's Legislative Requirements' (2017b) 4(2) Oslo Law Review 105.

Bygrave LA, *Data Privacy Law: An International Perspective* (Oxford University Press 2014a).

Bygrave LA, 'Data Privacy Law and the Internet: Policy Challenges' in N Witzleb et al (eds), *Emerging Challenges in Privacy Law: Comparative Perspectives* (Cambridge University Press 2014b).

Cavoukian A, 'Privacy by Design: The 7 Foundational Principles' (August 2009, revised January 2011) <https://www.ipc.on.ca/wp-content/uploads/Resources/7foundationalprinciples.pdf>.

Clifford D and Ausloos J, 'Data Protection Law and the Role of Fairness' (2018) 37 Yearbook of European Law 130.

Edwards L and Veale M, 'Slave to the Algorithm: Why a "Right to an Explanation" is Probably not the Remedy You are Looking for' (2017) 16(1) Duke Law & Technology Review 18.

European Union Agency for Network and Information Security (ENISA), *Privacy and Data Protection by Design—From Policy to Engineering* (ENISA 2014).

Ezrachi A and Stucke M, *Virtual Competition: The Promise and Perils of the Algorithm-Driven Economy* (Harvard University Press 2016).

Friedman B (ed), *Human Values and the Design of Computer Technology* (Cambridge University Press 1997).

Hes R and. Borking JJ, *Privacy-Enhancing Technologies: The Path to Anonymity* (Registratiekamer 1995).

Hildebrandt M and Koops B-J, 'The Challenges of Ambient Law and Legal Protection in the Profiling Era' (2010) 73(3) Modern Law Review 428.

Kamara I, 'Co-regulation in EU Personal Data Protection: The Case of Technical Standards and the Privacy by Design Standardisation "Mandate"' (2017) 8(1) European Journal of Law and Technology, no pagination.

Kaminski M, 'The Right to Explanation, Explained' (2018) University of Colorado Law Legal Studies Research Paper No. 18-24.

Mayer J and Narayanan A, 'Privacy Substitutes' (2013) 66 Stanford Law Review Online 89.

Mendoza I and Bygrave LA, 'The Right not to be Subject to Automated Decisions based on Profiling' in T Synodinou, P Jougleux, C Markou, and T Prastitou (eds), *EU Internet Law: Regulation and Enforcement* (Springer 2017).

Pasquale F, *The Black Box Society. The Secret Algorithms That Control Money and Information* (Harvard University Press 2015).

Purtova N, 'The Law of Everything. Broad Concept of Personal Data and Future of EU Data Protection Law' (2018) 10(1) Law, Innovation and Technology 40.

Reidenberg JR, 'Lex Informatica: The Formulation of Information Policy Rules through Technology' (1997) 76(3) Texas Law Review 553.

Schartum DW, 'Personvernforordningen og helt automatiserte avgjørelser innen forvaltningsretten' (2018a) 134(2) Lov&Data 4.

Schartum DW, 'From Facts to Decision Data: About the Factual Basis of Automated Individual Decisions' (2018b) 50 Scandinavian Studies in Law 379.

Selbst A and Powles J, 'Meaningful Information and the Right to Explanation' (2017) 7(4) International Data Privacy Law 233.

Spiekermann S, *Ethical IT Innovation: A Value-Based System Design Approach* (Taylor & Francis 2016).

Tamò-Larrieux A, *Designing for Privacy and its Legal Framework: Data Protection by Design and Default for the Internet of Things* (Springer 2018).

Tosoni L, 'The Right to Object to Automated Individual Decisions: Resolving the Ambiguity of Article 22(1) of the General Data Protection Regulation' (2019) 9 International Data Privacy Law (forthcoming).

Wachter S and Mittelstadt B, 'A Right to Reasonable Inferences: Re-Thinking Data Protection Law in the Age of Big Data and AI' (2019) (2) Columbia Business Law Review 1.

Wachter S, Mittelstadt B, and Floridi L, 'Why a Right to Explanation of Automated Decision-Making Does not Exist in the General Data Protection Regulation' (2017) 7 International Data Privacy Law 76.

Wiener N, *The Human Use of Human Beings: Cybernetics and Society* (Doubleday Anchor 1954).

Index

Note on index: *For the benefit of digital users, indexed terms that span two pages (e.g., 52–53) may, on occasion, appear on only one of those pages.*